HOT GIMMICK
CONTENTS

Hot Gimmick

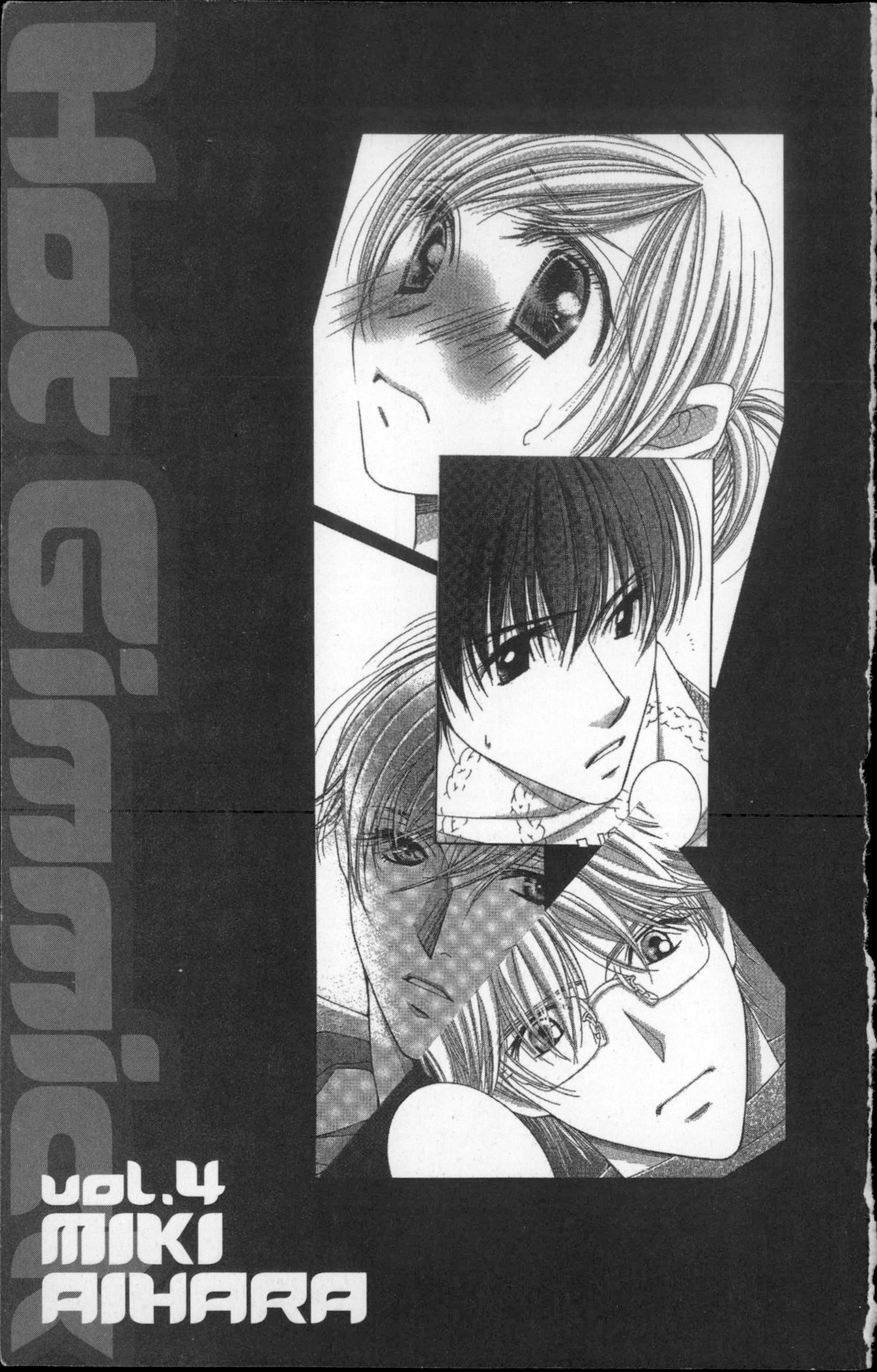

vol.4

MIKI AIHARA

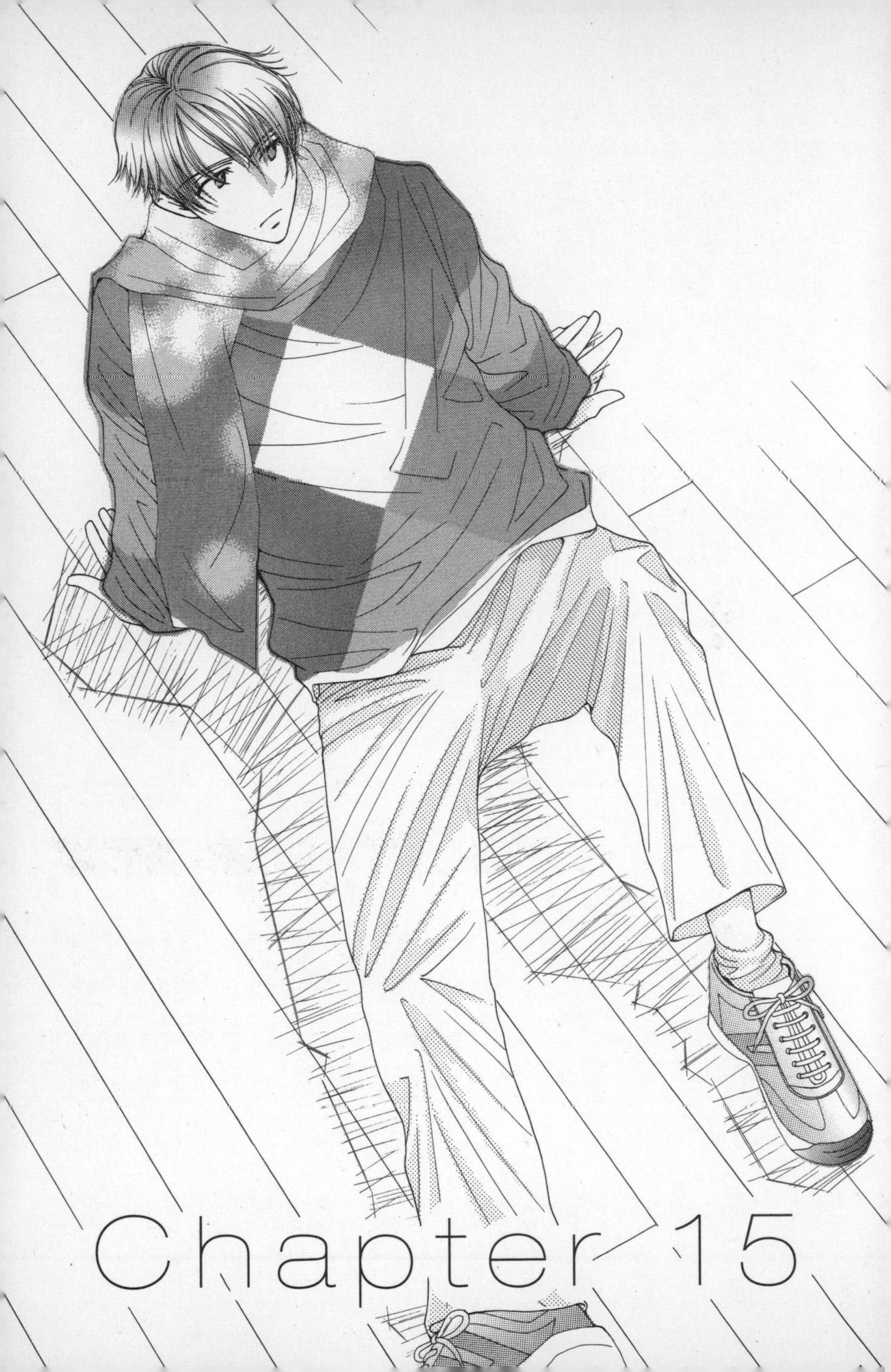

Chapter 15

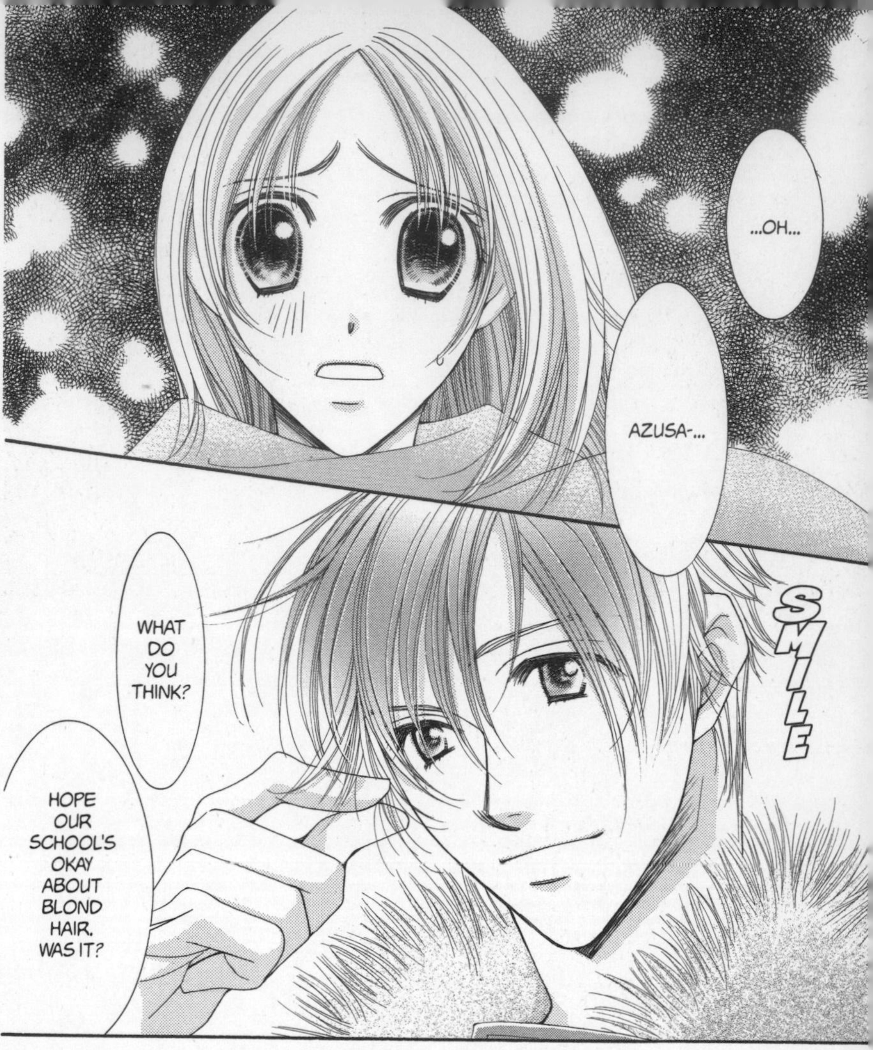
...OH...
AZUSA-...
SMILE
WHAT DO YOU THINK?
HOPE OUR SCHOOL'S OKAY ABOUT BLOND HAIR. WAS IT?

hot gimmick

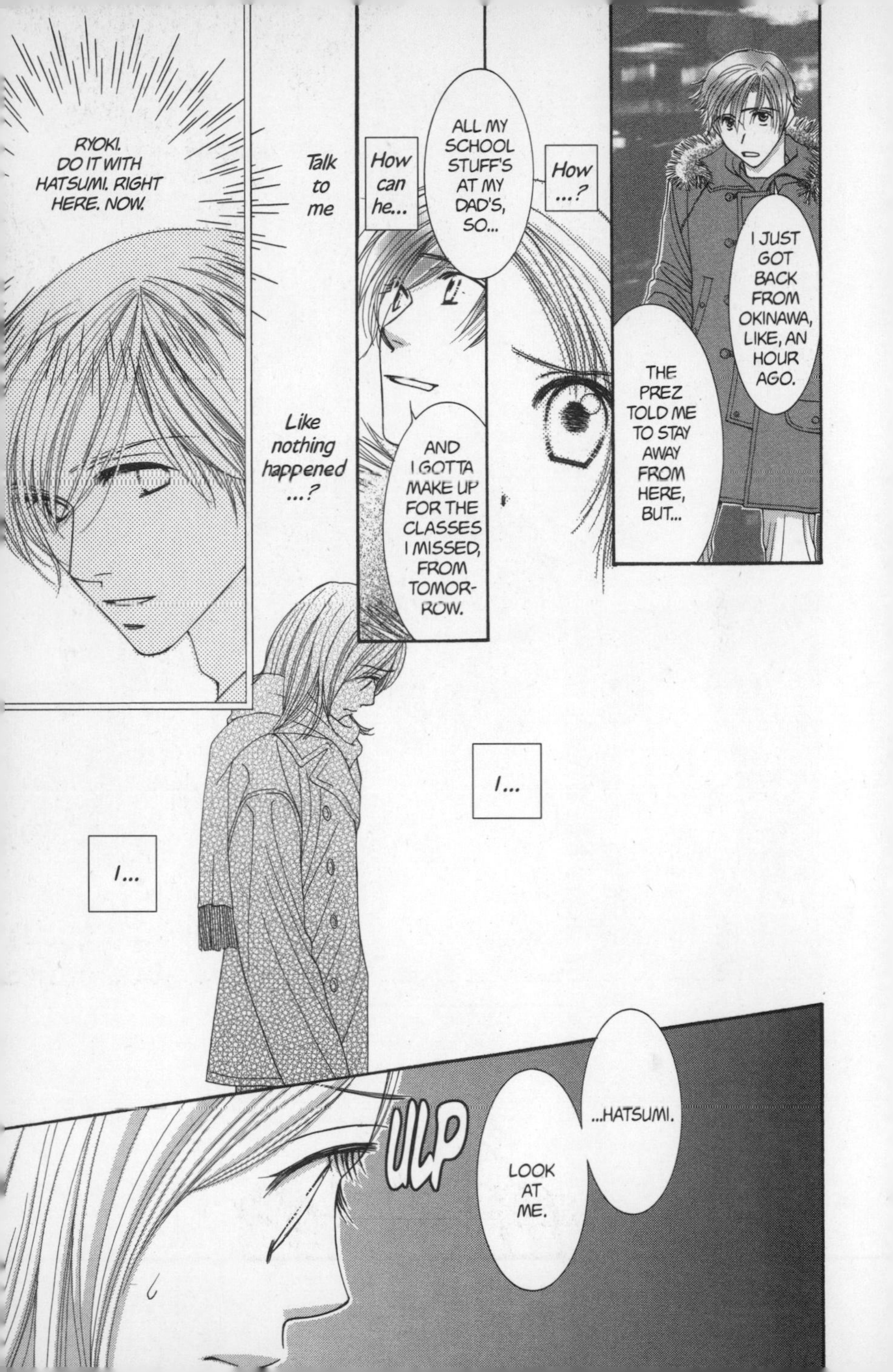
I JUST GOT BACK FROM OKINAWA, LIKE, AN HOUR AGO.
THE PREZ TOLD ME TO STAY AWAY FROM HERE, BUT...
How ...?
ALL MY SCHOOL STUFF'S AT MY DAD'S, SO...
How can he...
AND I GOTTA MAKE UP FOR THE CLASSES I MISSED, FROM TOMORROW.
Talk to me
Like nothing happened ...?
RYOKI. DO IT WITH HATSUMI. RIGHT HERE. NOW.
I...
I...
...HATSUMI.
LOOK AT ME.
ULP

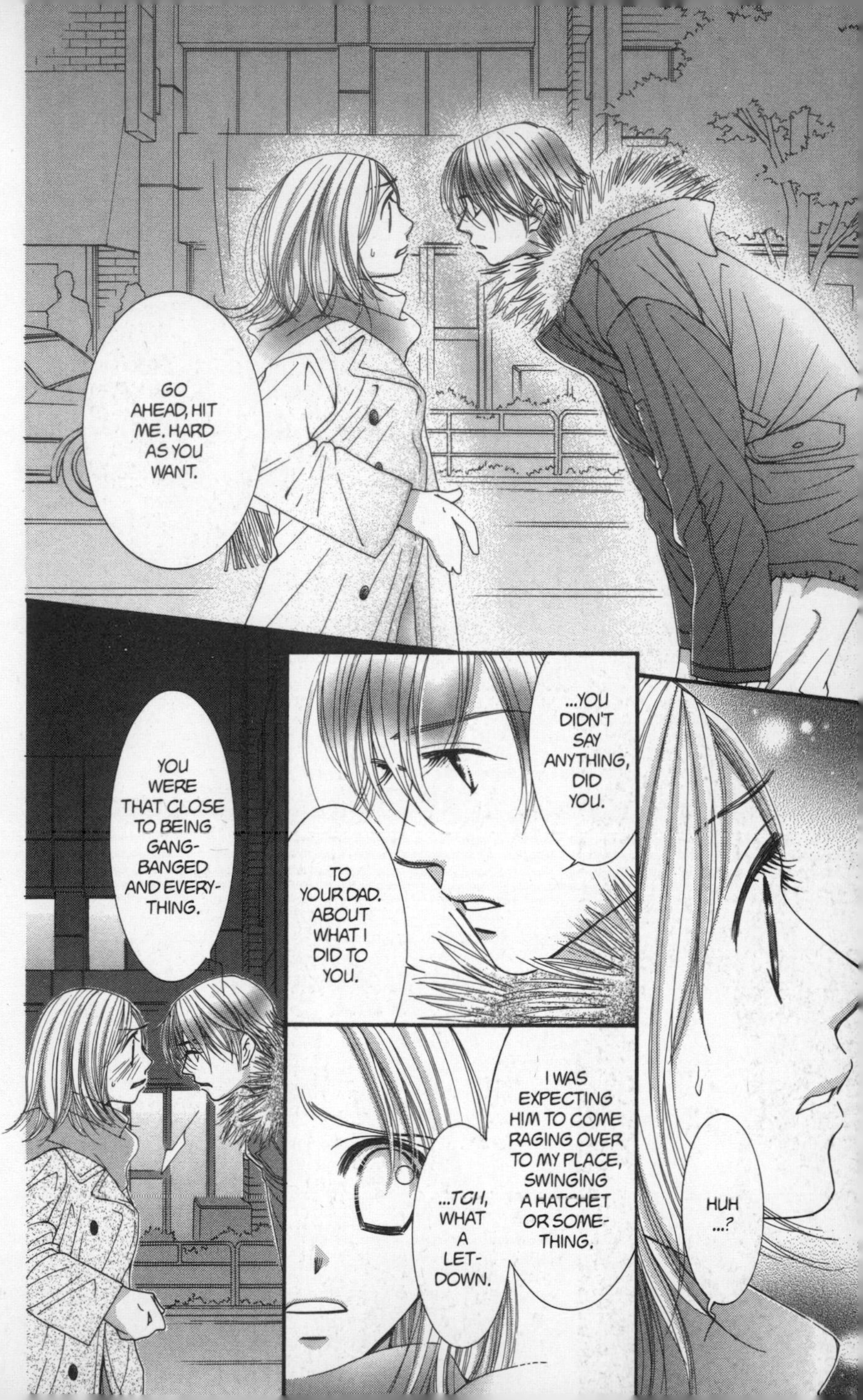
GO AHEAD, HIT ME. HARD AS YOU WANT.
HUH ...?
...YOU DIDN'T SAY ANYTHING, DID YOU.
TO YOUR DAD. ABOUT WHAT I DID TO YOU.
I WAS EXPECTING HIM TO COME RAGING OVER TO MY PLACE, SWINGING A HATCHET OR SOME-THING.
...TCH, WHAT A LET-DOWN.
YOU WERE THAT CLOSE TO BEING GANG-BANGED AND EVERY-THING.

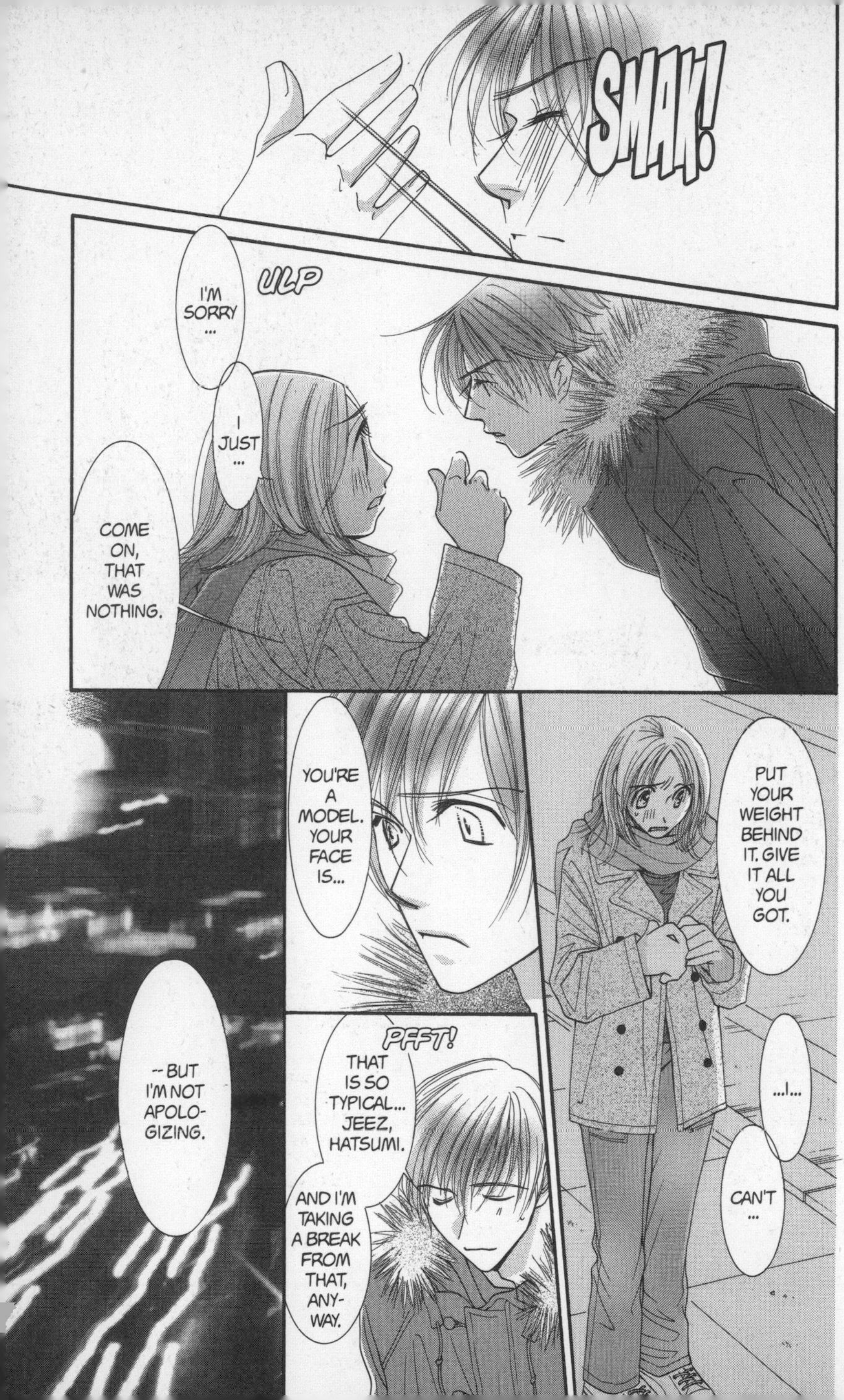
SMAK!
ULP
I'M SORRY ...
I JUST ...
COME ON, THAT WAS NOTHING.
PUT YOUR WEIGHT BEHIND IT. GIVE IT ALL YOU GOT.
...I...
CAN'T ...
YOU'RE A MODEL. YOUR FACE IS...
PFFT!
THAT IS SO TYPICAL... JEEZ, HATSUMI.
AND I'M TAKING A BREAK FROM THAT, ANY-WAY.
--BUT I'M NOT APOLO-GIZING.

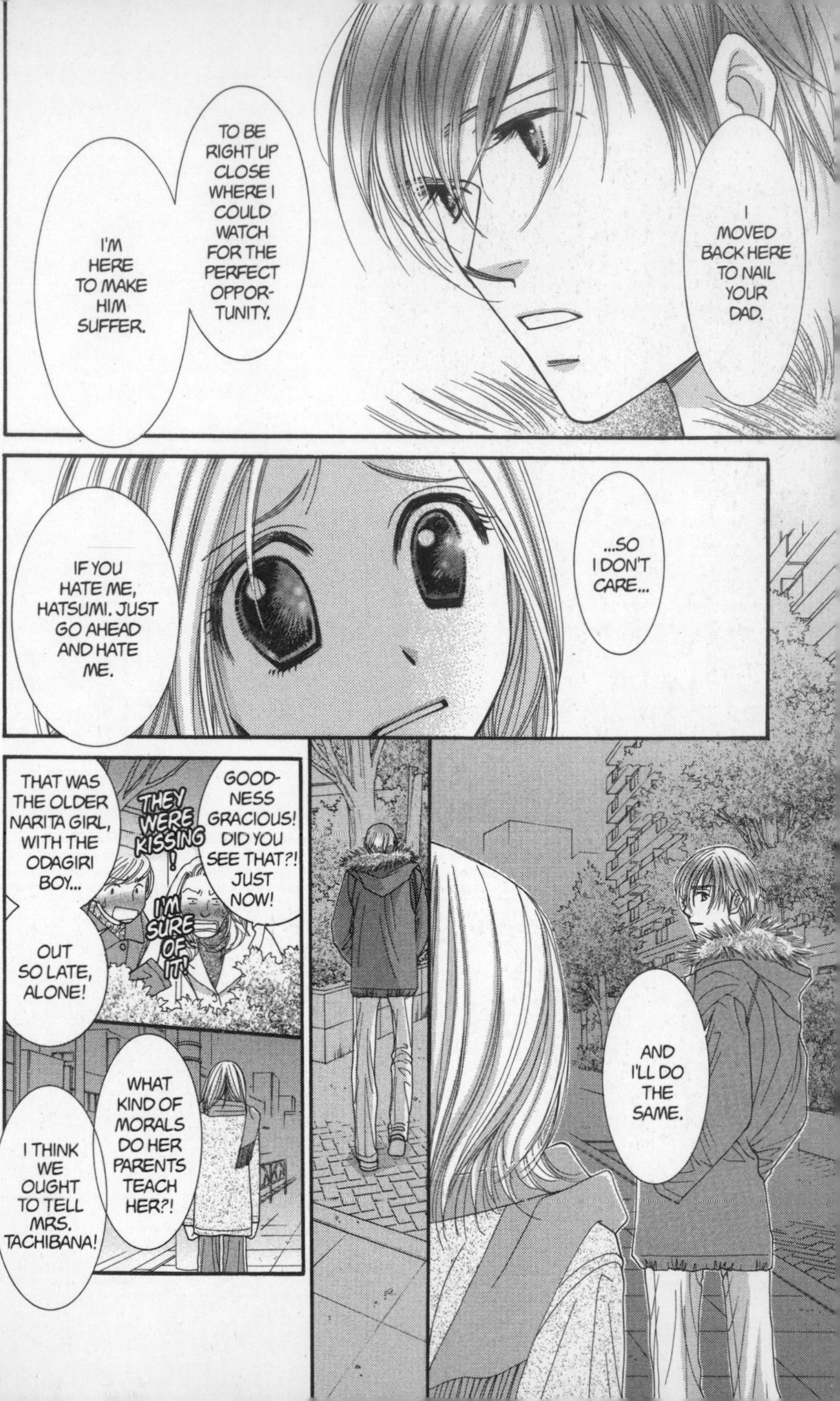
I MOVED BACK HERE TO NAIL YOUR DAD.
TO BE RIGHT UP CLOSE WHERE I COULD WATCH FOR THE PERFECT OPPOR-TUNITY.
I'M HERE TO MAKE HIM SUFFER.
...SO I DON'T CARE...
IF YOU HATE ME, HATSUMI. JUST GO AHEAD AND HATE ME.
AND I'LL DO THE SAME.
GOOD-NESS GRACIOUS! DID YOU SEE THAT?! JUST NOW!
THEY WERE KISSING!
I'M SURE OF IT!
THAT WAS THE OLDER NARITA GIRL, WITH THE ODAGIRI BOY...
OUT SO LATE, ALONE!
WHAT KIND OF MORALS DO HER PARENTS TEACH HER?!
I THINK WE OUGHT TO TELL MRS. TACHIBANA!

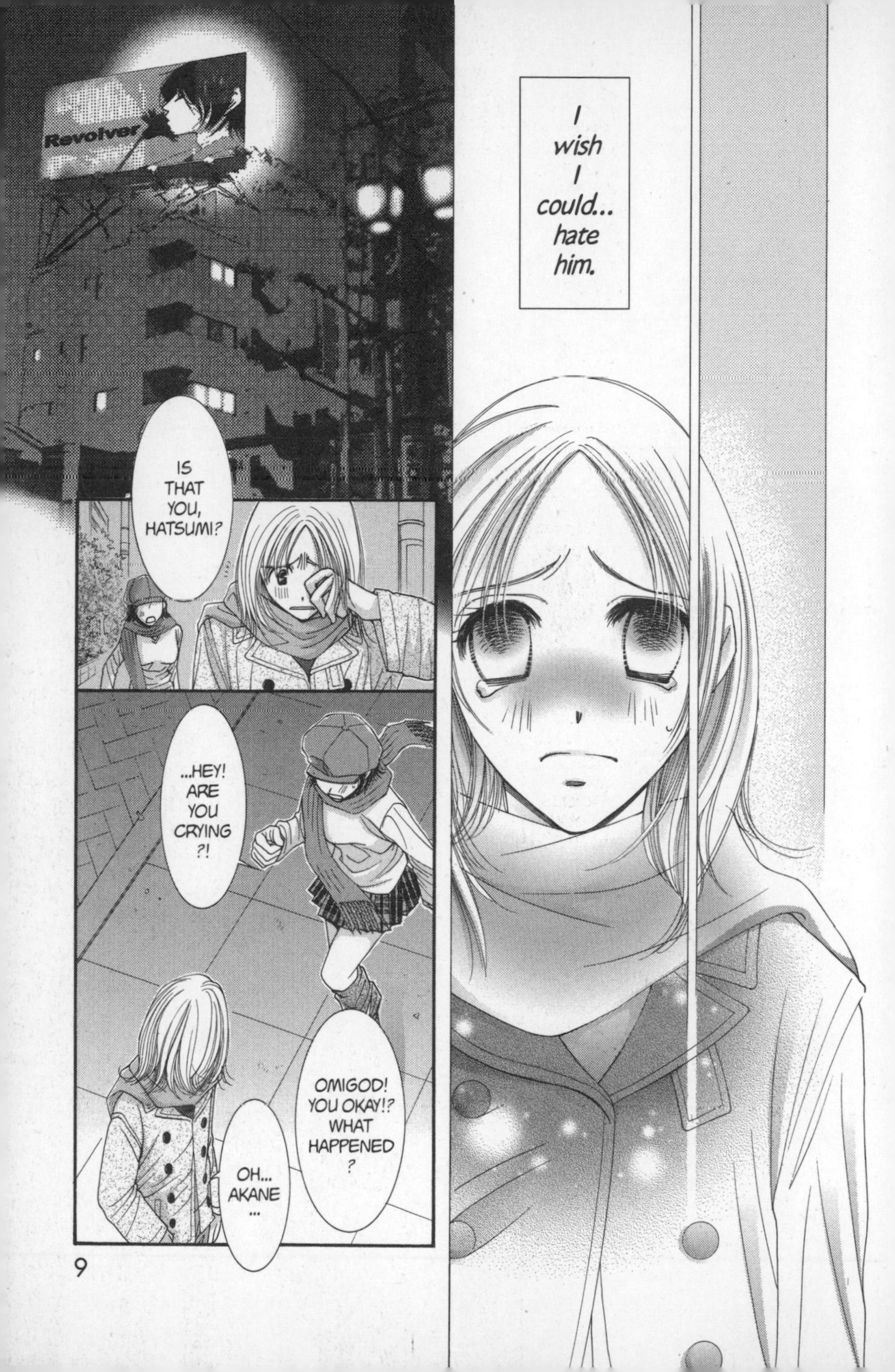
I wish I could... hate him.
Revolver
IS THAT YOU, HATSUMI?
...HEY! ARE YOU CRYING ?!
OMIGOD! YOU OKAY!? WHAT HAPPENED ?
OH... AKANE ...

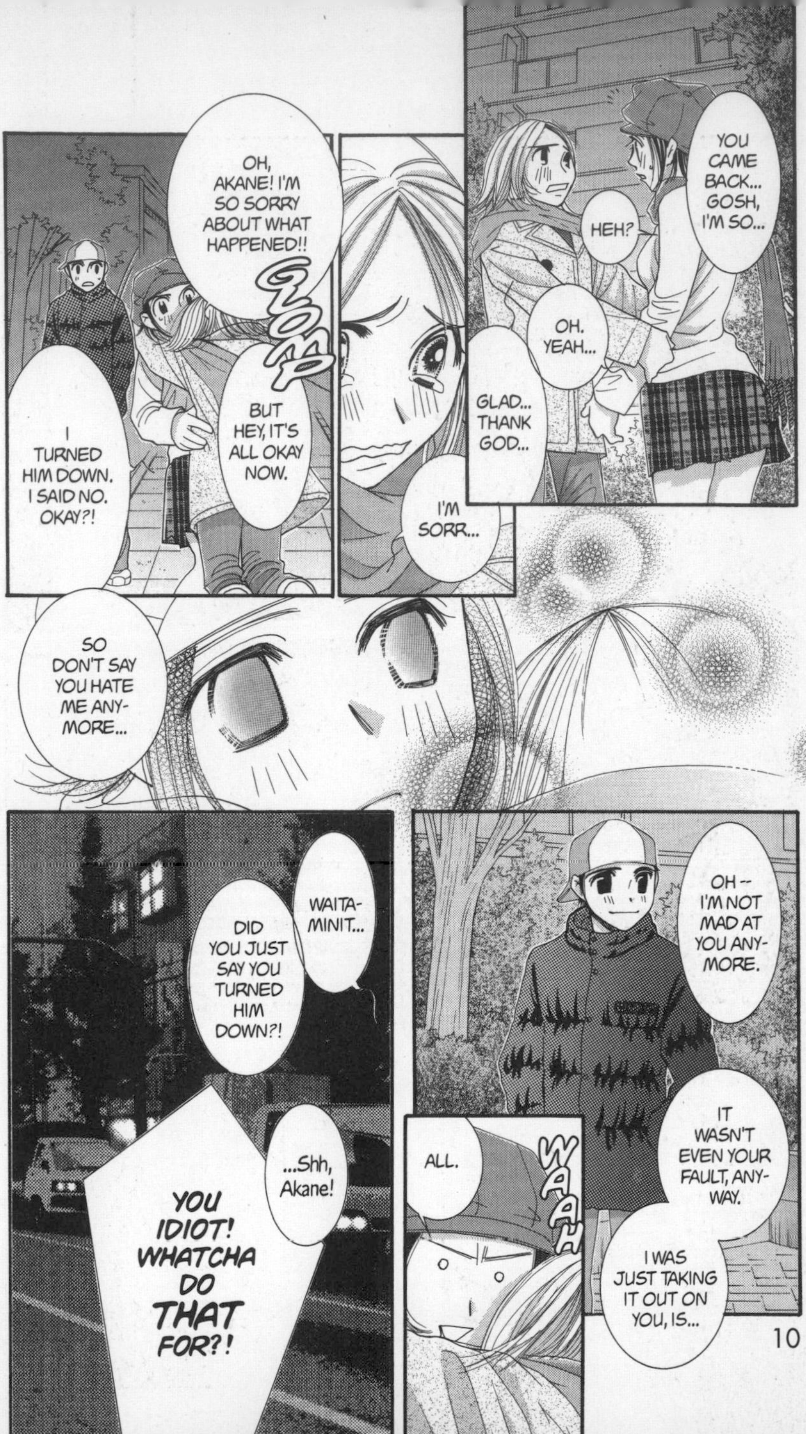
YOU CAME BACK... GOSH, I'M SO...
HEH?
OH. YEAH...
GLAD... THANK GOD...
I'M SORR...
OH, AKANE! I'M SO SORRY ABOUT WHAT HAPPENED!!
GLOMP
BUT HEY, IT'S ALL OKAY NOW.
I TURNED HIM DOWN. I SAID NO. OKAY?!
SO DON'T SAY YOU HATE ME ANY-MORE...
OH -- I'M NOT MAD AT YOU ANY-MORE.
IT WASN'T EVEN YOUR FAULT, ANY-WAY.
I WAS JUST TAKING IT OUT ON YOU, IS...
ALL.
WAAH
WAITA-MINIT...
DID YOU JUST SAY YOU TURNED HIM DOWN?!
...Shh, Akane!
YOU IDIOT! WHATCHA DO THAT FOR?!

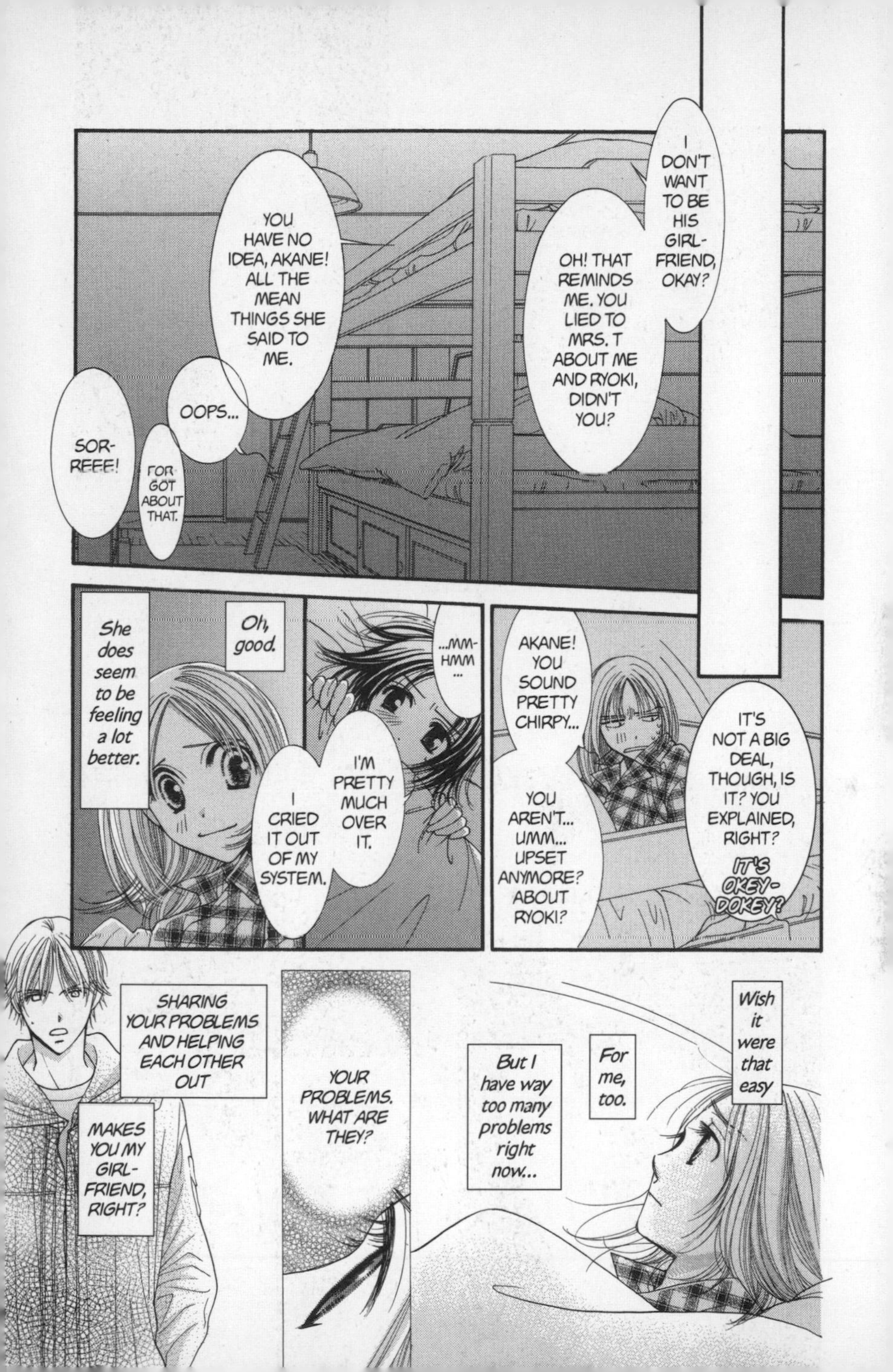
I DON'T WANT TO BE HIS GIRL-FRIEND, OKAY?
OH! THAT REMINDS ME. YOU LIED TO MRS. T ABOUT ME AND RYOKI, DIDN'T YOU?
YOU HAVE NO IDEA, AKANE! ALL THE MEAN THINGS SHE SAID TO ME.
OOPS...
FOR GOT ABOUT THAT.
SOR-REEE!
IT'S NOT A BIG DEAL, THOUGH, IS IT? YOU EXPLAINED, RIGHT?
IT'S OKEY-DOKEY?
AKANE! YOU SOUND PRETTY CHIRPY...
YOU AREN'T... UMM... UPSET ANYMORE? ABOUT RYOKI?
...MM-HMM...
I'M PRETTY MUCH OVER IT.
I CRIED IT OUT OF MY SYSTEM.
Oh, good.
She does seem to be feeling a lot better.
Wish it were that easy
For me, too.
But I have way too many problems right now...
YOUR PROBLEMS. WHAT ARE THEY?
SHARING YOUR PROBLEMS AND HELPING EACH OTHER OUT
MAKES YOU MY GIRL-FRIEND, RIGHT?

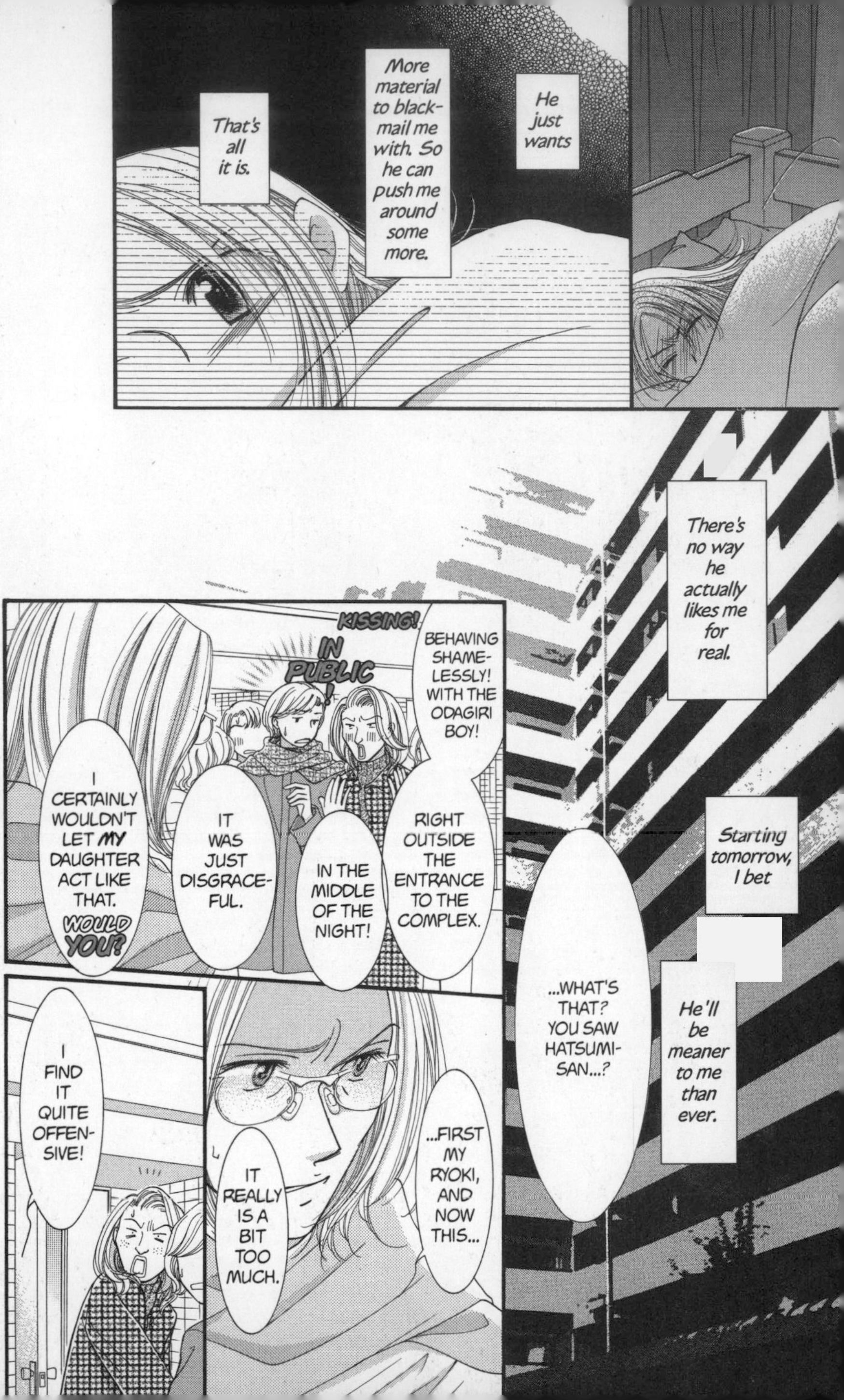
He just wants
More material to blackmail me with. So he can push me around some more.
That's all it is.
There's no way he actually likes me for real.
Starting tomorrow, I bet
He'll be meaner to me than ever.
KISSING!
IN PUBLIC!
BEHAVING SHAMELESSLY! WITH THE ODAGIRI BOY!
RIGHT OUTSIDE THE ENTRANCE TO THE COMPLEX.
IN THE MIDDLE OF THE NIGHT!
IT WAS JUST DISGRACEFUL.
I CERTAINLY WOULDN'T LET MY DAUGHTER ACT LIKE THAT.
WOULD YOU?
...WHAT'S THAT? YOU SAW HATSUMI-SAN...?
...FIRST MY RYOKI, AND NOW THIS...
IT REALLY IS A BIT TOO MUCH.
I FIND IT QUITE OFFENSIVE!

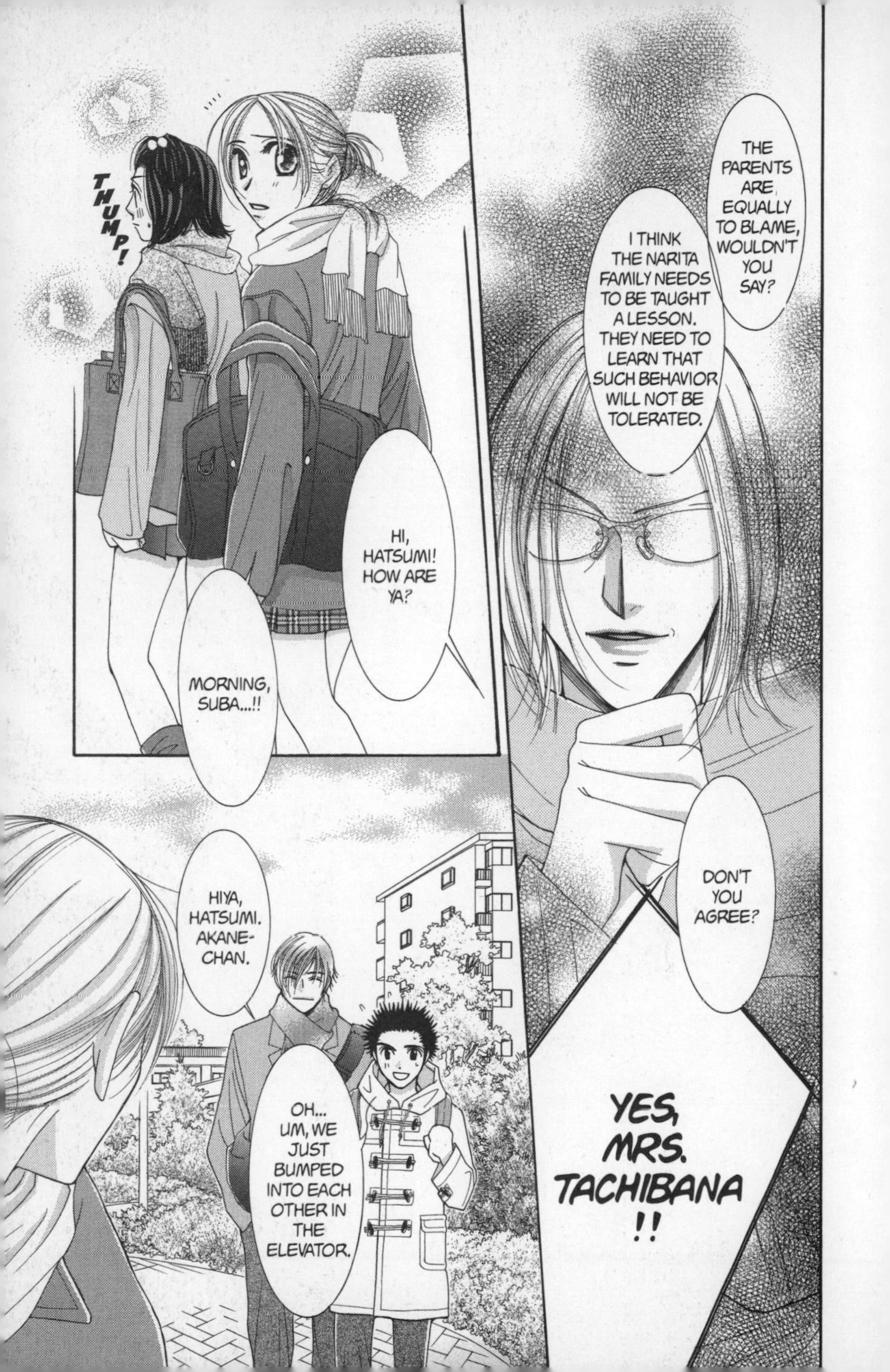
THE PARENTS ARE EQUALLY TO BLAME, WOULDN'T YOU SAY?
I THINK THE NARITA FAMILY NEEDS TO BE TAUGHT A LESSON. THEY NEED TO LEARN THAT SUCH BEHAVIOR WILL NOT BE TOLERATED.
DON'T YOU AGREE?
YES, MRS. TACHIBANA!!
THUMP!
HI, HATSUMI! HOW ARE YA?
MORNING, SUBA...!!
HIYA, HATSUMI. AKANE-CHAN.
OH... UM, WE JUST BUMPED INTO EACH OTHER IN THE ELEVATOR.

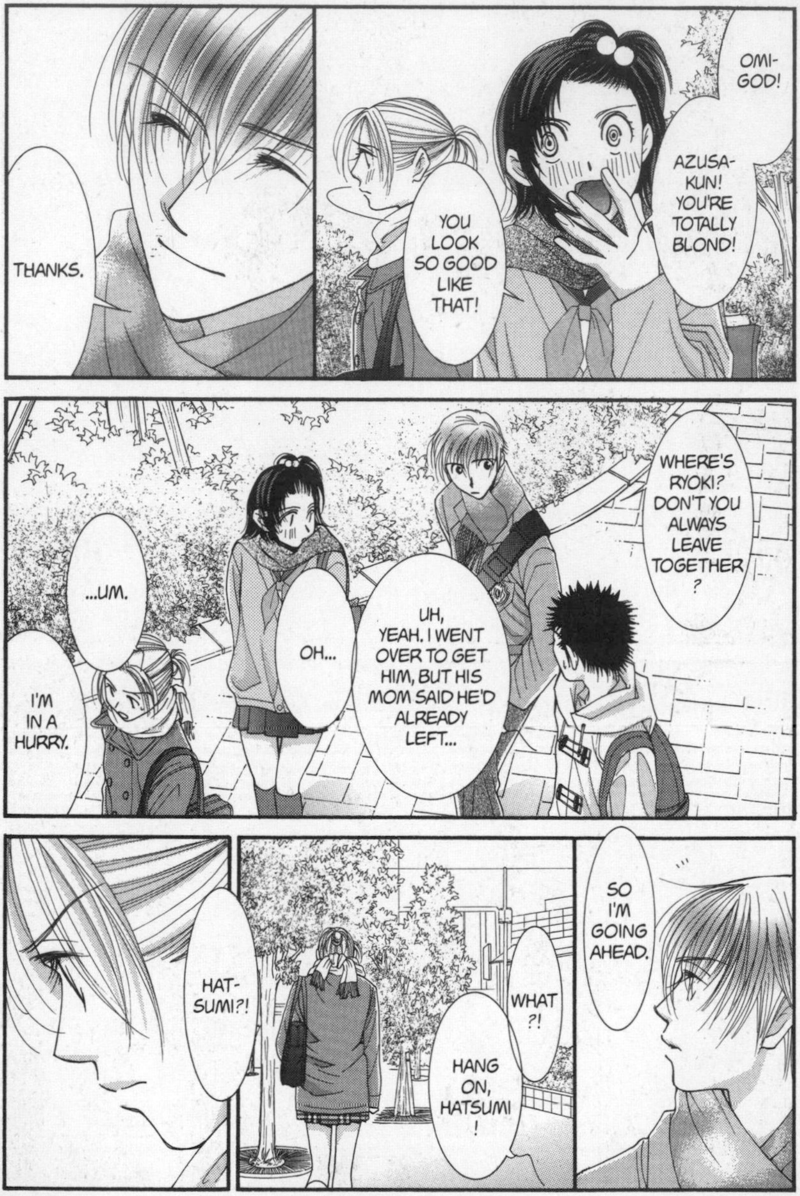
OMI-GOD!
AZUSA-KUN! YOU'RE TOTALLY BLOND!
YOU LOOK SO GOOD LIKE THAT!
THANKS.
WHERE'S RYOKI? DON'T YOU ALWAYS LEAVE TOGETHER?
UH, YEAH. I WENT OVER TO GET HIM, BUT HIS MOM SAID HE'D ALREADY LEFT...
OH...
...UM.
I'M IN A HURRY.
SO I'M GOING AHEAD.
WHAT?!
HANG ON, HATSUMI!
HAT-SUMI?!

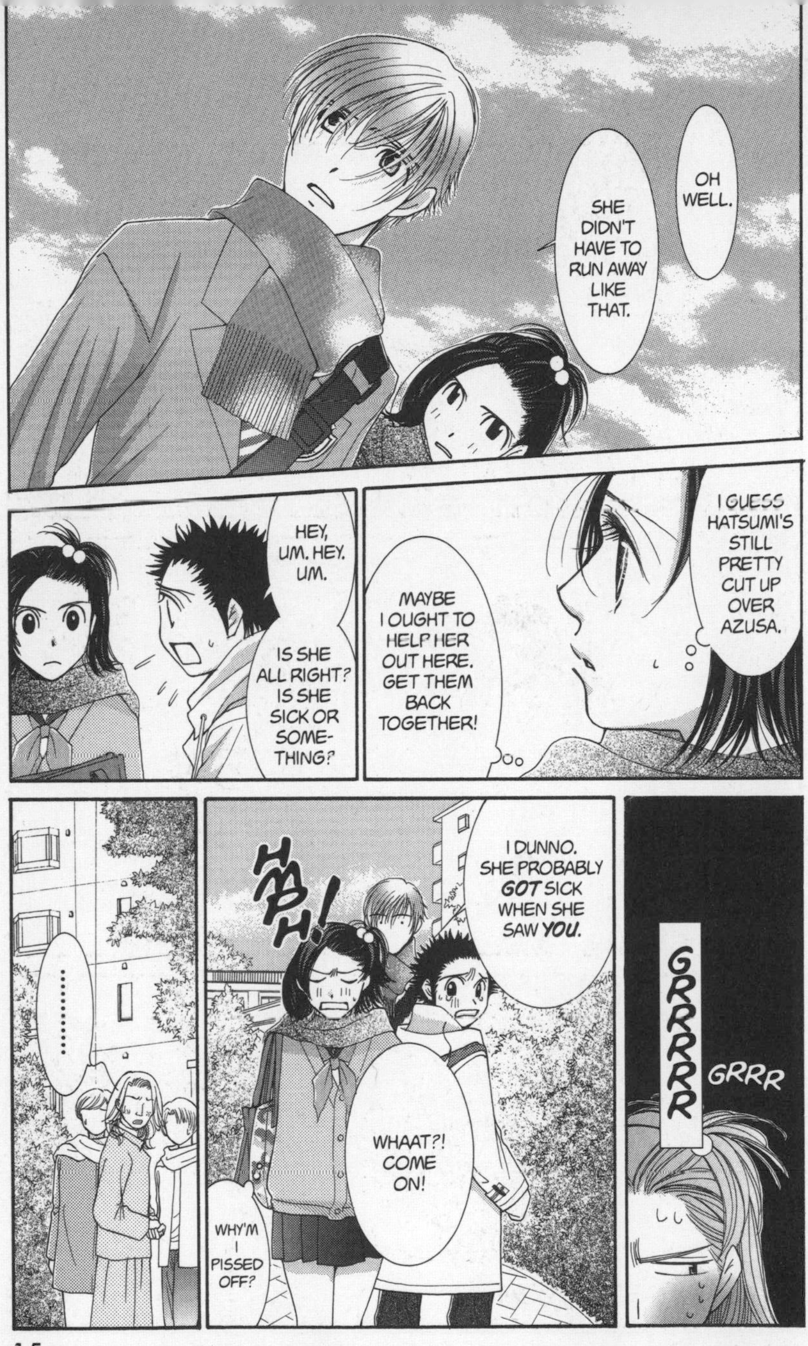
OH WELL.
SHE DIDN'T HAVE TO RUN AWAY LIKE THAT.
I GUESS HATSUMI'S STILL PRETTY CUT UP OVER AZUSA.
MAYBE I OUGHT TO HELP HER OUT HERE. GET THEM BACK TOGETHER!
HEY, UM. HEY. UM.
IS SHE ALL RIGHT? IS SHE SICK OR SOME-THING?
GRRRRR
GRRR
I DUNNO. SHE PROBABLY GOT SICK WHEN SHE SAW YOU.
HMPH!
WHAAT?! COME ON!
WHY'M I PISSED OFF?
....

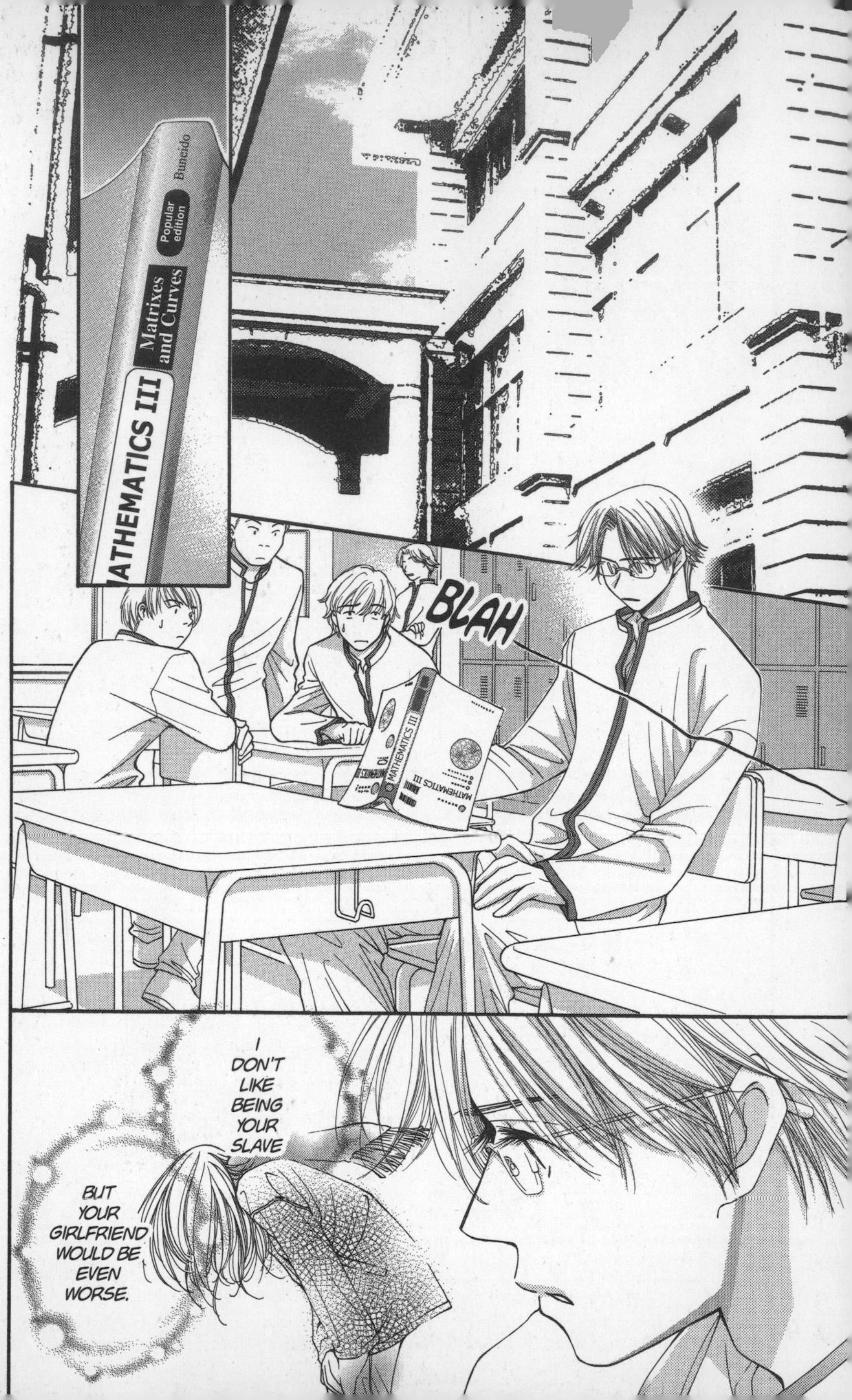

MATHEMATICS III
Matrixes and Curves
Popular edition
Buneido
BLAH
MATHEMATICS III
I DON'T LIKE BEING YOUR SLAVE
BUT YOUR GIRLFRIEND WOULD BE EVEN WORSE.

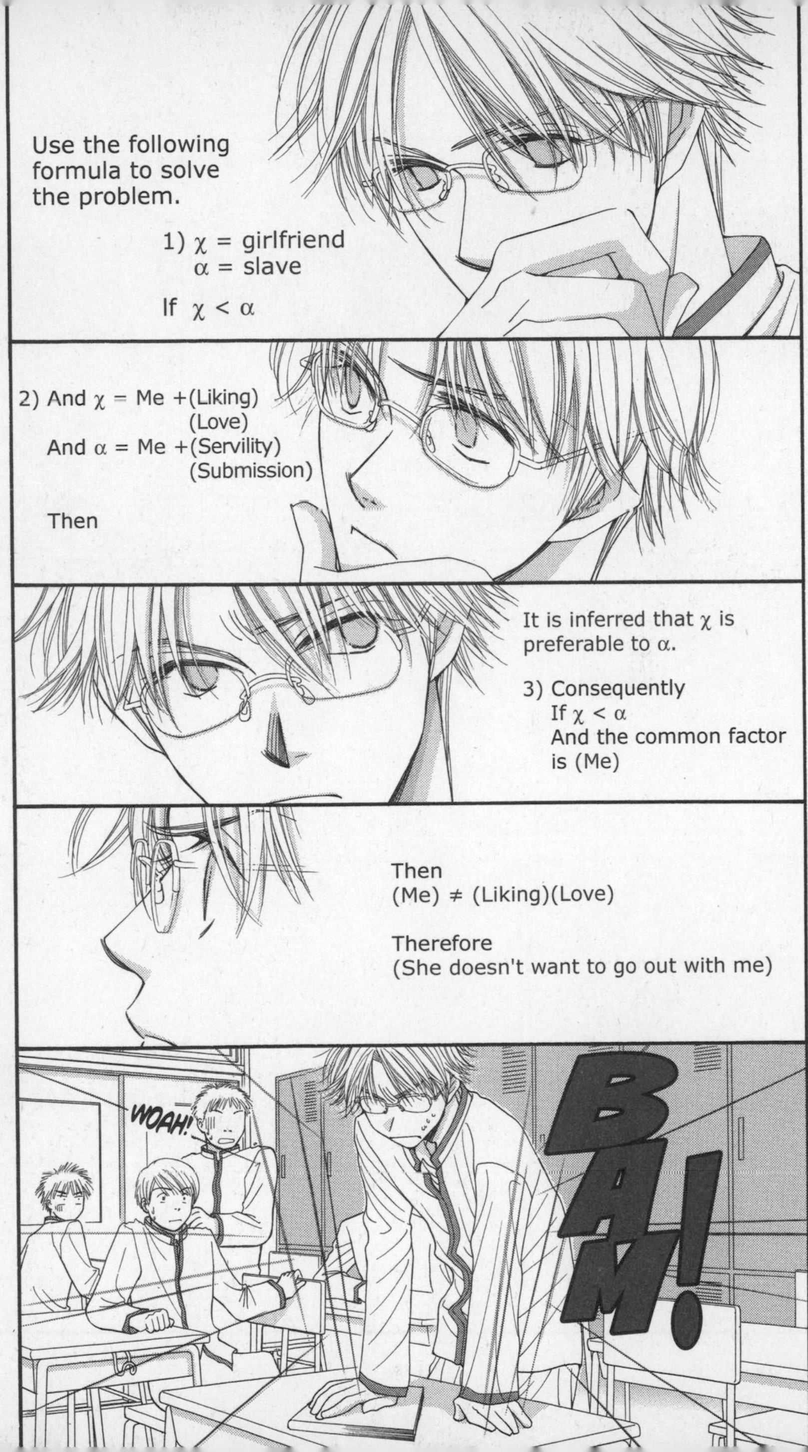
Use the following formula to solve the problem.
1) χ = girlfriend
α = slave
If $\chi < \alpha$
2) And χ = Me +(Liking)(Love)
And α = Me +(Servility)(Submission)
Then
It is inferred that χ is preferable to α.
3) Consequently
If $\chi < \alpha$
And the common factor is (Me)
Then
(Me) $\neq$ (Liking)(Love)
Therefore
(She doesn't want to go out with me)
BAM!
WOAH!

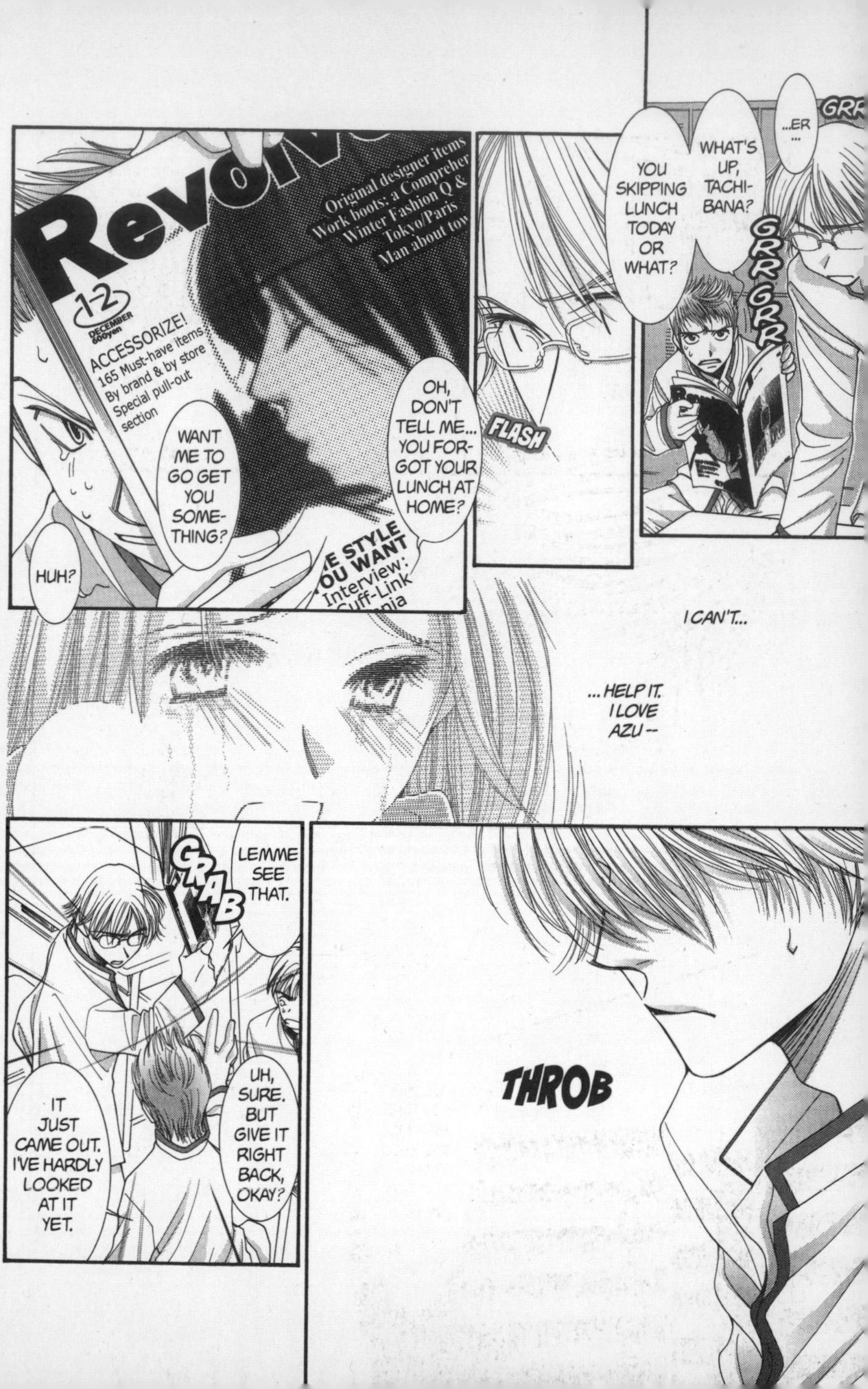
GRR
...ER ...
WHAT'S UP, TACHIBANA?
YOU SKIPPING LUNCH TODAY OR WHAT?
GRR GRR GRR
FLASH
Original designer items
Winter Fashion Q &
Tokyo/Paris
1-2
DECEMBER 600yen
ACCESSORIZE!
165 Must-have items
By brand & by store
Special pull-out section
Interview:
OH, DON'T TELL ME... YOU FORGOT YOUR LUNCH AT HOME?
WANT ME TO GO GET YOU SOMETHING?
HUH?
I CAN'T...
...HELP IT. I LOVE AZU--
THROB
LEMME SEE THAT.
GRAB
UH, SURE. BUT GIVE IT RIGHT BACK, OKAY?
IT JUST CAME OUT. I'VE HARDLY LOOKED AT IT YET.

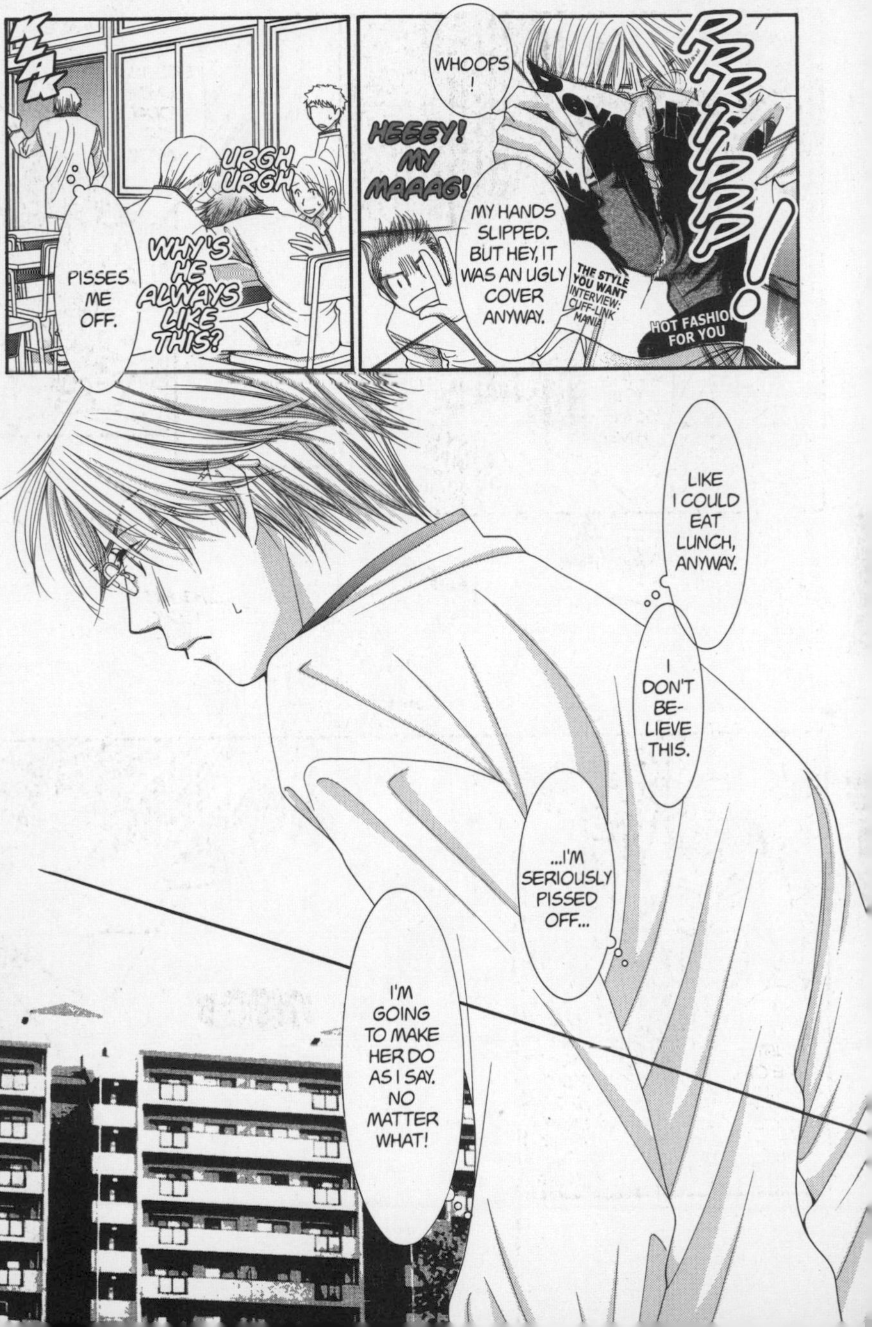
RRRIPPP!
WHOOPS!
HOT FASHIO FOR YOU
THE STYLE YOU WANT
INTERVIEW: CUFF-LINK MANIA
HEEEY! MY MAAAG!
MY HANDS SLIPPED. BUT HEY, IT WAS AN UGLY COVER ANYWAY.
KLAK
URGH URGH
WHY'S HE ALWAYS LIKE THIS?
PISSES ME OFF.
LIKE I COULD EAT LUNCH, ANYWAY.
I DON'T BE-LIEVE THIS.
...I'M SERIOUSLY PISSED OFF...
I'M GOING TO MAKE HER DO AS I SAY. NO MATTER WHAT!

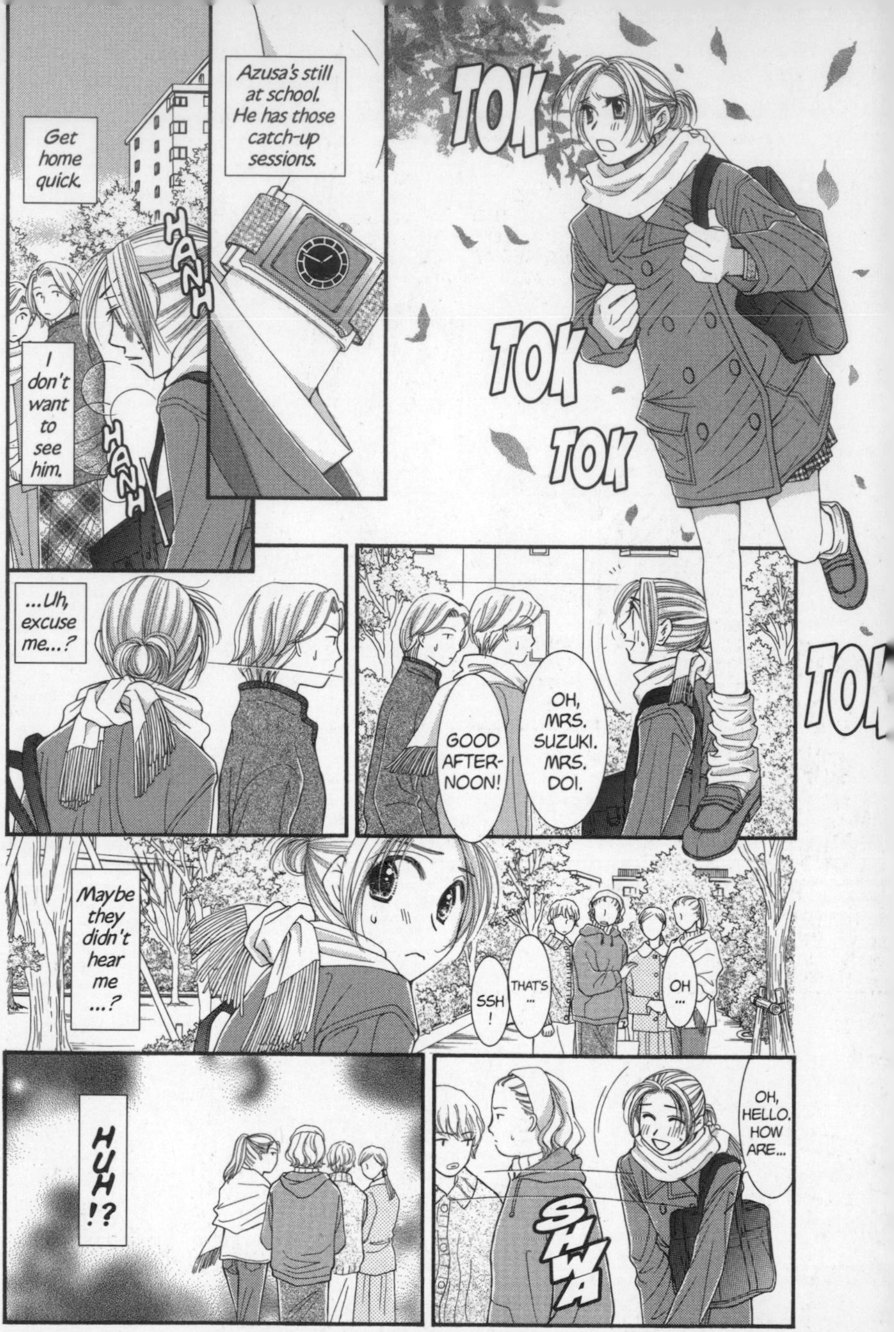
TOK
TOK
TOK
TOK
Azusa's still at school. He has those catch-up sessions.
Get home quick.
HANH
HANH
I don't want to see him.
OH, MRS. SUZUKI. MRS. DOI.
GOOD AFTER-NOON!
...Uh, excuse me...?
OH ...
THAT'S ...
SSH !
Maybe they didn't hear me ...?
OH, HELLO. HOW ARE...
SHWA
HUH!?

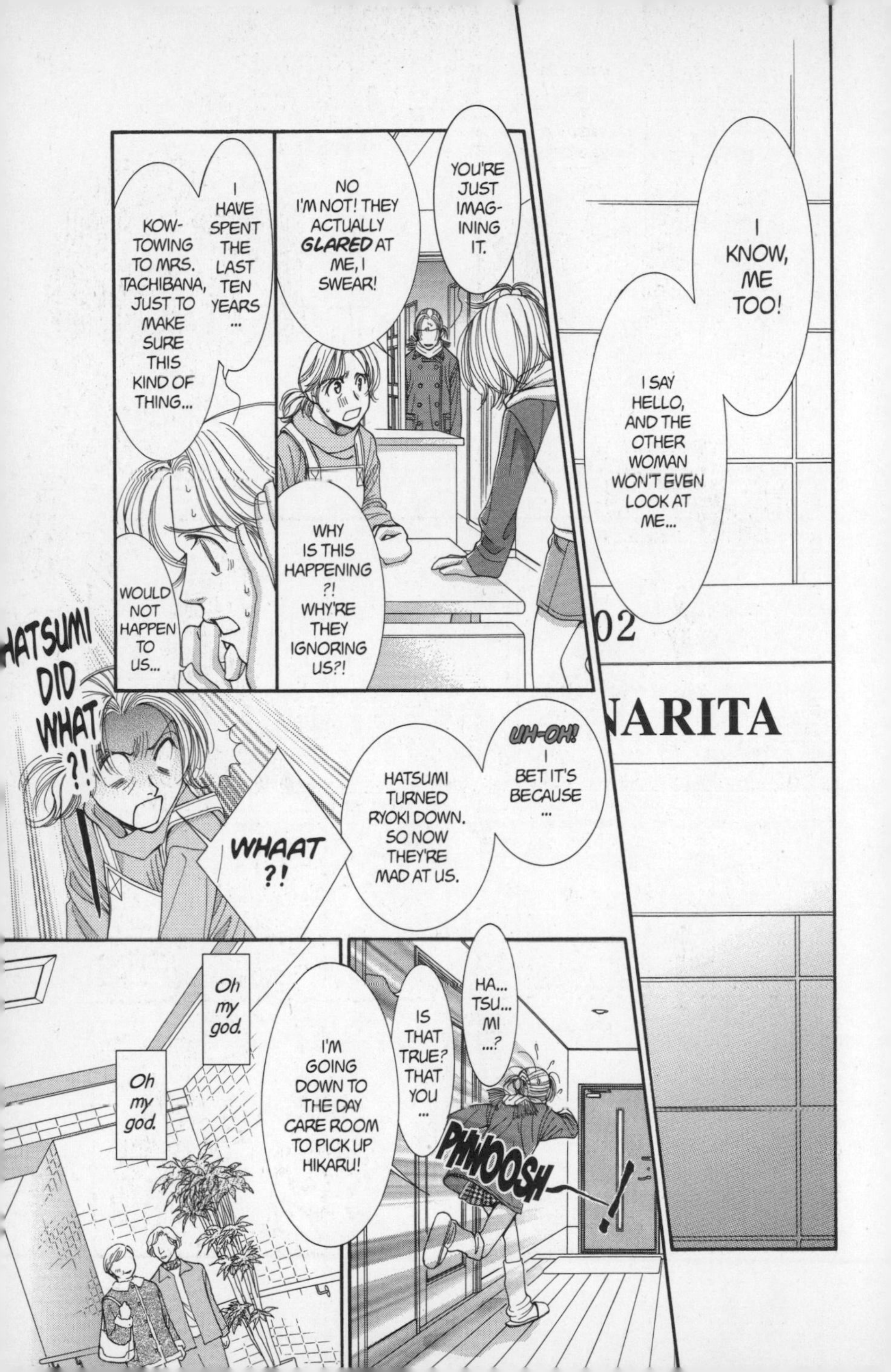
I KNOW, ME TOO!
I SAY HELLO, AND THE OTHER WOMAN WON'T EVEN LOOK AT ME...
02
NARITA
YOU'RE JUST IMAGINING IT.
NO I'M NOT! THEY ACTUALLY GLARED AT ME, I SWEAR!
WHY IS THIS HAPPENING?! WHY'RE THEY IGNORING US?!
I HAVE SPENT THE LAST TEN YEARS...
KOW-TOWING TO MRS. TACHIBANA, JUST TO MAKE SURE THIS KIND OF THING...
WOULD NOT HAPPEN TO US...
UH-OH! I BET IT'S BECAUSE...
HATSUMI TURNED RYOKI DOWN. SO NOW THEY'RE MAD AT US.
WHAAT?!
HATSUMI DID WHAT?!
HA... TSU... MI...?
IS THAT TRUE? THAT YOU...
I'M GOING DOWN TO THE DAY CARE ROOM TO PICK UP HIKARU!
PHWOOSH
Oh my god.
Oh my god.

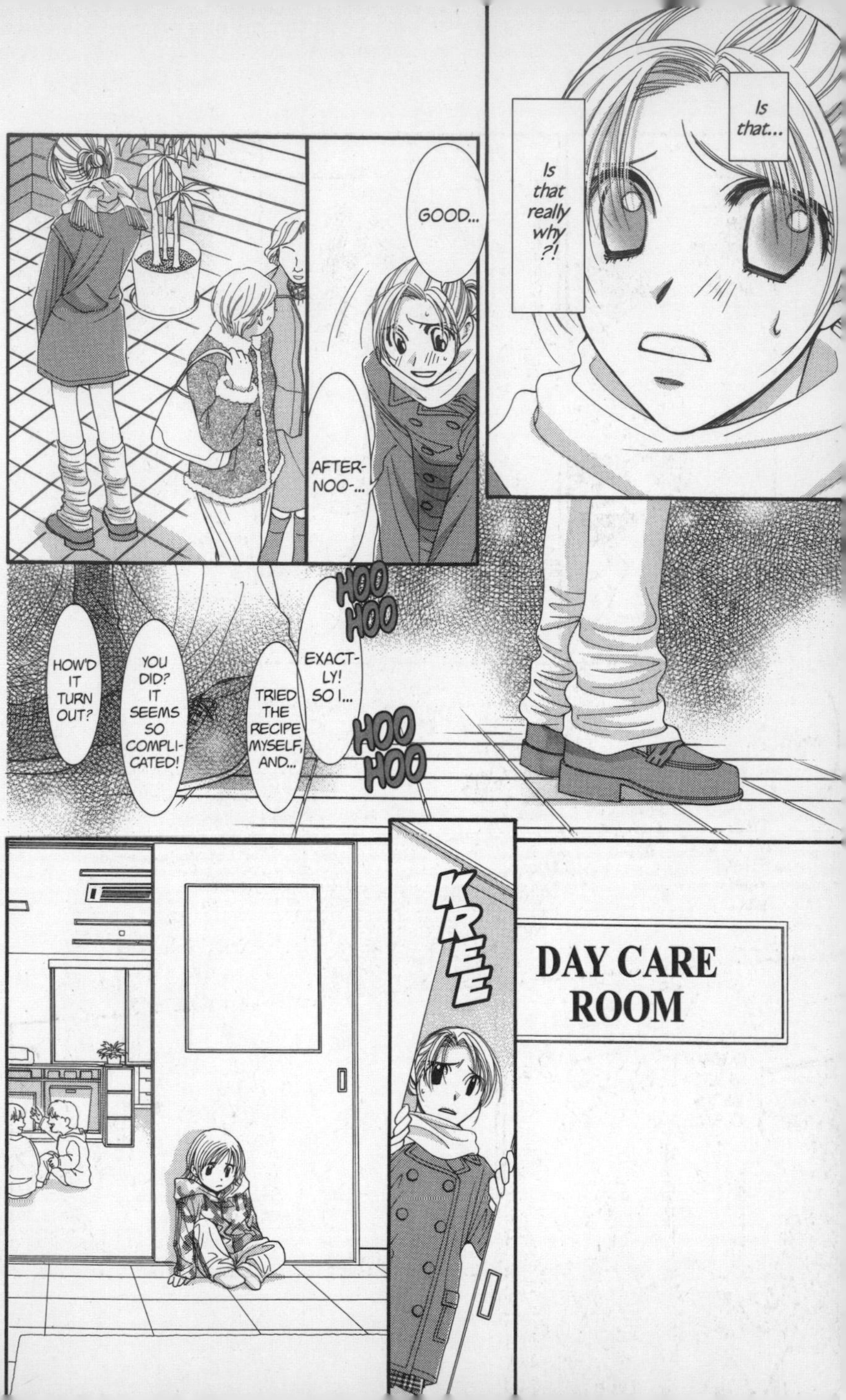

Is that...
Is that really why?!
GOOD...
AFTER-NOO-...
HOO HOO
EXACTLY! SO I...
TRIED THE RECIPE MYSELF, AND...
YOU DID? IT SEEMS SO COMPLICATED!
HOW'D IT TURN OUT?
HOO HOO
DAY CARE ROOM
KREE

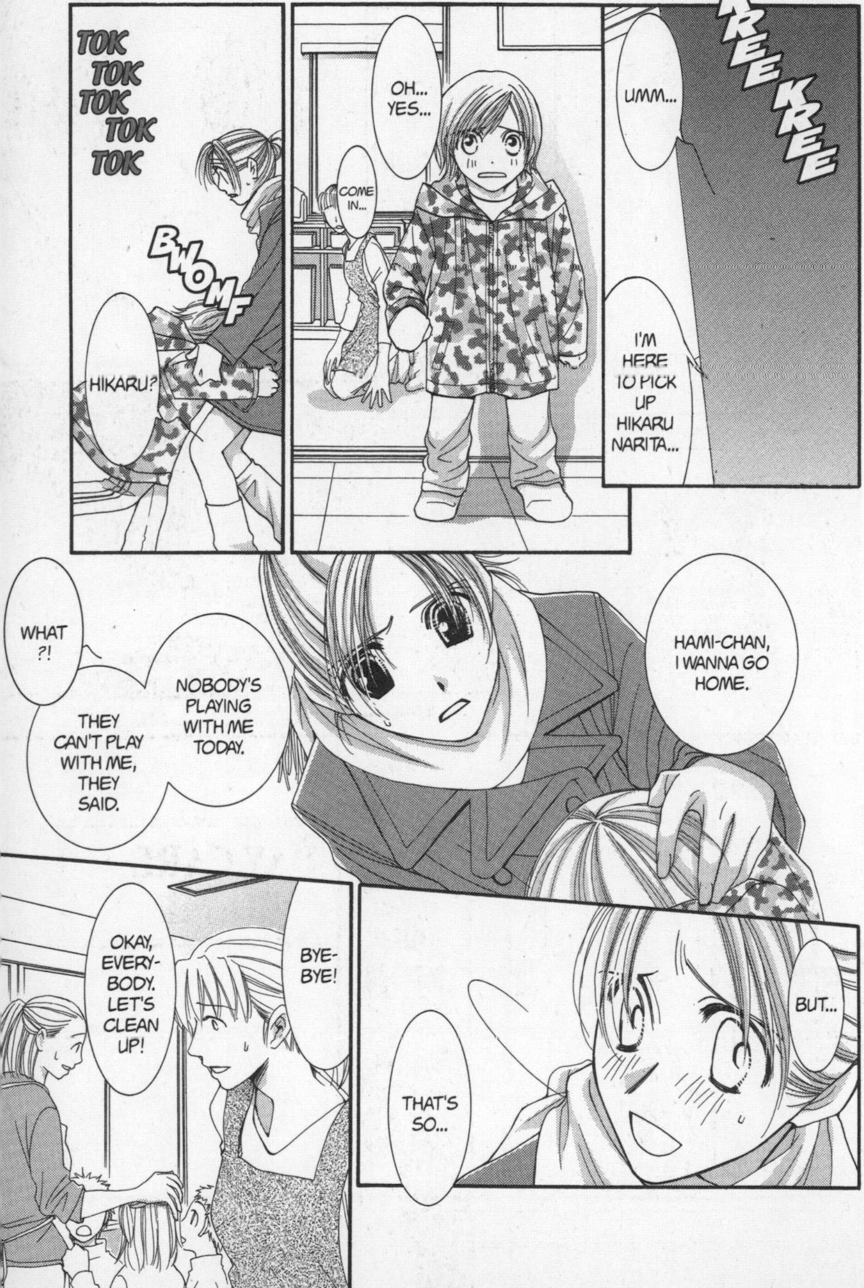
KREE KREE
UMM...
I'M HERE TO PICK UP HIKARU NARITA...
OH... YES...
COME IN...
TOK TOK TOK TOK TOK
BWOMF
HIKARU?
HAMI-CHAN, I WANNA GO HOME.
WHAT ?!
NOBODY'S PLAYING WITH ME TODAY.
THEY CAN'T PLAY WITH ME, THEY SAID.
BUT...
THAT'S SO...
BYE-BYE!
OKAY, EVERY-BODY. LET'S CLEAN UP!

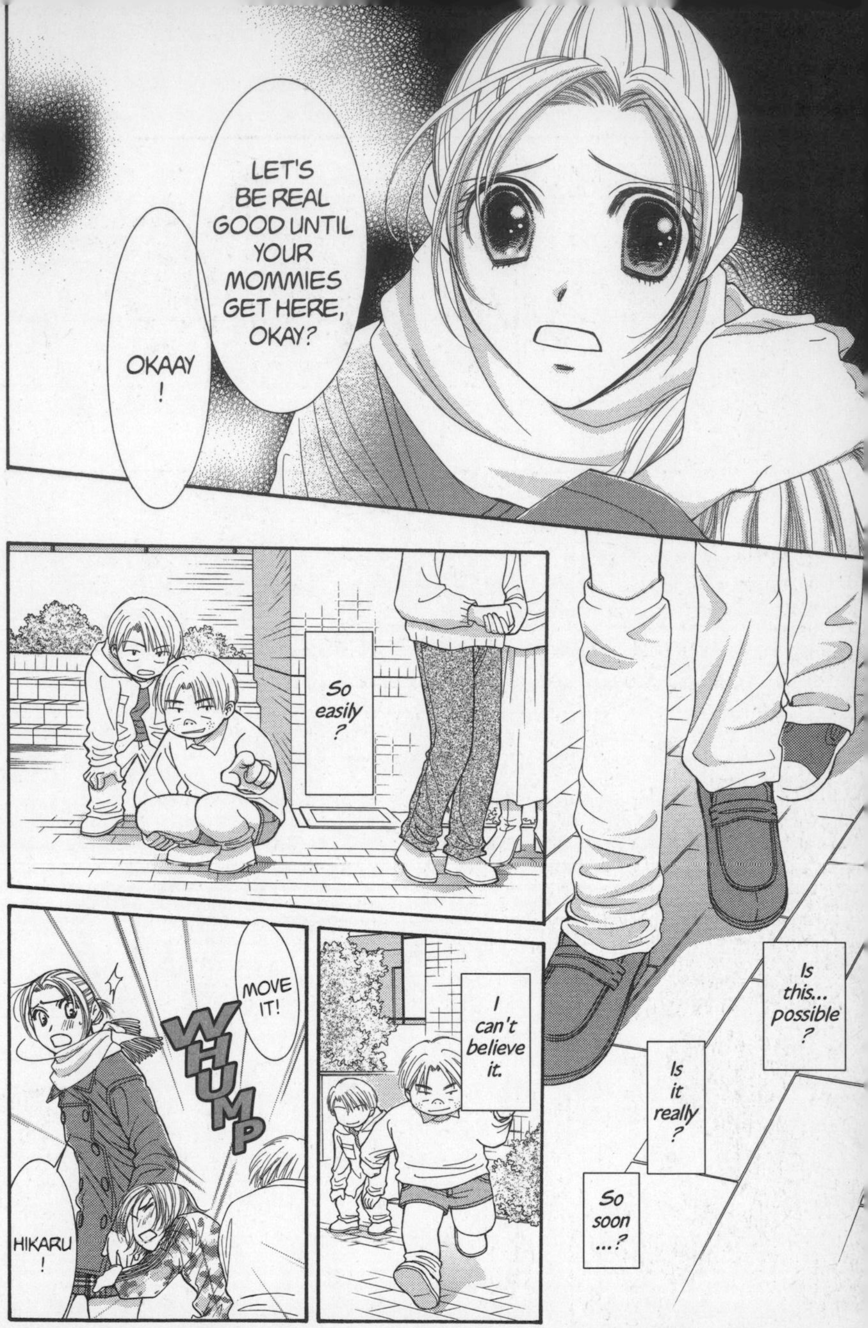
LET'S BE REAL GOOD UNTIL YOUR MOMMIES GET HERE, OKAY?
OKAAY!
Is this... possible?
Is it really?
So soon...?
So easily?
I can't believe it.
MOVE IT!
WHUMP
HIKARU!

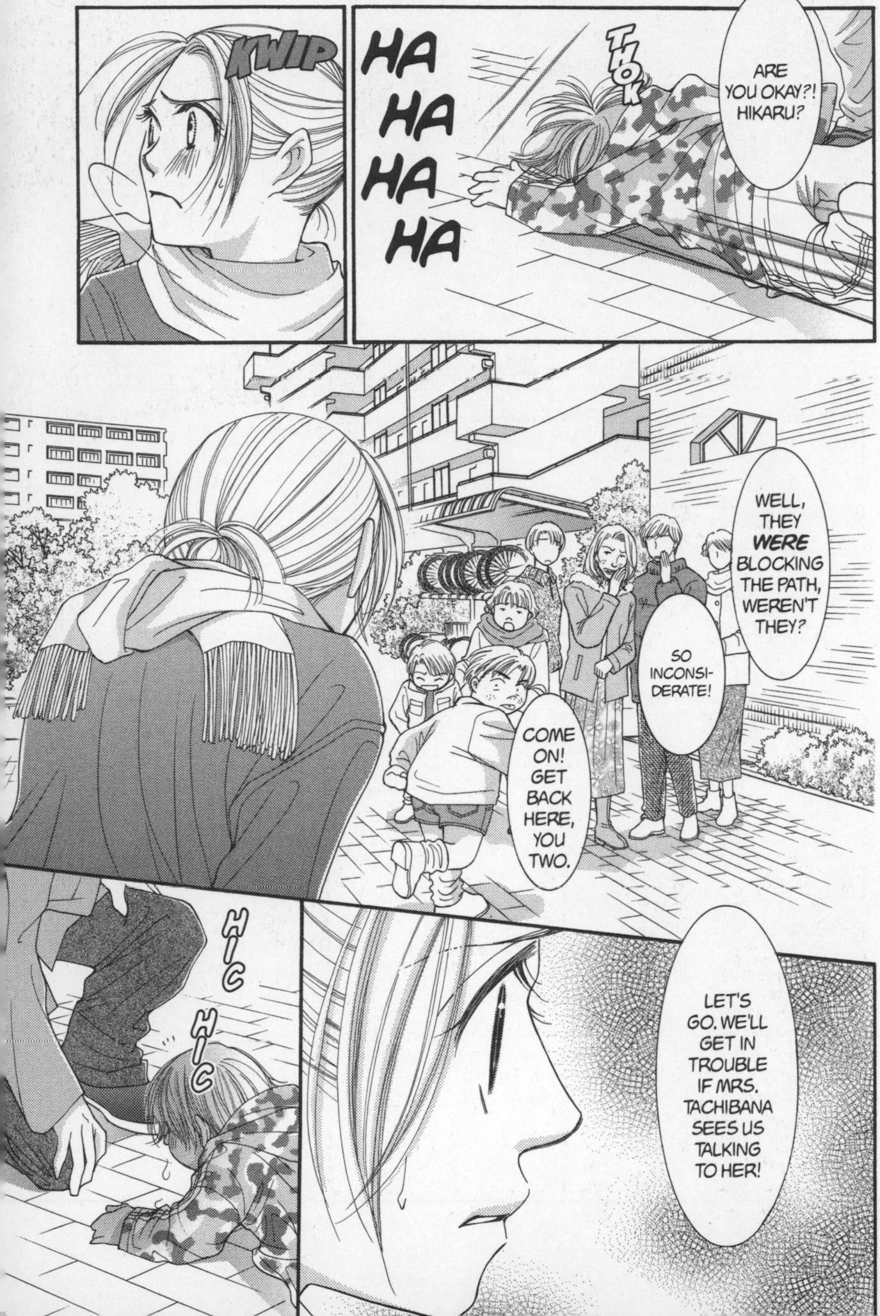
ARE YOU OKAY?! HIKARU?
THOK
HA HA HA HA
KWIP
WELL, THEY **WERE** BLOCKING THE PATH, WEREN'T THEY?
SO INCONSIDERATE!
COME ON! GET BACK HERE, YOU TWO.
LET'S GO. WE'LL GET IN TROUBLE IF MRS. TACHIBANA SEES US TALKING TO HER!
HIC HIC

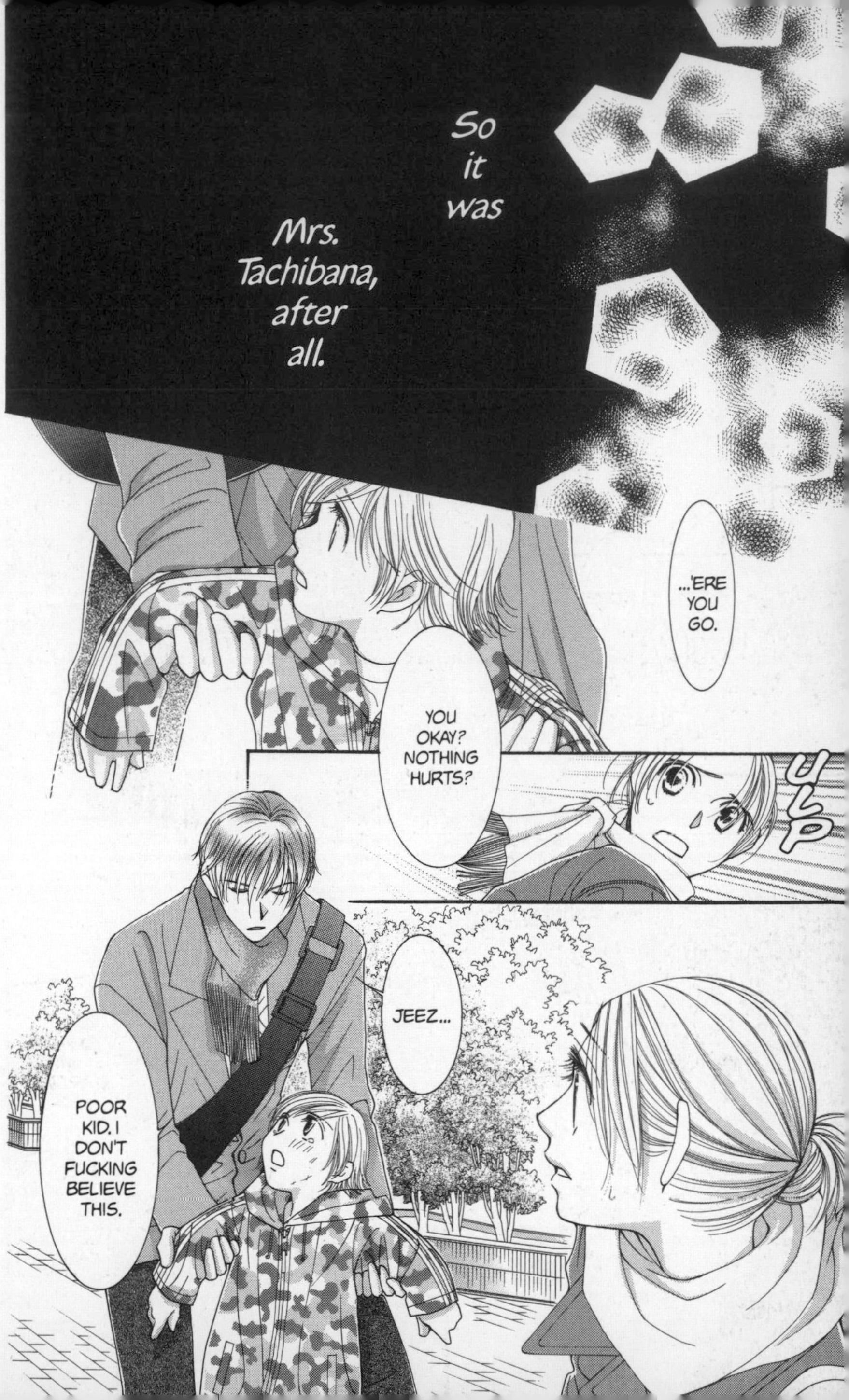
So it was Mrs. Tachibana, after all.
...'ERE YOU GO.
YOU OKAY? NOTHING HURTS?
ULP
JEEZ...
POOR KID. I DON'T FUCKING BELIEVE THIS.

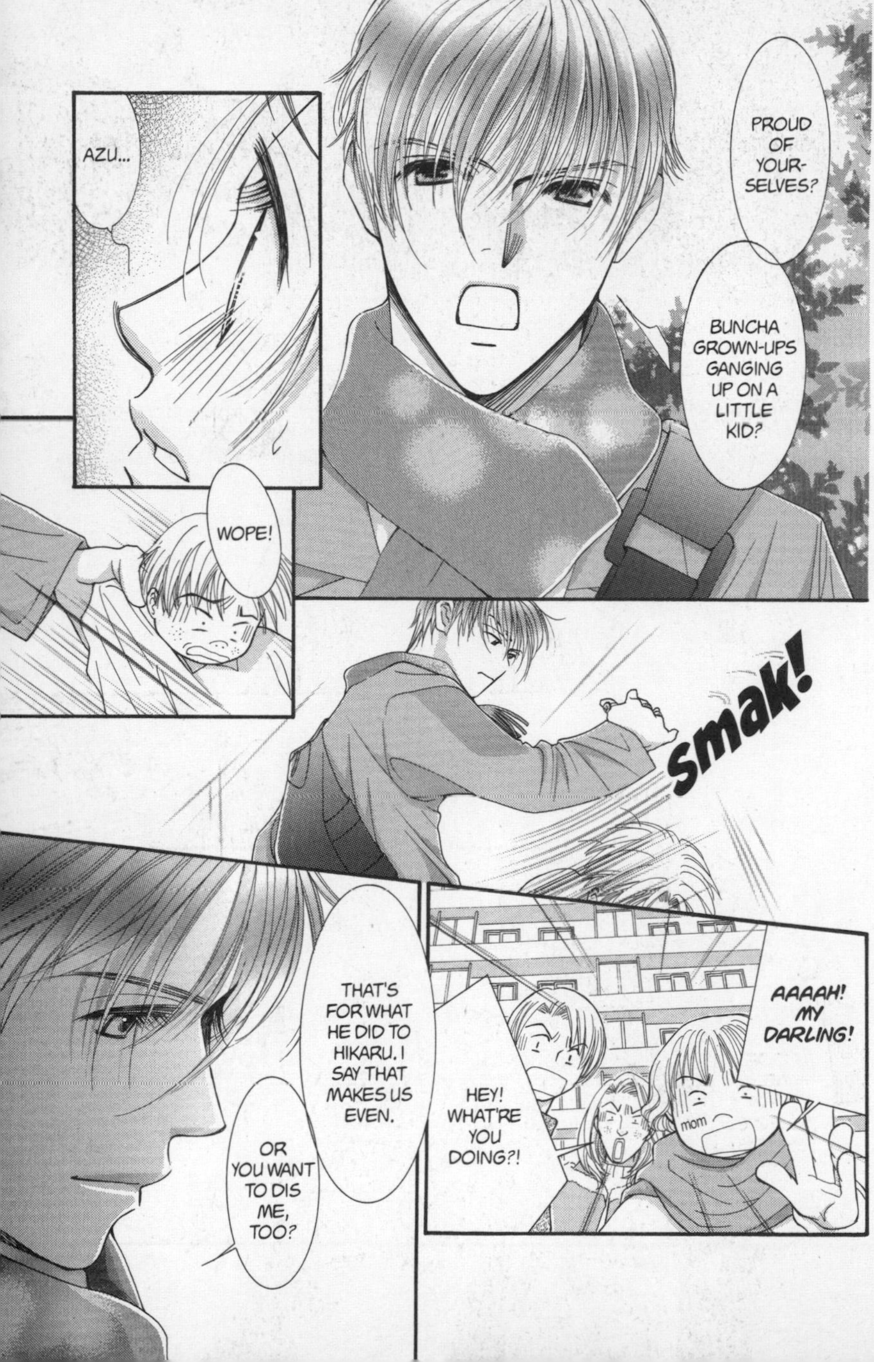
PROUD OF YOUR-SELVES?
BUNCHA GROWN-UPS GANGING UP ON A LITTLE KID?
AZU...
WOPE!
SMAK!
AAAAH! MY DARLING!
mom
HEY! WHAT'RE YOU DOING?!
THAT'S FOR WHAT HE DID TO HIKARU. I SAY THAT MAKES US EVEN.
OR YOU WANT TO DIS ME, TOO?

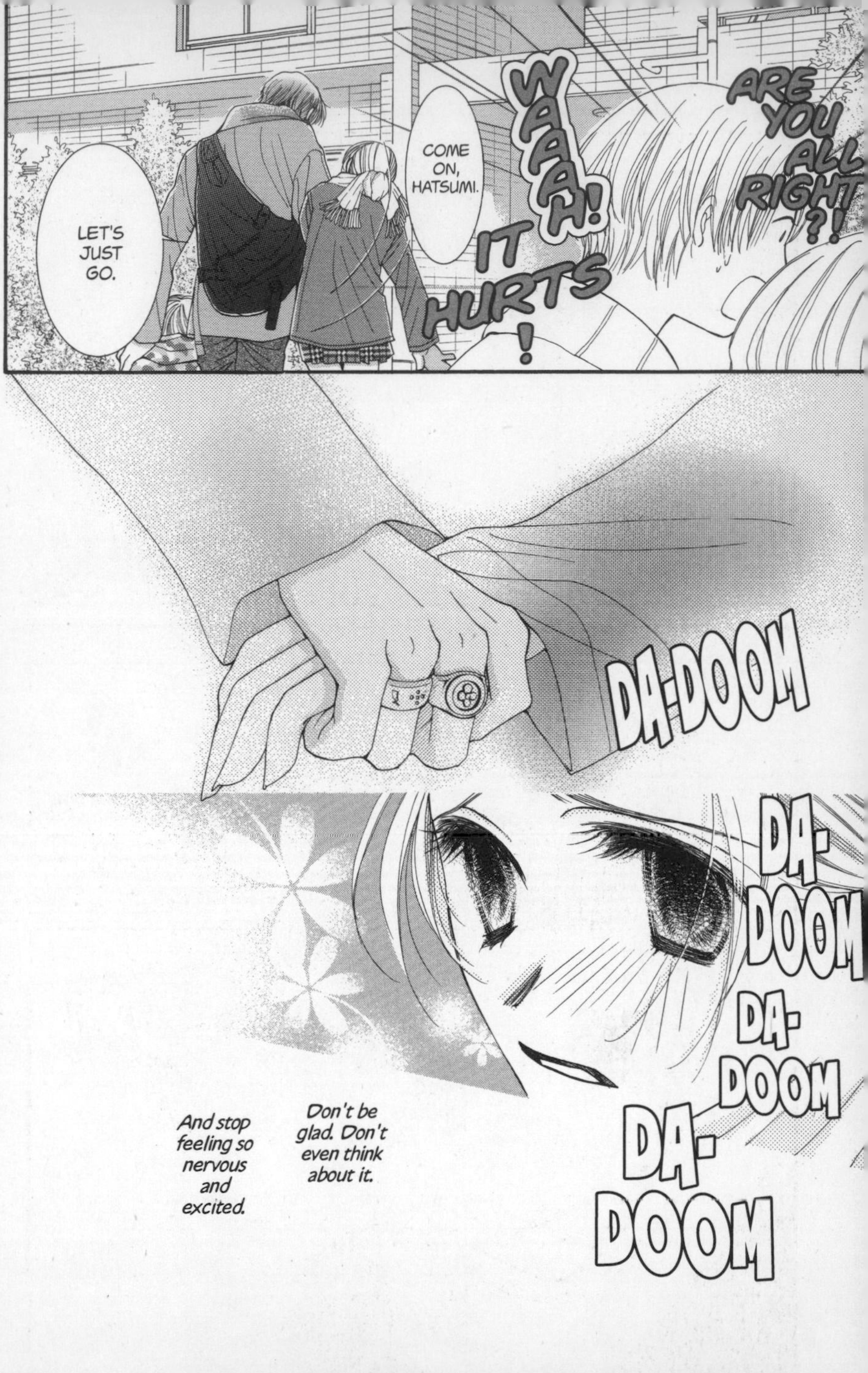
ARE YOU ALL RIGHT?!
WAAAH! IT HURTS!
COME ON, HATSUMI.
LET'S JUST GO.
DA-DOOM
DA-DOOM
DA-DOOM
DA-DOOM
Don't be glad. Don't even think about it.
And stop feeling so nervous and excited.

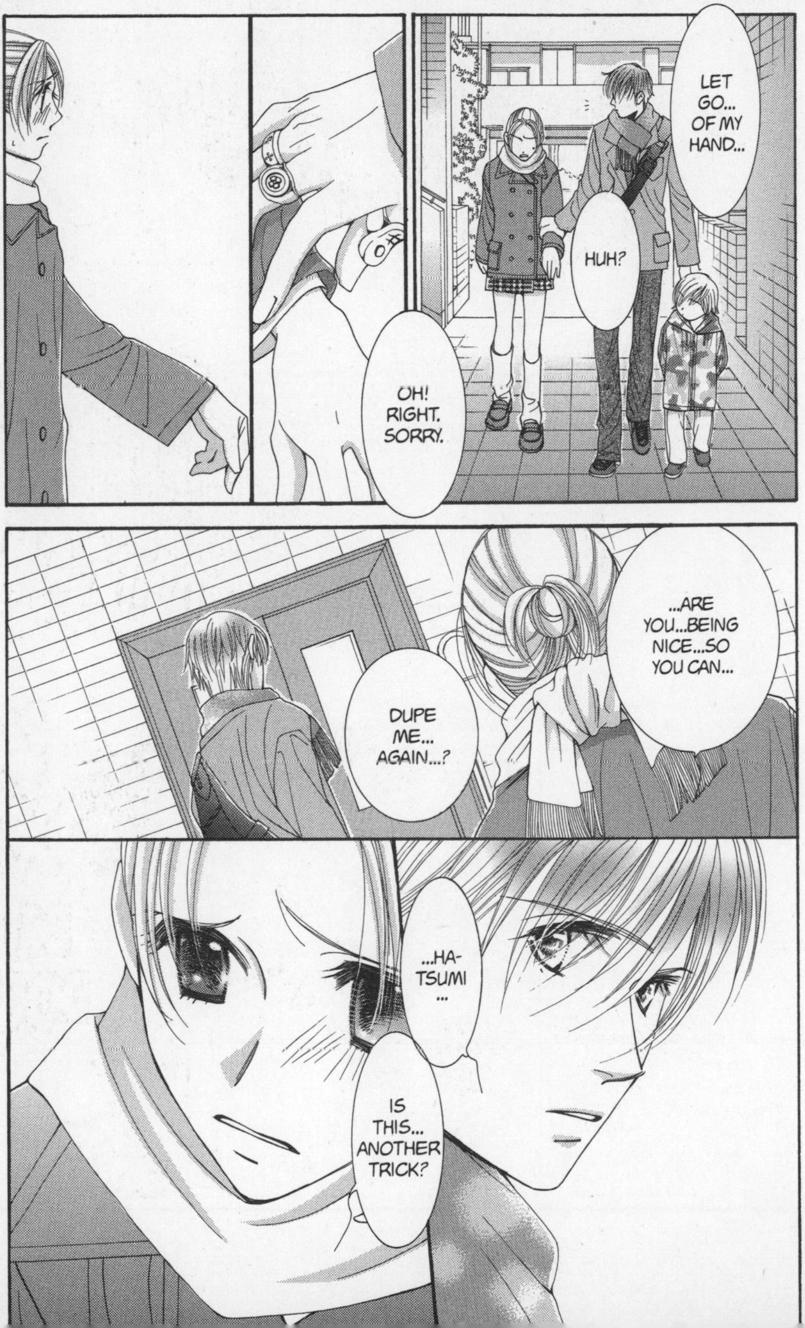
LET GO... OF MY HAND...
HUH?
OH! RIGHT. SORRY.
...ARE YOU...BEING NICE...SO YOU CAN...
DUPE ME... AGAIN...?
...HA-TSUMI...
IS THIS... ANOTHER TRICK?

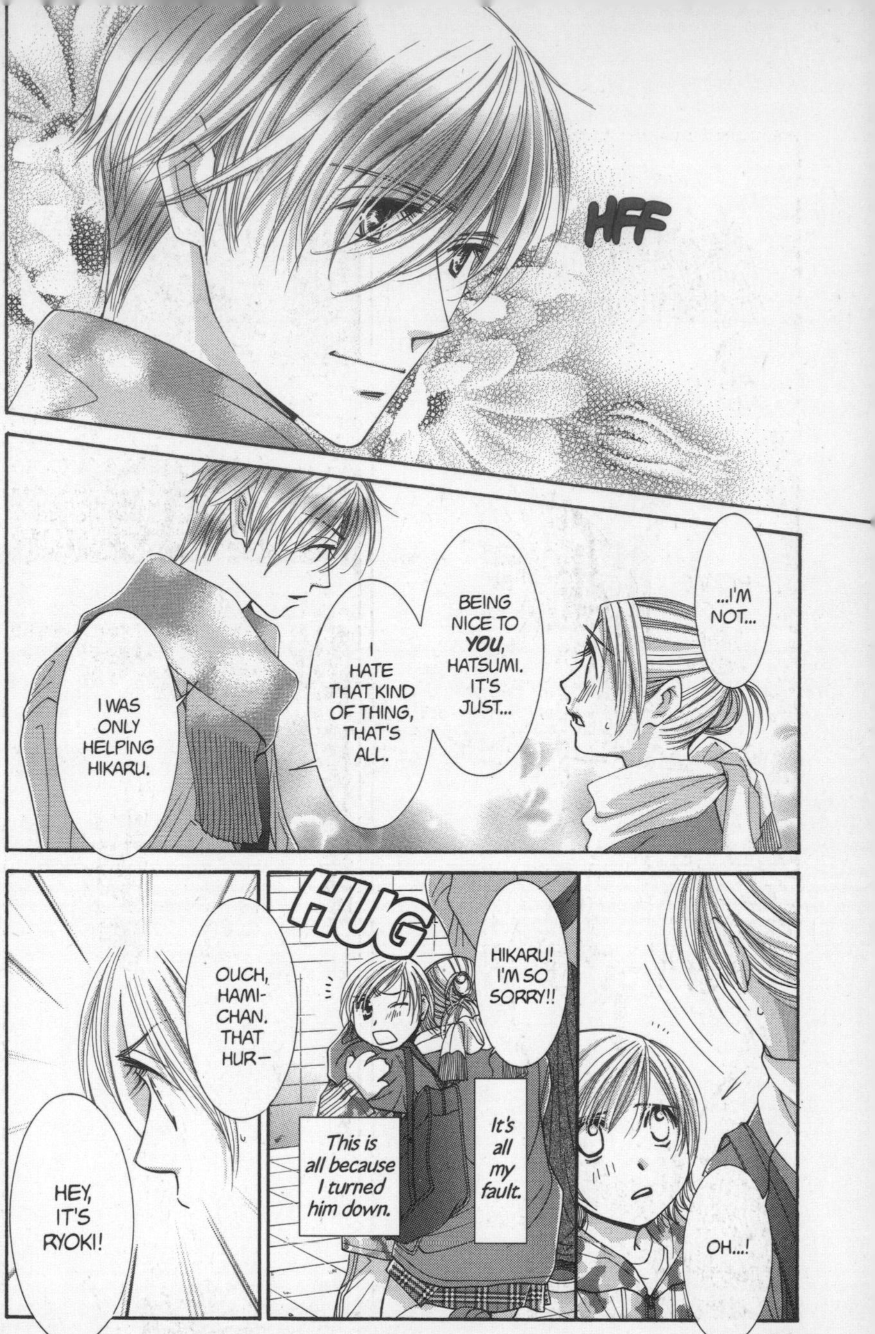
HFF
...I'M NOT...
BEING NICE TO YOU, HATSUMI. IT'S JUST...
I HATE THAT KIND OF THING, THAT'S ALL.
I WAS ONLY HELPING HIKARU.
OH...!
HUG
HIKARU! I'M SO SORRY!!
It's all my fault.
This is all because I turned him down.
OUCH, HAMI-CHAN. THAT HUR—
HEY, IT'S RYOKI!

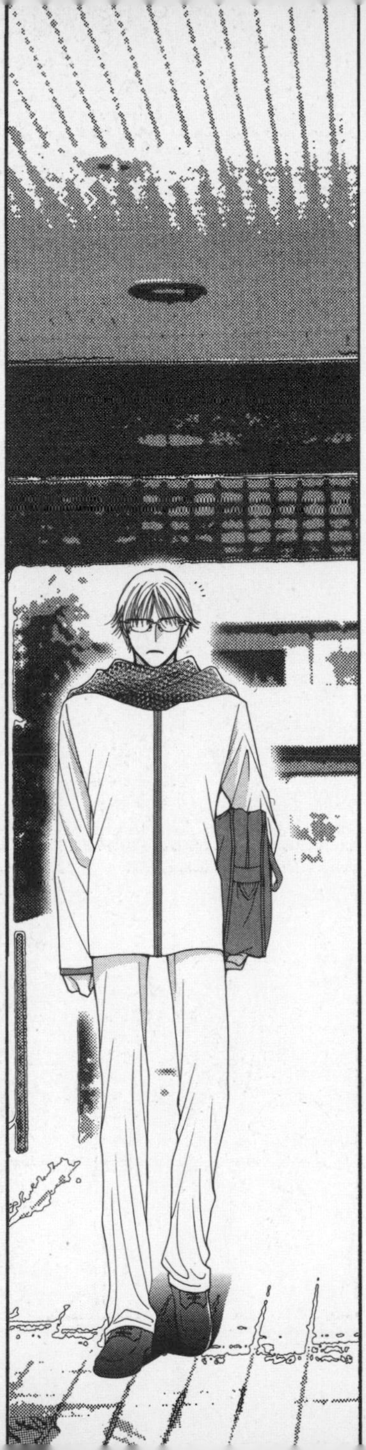

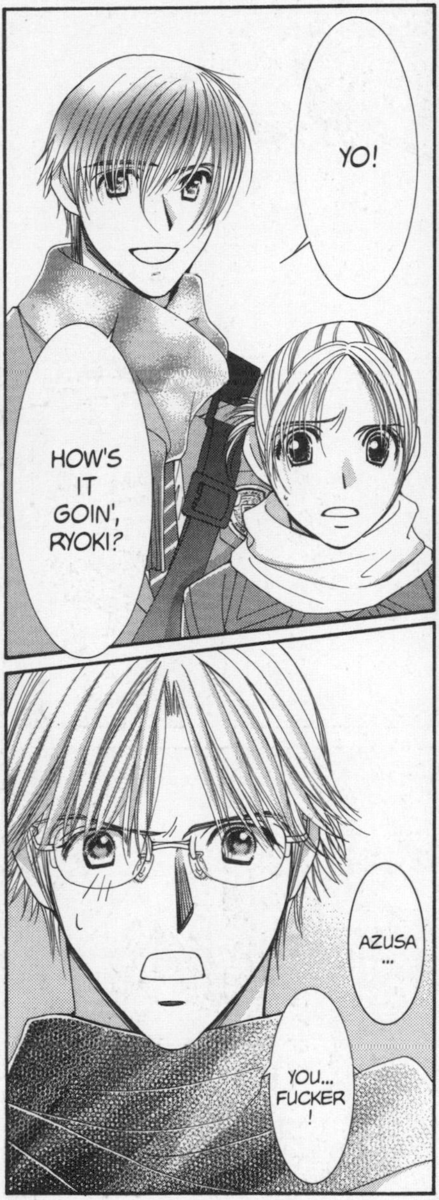
YO!
HOW'S IT GOIN', RYOKI?
AZUSA ...
YOU... FUCKER !

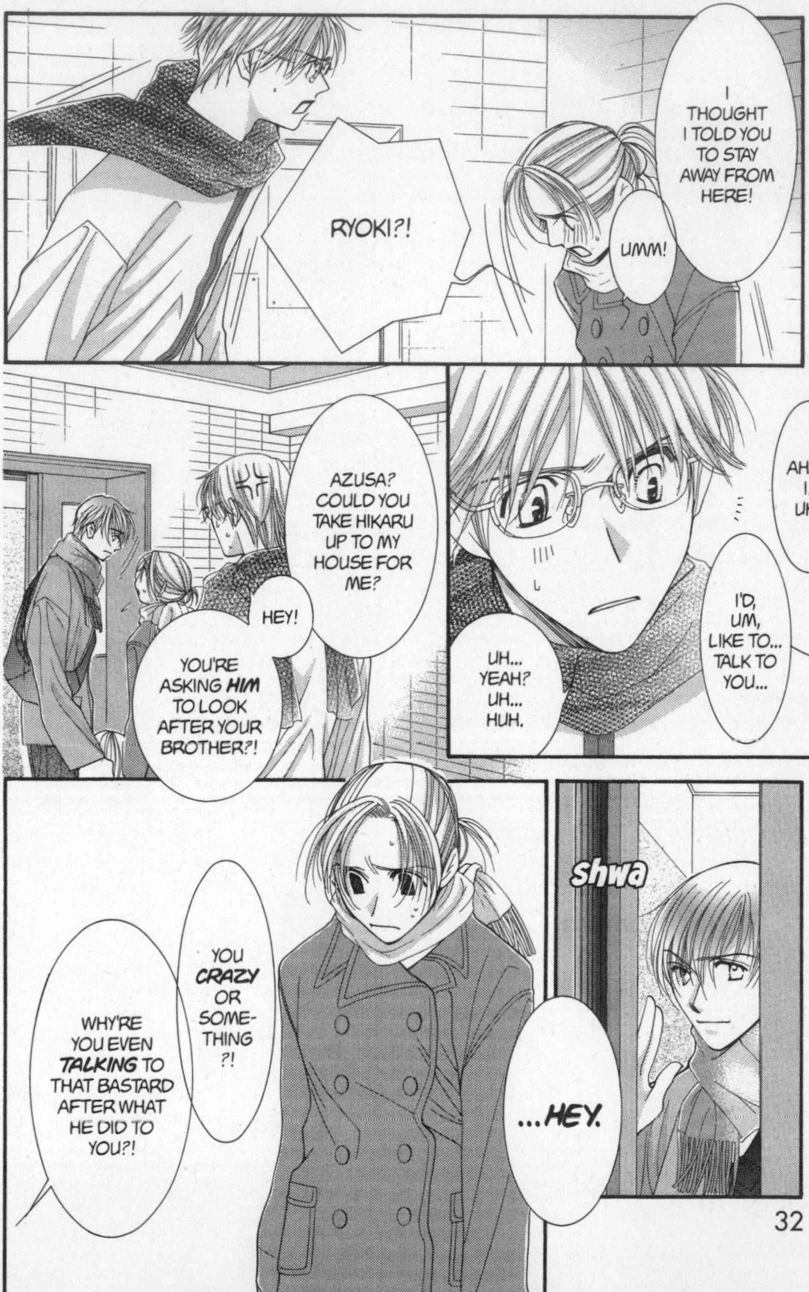
I THOUGHT I TOLD YOU TO STAY AWAY FROM HERE!
UMM!
RYOKI?!
AHM... I... UH...
I'D, UM, LIKE TO... TALK TO YOU...
UH... YEAH? UH... HUH.
AZUSA? COULD YOU TAKE HIKARU UP TO MY HOUSE FOR ME?
HEY!
YOU'RE ASKING **HIM** TO LOOK AFTER YOUR BROTHER?!
Shwa
...**HEY.**
YOU **CRAZY** OR SOME-THING?!
WHY'RE YOU EVEN **TALKING** TO THAT BASTARD AFTER WHAT HE DID TO YOU?!

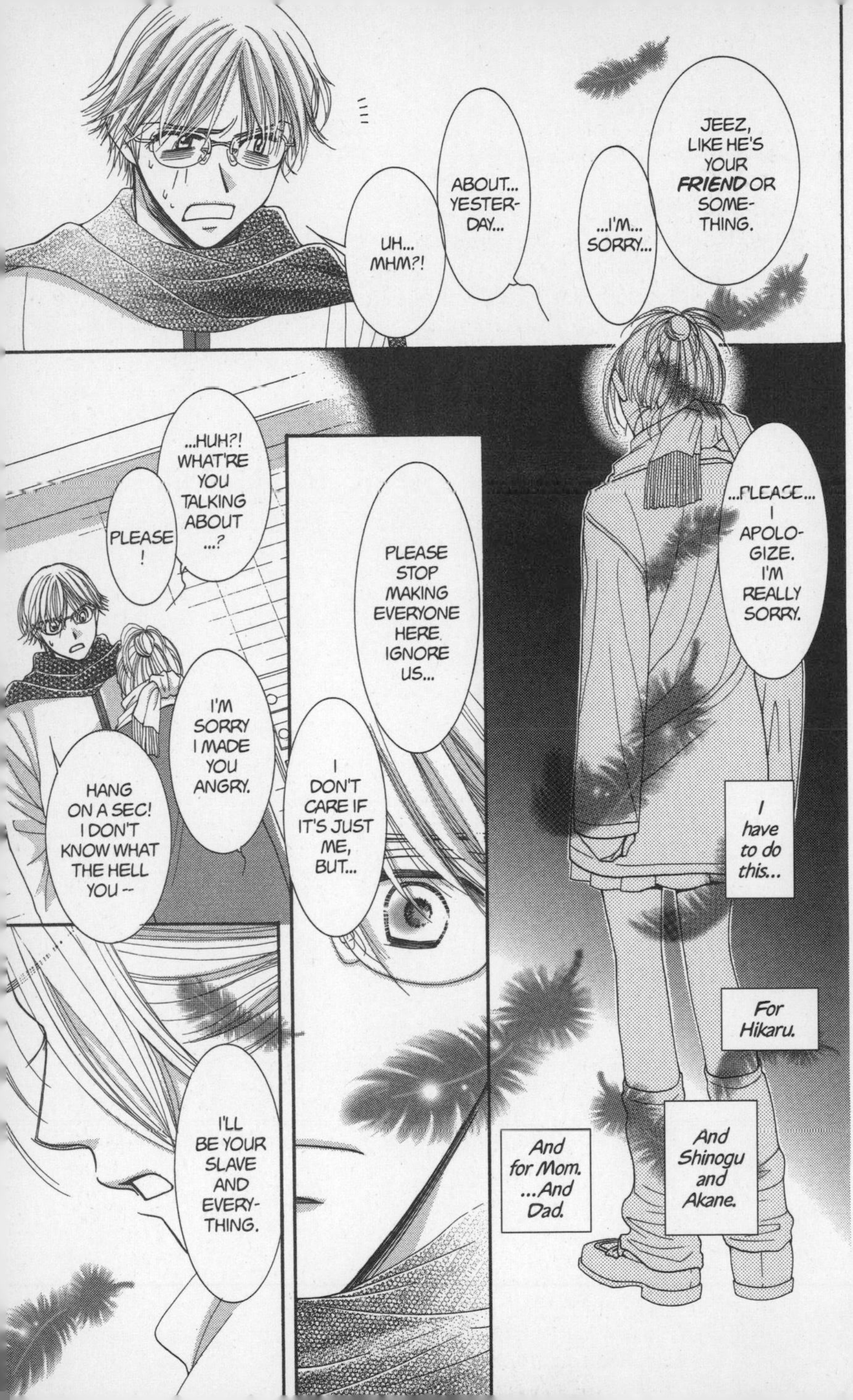

JEEZ, LIKE HE'S YOUR **FRIEND** OR SOMETHING.
...I'M... SORRY...
ABOUT... YESTERDAY...
UH... MHM?!
...PLEASE... I APOLOGIZE. I'M REALLY SORRY.
I have to do this...
For Hikaru.
And Shinogu and Akane.
And for Mom. ...And Dad.
PLEASE STOP MAKING EVERYONE HERE IGNORE US...
I DON'T CARE IF IT'S JUST ME, BUT...
...HUH?! WHAT'RE YOU TALKING ABOUT ...?
PLEASE!
I'M SORRY I MADE YOU ANGRY.
HANG ON A SEC! I DON'T KNOW WHAT THE HELL YOU --
I'LL BE YOUR SLAVE AND EVERYTHING.

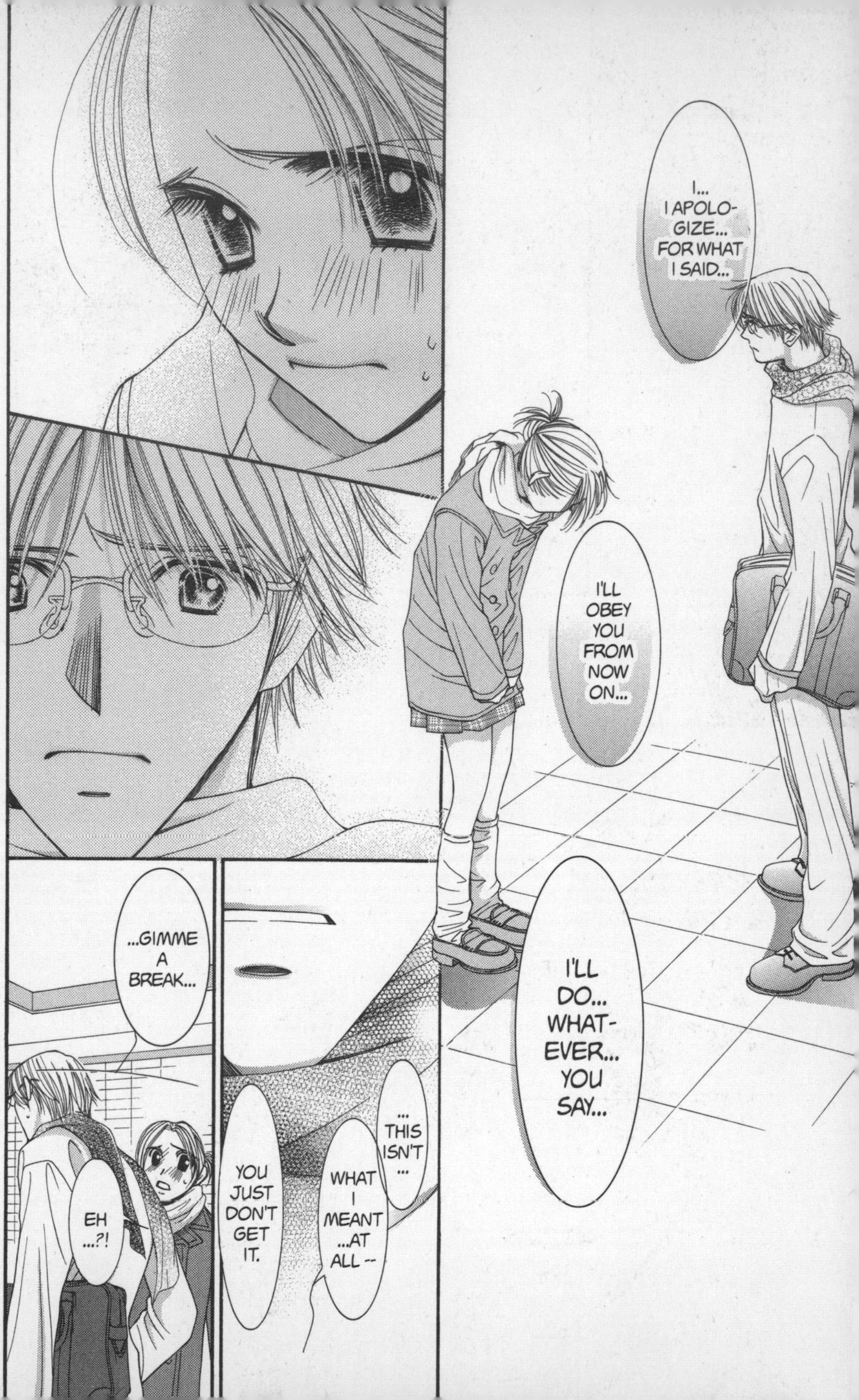
I... I APOLOGIZE... FOR WHAT I SAID...
I'LL OBEY YOU FROM NOW ON...
I'LL DO... WHATEVER... YOU SAY...
... THIS ISN'T ...
WHAT I MEANT ...AT ALL --
YOU JUST DON'T GET IT.
...GIMME A BREAK...
EH ...?!

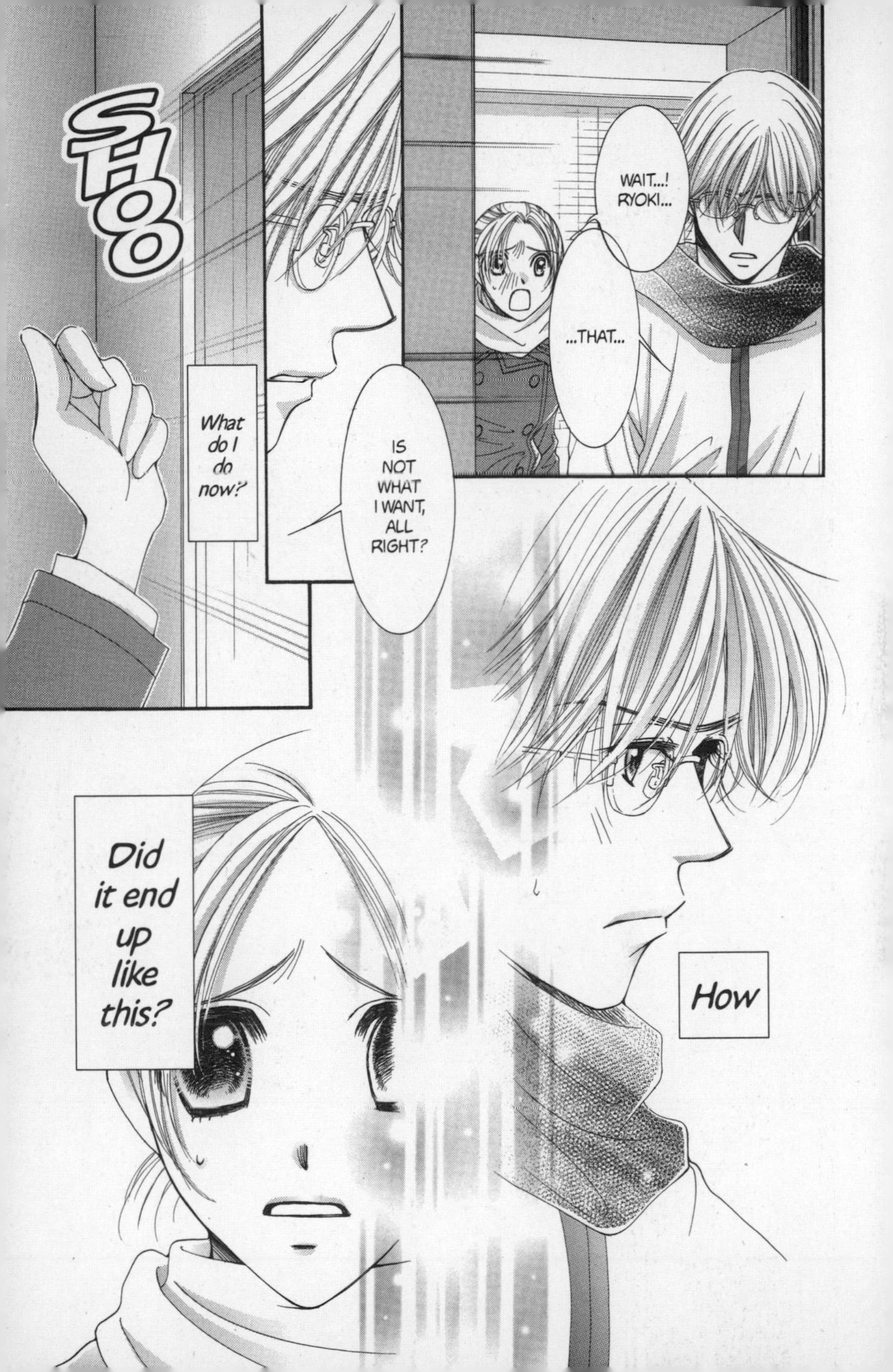
WAIT...! RYOKI...
...THAT...
IS NOT WHAT I WANT, ALL RIGHT?
SHOO
What do I do now?
How
Did it end up like this?

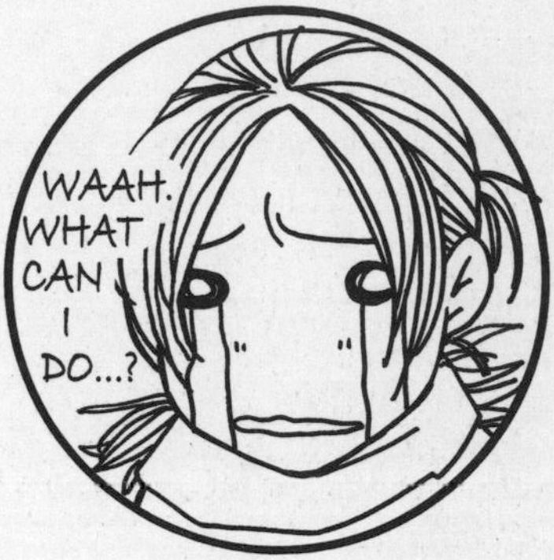
WAAH. WHAT CAN I DO...?

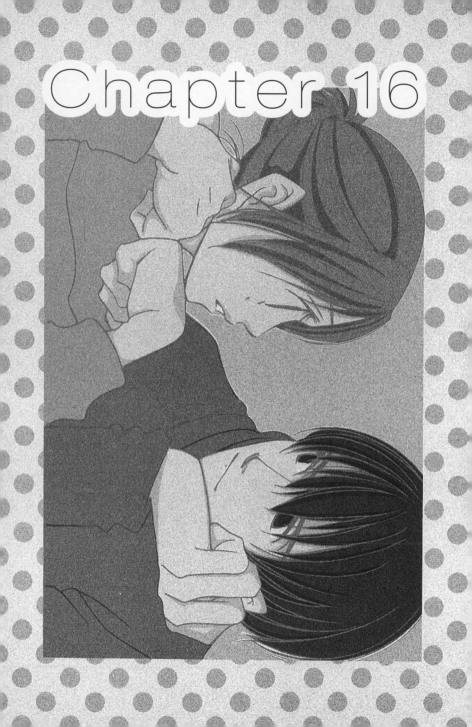

Chapter 16

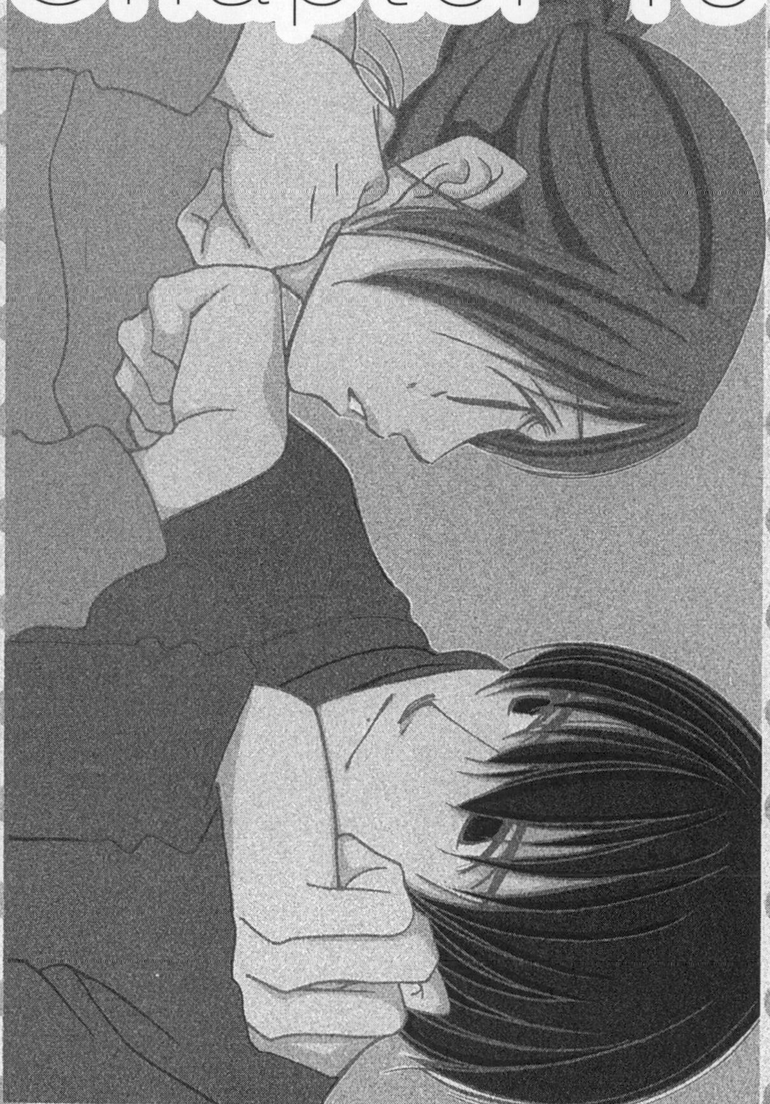

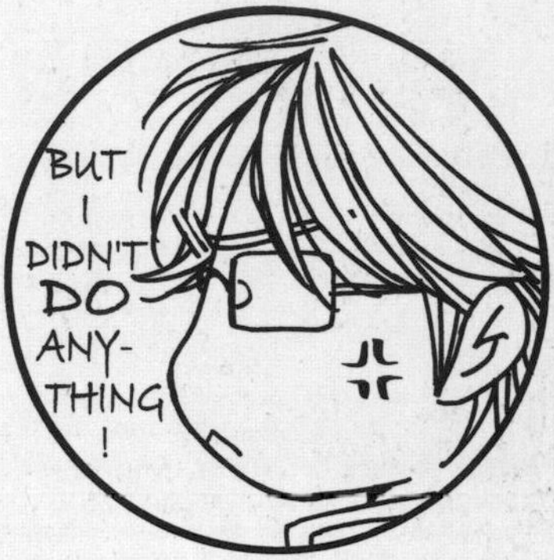
BUT I DIDN'T DO ANYTHING!

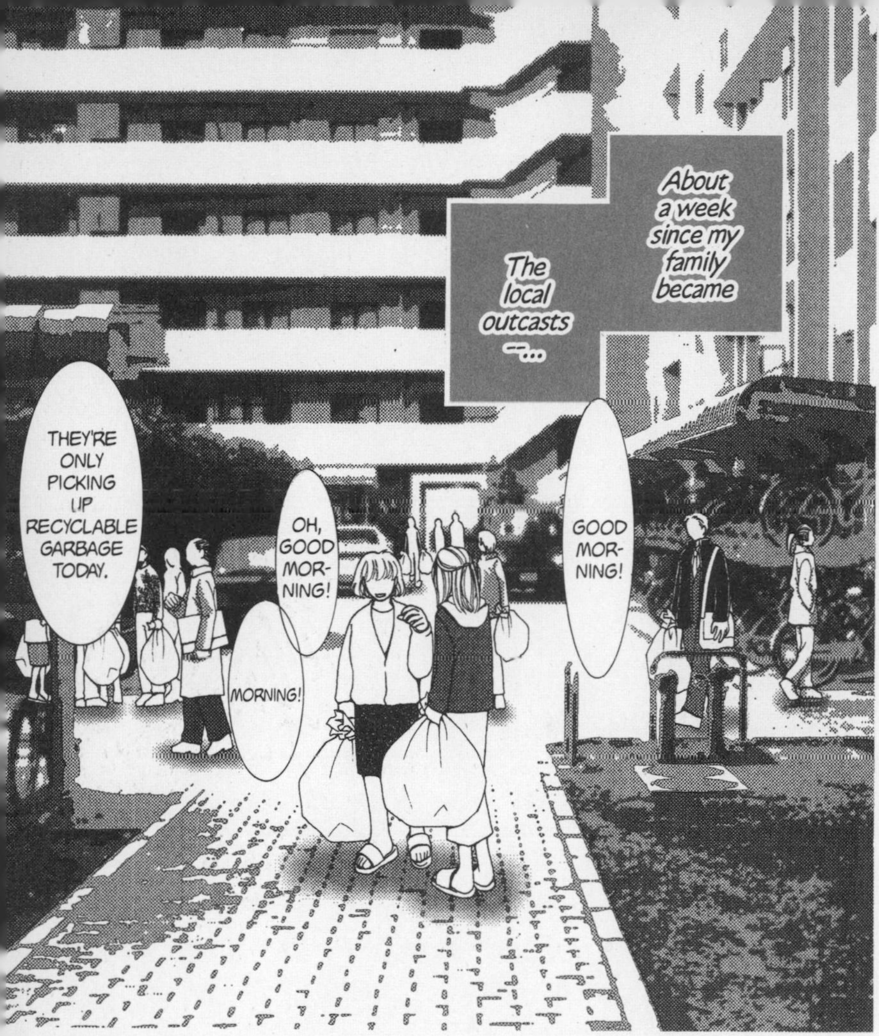
About a week since my family became
The local outcasts --...
GOOD MOR-NING!
OH, GOOD MOR-NING!
MORNING!
THEY'RE ONLY PICKING UP RECYCLABLE GARBAGE TODAY.

hot gimmick

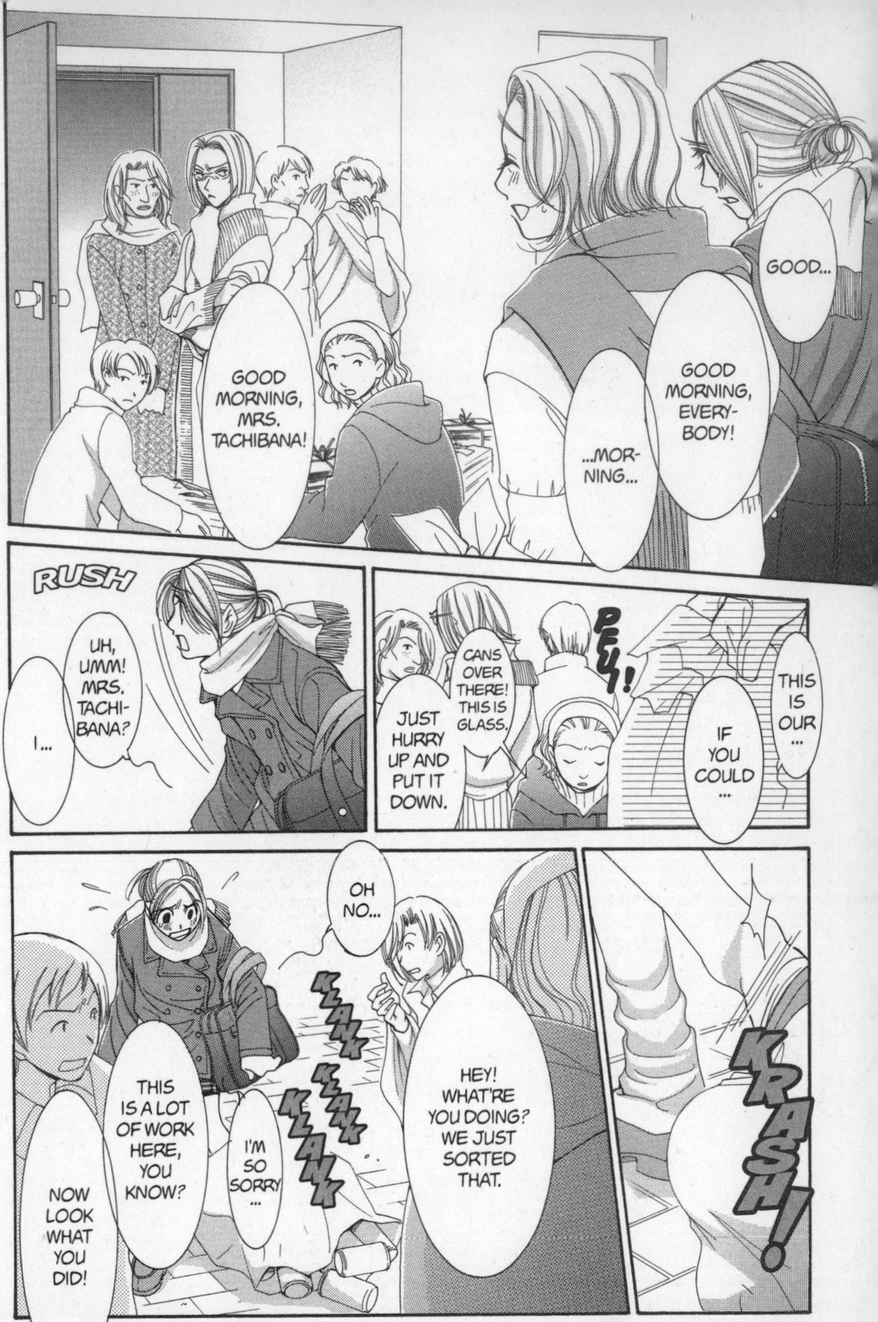
GOOD...
GOOD MORNING, EVERY-BODY!
...MOR-NING...
GOOD MORNING, MRS. TACHIBANA!
THIS IS OUR ...
IF YOU COULD ...
PEU!
CANS OVER THERE! THIS IS GLASS.
JUST HURRY UP AND PUT IT DOWN.
RUSH
UH, UMM! MRS. TACHI-BANA?
I...
KRASH!
OH NO...
HEY! WHAT'RE YOU DOING? WE JUST SORTED THAT.
KLANK KLANK KLANK
I'M SO SORRY ...
THIS IS A LOT OF WORK HERE, YOU KNOW?
NOW LOOK WHAT YOU DID!

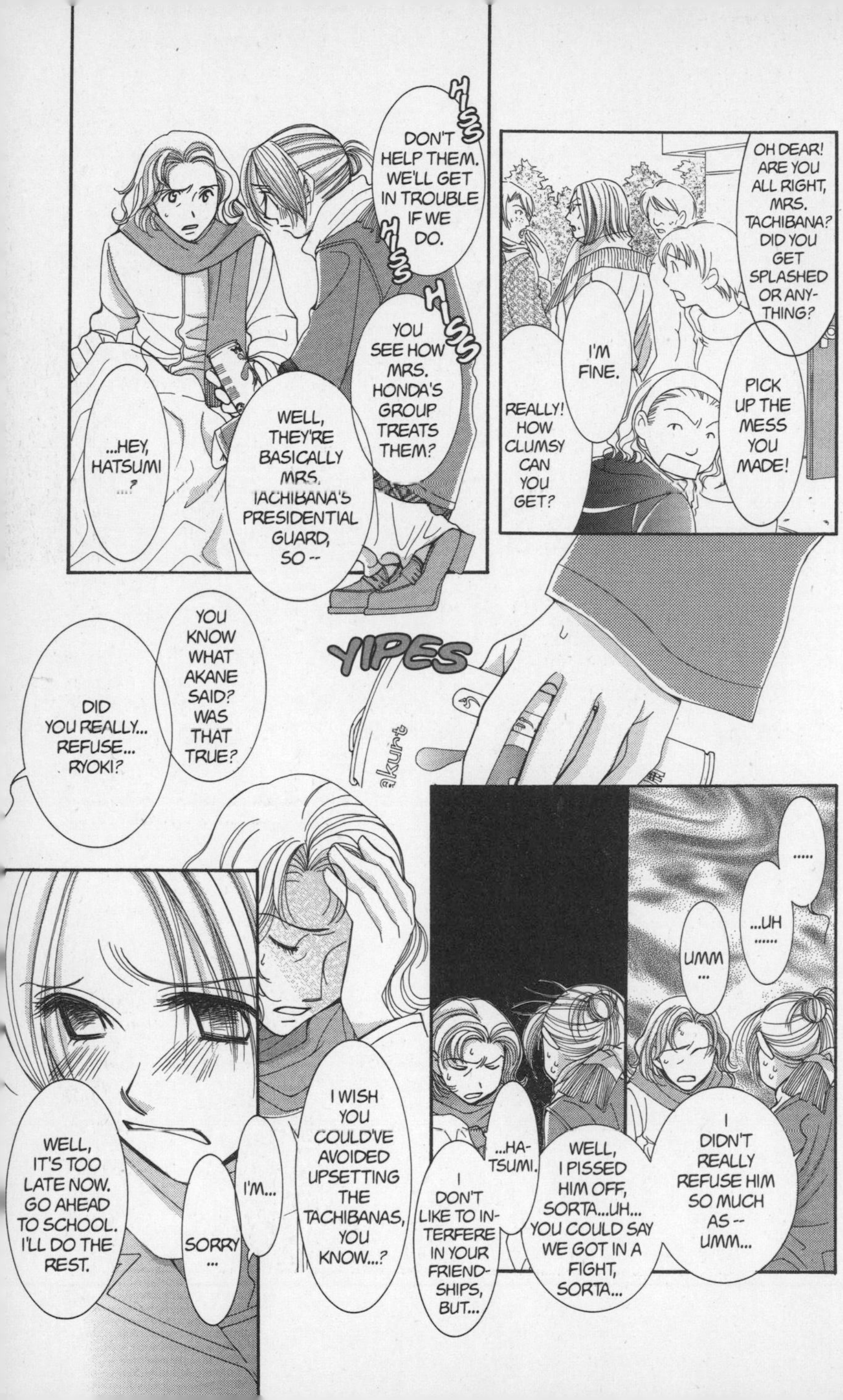
OH DEAR! ARE YOU ALL RIGHT, MRS. TACHIBANA? DID YOU GET SPLASHED OR ANYTHING?
PICK UP THE MESS YOU MADE!
I'M FINE.
REALLY! HOW CLUMSY CAN YOU GET?
HISS
DON'T HELP THEM. WE'LL GET IN TROUBLE IF WE DO.
HISS
HISS
YOU SEE HOW MRS. HONDA'S GROUP TREATS THEM?
WELL, THEY'RE BASICALLY MRS. TACHIBANA'S PRESIDENTIAL GUARD, SO --
...HEY, HATSUMI ...?
YIPES
YOU KNOW WHAT AKANE SAID? WAS THAT TRUE?
DID YOU REALLY... REFUSE... RYOKI?
......
...UH ......
UMM ...
I DIDN'T REALLY REFUSE HIM SO MUCH AS -- UMM...
WELL, I PISSED HIM OFF, SORTA...UH... YOU COULD SAY WE GOT IN A FIGHT, SORTA...
...HA-TSUMI.
I DON'T LIKE TO IN-TERFERE IN YOUR FRIEND-SHIPS, BUT...
I WISH YOU COULD'VE AVOIDED UPSETTING THE TACHIBANAS, YOU KNOW...?
I'M...
SORRY ...
WELL, IT'S TOO LATE NOW. GO AHEAD TO SCHOOL. I'LL DO THE REST.

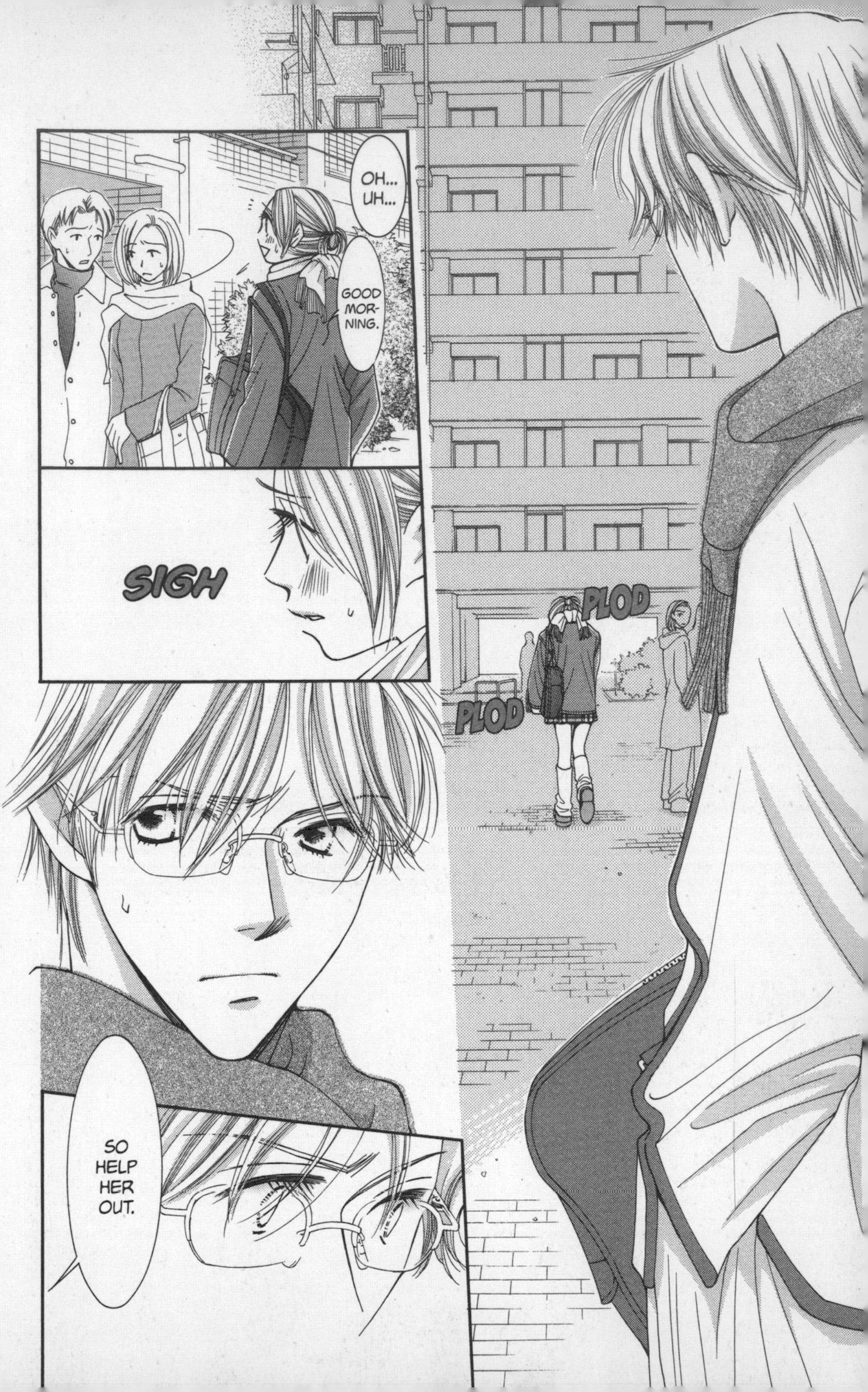
PLOD
PLOD
OH... UH...
GOOD MORNING.
SIGH
SO HELP HER OUT.

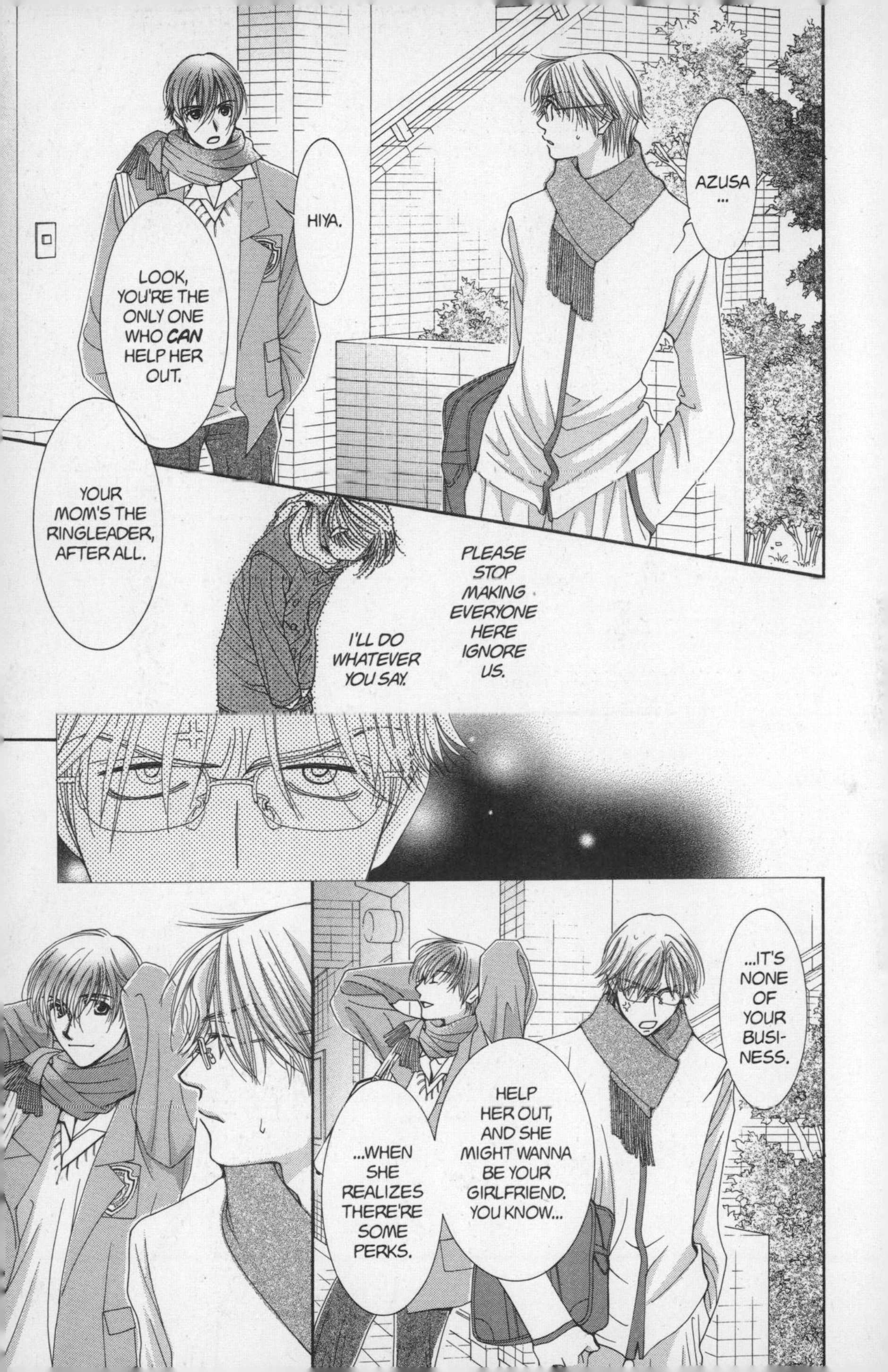
AZUSA ...
HIYA.
LOOK, YOU'RE THE ONLY ONE WHO **CAN** HELP HER OUT.
YOUR MOM'S THE RINGLEADER, AFTER ALL.
PLEASE STOP MAKING EVERYONE HERE IGNORE US.
I'LL DO WHATEVER YOU SAY.
...IT'S NONE OF YOUR BUSI-NESS.
HELP HER OUT, AND SHE MIGHT WANNA BE YOUR GIRLFRIEND. YOU KNOW...
...WHEN SHE REALIZES THERE'RE SOME PERKS.

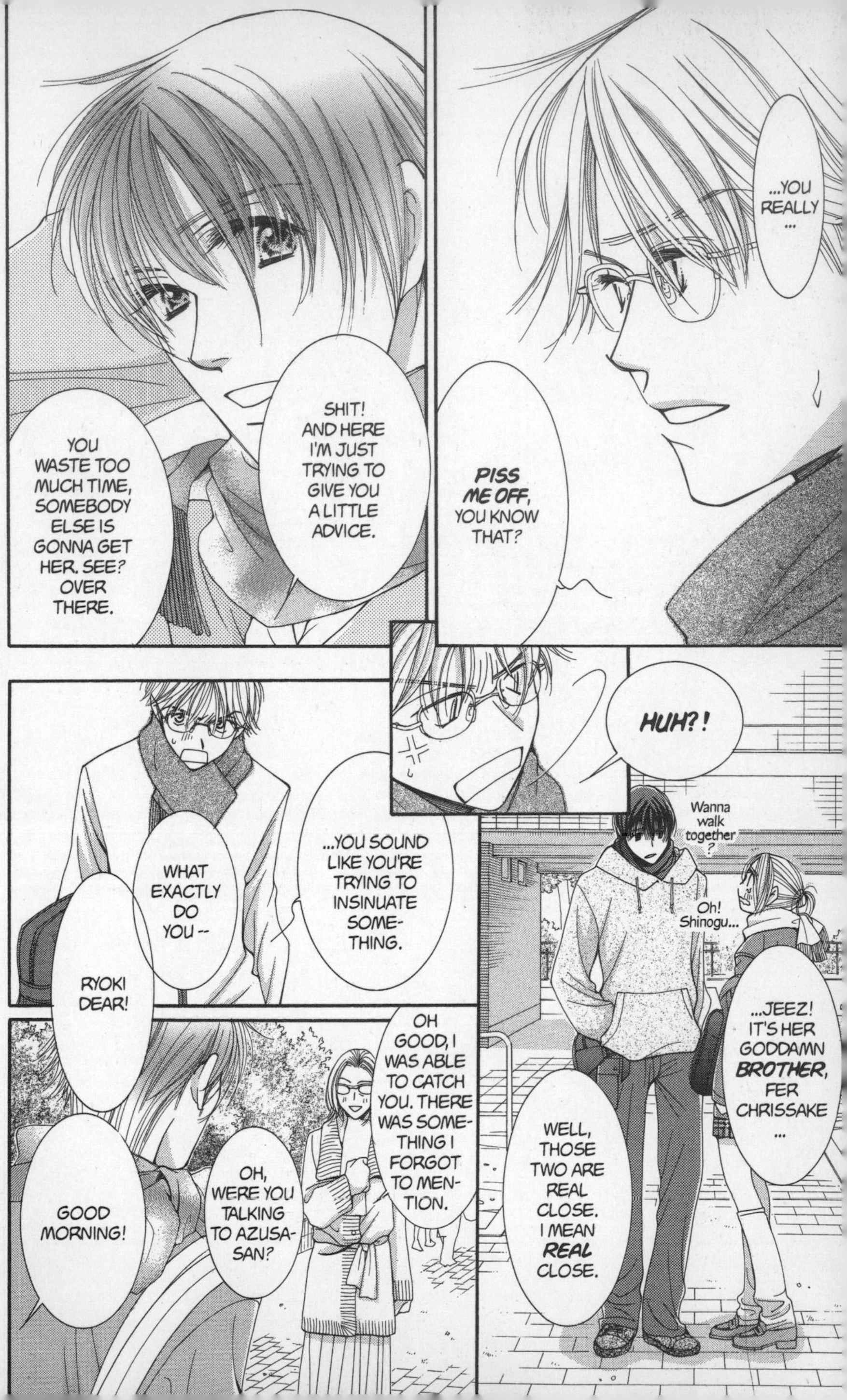
...YOU REALLY ...
PISS ME OFF, YOU KNOW THAT?
SHIT! AND HERE I'M JUST TRYING TO GIVE YOU A LITTLE ADVICE.
YOU WASTE TOO MUCH TIME, SOMEBODY ELSE IS GONNA GET HER. SEE? OVER THERE.
HUH?!
Wanna walk together?
Oh! Shinogu...
...JEEZ! IT'S HER GODDAMN BROTHER, FER CHRISSAKE ...
WELL, THOSE TWO ARE REAL CLOSE. I MEAN REAL CLOSE.
...YOU SOUND LIKE YOU'RE TRYING TO INSINUATE SOME-THING.
WHAT EXACTLY DO YOU --
RYOKI DEAR!
OH GOOD, I WAS ABLE TO CATCH YOU. THERE WAS SOME-THING I FORGOT TO MEN-TION.
OH, WERE YOU TALKING TO AZUSA-SAN?
GOOD MORNING!

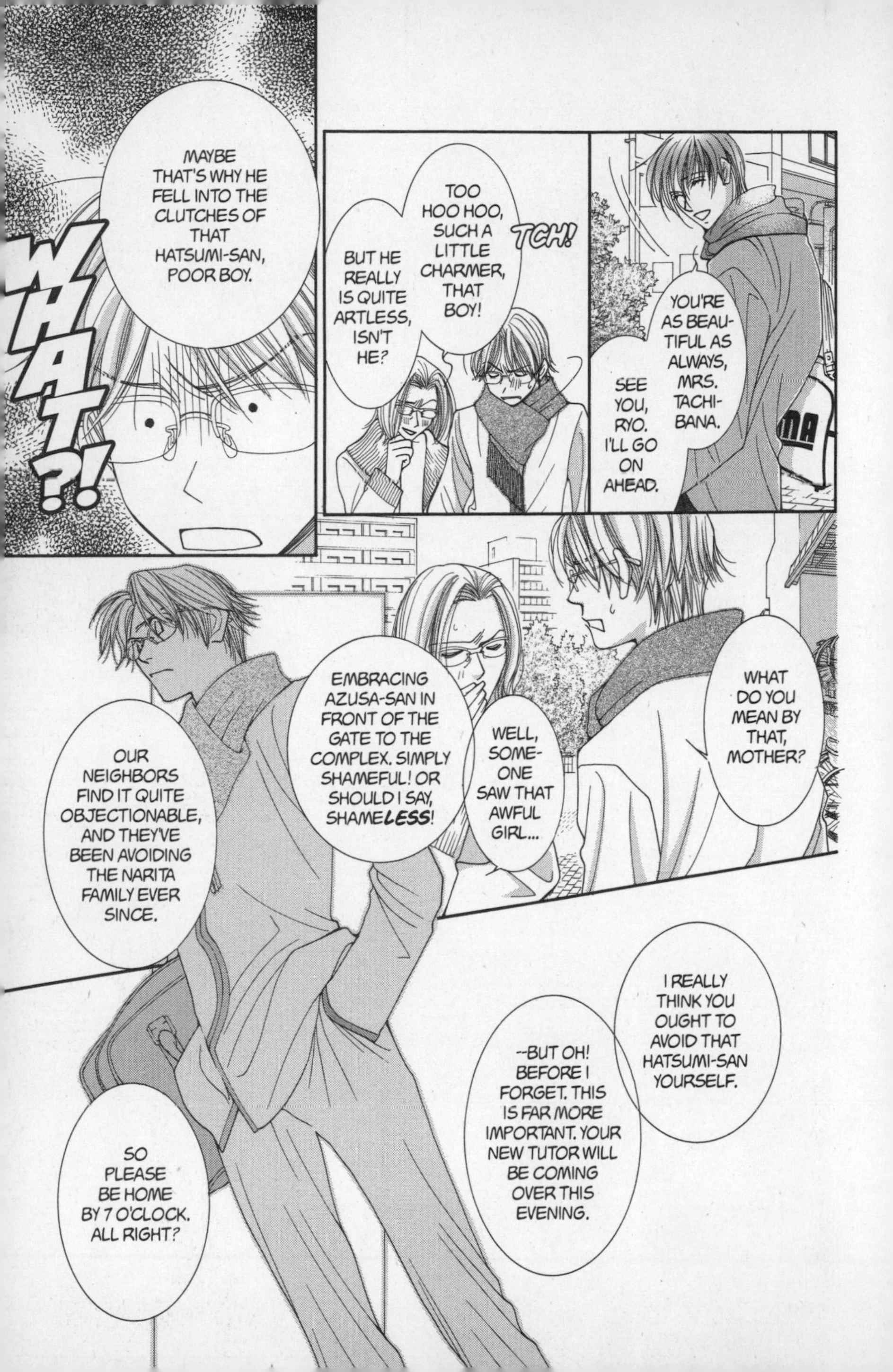

YOU'RE AS BEAUTIFUL AS ALWAYS, MRS. TACHIBANA.
SEE YOU, RYO. I'LL GO ON AHEAD.
TCH!
TOO HOO HOO, SUCH A LITTLE CHARMER, THAT BOY!
BUT HE REALLY IS QUITE ARTLESS, ISN'T HE?
MAYBE THAT'S WHY HE FELL INTO THE CLUTCHES OF THAT HATSUMI-SAN, POOR BOY.
WHAT?!
WHAT DO YOU MEAN BY THAT, MOTHER?
WELL, SOMEONE SAW THAT AWFUL GIRL...
EMBRACING AZUSA-SAN IN FRONT OF THE GATE TO THE COMPLEX. SIMPLY SHAMEFUL! OR SHOULD I SAY, SHAMELESS!
OUR NEIGHBORS FIND IT QUITE OBJECTIONABLE, AND THEY'VE BEEN AVOIDING THE NARITA FAMILY EVER SINCE.
I REALLY THINK YOU OUGHT TO AVOID THAT HATSUMI-SAN YOURSELF.
--BUT OH! BEFORE I FORGET. THIS IS FAR MORE IMPORTANT. YOUR NEW TUTOR WILL BE COMING OVER THIS EVENING.
SO PLEASE BE HOME BY 7 O'CLOCK. ALL RIGHT?

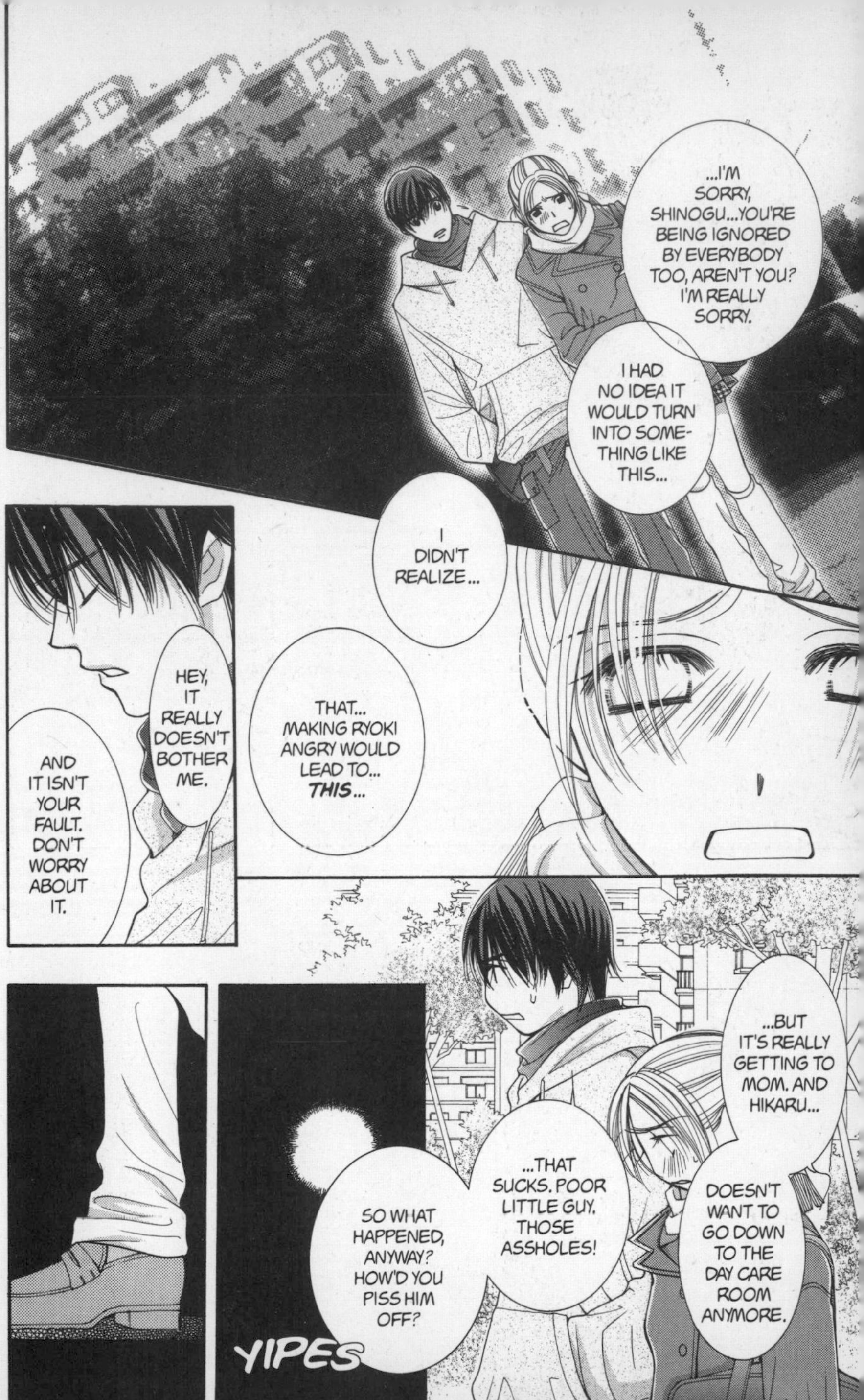
...I'M SORRY, SHINOGU...YOU'RE BEING IGNORED BY EVERYBODY TOO, AREN'T YOU? I'M REALLY SORRY.
I HAD NO IDEA IT WOULD TURN INTO SOME-THING LIKE THIS...
I DIDN'T REALIZE...
THAT... MAKING RYOKI ANGRY WOULD LEAD TO... *THIS*...
HEY, IT REALLY DOESN'T BOTHER ME.
AND IT ISN'T YOUR FAULT. DON'T WORRY ABOUT IT.
...BUT IT'S REALLY GETTING TO MOM. AND HIKARU...
DOESN'T WANT TO GO DOWN TO THE DAY CARE ROOM ANYMORE.
...THAT SUCKS. POOR LITTLE GUY. THOSE ASSHOLES!
SO WHAT HAPPENED, ANYWAY? HOW'D YOU PISS HIM OFF?
YIPES

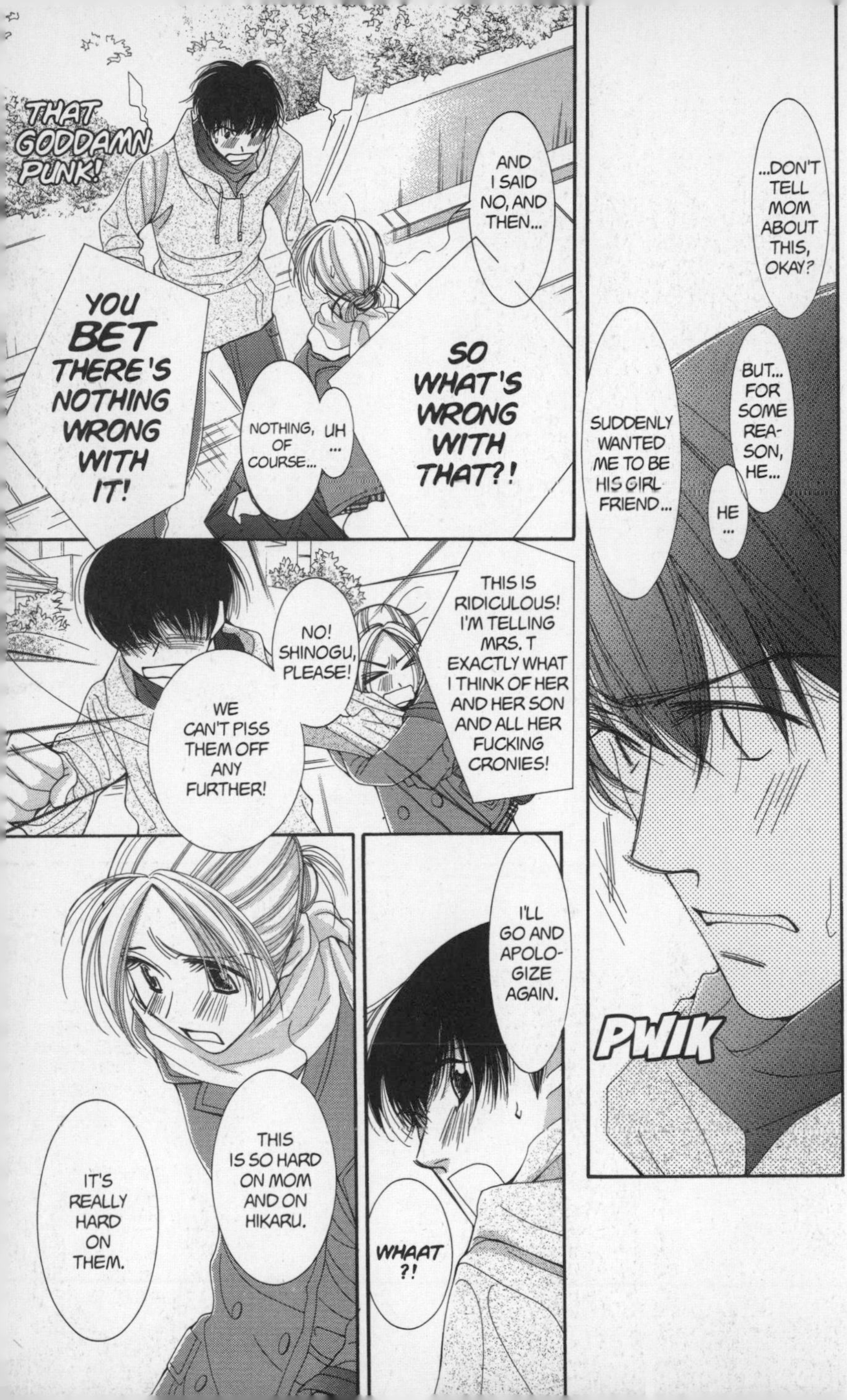
...DON'T TELL MOM ABOUT THIS, OKAY?
BUT... FOR SOME REA-SON, HE...
HE ...
SUDDENLY WANTED ME TO BE HIS GIRL FRIEND...
PWIK
AND I SAID NO, AND THEN...
SO WHAT'S WRONG WITH THAT?!
UH ...
NOTHING, OF COURSE...
YOU BET THERE'S NOTHING WRONG WITH IT!
THAT GODDAMN PUNK!
THIS IS RIDICULOUS! I'M TELLING MRS. T EXACTLY WHAT I THINK OF HER AND HER SON AND ALL HER FUCKING CRONIES!
NO! SHINOGU, PLEASE!
WE CAN'T PISS THEM OFF ANY FURTHER!
I'LL GO AND APOLOGIZE AGAIN.
WHAAT ?!
THIS IS SO HARD ON MOM AND ON HIKARU.
IT'S REALLY HARD ON THEM.

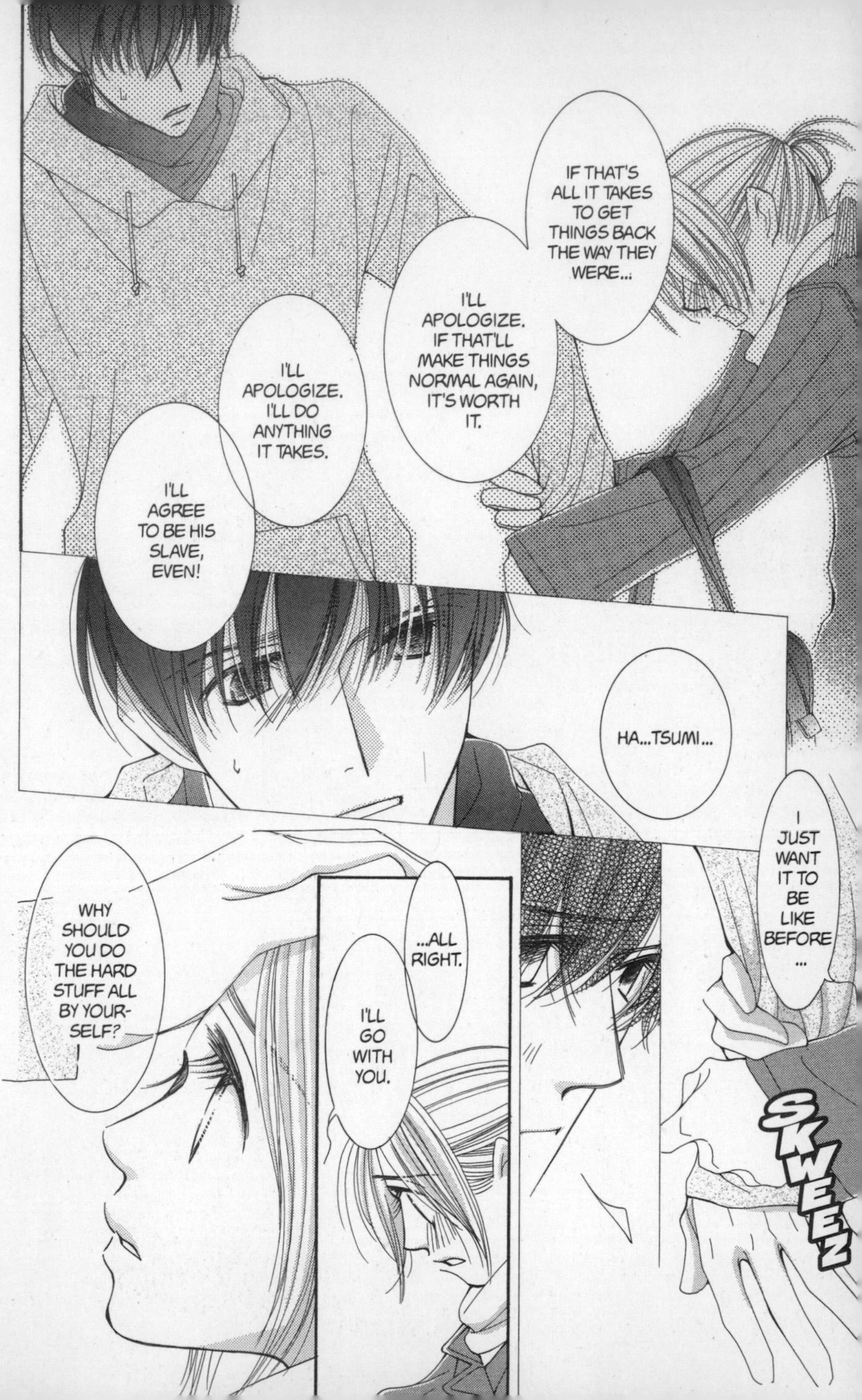
IF THAT'S ALL IT TAKES TO GET THINGS BACK THE WAY THEY WERE...
I'LL APOLOGIZE. IF THAT'LL MAKE THINGS NORMAL AGAIN, IT'S WORTH IT.
I'LL APOLOGIZE. I'LL DO ANYTHING IT TAKES.
I'LL AGREE TO BE HIS SLAVE, EVEN!
HA...TSUMI...
I JUST WANT IT TO BE LIKE BEFORE ...
SKWEEZ
...ALL RIGHT.
I'LL GO WITH YOU.
WHY SHOULD YOU DO THE HARD STUFF ALL BY YOUR-SELF?!

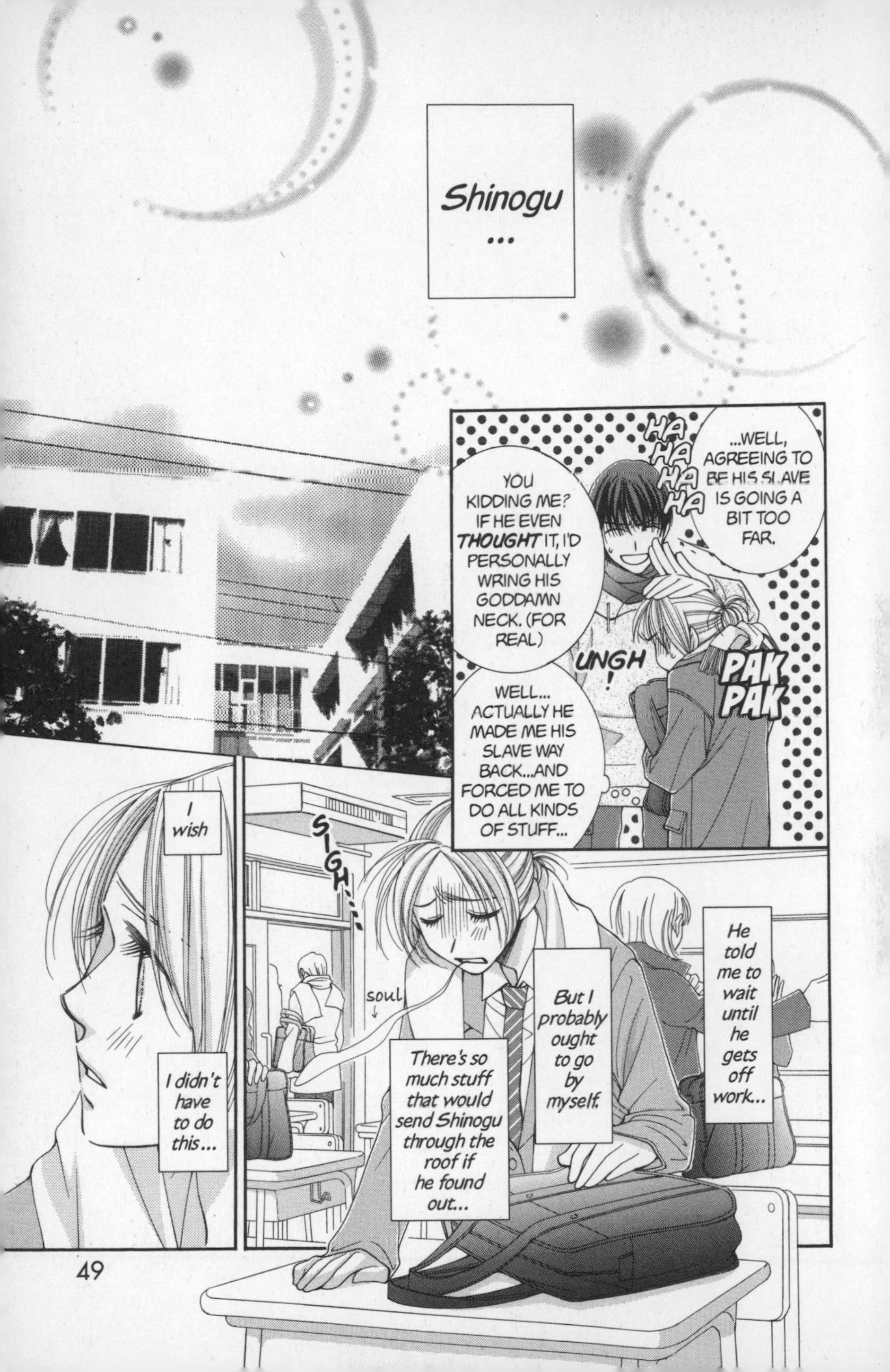
Shinogu ...
...WELL, AGREEING TO BE HIS SLAVE IS GOING A BIT TOO FAR.
HA HA HA HA
YOU KIDDING ME? IF HE EVEN THOUGHT IT, I'D PERSONALLY WRING HIS GODDAMN NECK. (FOR REAL)
PAK PAK
UNGH!
WELL... ACTUALLY HE MADE ME HIS SLAVE WAY BACK...AND FORCED ME TO DO ALL KINDS OF STUFF...
He told me to wait until he gets off work...
But I probably ought to go by myself.
There's so much stuff that would send Shinogu through the roof if he found out...
SIGH...
soul
I wish
I didn't have to do this...

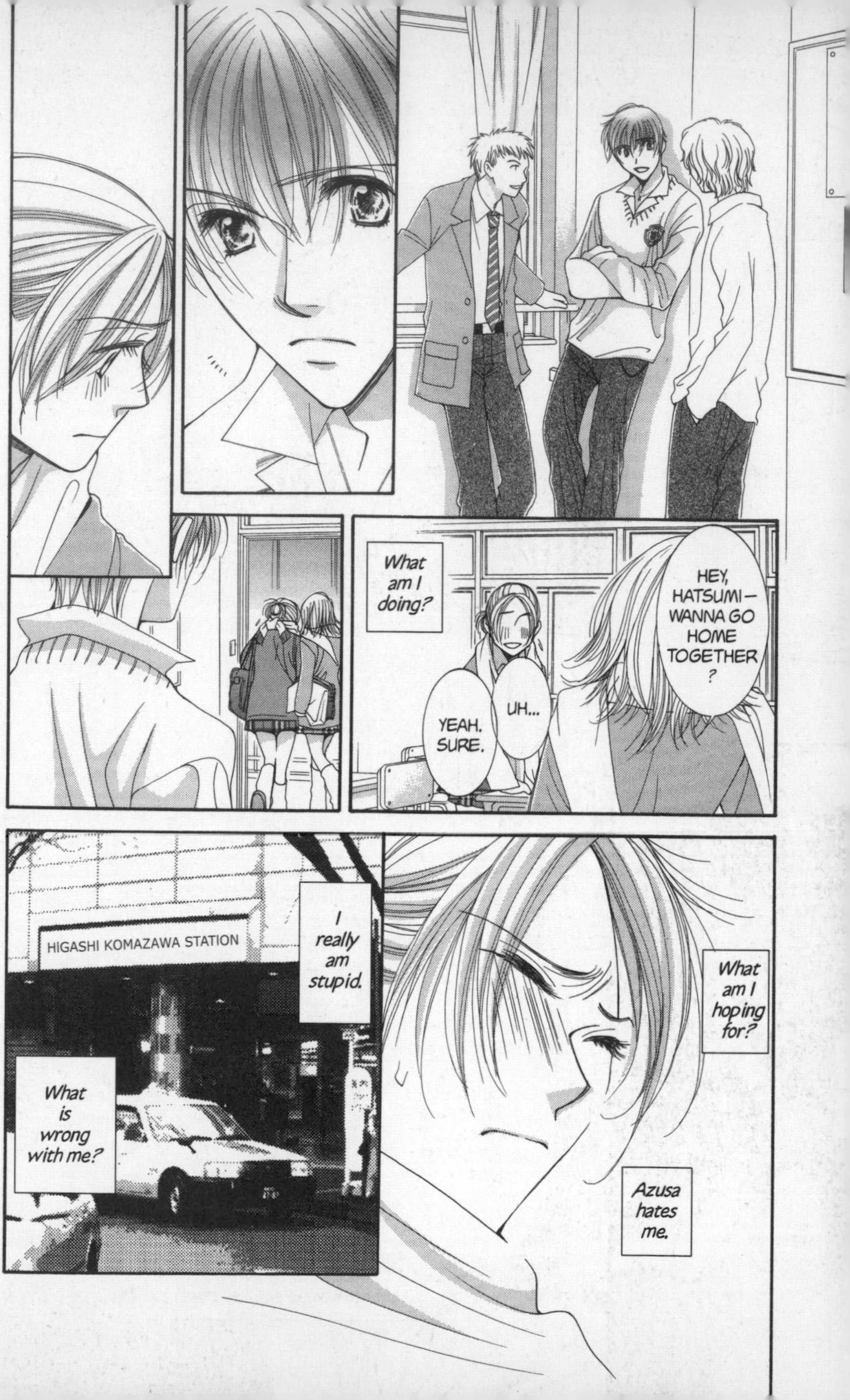
HEY, HATSUMI— WANNA GO HOME TOGETHER?
UH...
YEAH. SURE.
What am I doing?
What am I hoping for?
Azusa hates me.
I really am stupid.
HIGASHI KOMAZAWA STATION
What is wrong with me?

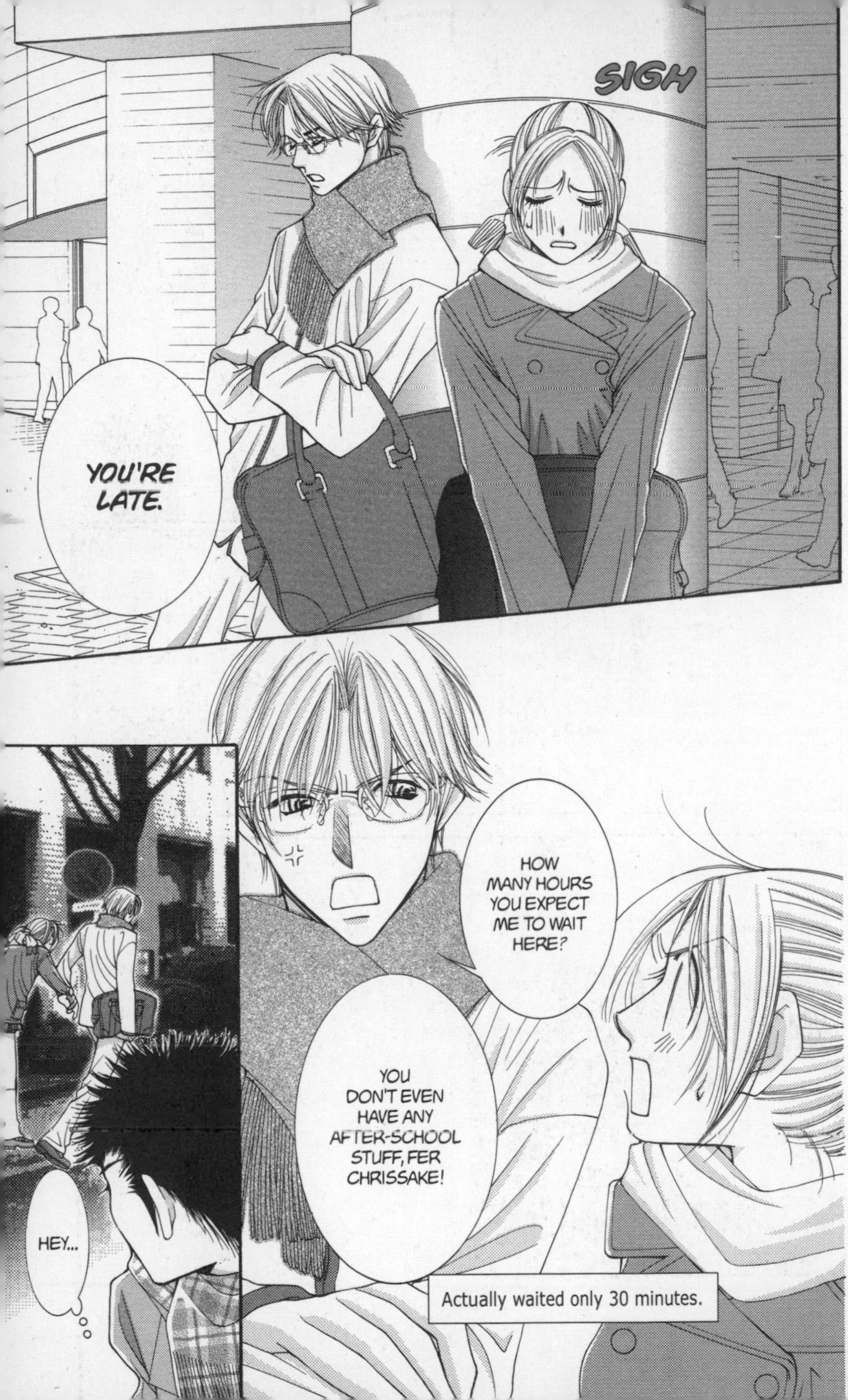
SIGH
YOU'RE LATE.
HOW MANY HOURS YOU EXPECT ME TO WAIT HERE?
YOU DON'T EVEN HAVE ANY AFTER-SCHOOL STUFF, FER CHRISSAKE!
Actually waited only 30 minutes.
HEY...

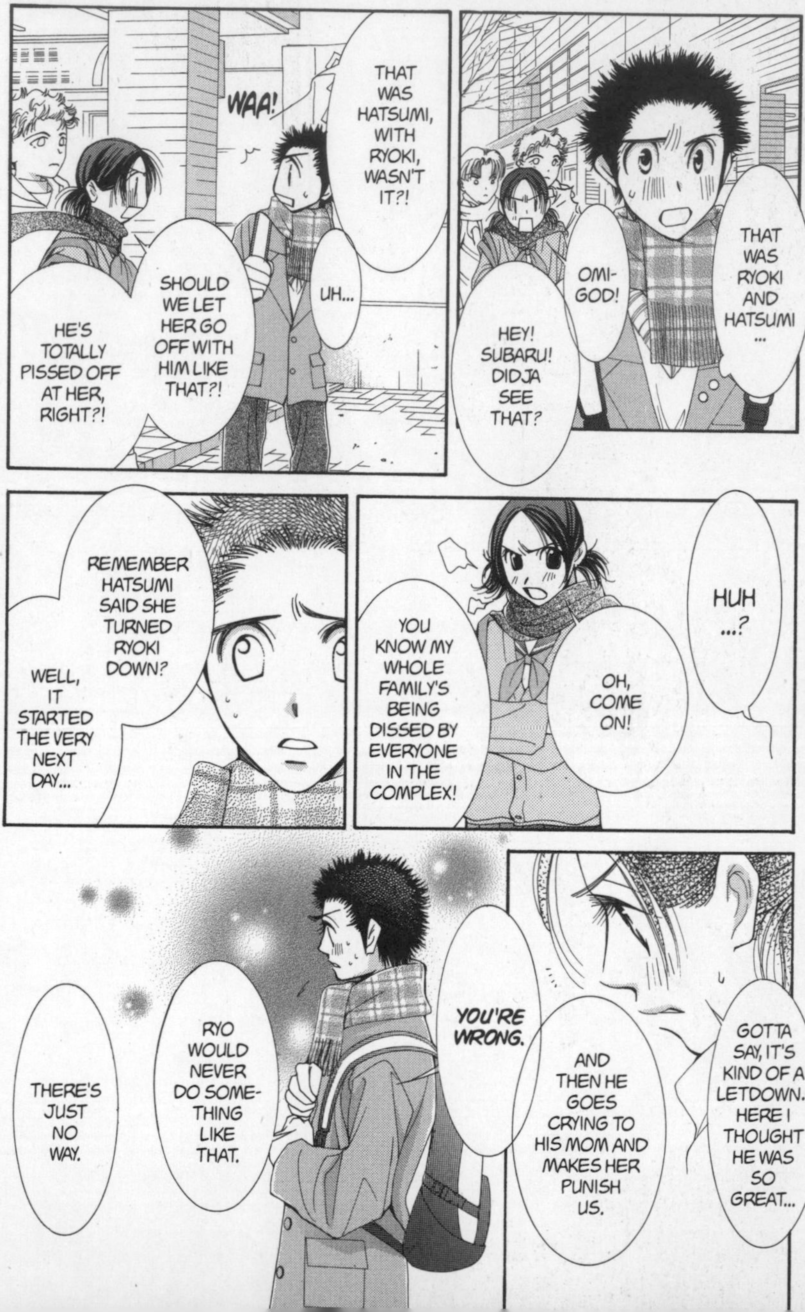
THAT WAS RYOKI AND HATSUMI ...
OMI-GOD!
HEY! SUBARU! DIDJA SEE THAT?
WAA!
THAT WAS HATSUMI, WITH RYOKI, WASN'T IT?!
UH...
SHOULD WE LET HER GO OFF WITH HIM LIKE THAT?!
HE'S TOTALLY PISSED OFF AT HER, RIGHT?!
HUH ...?
OH, COME ON!
YOU KNOW MY WHOLE FAMILY'S BEING DISSED BY EVERYONE IN THE COMPLEX!
REMEMBER HATSUMI SAID SHE TURNED RYOKI DOWN?
WELL, IT STARTED THE VERY NEXT DAY...
GOTTA SAY, IT'S KIND OF A LETDOWN... HERE I THOUGHT HE WAS SO GREAT...
AND THEN HE GOES CRYING TO HIS MOM AND MAKES HER PUNISH US.
YOU'RE WRONG.
RYO WOULD NEVER DO SOME-THING LIKE THAT.
THERE'S JUST NO WAY.

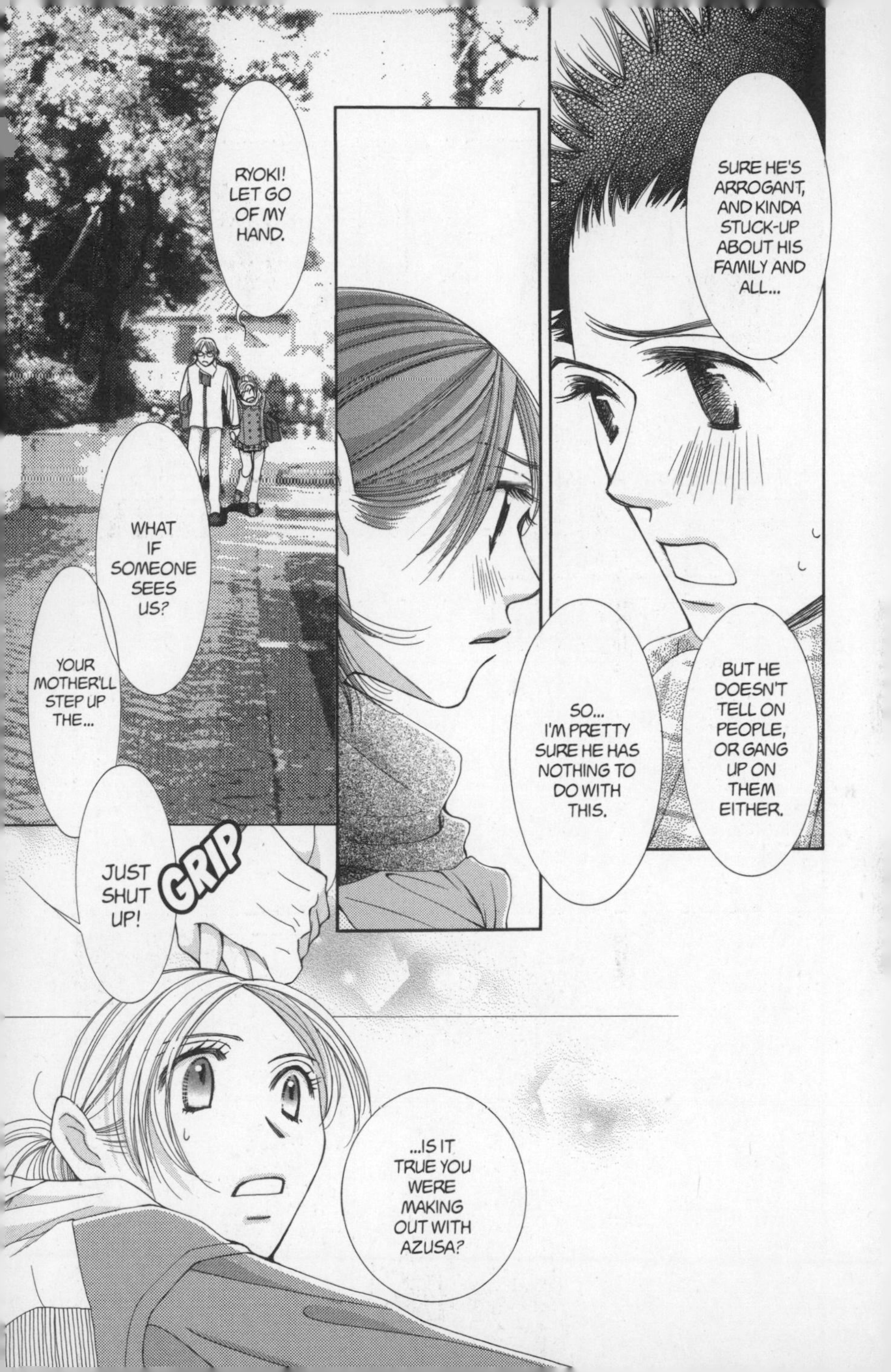
SURE HE'S ARROGANT, AND KINDA STUCK-UP ABOUT HIS FAMILY AND ALL...
BUT HE DOESN'T TELL ON PEOPLE, OR GANG UP ON THEM EITHER.
SO... I'M PRETTY SURE HE HAS NOTHING TO DO WITH THIS.
RYOKI! LET GO OF MY HAND.
WHAT IF SOMEONE SEES US?
YOUR MOTHER'LL STEP UP THE...
GRIP
JUST SHUT UP!
...IS IT TRUE YOU WERE MAKING OUT WITH AZUSA?

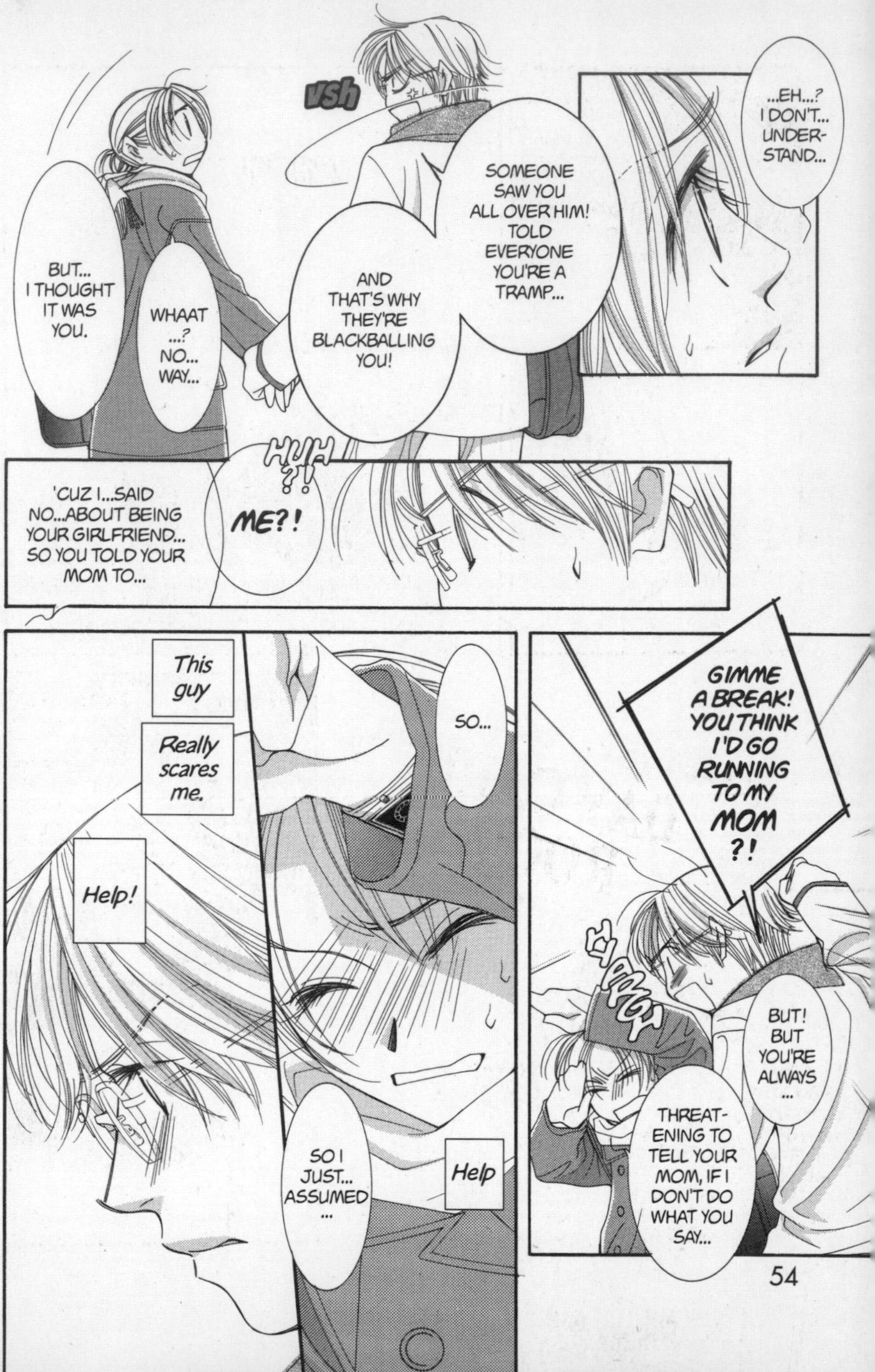
...EH...? I DON'T... UNDER-STAND...
vsh
SOMEONE SAW YOU ALL OVER HIM! TOLD EVERYONE YOU'RE A TRAMP...
AND THAT'S WHY THEY'RE BLACKBALLING YOU!
WHAAT ...? NO... WAY...
BUT... I THOUGHT IT WAS YOU.
HUH ?!
ME?!
'CUZ I...SAID NO...ABOUT BEING YOUR GIRLFRIEND... SO YOU TOLD YOUR MOM TO...
GIMME A BREAK! YOU THINK I'D GO RUNNING TO MY MOM ?!
BUT! BUT YOU'RE ALWAYS ...
THREAT-ENING TO TELL YOUR MOM, IF I DON'T DO WHAT YOU SAY...
SO...
This guy
Really scares me.
Help!
Help
SO I JUST... ASSUMED ...

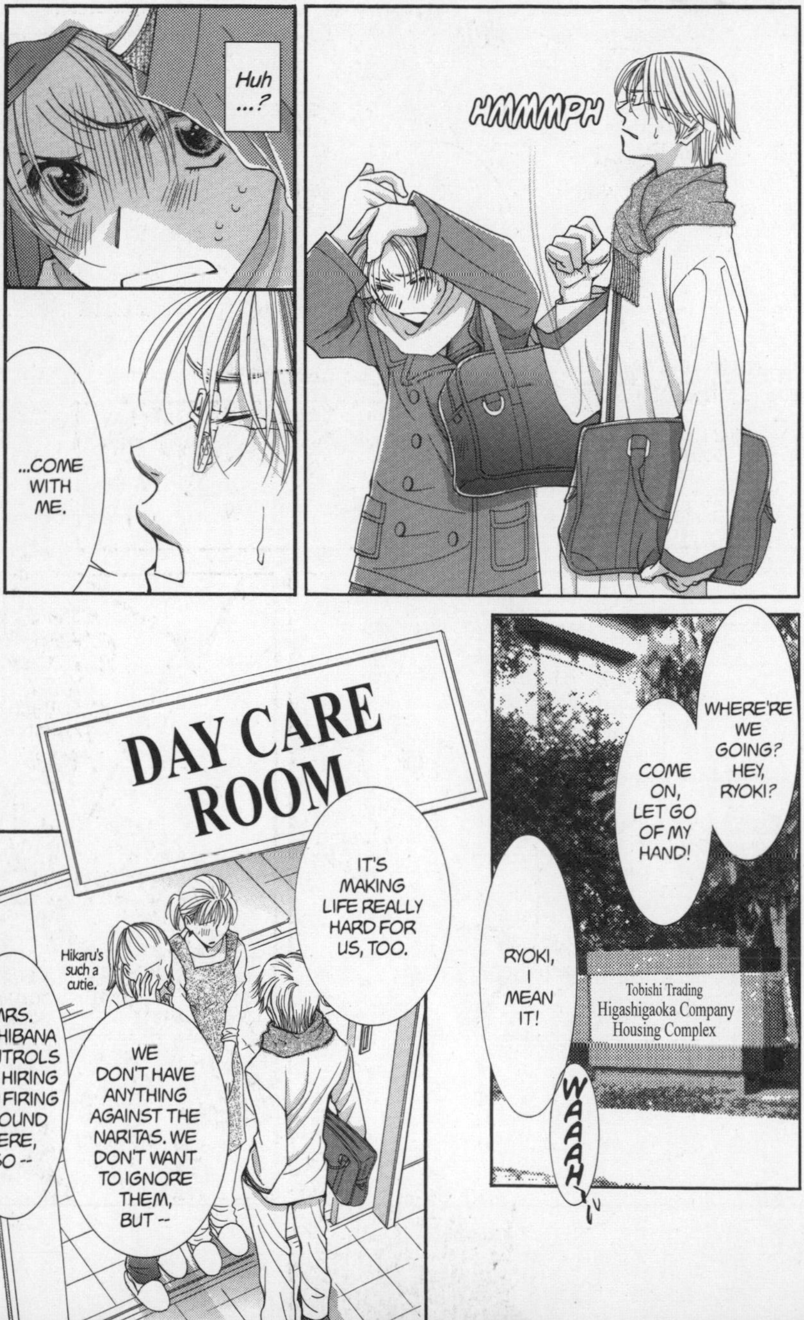

HMMMPH
Huh ...?
...COME WITH ME.
WHERE'RE WE GOING? HEY, RYOKI?
COME ON, LET GO OF MY HAND!
RYOKI, I MEAN IT!
Tobishi Trading
Higashigaoka Company
Housing Complex
WAAAH
DAY CARE ROOM
IT'S MAKING LIFE REALLY HARD FOR US, TOO.
Hikaru's such a cutie.
WE DON'T HAVE ANYTHING AGAINST THE NARITAS. WE DON'T WANT TO IGNORE THEM, BUT --
MRS. TACHIBANA CONTROLS THE HIRING AND FIRING AROUND HERE, SO --

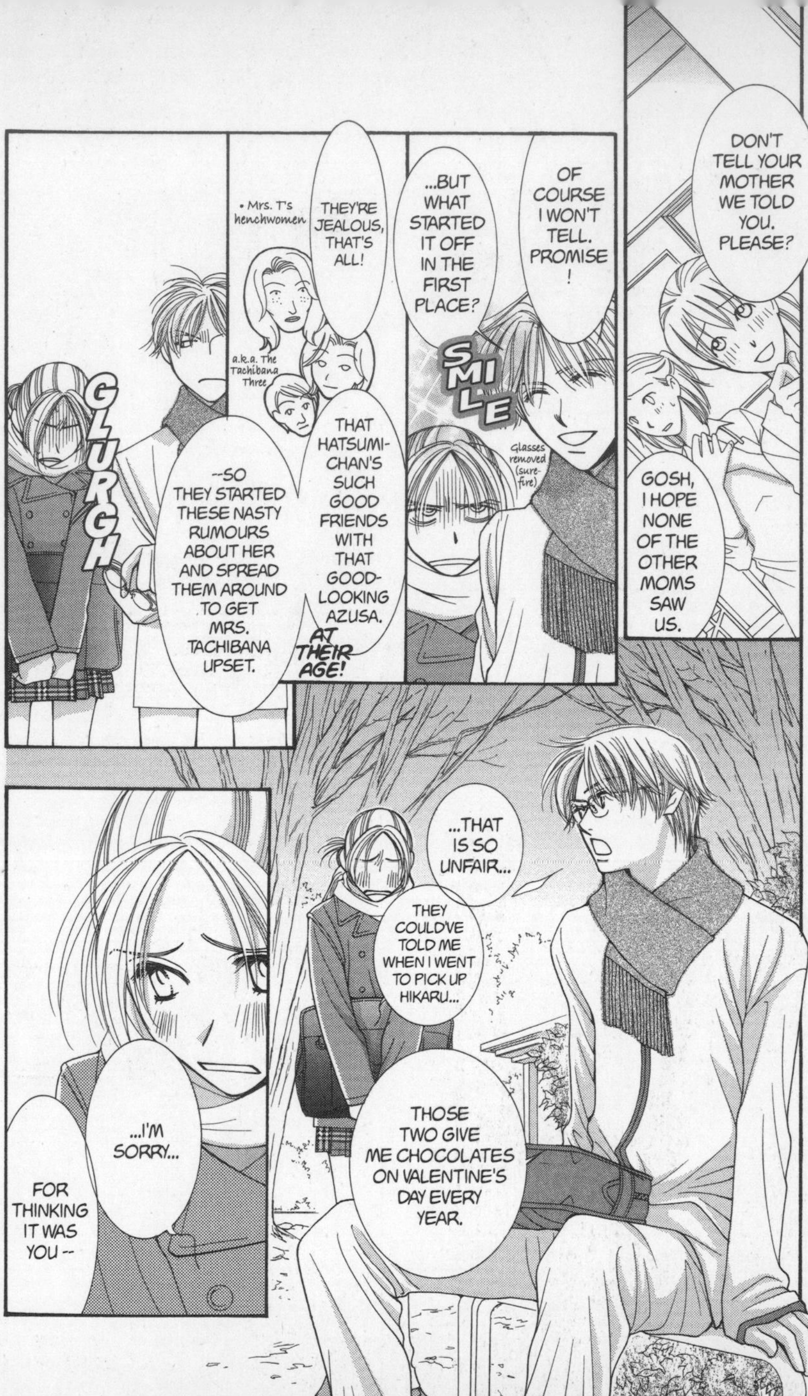
DON'T TELL YOUR MOTHER WE TOLD YOU. PLEASE?
GOSH, I HOPE NONE OF THE OTHER MOMS SAW US.
OF COURSE I WON'T TELL. PROMISE!
...BUT WHAT STARTED IT OFF IN THE FIRST PLACE?
SMILE
Glasses removed (sure-fire)
THEY'RE JEALOUS, THAT'S ALL!
• Mrs. T's henchwomen
a.k.a. The Tachibana Three
THAT HATSUMI-CHAN'S SUCH GOOD FRIENDS WITH THAT GOOD-LOOKING AZUSA.
AT THEIR AGE!
--SO THEY STARTED THESE NASTY RUMOURS ABOUT HER AND SPREAD THEM AROUND TO GET MRS. TACHIBANA UPSET.
GLURGH
...THAT IS SO UNFAIR...
THEY COULD'VE TOLD ME WHEN I WENT TO PICK UP HIKARU...
THOSE TWO GIVE ME CHOCOLATES ON VALENTINE'S DAY EVERY YEAR.
...I'M SORRY...
FOR THINKING IT WAS YOU --

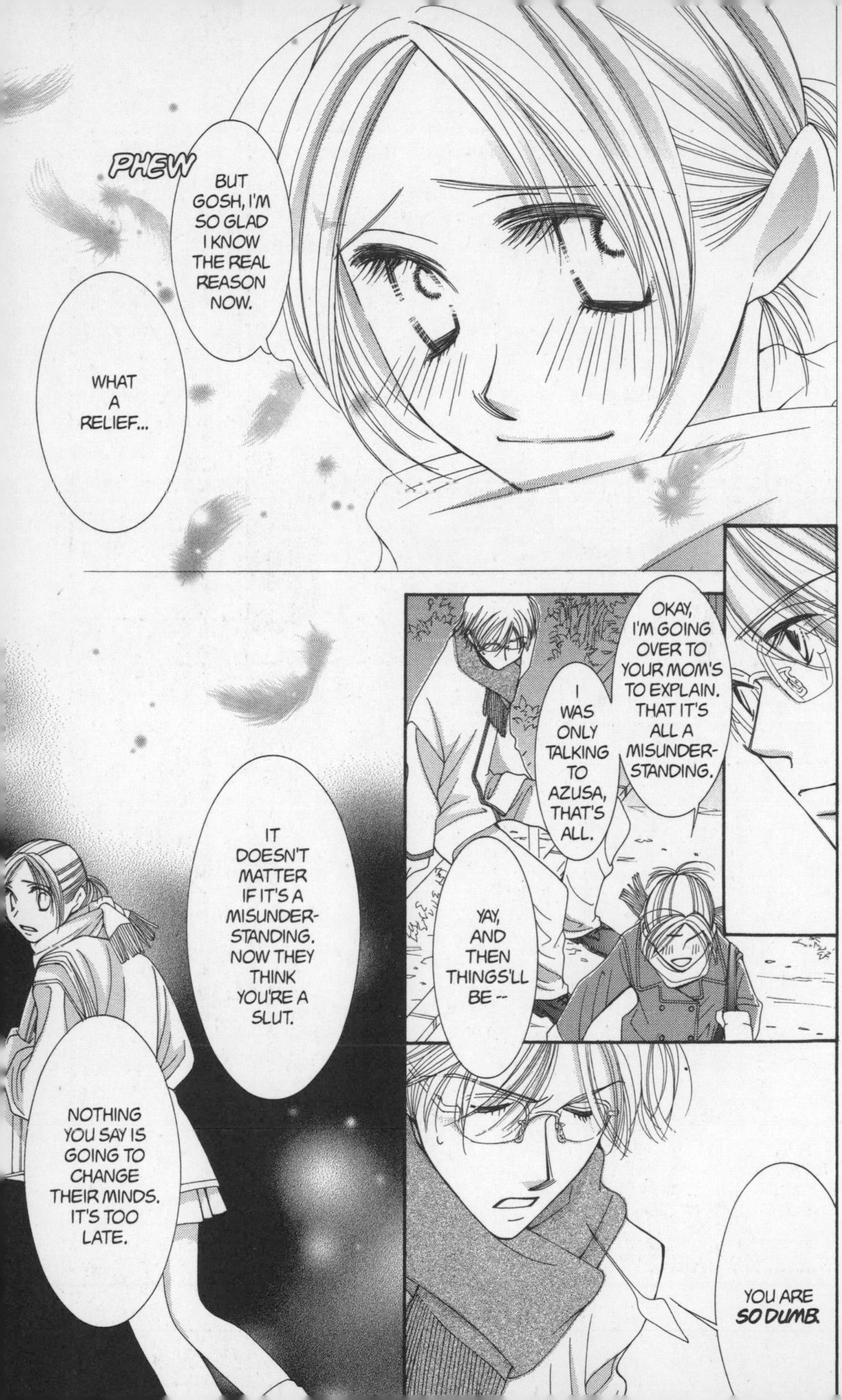

PHEW
BUT GOSH, I'M SO GLAD I KNOW THE REAL REASON NOW.
WHAT A RELIEF...
OKAY, I'M GOING OVER TO YOUR MOM'S TO EXPLAIN. THAT IT'S ALL A MISUNDER-STANDING.
I WAS ONLY TALKING TO AZUSA, THAT'S ALL.
YAY, AND THEN THINGS'LL BE --
YOU ARE SO DUMB.
IT DOESN'T MATTER IF IT'S A MISUNDER-STANDING. NOW THEY THINK YOU'RE A SLUT.
NOTHING YOU SAY IS GOING TO CHANGE THEIR MINDS. IT'S TOO LATE.

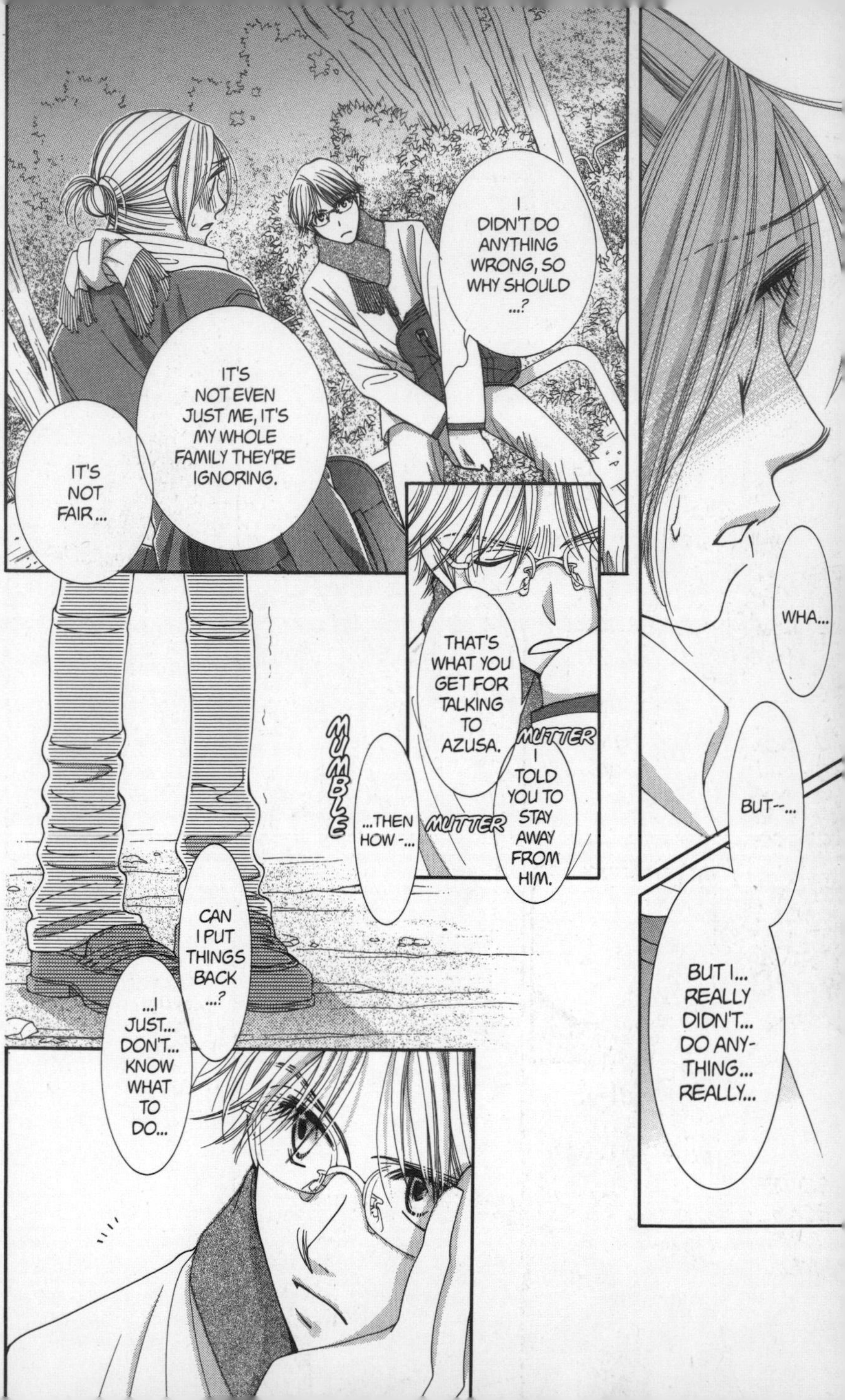
WHA...
BUT--...
BUT I... REALLY DIDN'T... DO ANY-THING... REALLY...
I DIDN'T DO ANYTHING WRONG, SO WHY SHOULD ...?
IT'S NOT EVEN JUST ME, IT'S MY WHOLE FAMILY THEY'RE IGNORING.
IT'S NOT FAIR...
THAT'S WHAT YOU GET FOR TALKING TO AZUSA.
MUTTER
I TOLD YOU TO STAY AWAY FROM HIM.
MUTTER
...THEN HOW -...
MUMBLE
CAN I PUT THINGS BACK ...?
...I JUST... DON'T... KNOW WHAT TO DO...

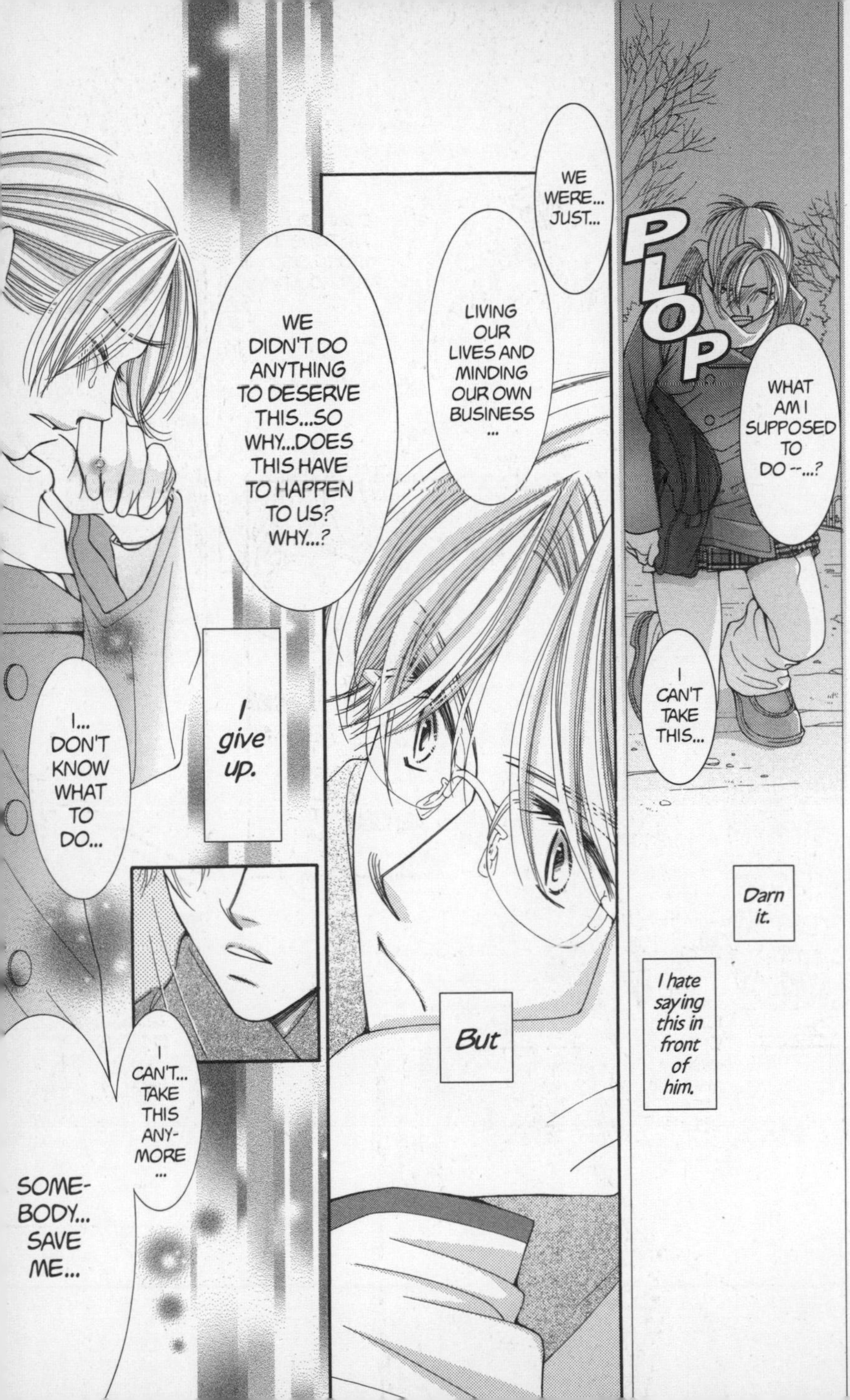
PLOP
WHAT AM I SUPPOSED TO DO --...?
I CAN'T TAKE THIS...
Darn it.
I hate saying this in front of him.
WE WERE... JUST...
LIVING OUR LIVES AND MINDING OUR OWN BUSINESS ...
WE DIDN'T DO ANYTHING TO DESERVE THIS...SO WHY...DOES THIS HAVE TO HAPPEN TO US? WHY...?
But
I give up.
I... DON'T KNOW WHAT TO DO...
I CAN'T... TAKE THIS ANY-MORE ...
SOME-BODY... SAVE ME...

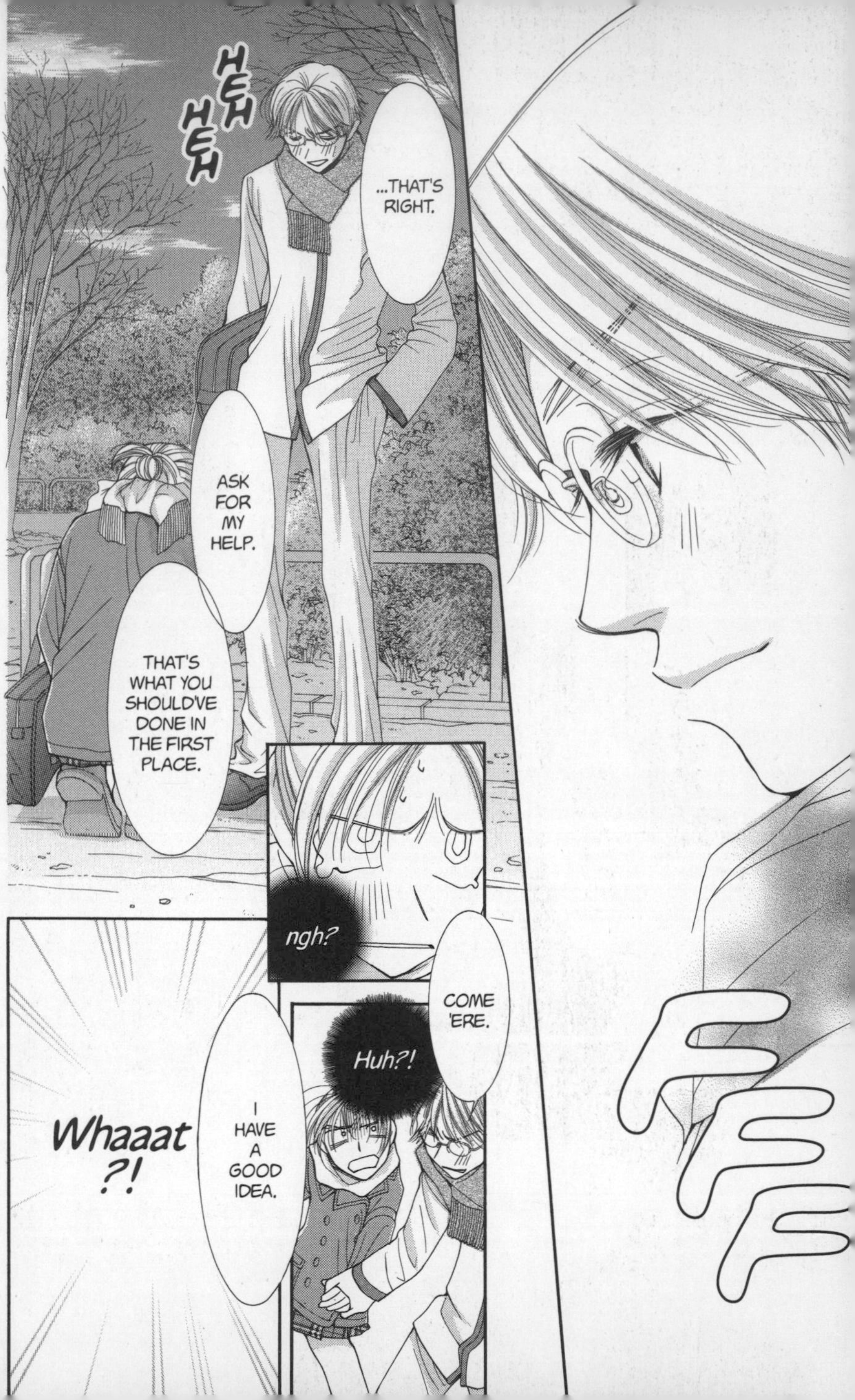
FFF
...THAT'S RIGHT.
HEH HEH
ASK FOR MY HELP.
THAT'S WHAT YOU SHOULD'VE DONE IN THE FIRST PLACE.
ngh?
COME 'ERE.
Huh?!
I HAVE A GOOD IDEA.
Whaaat ?!

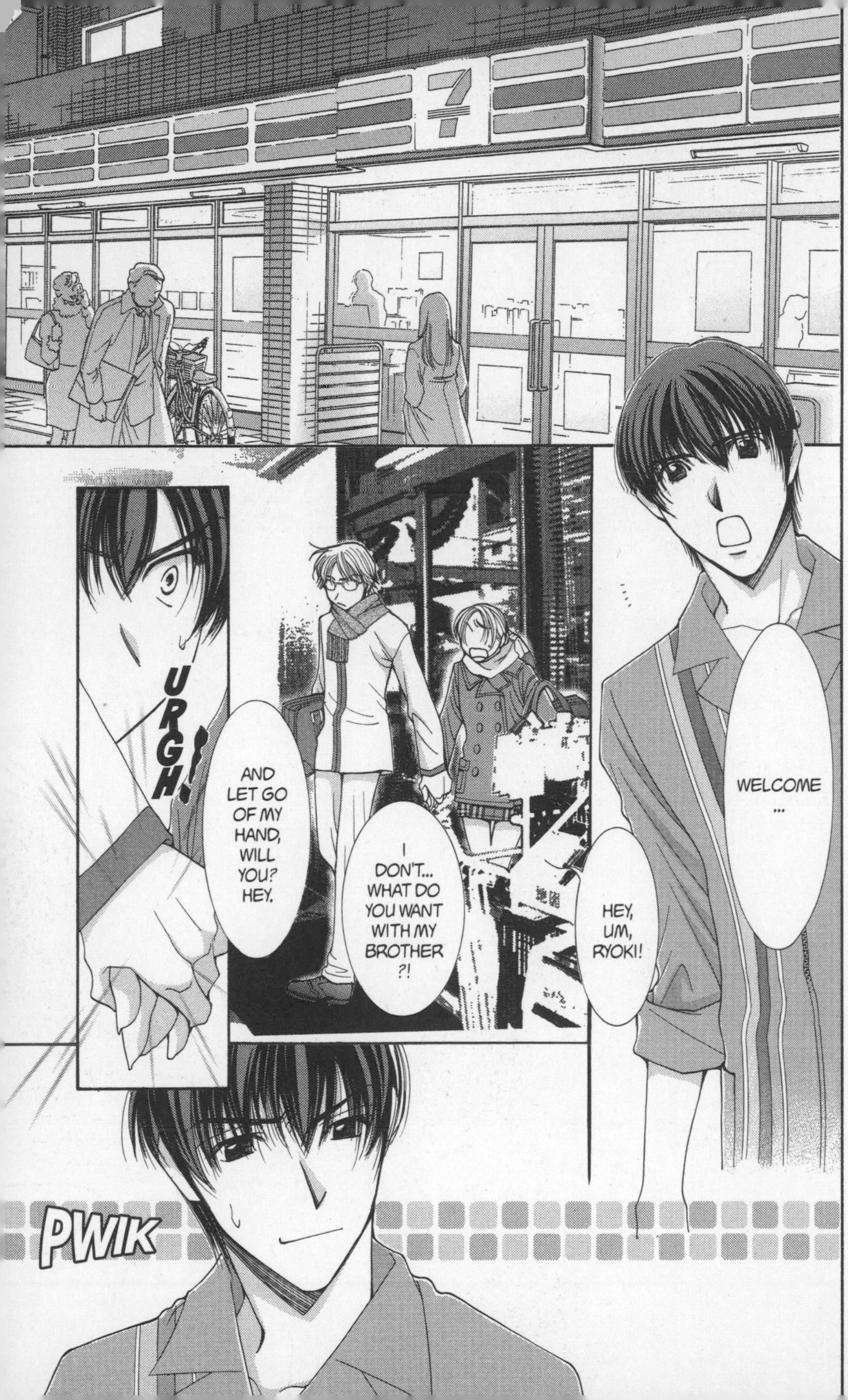
WELCOME ...
HEY, UM, RYOKI!
I DON'T... WHAT DO YOU WANT WITH MY BROTHER ?!
AND LET GO OF MY HAND, WILL YOU? HEY.
URGH!
PWIK

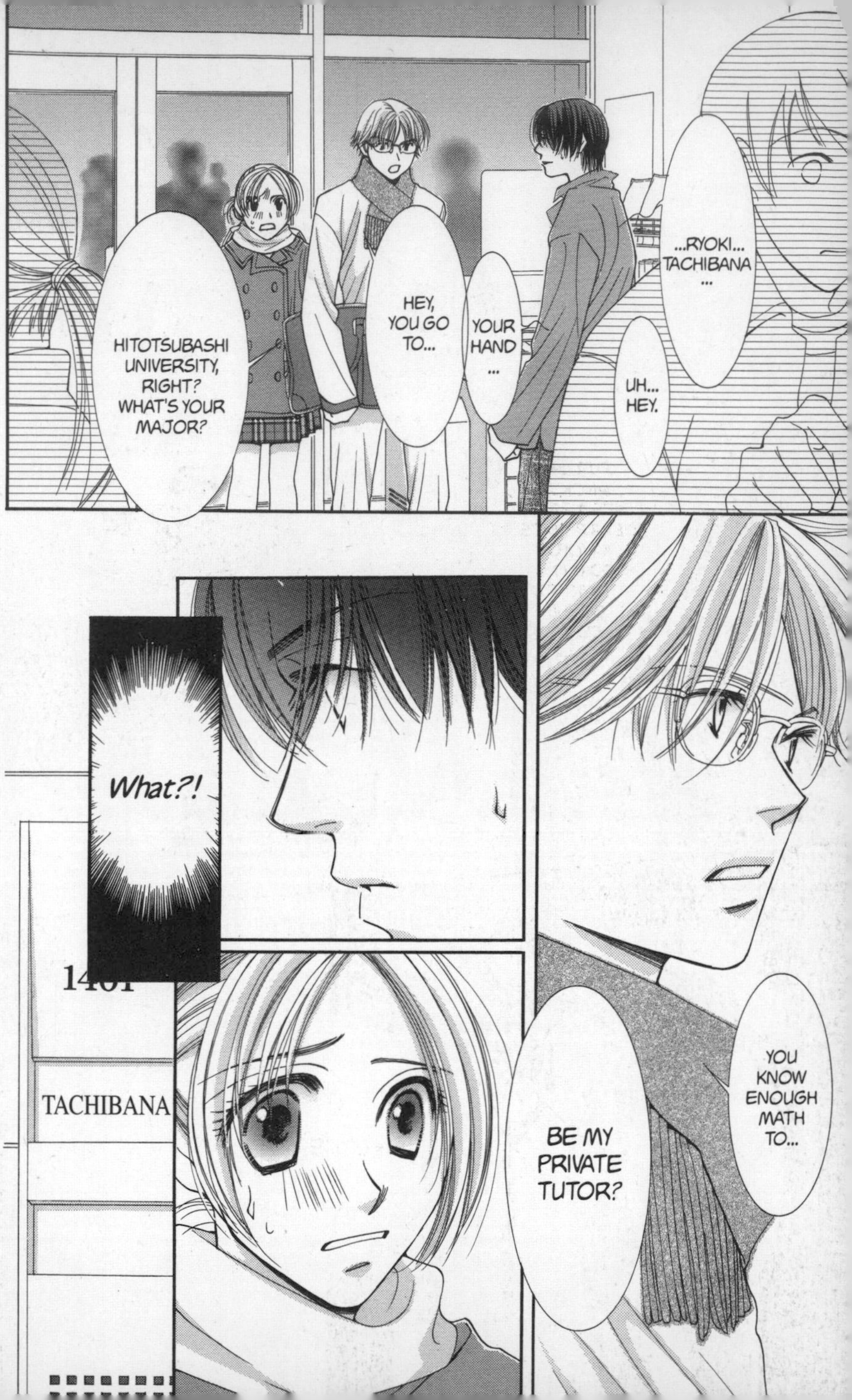
...RYOKI... TACHIBANA ...
UH... HEY.
YOUR HAND ...
HEY, YOU GO TO...
HITOTSUBASHI UNIVERSITY, RIGHT? WHAT'S YOUR MAJOR?
YOU KNOW ENOUGH MATH TO...
BE MY PRIVATE TUTOR?
What?!
1401
TACHIBANA

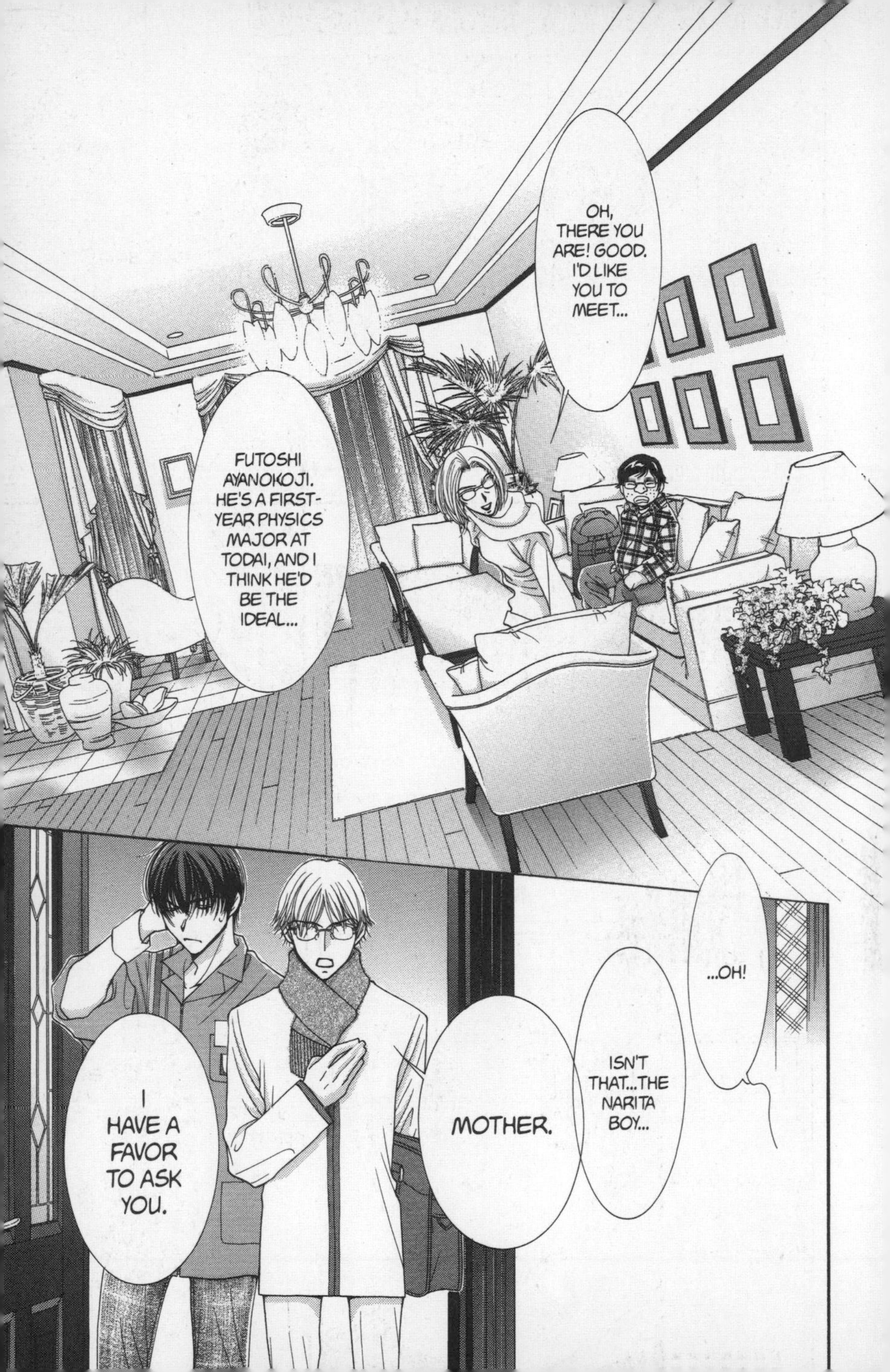
OH, THERE YOU ARE! GOOD. I'D LIKE YOU TO MEET...
FUTOSHI AYANOKOJI. HE'S A FIRST-YEAR PHYSICS MAJOR AT TODAI, AND I THINK HE'D BE THE IDEAL...
...OH!
ISN'T THAT...THE NARITA BOY...
MOTHER.
I HAVE A FAVOR TO ASK YOU.

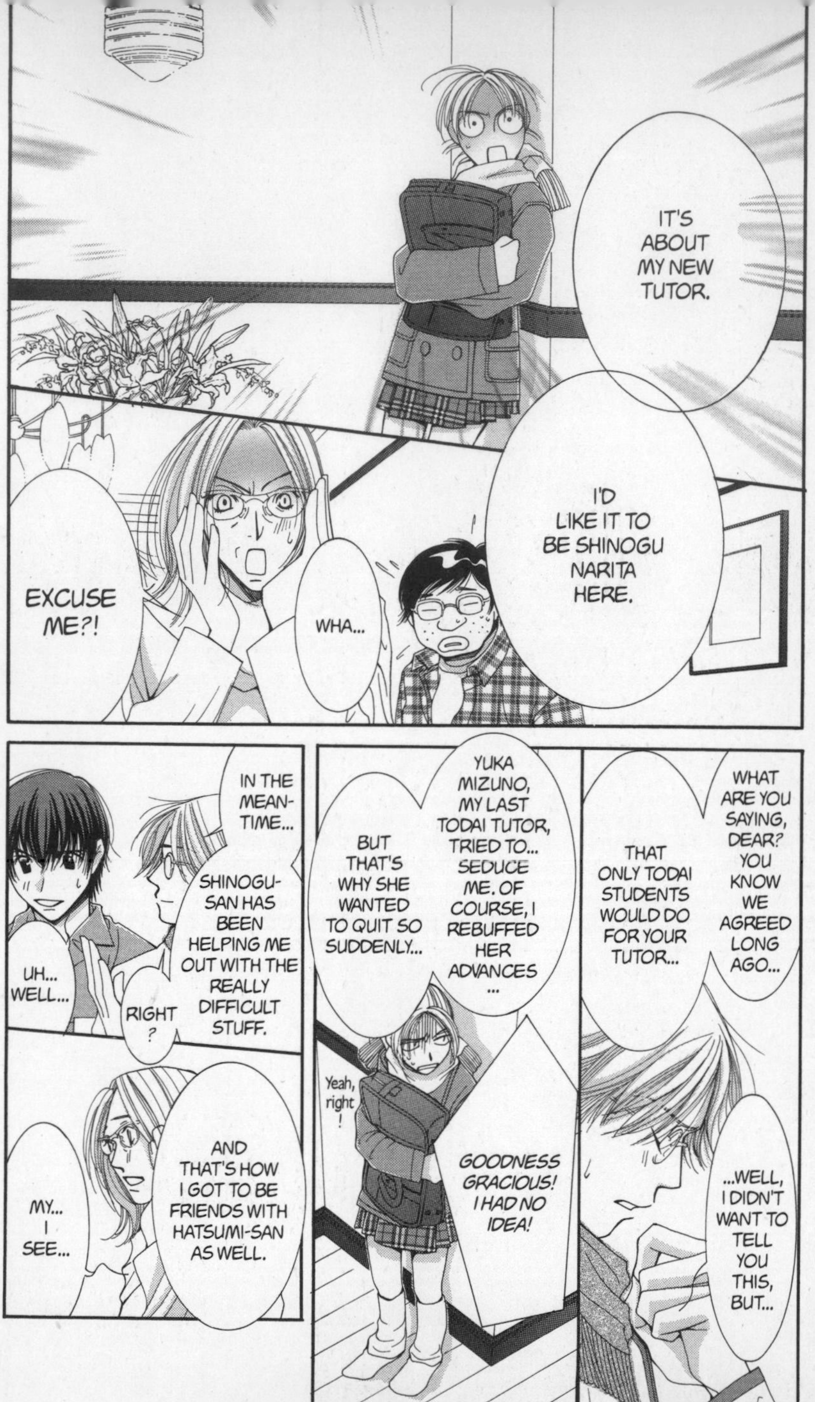
IT'S ABOUT MY NEW TUTOR.
I'D LIKE IT TO BE SHINOGU NARITA HERE.
WHA...
EXCUSE ME?!
WHAT ARE YOU SAYING, DEAR? YOU KNOW WE AGREED LONG AGO...
THAT ONLY TODAI STUDENTS WOULD DO FOR YOUR TUTOR...
...WELL, I DIDN'T WANT TO TELL YOU THIS, BUT...
YUKA MIZUNO, MY LAST TODAI TUTOR, TRIED TO... SEDUCE ME. OF COURSE, I REBUFFED HER ADVANCES...
BUT THAT'S WHY SHE WANTED TO QUIT SO SUDDENLY...
GOODNESS GRACIOUS! I HAD NO IDEA!
Yeah, right!
IN THE MEAN-TIME...
SHINOGU-SAN HAS BEEN HELPING ME OUT WITH THE REALLY DIFFICULT STUFF.
RIGHT?
UH... WELL...
AND THAT'S HOW I GOT TO BE FRIENDS WITH HATSUMI-SAN AS WELL.
MY... I SEE...

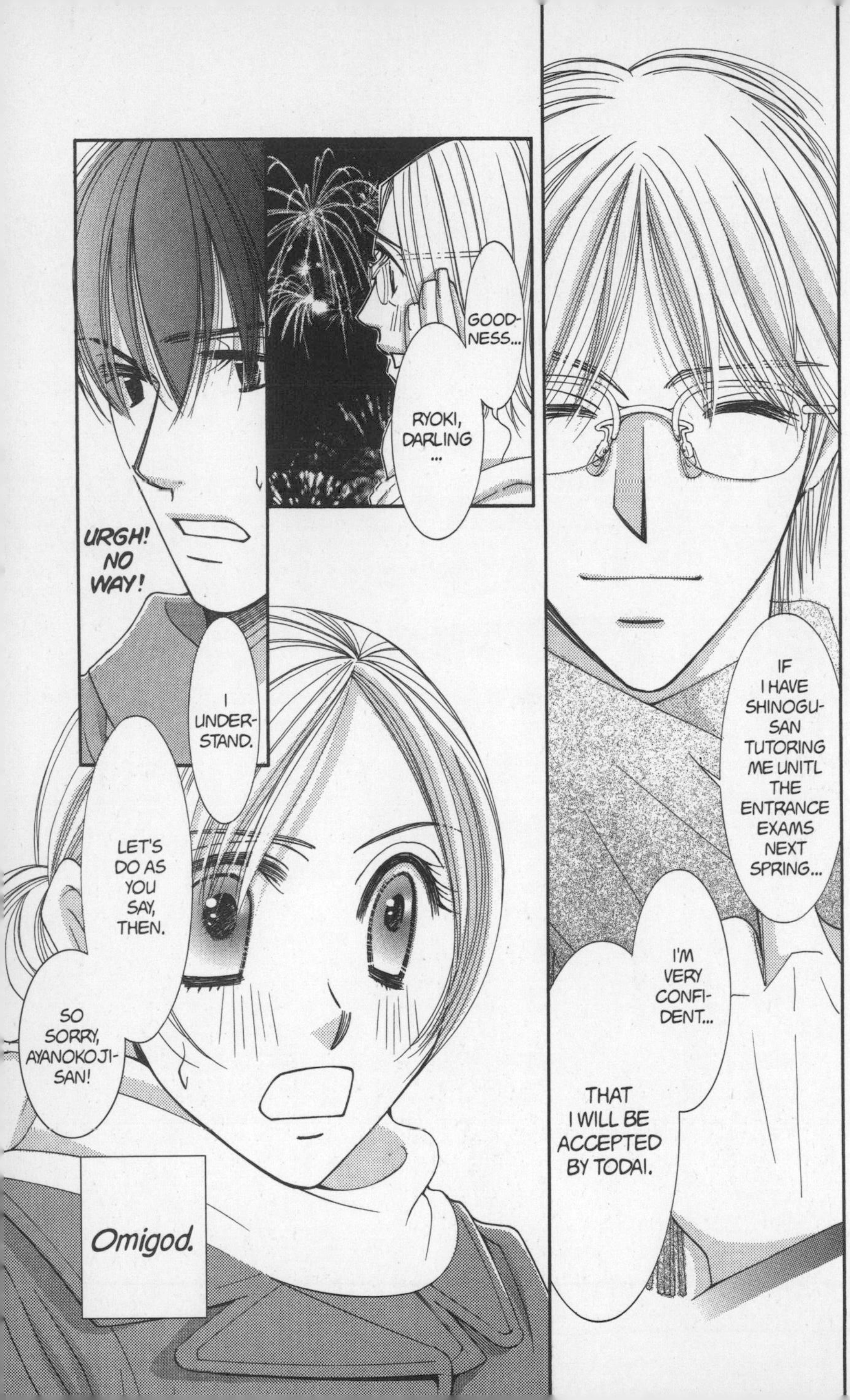
IF I HAVE SHINOGU-SAN TUTORING ME UNITL THE ENTRANCE EXAMS NEXT SPRING...
I'M VERY CONFI-DENT...
THAT I WILL BE ACCEPTED BY TODAI.
GOOD-NESS...
RYOKI, DARLING ...
URGH! NO WAY!
I UNDER-STAND.
LET'S DO AS YOU SAY, THEN.
SO SORRY, AYANOKOJI-SAN!
Omigod.

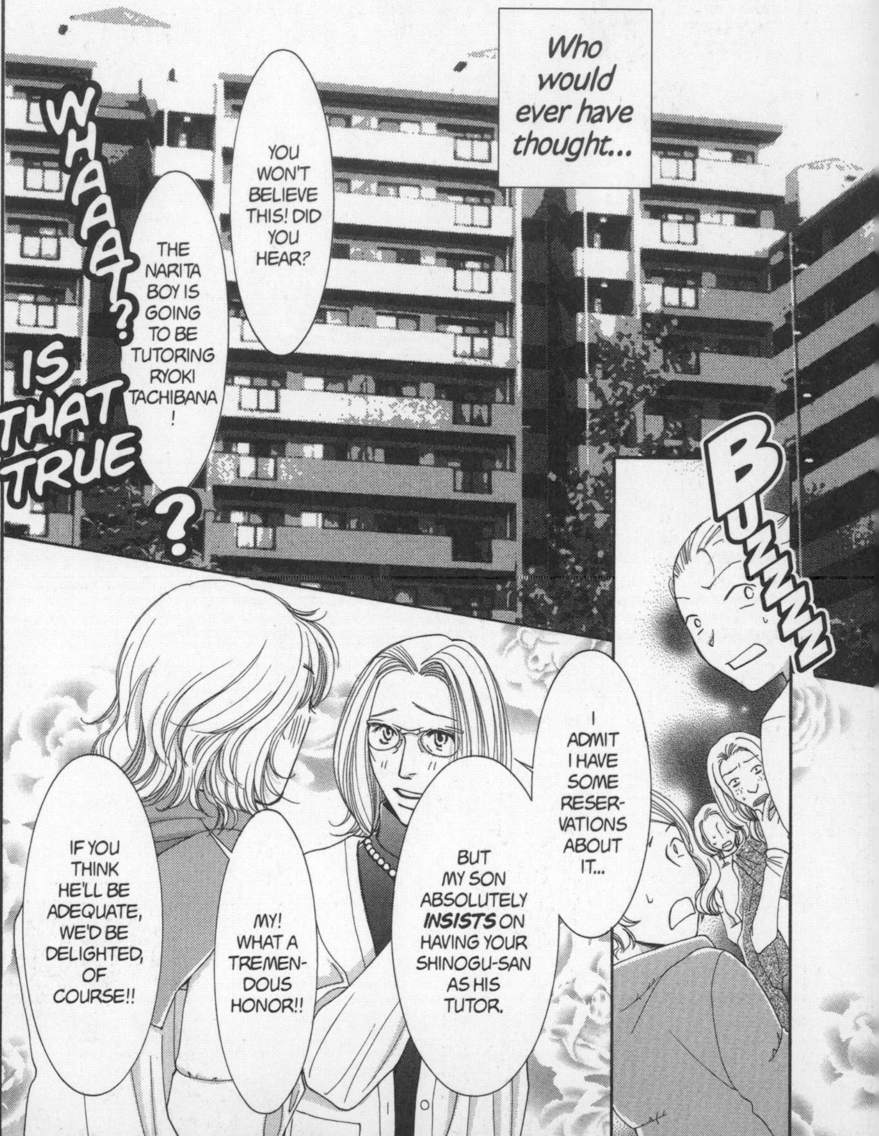
Who would ever have thought...
YOU WON'T BELIEVE THIS! DID YOU HEAR?
THE NARITA BOY IS GOING TO BE TUTORING RYOKI TACHIBANA!
WHAAAT?! IS THAT TRUE?
BUNNNN
I ADMIT I HAVE SOME RESERVATIONS ABOUT IT...
BUT MY SON ABSOLUTELY ***INSISTS*** ON HAVING YOUR SHINOGU-SAN AS HIS TUTOR.
MY! WHAT A TREMENDOUS HONOR!!
IF YOU THINK HE'LL BE ADEQUATE, WE'D BE DELIGHTED, OF COURSE!!

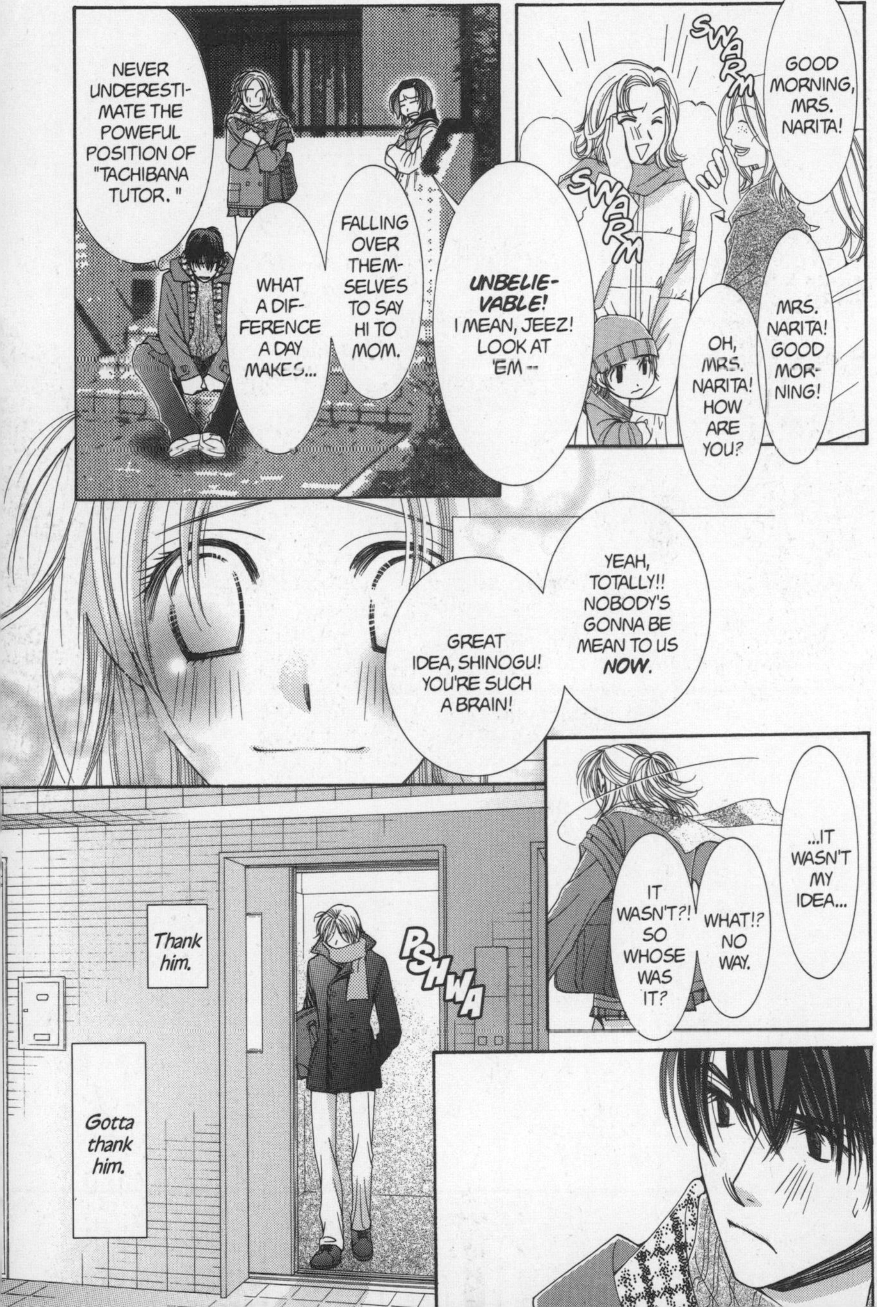
GOOD MORNING, MRS. NARITA!
SWARM
SWARM
MRS. NARITA! GOOD MORNING!
OH, MRS. NARITA! HOW ARE YOU?
UNBELIEVABLE! I MEAN, JEEZ! LOOK AT 'EM --
FALLING OVER THEMSELVES TO SAY HI TO MOM.
WHAT A DIFFERENCE A DAY MAKES...
NEVER UNDERESTIMATE THE POWEFUL POSITION OF "TACHIBANA TUTOR."
YEAH, TOTALLY!! NOBODY'S GONNA BE MEAN TO US NOW.
GREAT IDEA, SHINOGU! YOU'RE SUCH A BRAIN!
...IT WASN'T MY IDEA...
WHAT!? NO WAY.
IT WASN'T?! SO WHOSE WAS IT?
PSHWA
Thank him.
Gotta thank him.

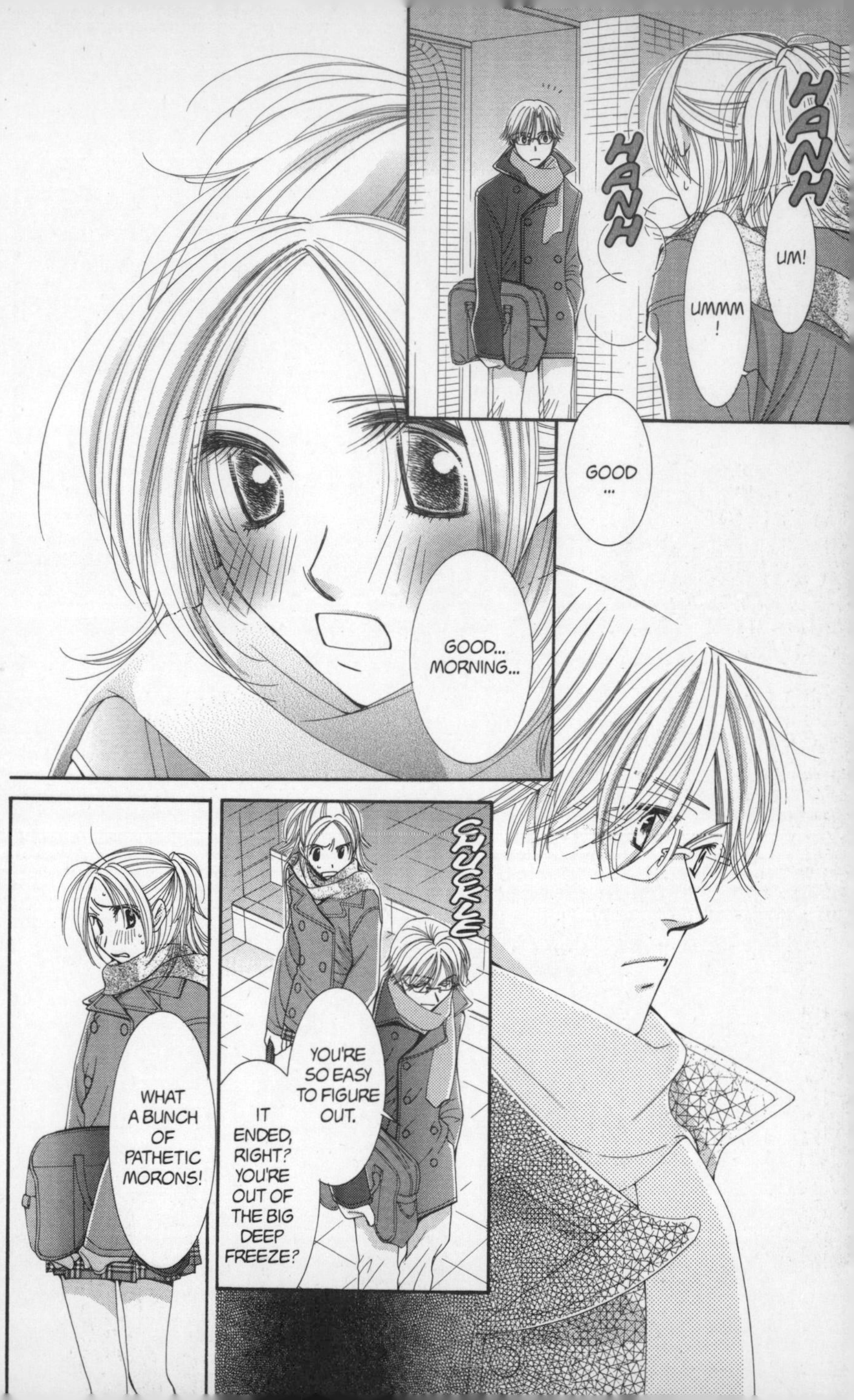

HANH HANH
UM!
UMMM!
HANH HANH
GOOD ...
GOOD... MORNING...
CHUCKLE
YOU'RE SO EASY TO FIGURE OUT.
IT ENDED, RIGHT? YOU'RE OUT OF THE BIG DEEP FREEZE?
WHAT A BUNCH OF PATHETIC MORONS!

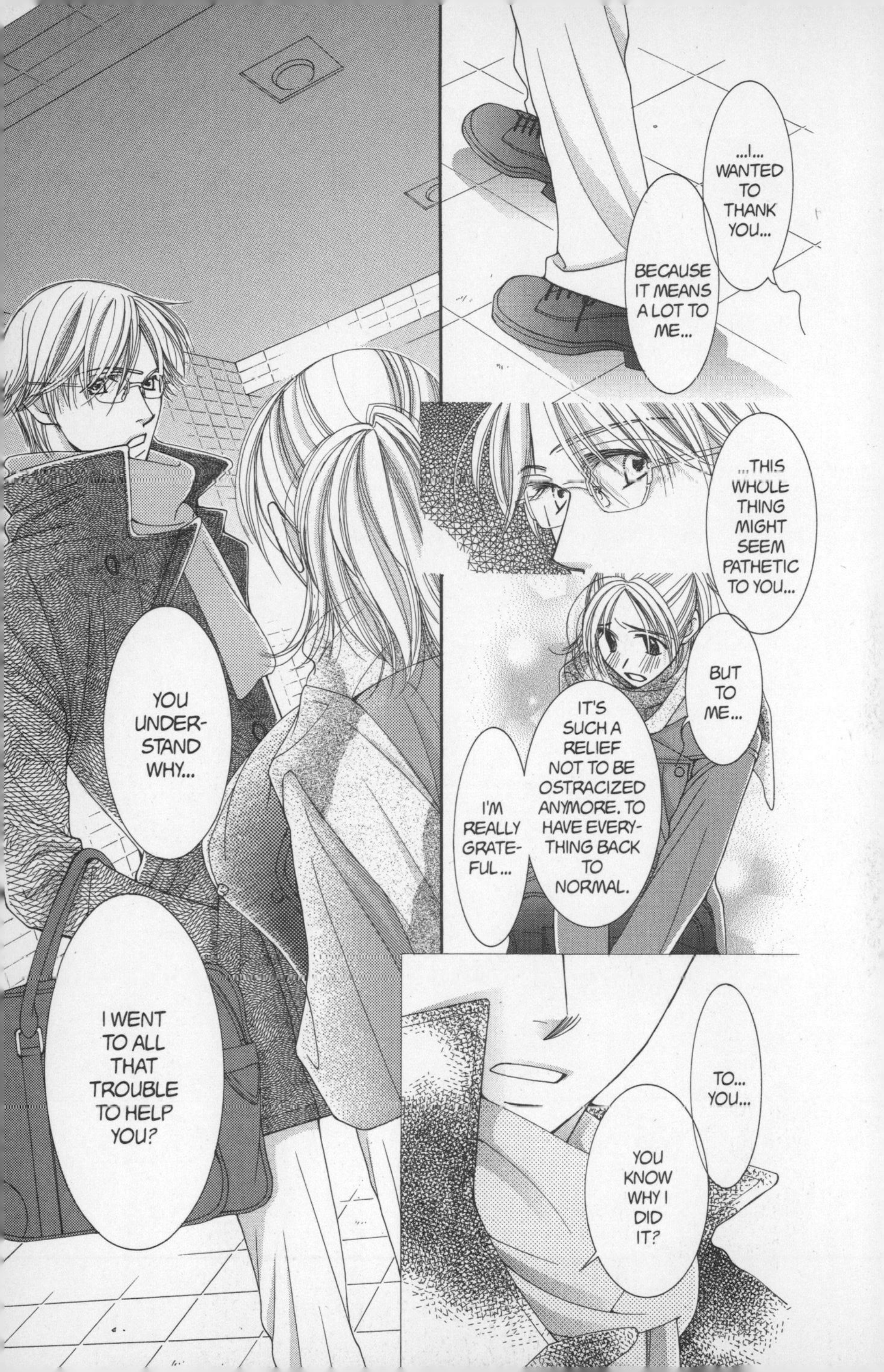
...I... WANTED TO THANK YOU...
BECAUSE IT MEANS A LOT TO ME...
...THIS WHOLE THING MIGHT SEEM PATHETIC TO YOU...
BUT TO ME...
IT'S SUCH A RELIEF NOT TO BE OSTRACIZED ANYMORE. TO HAVE EVERY-THING BACK TO NORMAL.
I'M REALLY GRATE-FUL...
TO... YOU...
YOU KNOW WHY I DID IT?
YOU UNDER-STAND WHY...
I WENT TO ALL THAT TROUBLE TO HELP YOU?

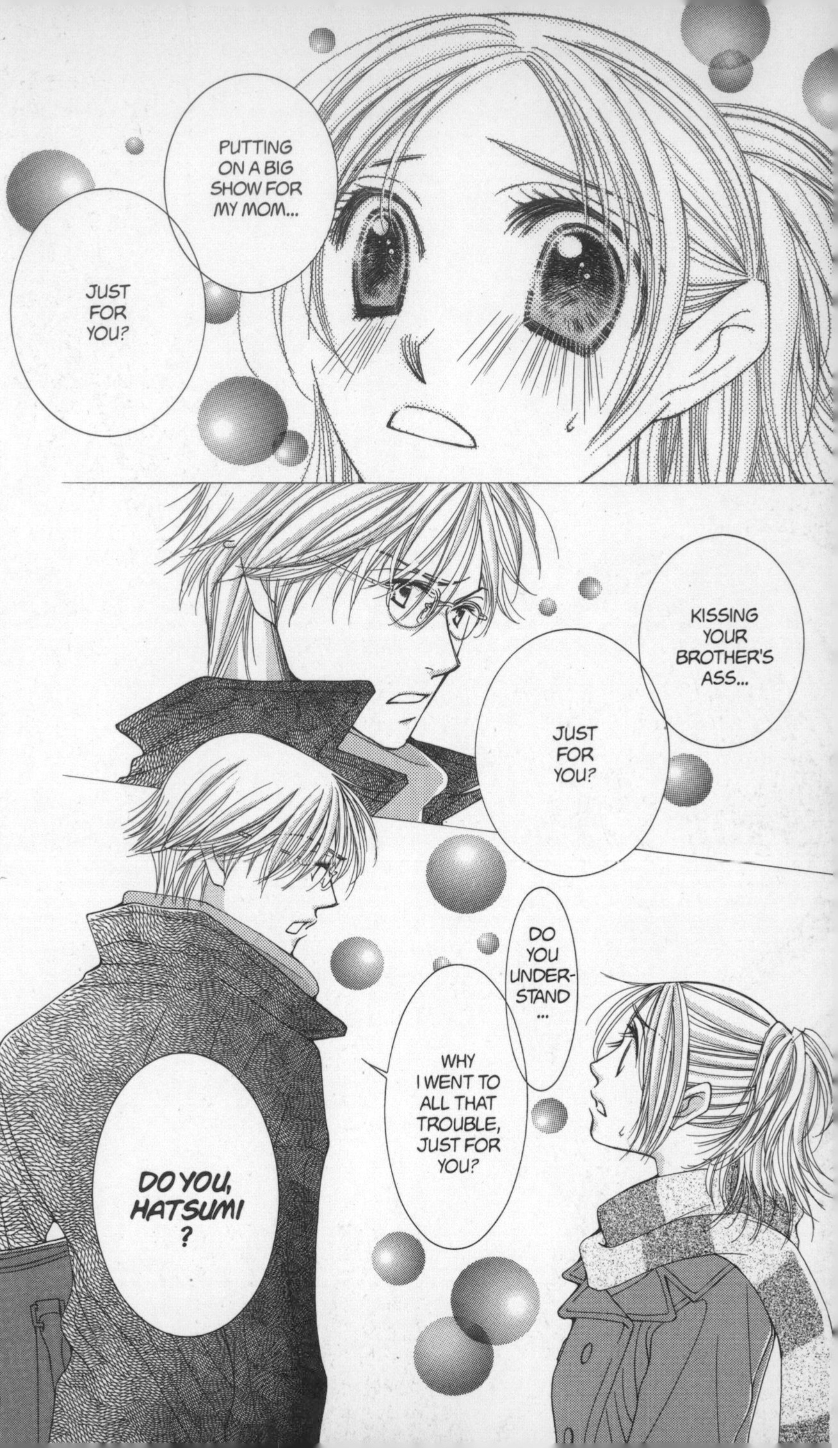
PUTTING ON A BIG SHOW FOR MY MOM...
JUST FOR YOU?
KISSING YOUR BROTHER'S ASS...
JUST FOR YOU?
DO YOU UNDER-STAND...
WHY I WENT TO ALL THAT TROUBLE, JUST FOR YOU?
DO YOU, HATSUMI?

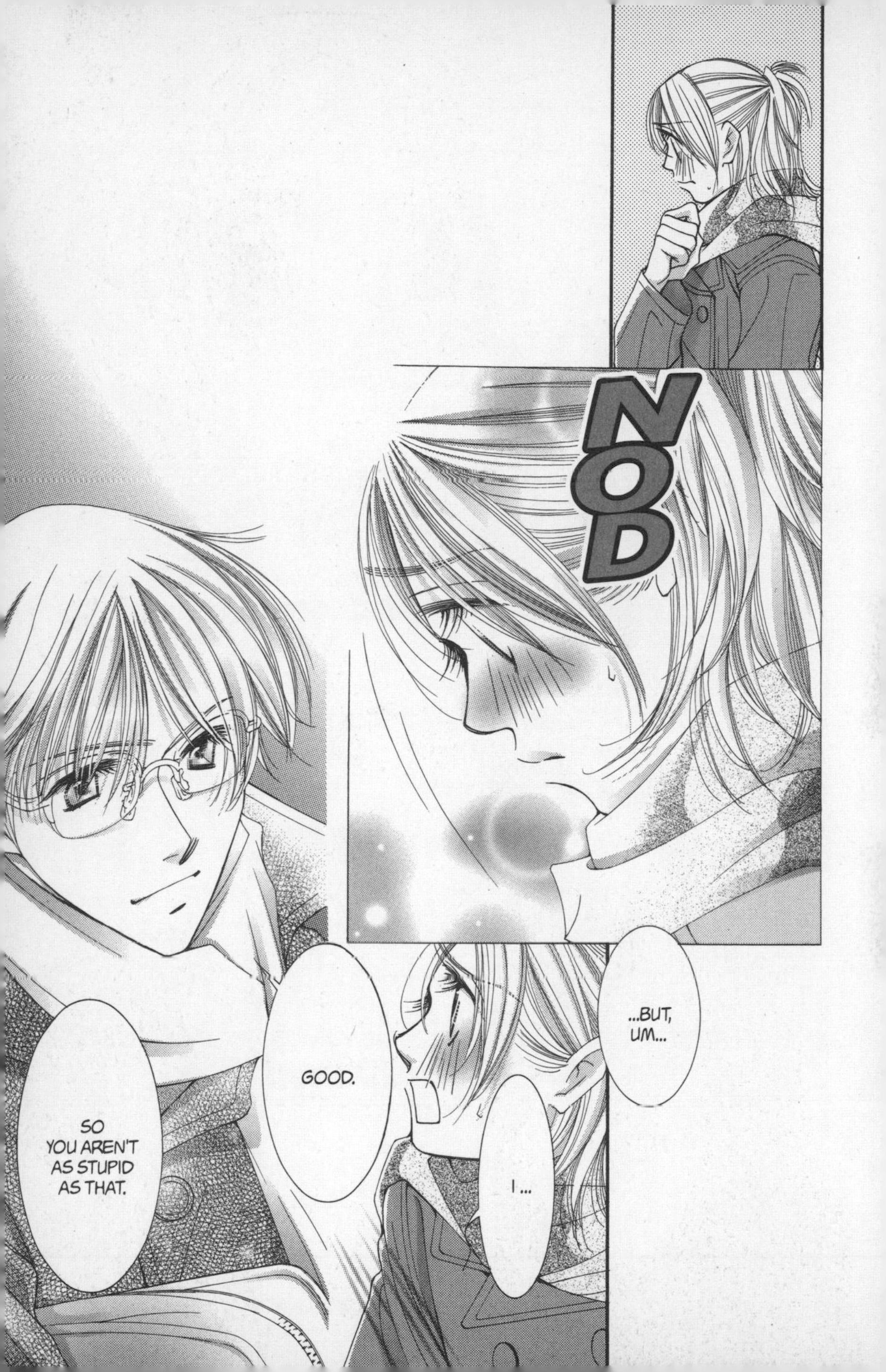
NOD
...BUT, UM...
I...
GOOD.
SO YOU AREN'T AS STUPID AS THAT.

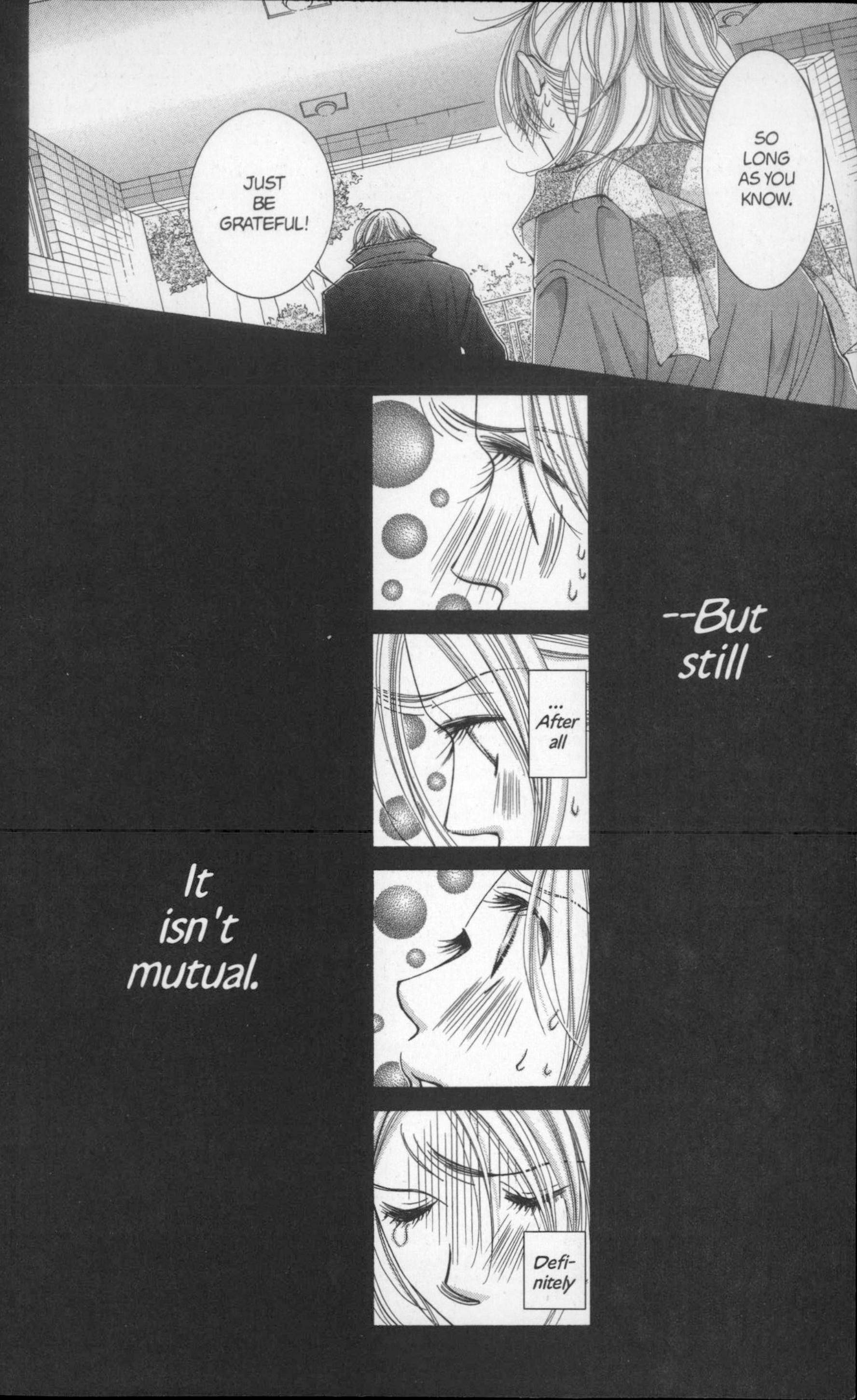
SO LONG AS YOU KNOW.
JUST BE GRATEFUL!
--But still
...After all
It isn't mutual.
Defi-nitely

Chapter 17

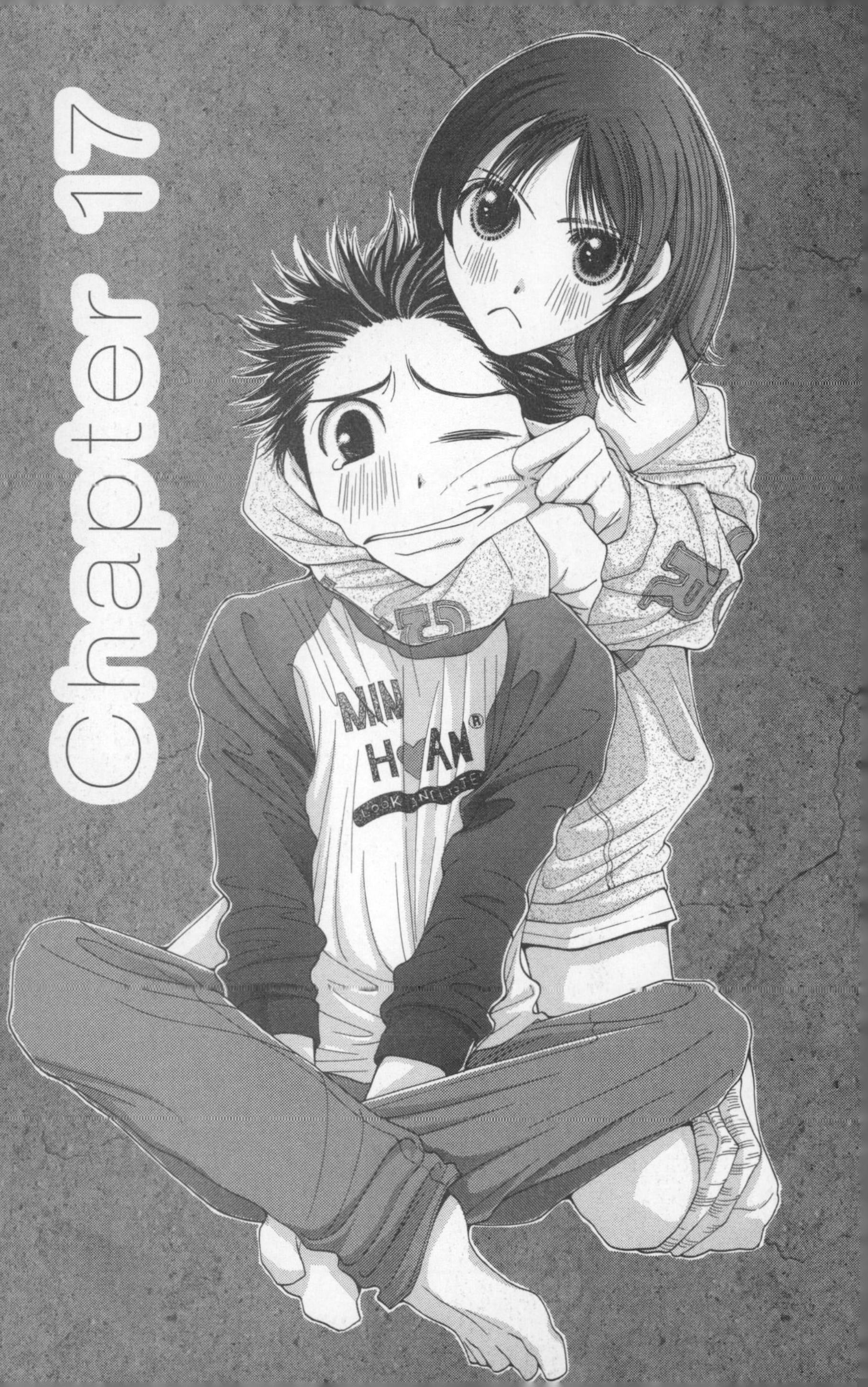

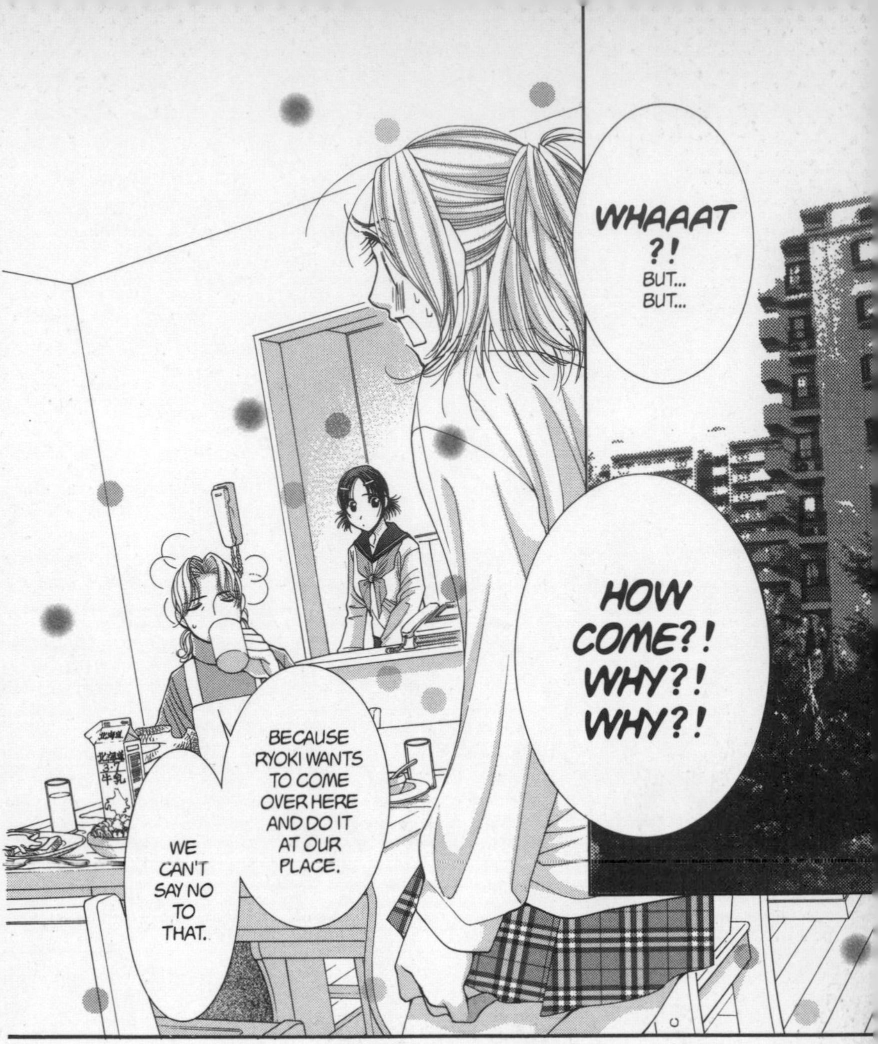
WHAAAT?! BUT... BUT...
HOW COME?! WHY?! WHY?!
BECAUSE RYOKI WANTS TO COME OVER HERE AND DO IT AT OUR PLACE.
WE CAN'T SAY NO TO THAT.

hot gimmick

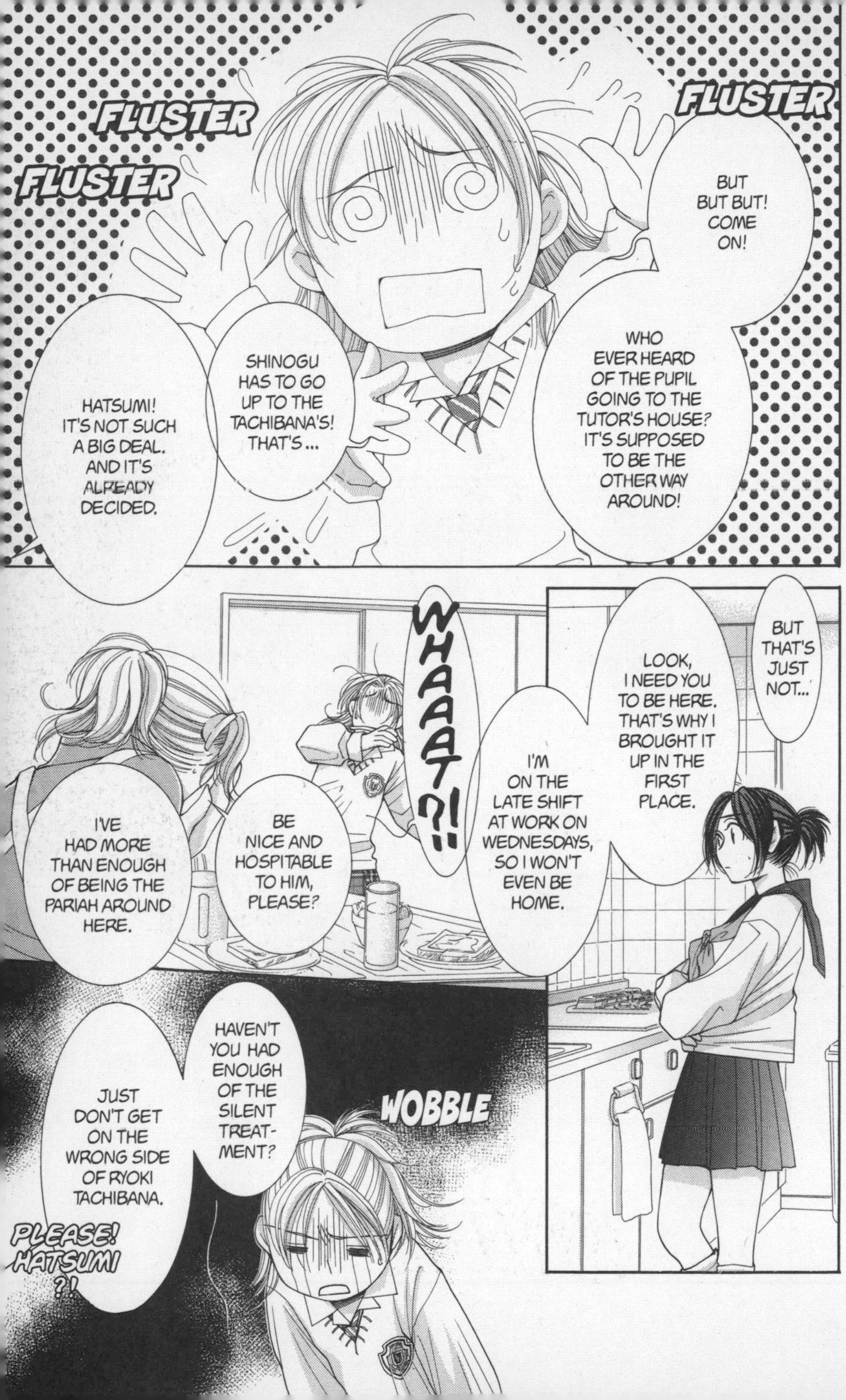
FLUSTER
BUT BUT BUT! COME ON!
FLUSTER
FLUSTER
WHO EVER HEARD OF THE PUPIL GOING TO THE TUTOR'S HOUSE? IT'S SUPPOSED TO BE THE OTHER WAY AROUND!
SHINOGU HAS TO GO UP TO THE TACHIBANA'S! THAT'S...
HATSUMI! IT'S NOT SUCH A BIG DEAL. AND IT'S ALREADY DECIDED.
BUT THAT'S JUST NOT...
LOOK, I NEED YOU TO BE HERE. THAT'S WHY I BROUGHT IT UP IN THE FIRST PLACE.
I'M ON THE LATE SHIFT AT WORK ON WEDNESDAYS, SO I WON'T EVEN BE HOME.
WHAAAT?!!
BE NICE AND HOSPITABLE TO HIM, PLEASE?
I'VE HAD MORE THAN ENOUGH OF BEING THE PARIAH AROUND HERE.
WOBBLE
HAVEN'T YOU HAD ENOUGH OF THE SILENT TREAT-MENT?
JUST DON'T GET ON THE WRONG SIDE OF RYOKI TACHIBANA.
PLEASE! HATSUMI?!

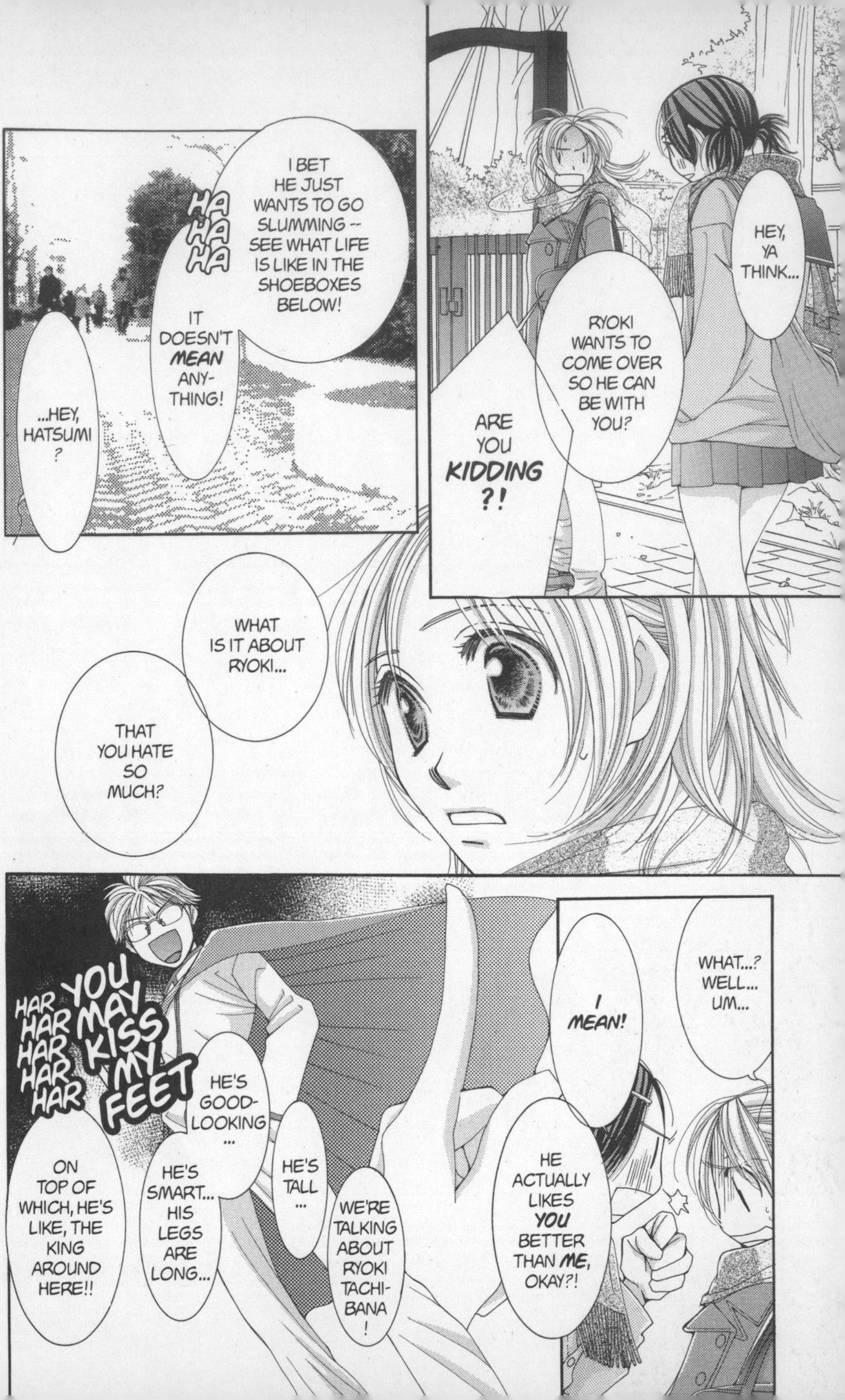
HEY, YA THINK...
RYOKI WANTS TO COME OVER SO HE CAN BE WITH YOU?
ARE YOU KIDDING?!
I BET HE JUST WANTS TO GO SLUMMING -- SEE WHAT LIFE IS LIKE IN THE SHOEBOXES BELOW!
HA HA HA
IT DOESN'T MEAN ANY-THING!
...HEY, HATSUMI?
WHAT IS IT ABOUT RYOKI...
THAT YOU HATE SO MUCH?
WHAT...? WELL... UM...
I MEAN!
HE ACTUALLY LIKES YOU BETTER THAN ME, OKAY?!
WE'RE TALKING ABOUT RYOKI TACHI-BANA!
HE'S TALL...
HE'S GOOD-LOOKING...
HE'S SMART... HIS LEGS ARE LONG...
ON TOP OF WHICH, HE'S LIKE, THE KING AROUND HERE!!
YOU MAY KISS MY FEET
HAR HAR HAR HAR HAR

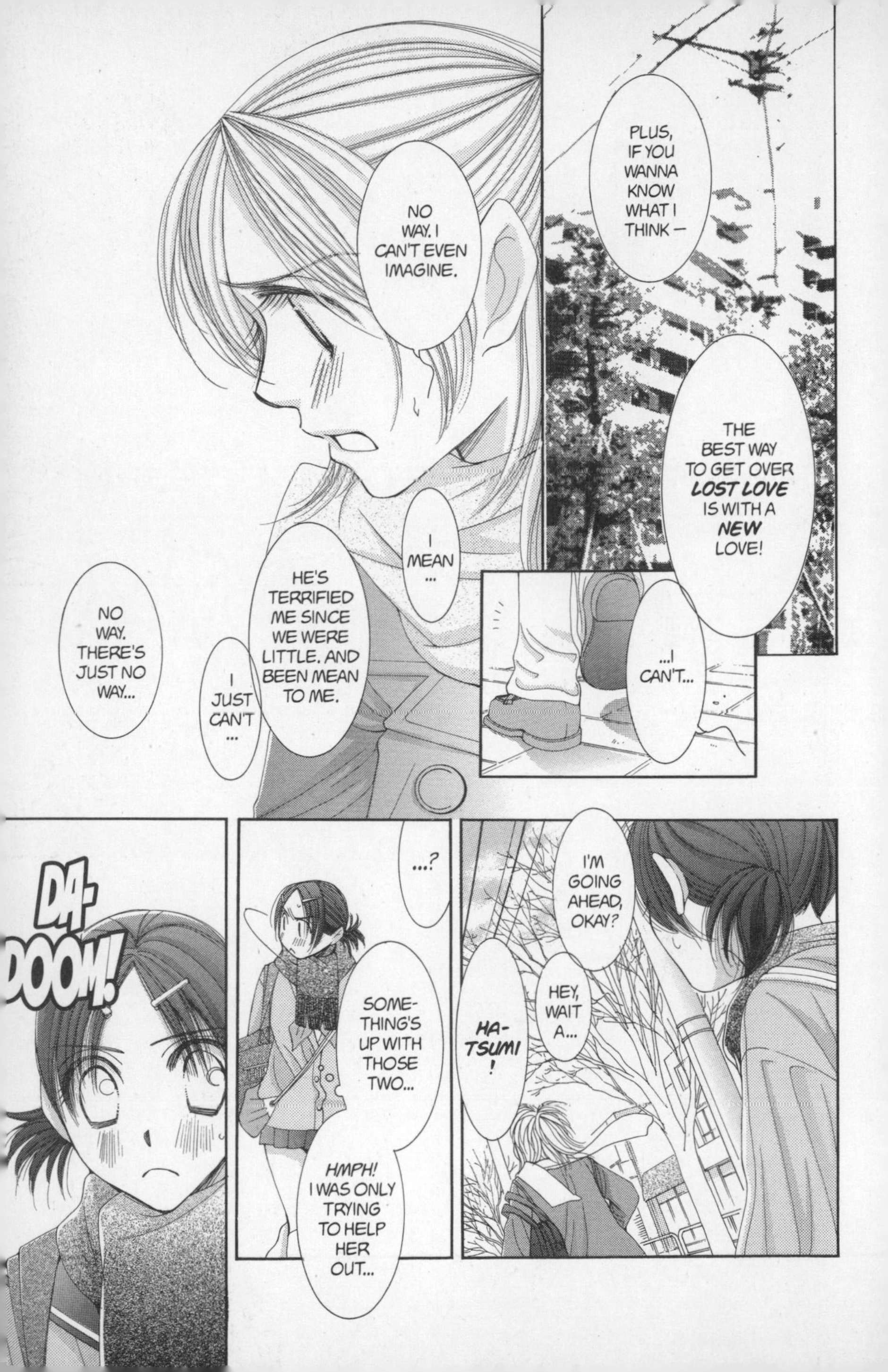
PLUS, IF YOU WANNA KNOW WHAT I THINK —
THE BEST WAY TO GET OVER LOST LOVE IS WITH A NEW LOVE!
...I CAN'T...
NO WAY. I CAN'T EVEN IMAGINE.
I MEAN...
HE'S TERRIFIED ME SINCE WE WERE LITTLE. AND BEEN MEAN TO ME.
I JUST CAN'T...
NO WAY. THERE'S JUST NO WAY...
I'M GOING AHEAD, OKAY?
HEY, WAIT A...
HA-TSUMI!
...?
SOME-THING'S UP WITH THOSE TWO...
HMPH! I WAS ONLY TRYING TO HELP HER OUT...
DA-DOOM!

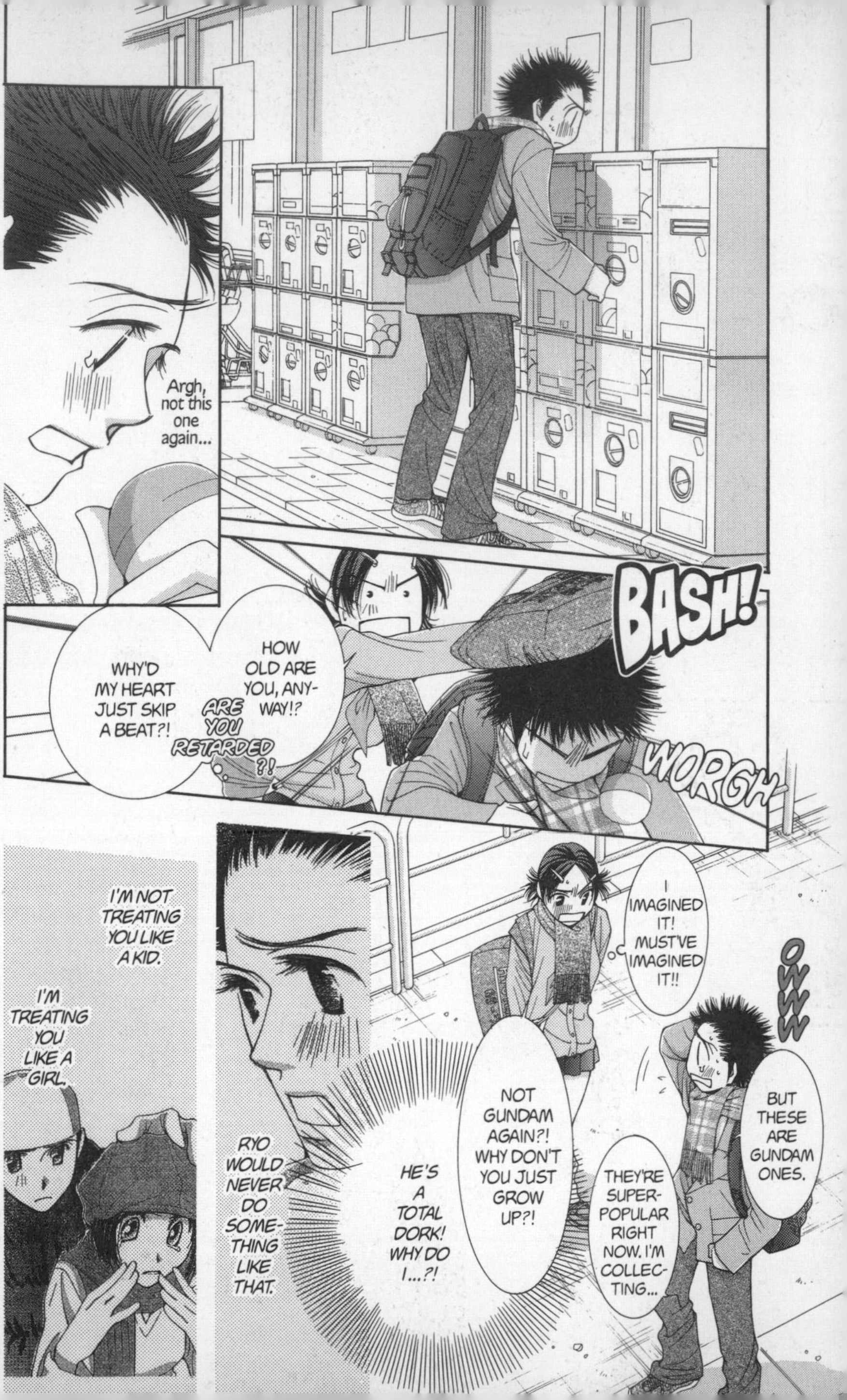
Argh, not this one again...
BASH!
HOW OLD ARE YOU, ANYWAY!?
ARE YOU RETARDED?!
WHY'D MY HEART JUST SKIP A BEAT?!
WORGH
OWW
I IMAGINED IT! MUST'VE IMAGINED IT!!
NOT GUNDAM AGAIN?! WHY DON'T YOU JUST GROW UP?!
BUT THESE ARE GUNDAM ONES.
THEY'RE SUPER-POPULAR RIGHT NOW. I'M COLLECTING...
HE'S A TOTAL DORK! WHY DO I...?!
RYO WOULD NEVER DO SOMETHING LIKE THAT.
I'M NOT TREATING YOU LIKE A KID.
I'M TREATING YOU LIKE A GIRL.

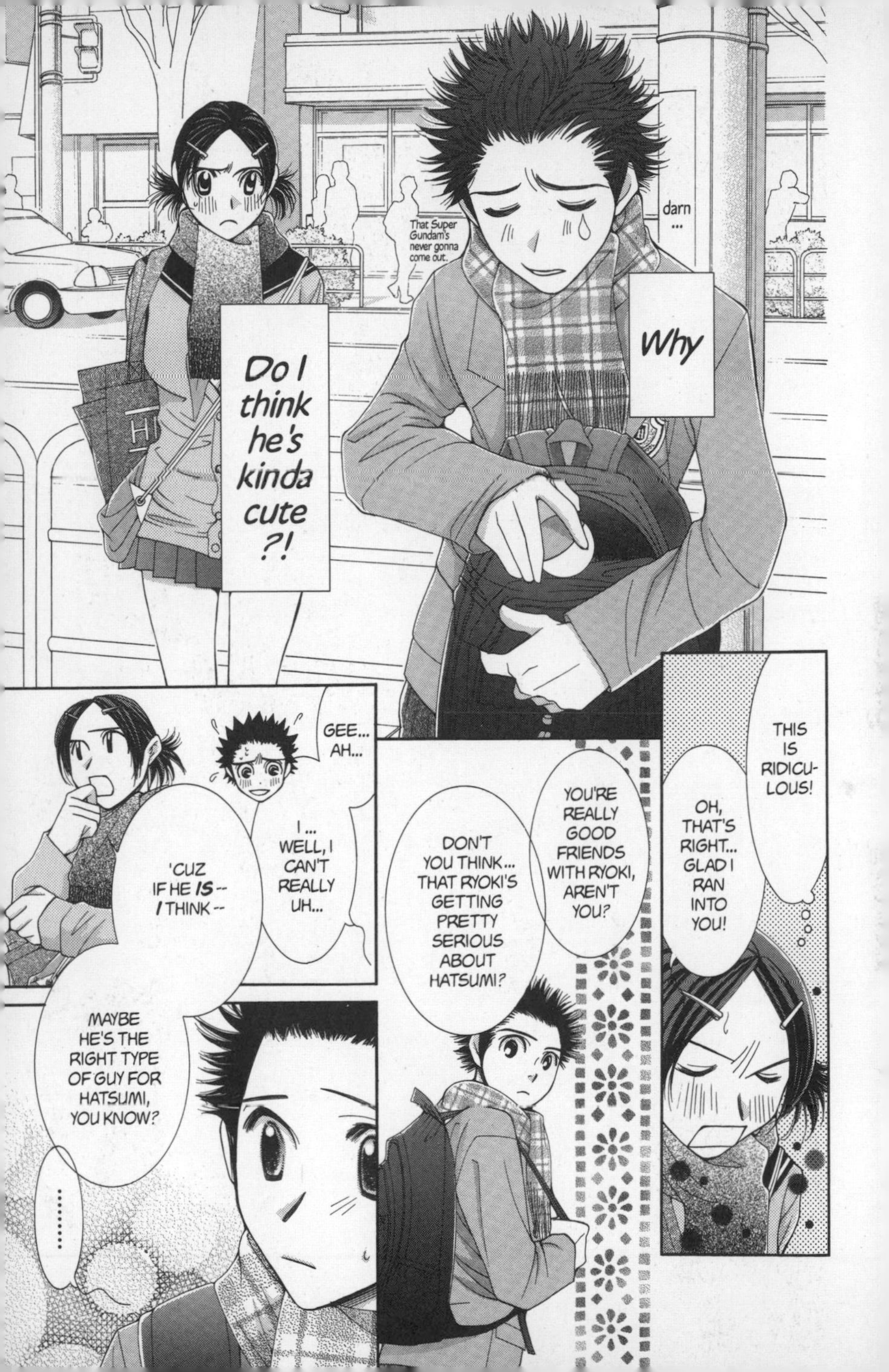
darn ...
That Super Gundam's never gonna come out.
Why
Do I think he's kinda cute ?!
THIS IS RIDICU-LOUS!
OH, THAT'S RIGHT... GLAD I RAN INTO YOU!
YOU'RE REALLY GOOD FRIENDS WITH RYOKI, AREN'T YOU?
DON'T YOU THINK... THAT RYOKI'S GETTING PRETTY SERIOUS ABOUT HATSUMI?
GEE... AH...
I ... WELL, I CAN'T REALLY UH...
'CUZ IF HE *IS* -- I THINK --
MAYBE HE'S THE RIGHT TYPE OF GUY FOR HATSUMI, YOU KNOW?
......

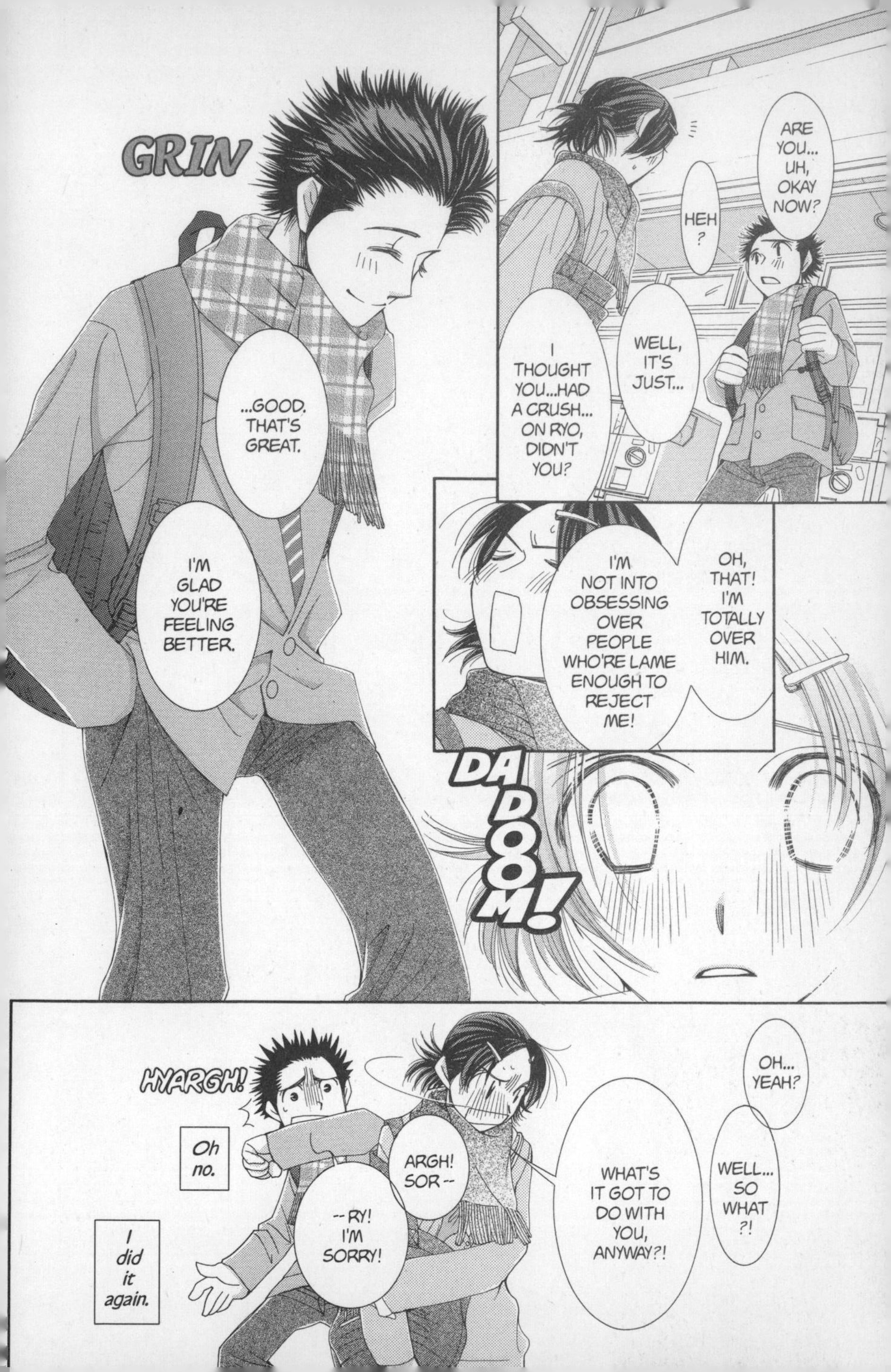
ARE YOU... UH, OKAY NOW?
HEH?
WELL, IT'S JUST...
I THOUGHT YOU...HAD A CRUSH... ON RYO, DIDN'T YOU?
OH, THAT! I'M TOTALLY OVER HIM.
I'M NOT INTO OBSESSING OVER PEOPLE WHO'RE LAME ENOUGH TO REJECT ME!
DADOOM!
GRIN
...GOOD. THAT'S GREAT.
I'M GLAD YOU'RE FEELING BETTER.
OH... YEAH?
WELL... SO WHAT?!
WHAT'S IT GOT TO DO WITH YOU, ANYWAY?!
ARGH! SOR --
HYARGH!
--RY! I'M SORRY!
Oh no.
I did it again.

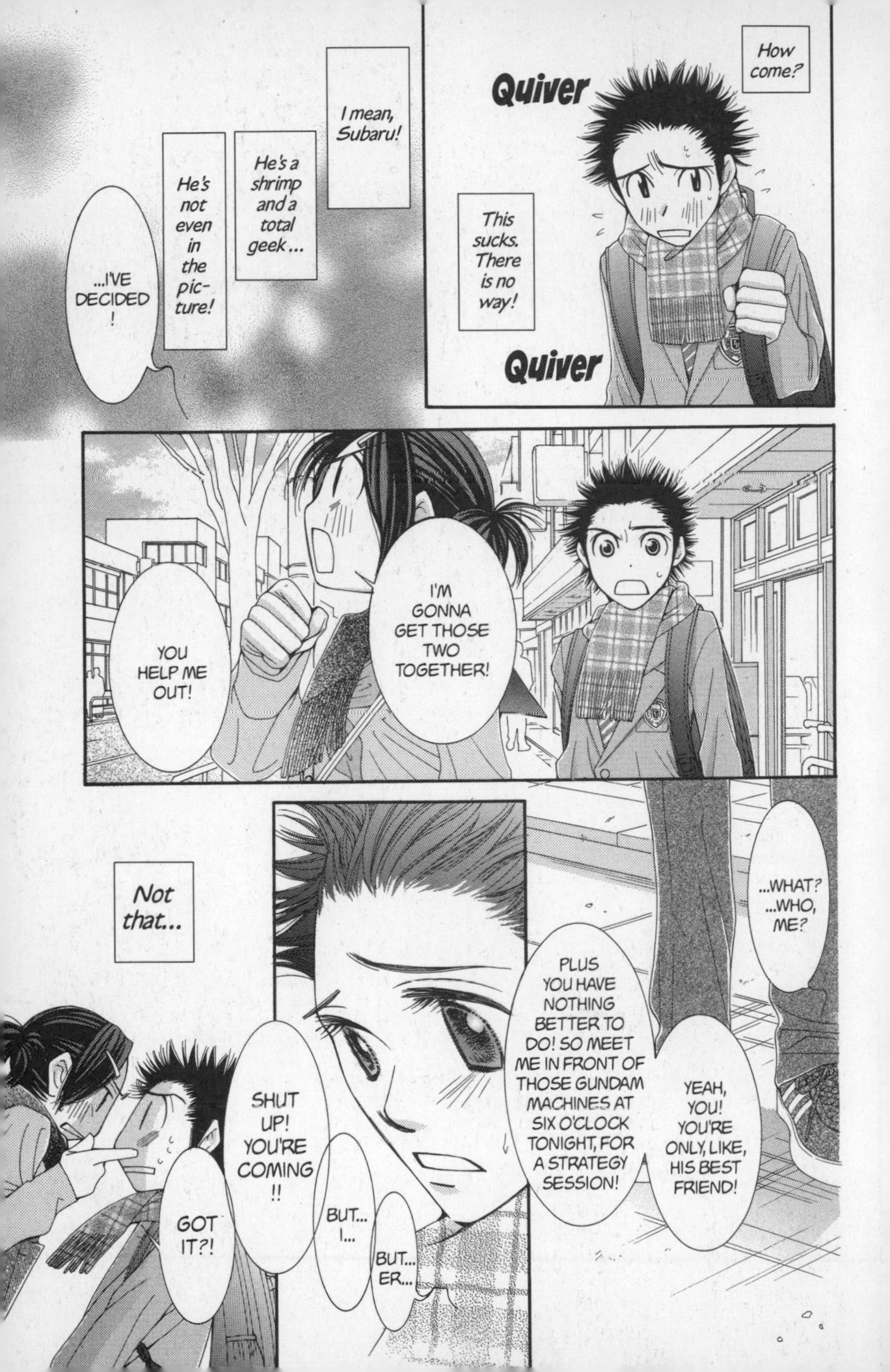
How come?
Quiver
This sucks. There is no way!
Quiver
I mean, Subaru!
He's a shrimp and a total geek...
He's not even in the pic-ture!
...I'VE DECIDED!
I'M GONNA GET THOSE TWO TOGETHER!
YOU HELP ME OUT!
...WHAT? ...WHO, ME?
YEAH, YOU! YOU'RE ONLY, LIKE, HIS BEST FRIEND!
PLUS YOU HAVE NOTHING BETTER TO DO! SO MEET ME IN FRONT OF THOSE GUNDAM MACHINES AT SIX O'CLOCK TONIGHT, FOR A STRATEGY SESSION!
SHUT UP! YOU'RE COMING!!
BUT... I...
BUT... ER...
GOT IT?!
Not that...

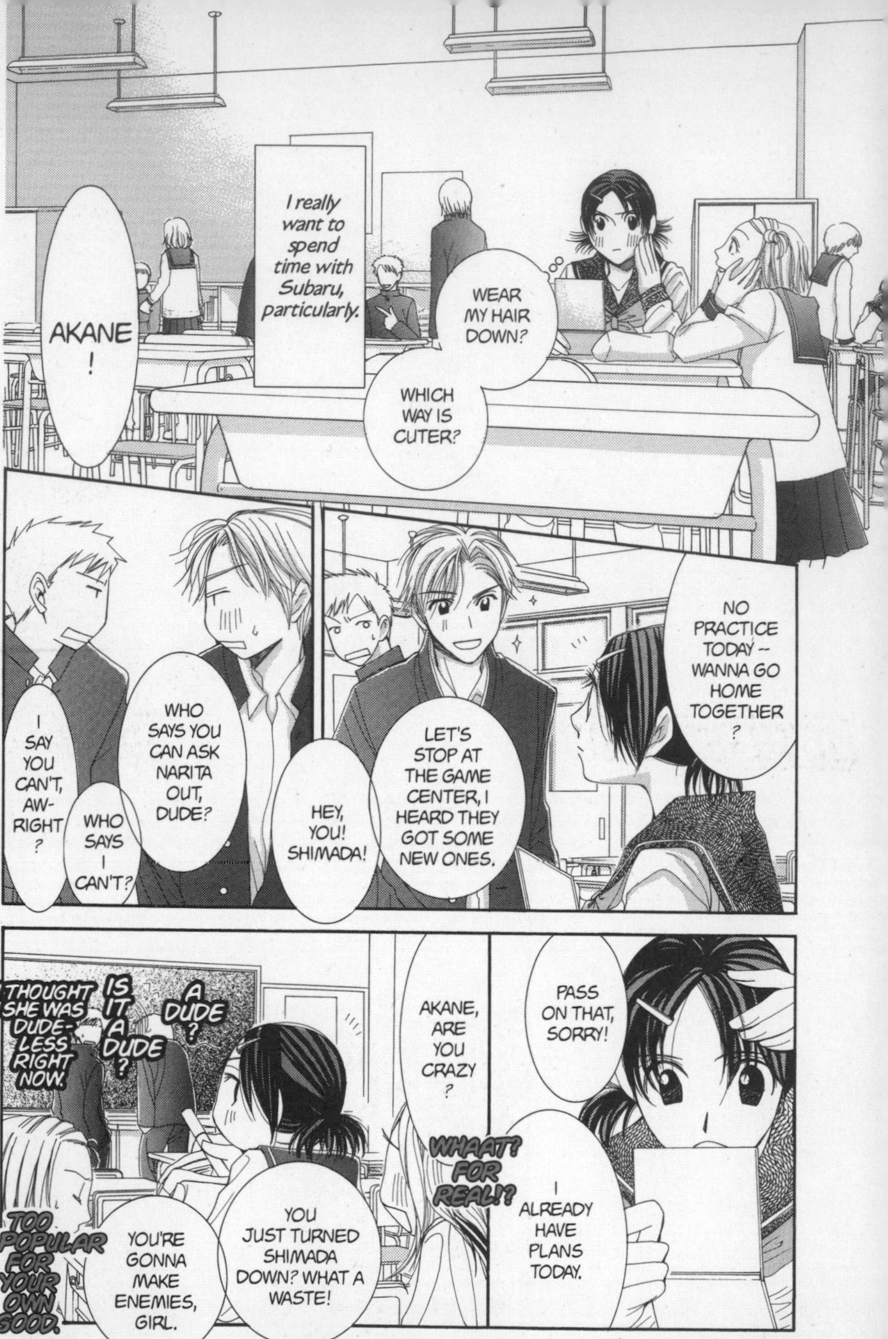

WEAR MY HAIR DOWN?
WHICH WAY IS CUTER?
I really want to spend time with Subaru, particularly.
AKANE!
NO PRACTICE TODAY -- WANNA GO HOME TOGETHER?
LET'S STOP AT THE GAME CENTER, I HEARD THEY GOT SOME NEW ONES.
HEY, YOU! SHIMADA!
WHO SAYS YOU CAN ASK NARITA OUT, DUDE?
I SAY YOU CAN'T, AW-RIGHT?
WHO SAYS I CAN'T?
PASS ON THAT, SORRY!
I ALREADY HAVE PLANS TODAY.
AKANE, ARE YOU CRAZY?
WHAAT? FOR REAL!?
YOU JUST TURNED SHIMADA DOWN? WHAT A WASTE!
A DUDE?
IS IT A DUDE?
I THOUGHT SHE WAS DUDE-LESS RIGHT NOW.
YOU'RE GONNA MAKE ENEMIES, GIRL.
TOO POPULAR FOR YOUR OWN GOOD.

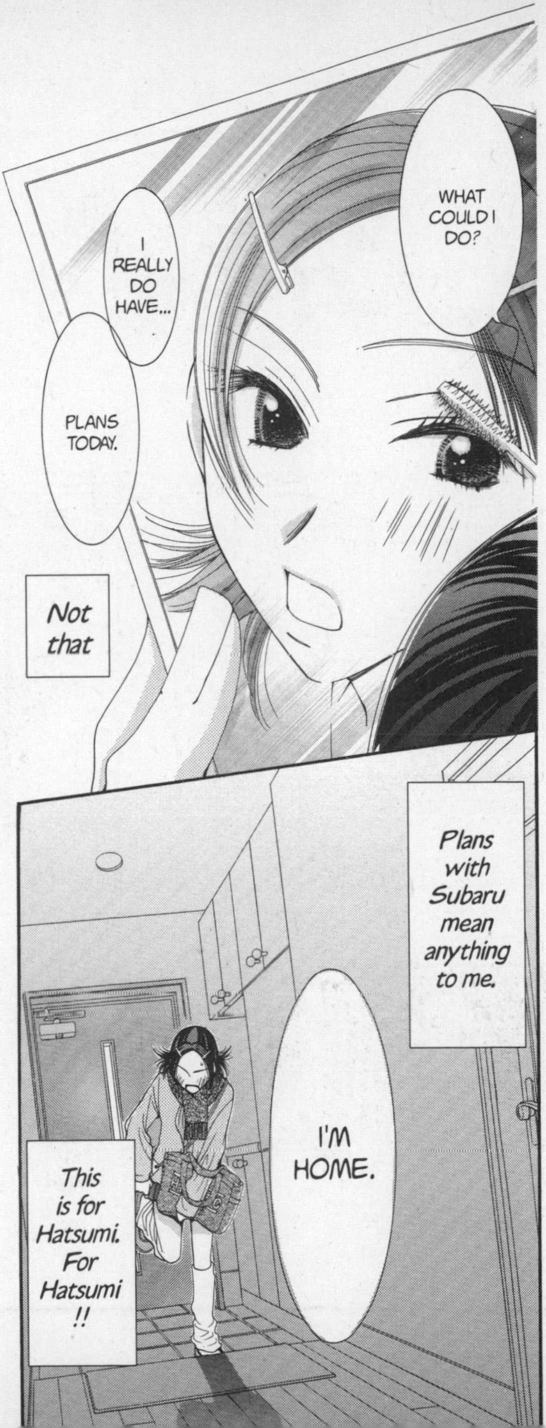
WHAT COULD I DO?
I REALLY DO HAVE...
PLANS TODAY.
Not that
Plans with Subaru mean anything to me.
I'M HOME.
This is for Hatsumi. For Hatsumi !!

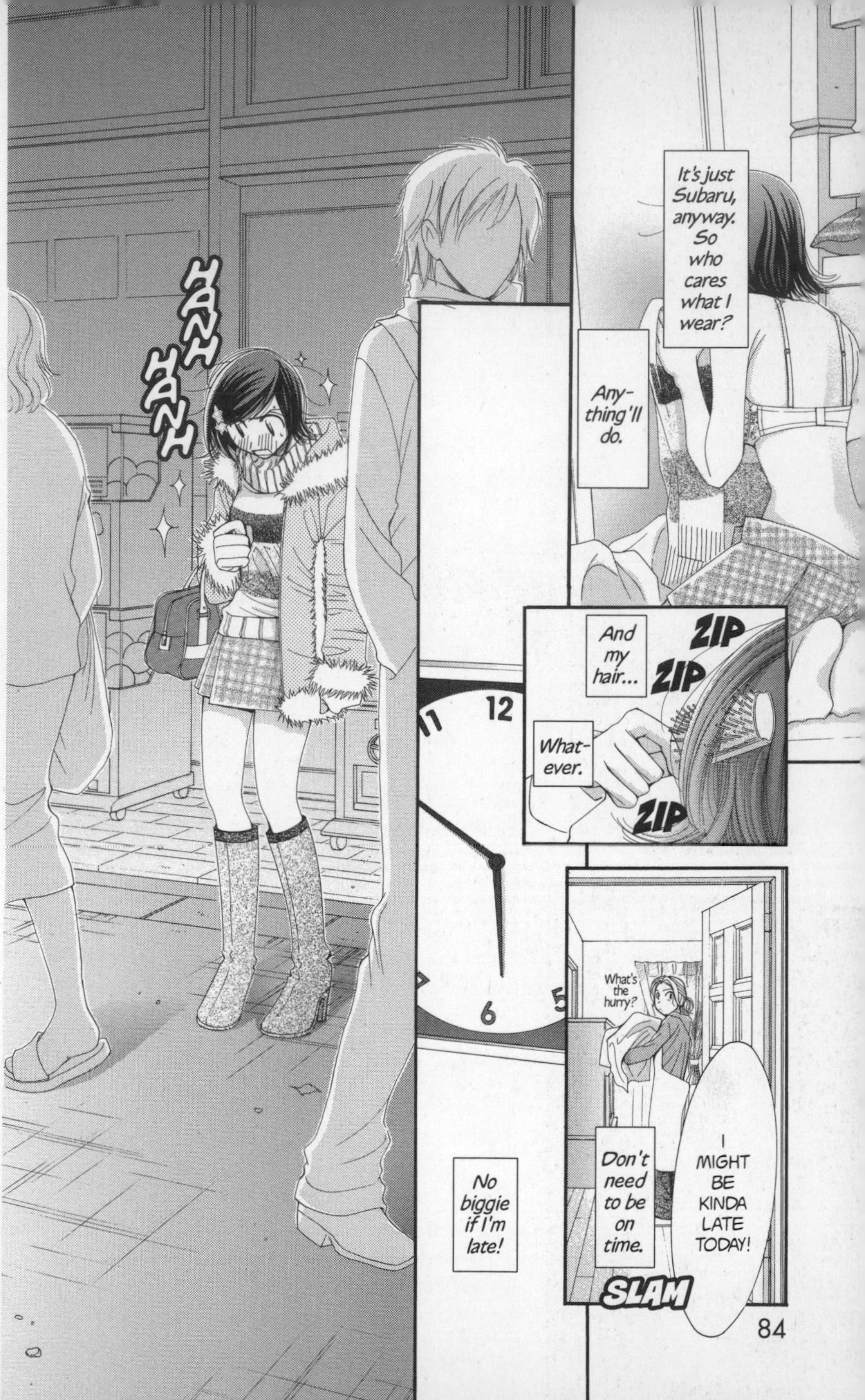
It's just Subaru, anyway. So who cares what I wear?
Any-thing'll do.
And my hair...
ZIP
ZIP
Whatever.
ZIP
I MIGHT BE KINDA LATE TODAY!
What's the hurry?
Don't need to be on time.
SLAM
12
11
6
5
No biggie if I'm late!
HANH
HANH

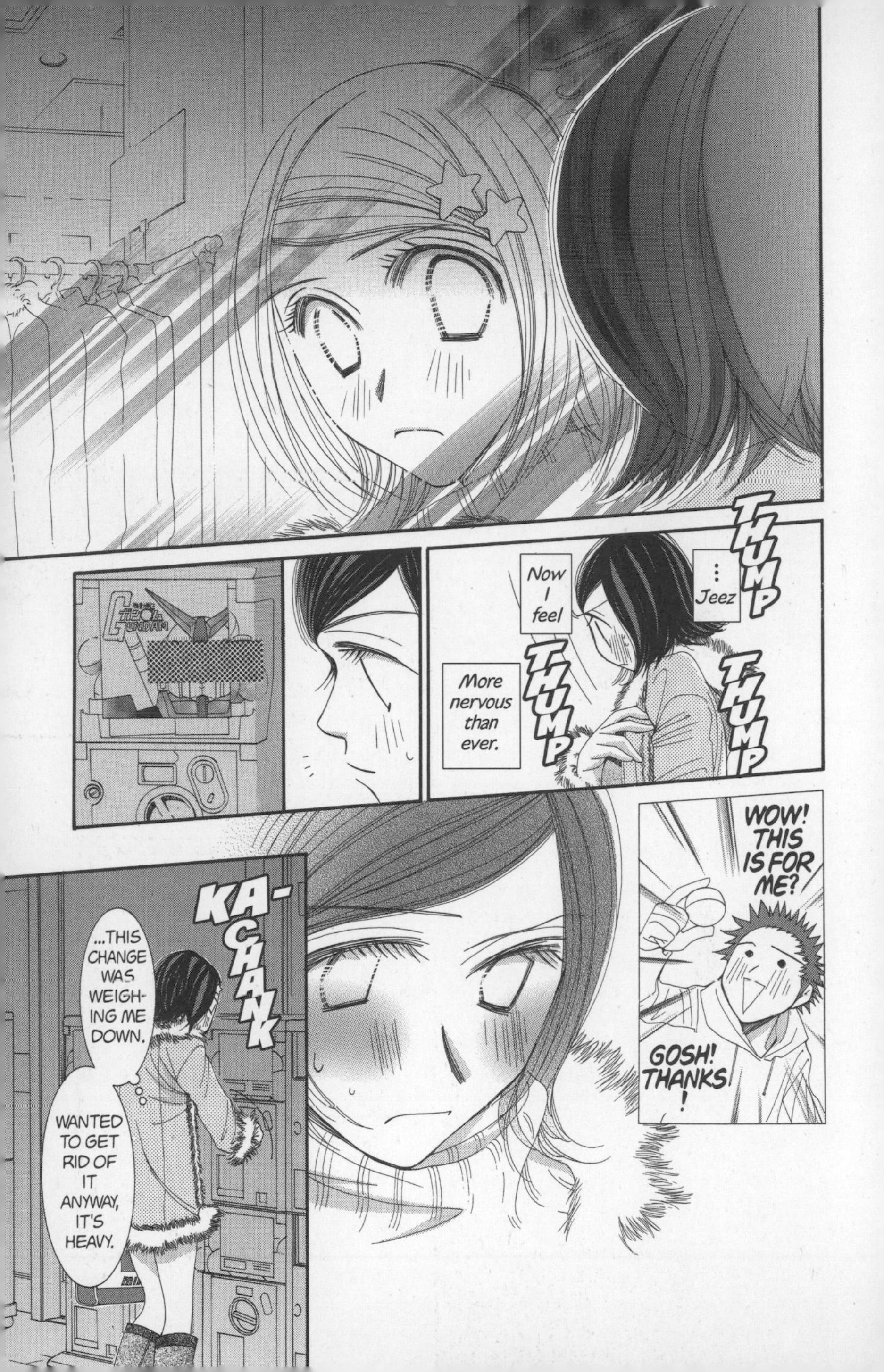
THUMP
...Jeez
Now I feel
THUMP
More nervous than ever.
THUMP
GUNDAM
WOW! THIS IS FOR ME?
GOSH! THANKS!
KA-CHANK
...THIS CHANGE WAS WEIGHING ME DOWN.
WANTED TO GET RID OF IT ANYWAY, IT'S HEAVY.

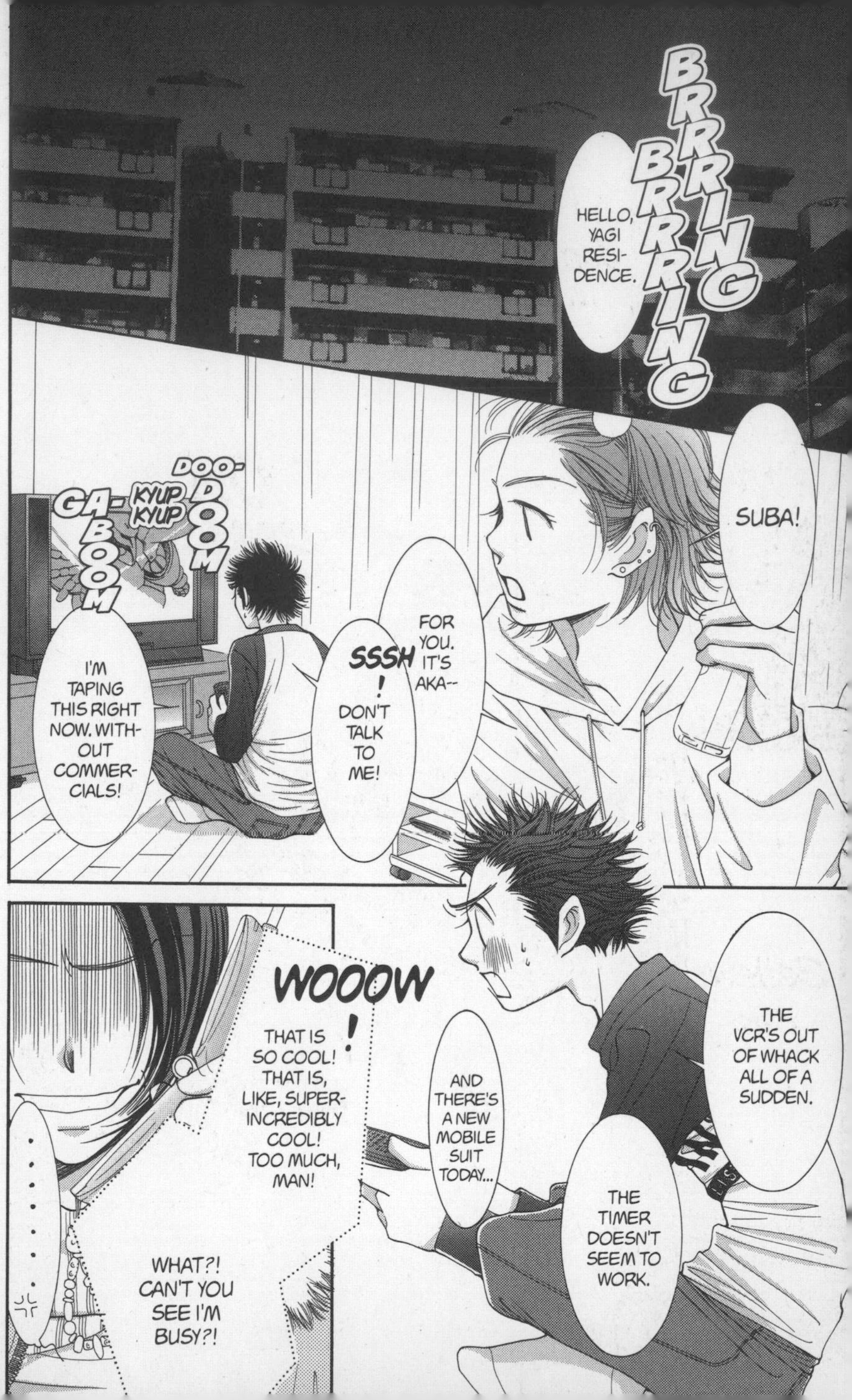
BRRRING
BRRRING
HELLO, YAGI RESIDENCE.
SUBA!
FOR YOU. IT'S AKA--
SSSH! DON'T TALK TO ME!
DOO-DOOM
KYUP KYUP
GA-BOOM
I'M TAPING THIS RIGHT NOW. WITHOUT COMMERCIALS!
THE VCR'S OUT OF WHACK ALL OF A SUDDEN.
THE TIMER DOESN'T SEEM TO WORK.
AND THERE'S A NEW MOBILE SUIT TODAY...
WOOOW!
THAT IS SO COOL! THAT IS, LIKE, SUPER-INCREDIBLY COOL! TOO MUCH, MAN!
......
WHAT?! CAN'T YOU SEE I'M BUSY?!

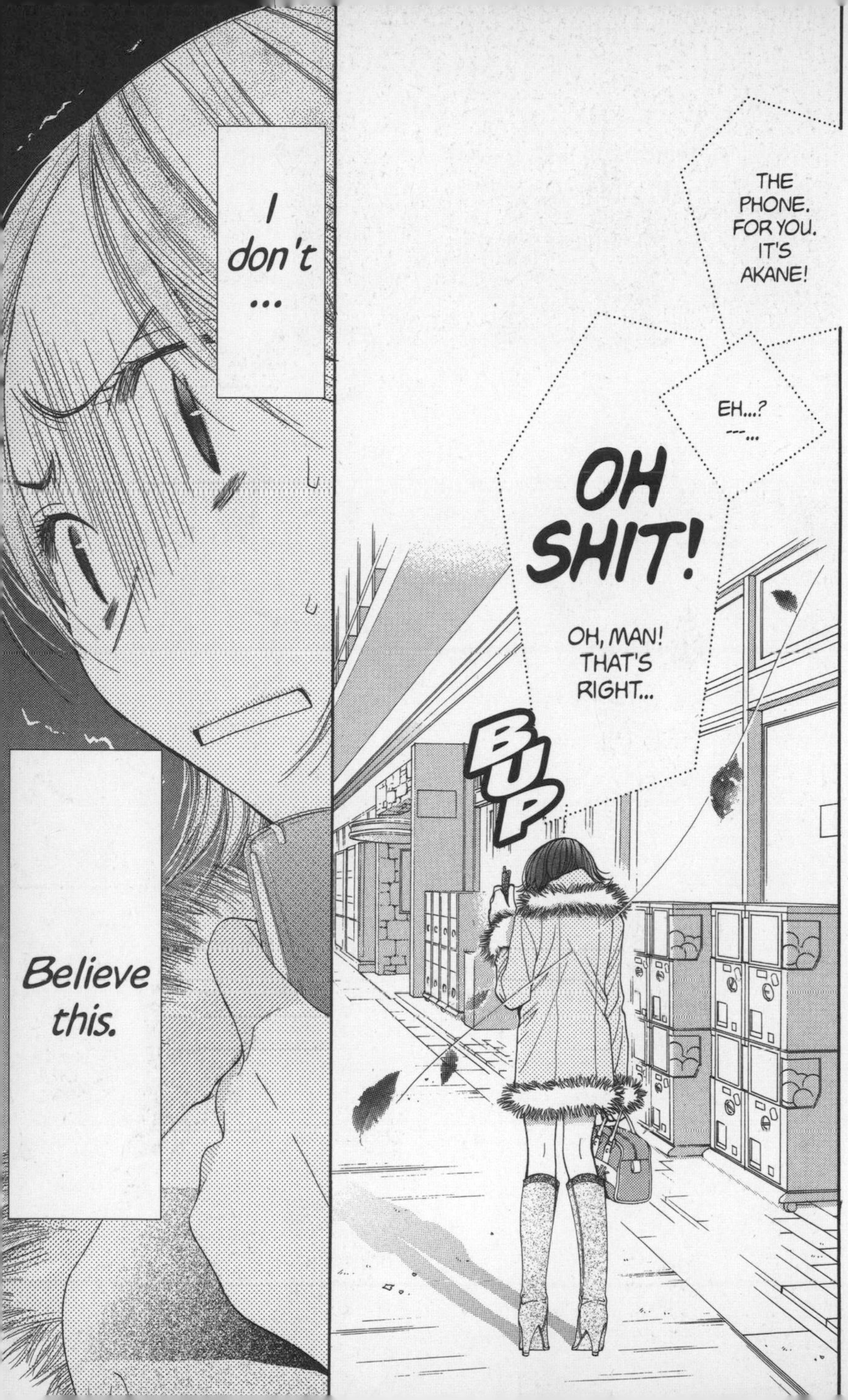
THE PHONE. FOR YOU. IT'S AKANE!
EH...? ---...
OH SHIT!
OH, MAN! THAT'S RIGHT...
BUP
I don't ...
Believe this.

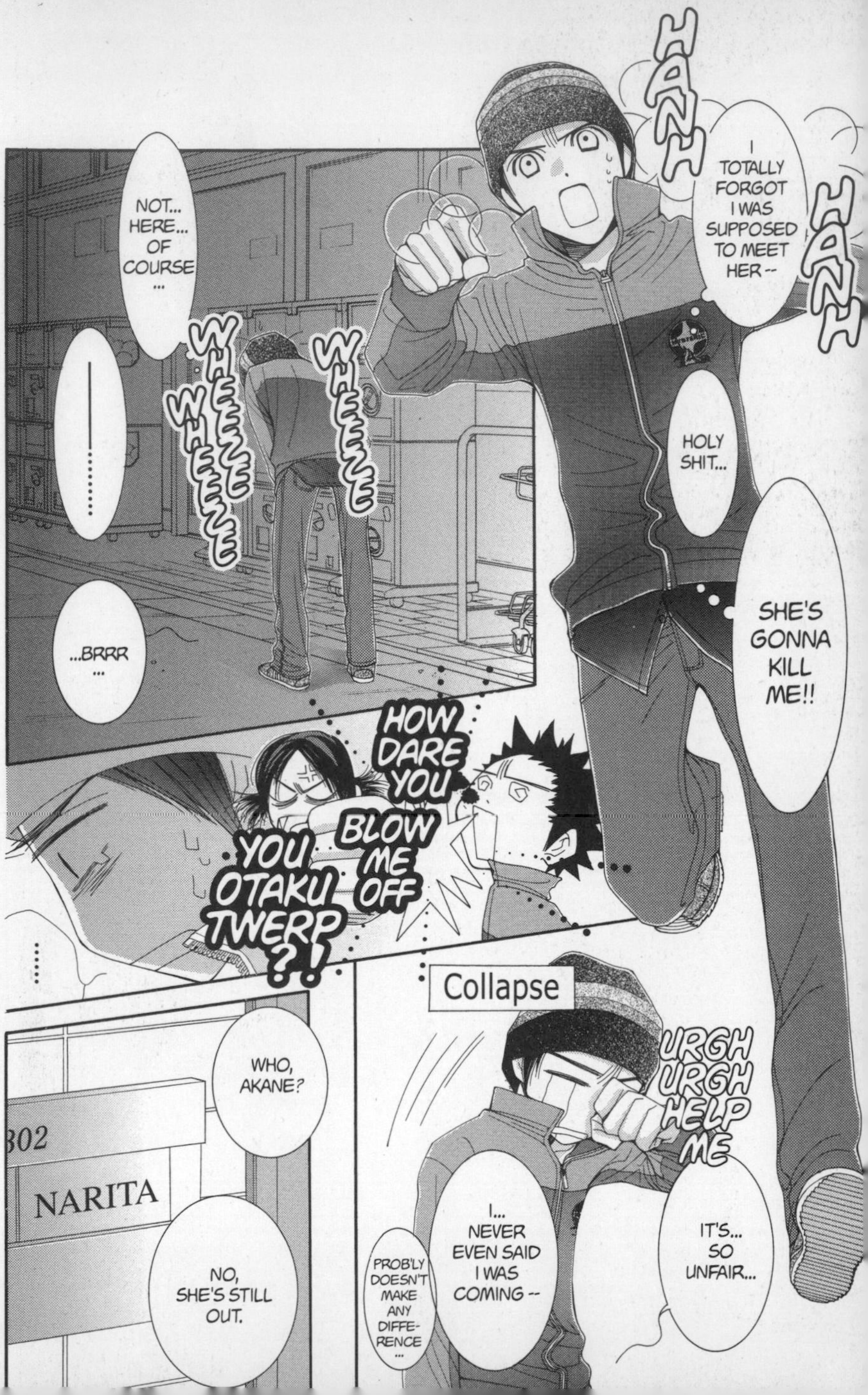
HANH
I TOTALLY FORGOT I WAS SUPPOSED TO MEET HER --
HANH
HOLY SHIT...
SHE'S GONNA KILL ME!!
NOT... HERE... OF COURSE...
——......
WHEEZE
WHEEZE WHEEZE
...BRRR...
HOW DARE YOU BLOW ME OFF
YOU OTAKU TWERP?!
......
Collapse
URGH URGH HELP ME
IT'S... SO UNFAIR...
I... NEVER EVEN SAID I WAS COMING --
PROB'LY DOESN'T MAKE ANY DIFFE-RENCE...
302
NARITA
WHO, AKANE?
NO, SHE'S STILL OUT.

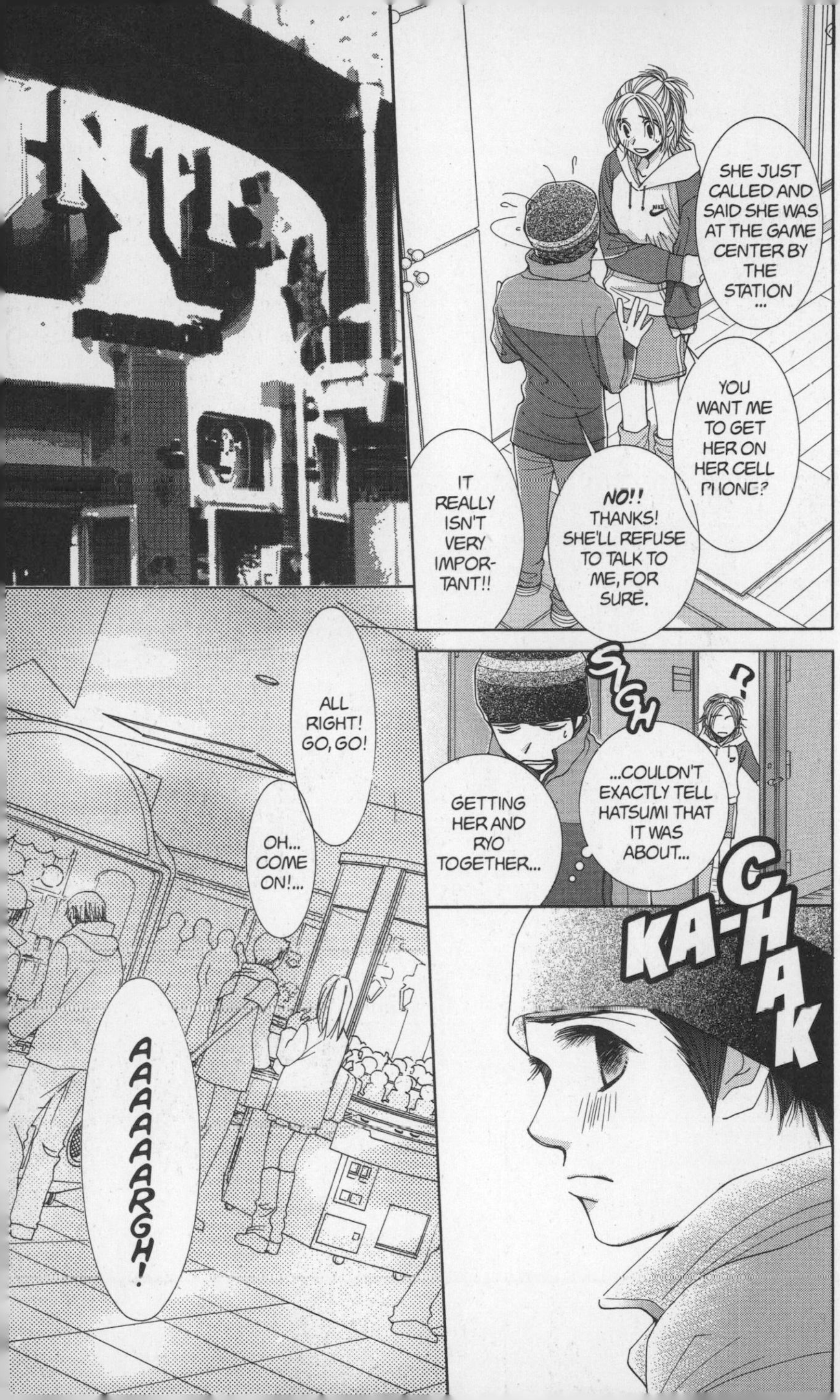
SHE JUST CALLED AND SAID SHE WAS AT THE GAME CENTER BY THE STATION ...
YOU WANT ME TO GET HER ON HER CELL PHONE?
NO!! THANKS! SHE'LL REFUSE TO TALK TO ME, FOR SURE.
IT REALLY ISN'T VERY IMPOR-TANT!!
SIGH
?
...COULDN'T EXACTLY TELL HATSUMI THAT IT WAS ABOUT...
GETTING HER AND RYO TOGETHER...
KA-CHAK
ALL RIGHT! GO, GO!
OH... COME ON!...
AAAAAAARGH!

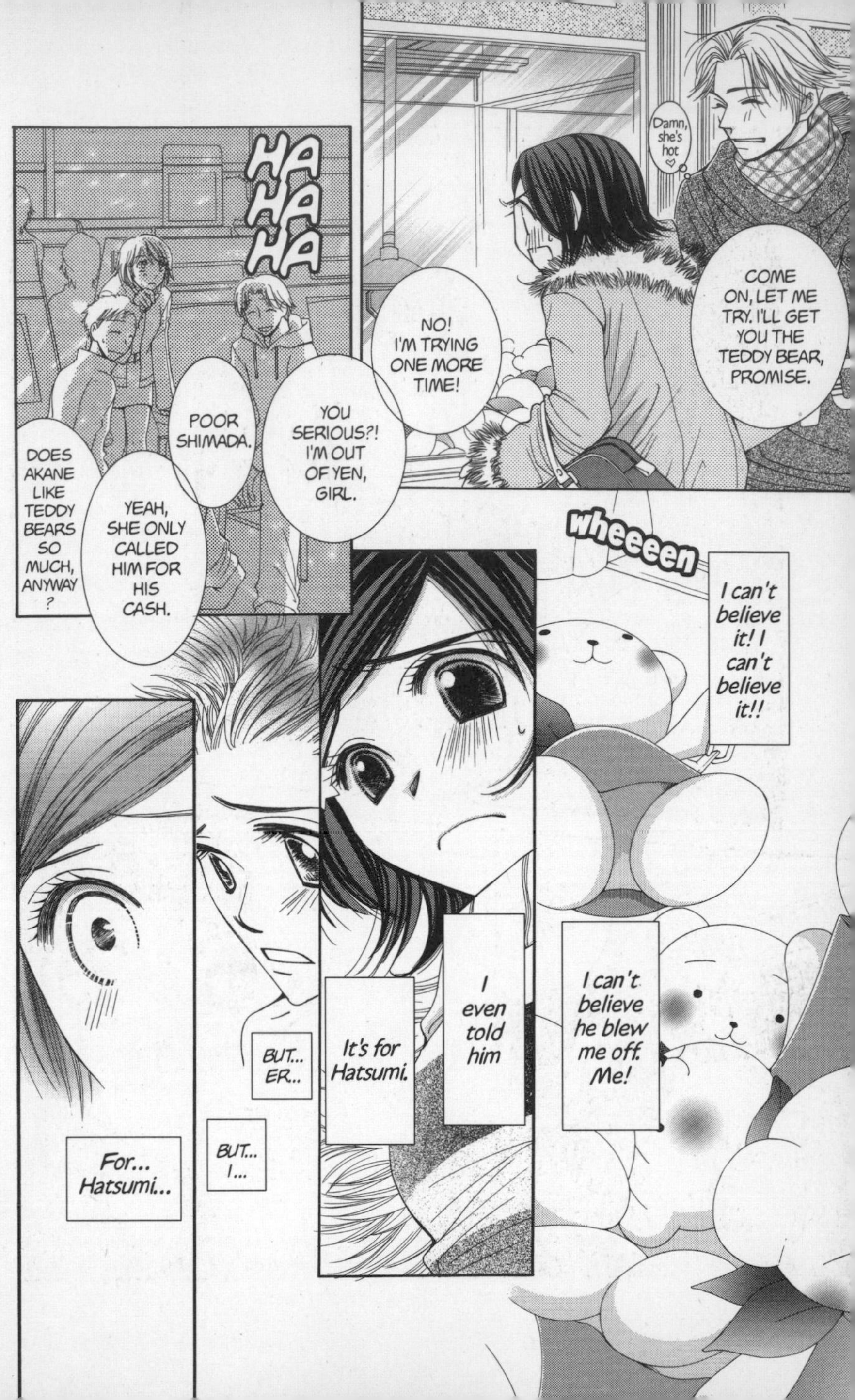
Damn, she's hot ♡
COME ON, LET ME TRY. I'LL GET YOU THE TEDDY BEAR, PROMISE.
NO! I'M TRYING ONE MORE TIME!
YOU SERIOUS?! I'M OUT OF YEN, GIRL.
HA HA HA
POOR SHIMADA.
DOES AKANE LIKE TEDDY BEARS SO MUCH, ANYWAY?
YEAH, SHE ONLY CALLED HIM FOR HIS CASH.
wheeeeen
I can't believe it! I can't believe it!!
I can't believe he blew me off. Me!
I even told him
It's for Hatsumi.
BUT... ER...
BUT... I...
For... Hatsumi...

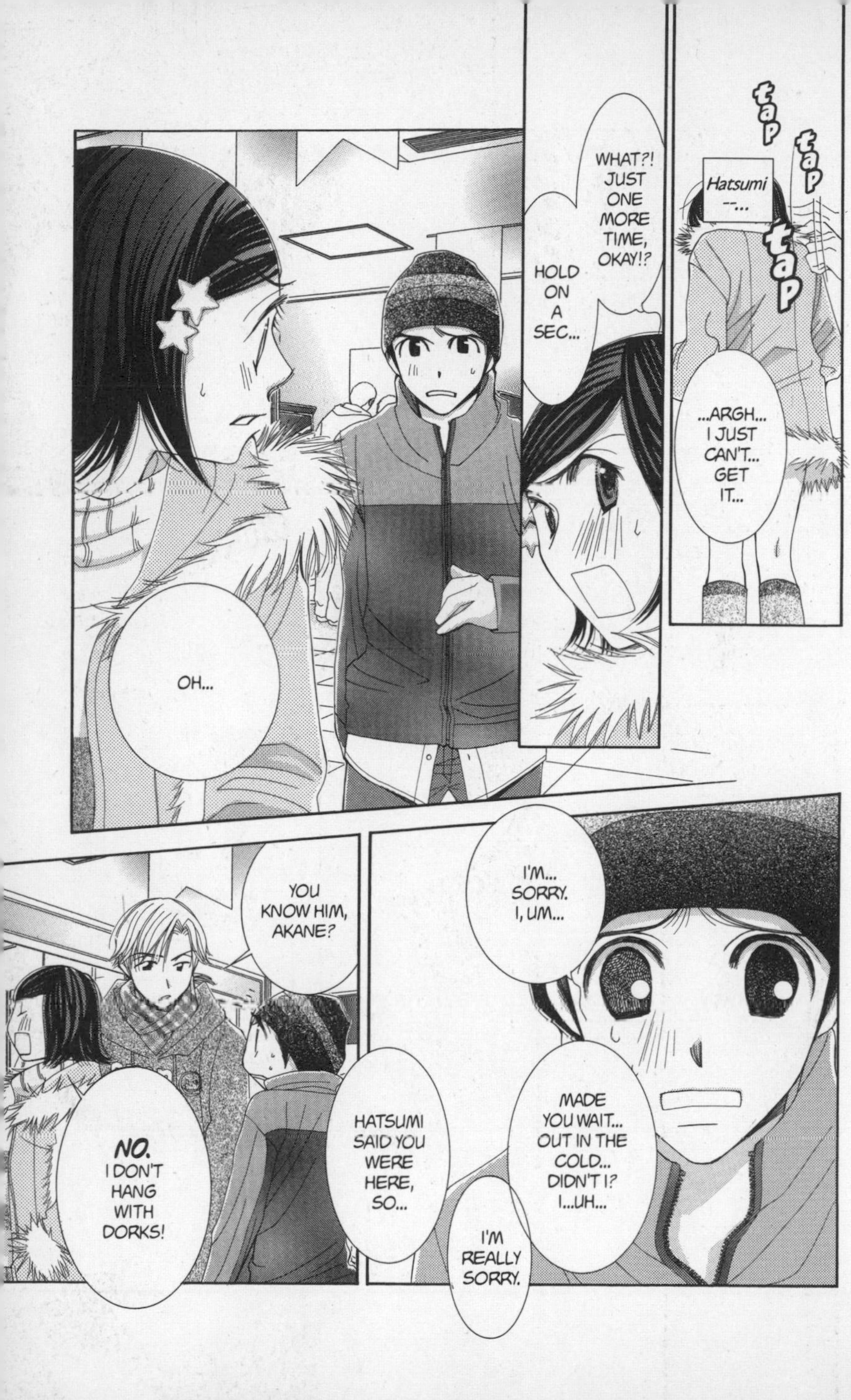
tap
tap
tap
Hatsumi --...
...ARGH... I JUST CAN'T... GET IT...
WHAT?! JUST ONE MORE TIME, OKAY!?
HOLD ON A SEC...
OH...
I'M... SORRY. I, UM...
MADE YOU WAIT... OUT IN THE COLD... DIDN'T I? I...UH...
I'M REALLY SORRY.
YOU KNOW HIM, AKANE?
HATSUMI SAID YOU WERE HERE, SO...
NO. I DON'T HANG WITH DORKS!

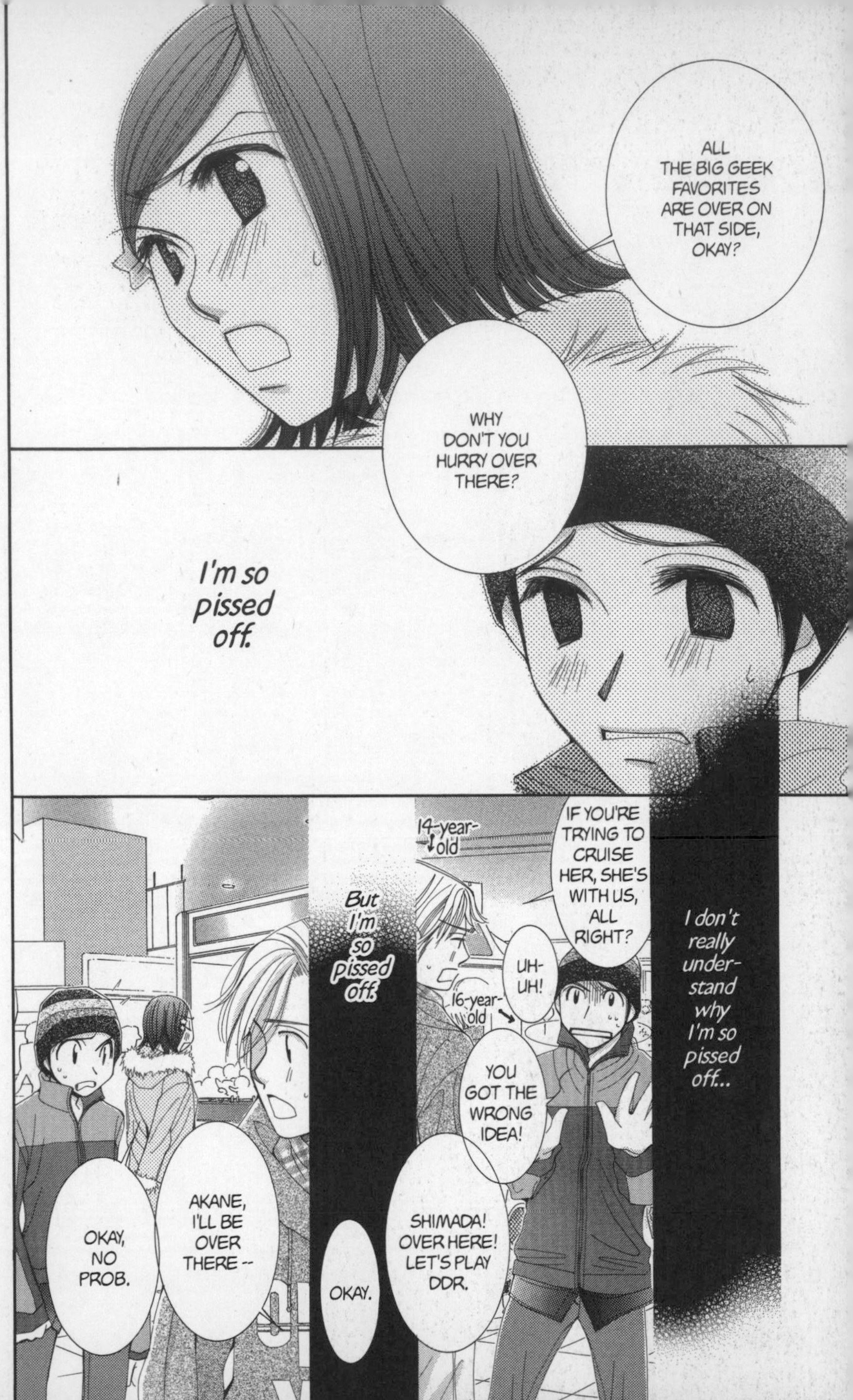
ALL THE BIG GEEK FAVORITES ARE OVER ON THAT SIDE, OKAY?
WHY DON'T YOU HURRY OVER THERE?
I'm so pissed off.
I don't really under-stand why I'm so pissed off...
IF YOU'RE TRYING TO CRUISE HER, SHE'S WITH US, ALL RIGHT?
14-year-old
UH-UH!
16-year-old
YOU GOT THE WRONG IDEA!
SHIMADA! OVER HERE! LET'S PLAY DDR.
OKAY.
But I'm so pissed off.
AKANE, I'LL BE OVER THERE --
OKAY, NO PROB.

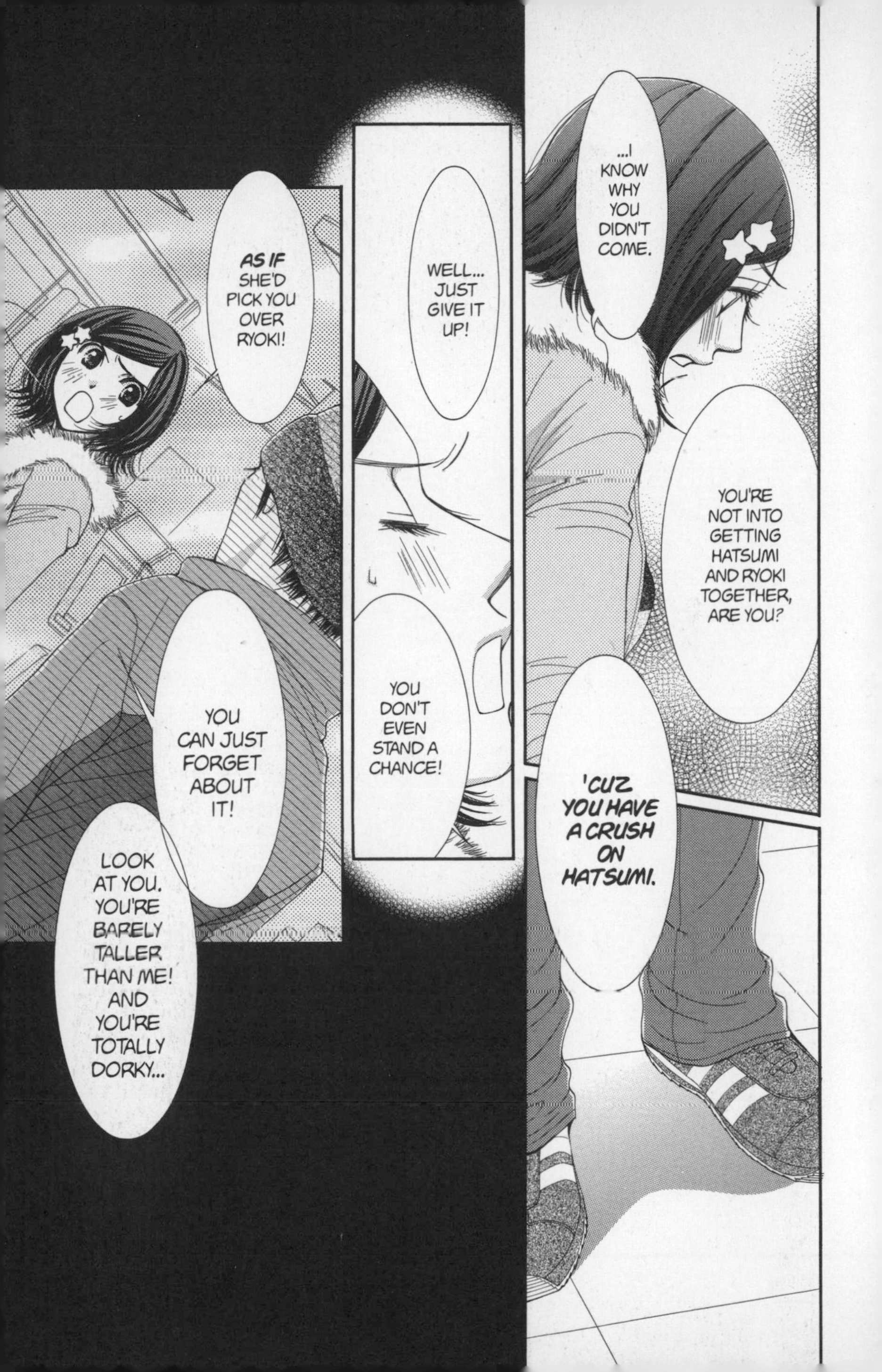
...I KNOW WHY YOU DIDN'T COME.
YOU'RE NOT INTO GETTING HATSUMI AND RYOKI TOGETHER, ARE YOU?
'CUZ YOU HAVE A CRUSH ON HATSUMI.
WELL... JUST GIVE IT UP!
YOU DON'T EVEN STAND A CHANCE!
AS IF SHE'D PICK YOU OVER RYOKI!
YOU CAN JUST FORGET ABOUT IT!
LOOK AT YOU. YOU'RE BARELY TALLER THAN ME! AND YOU'RE TOTALLY DORKY...

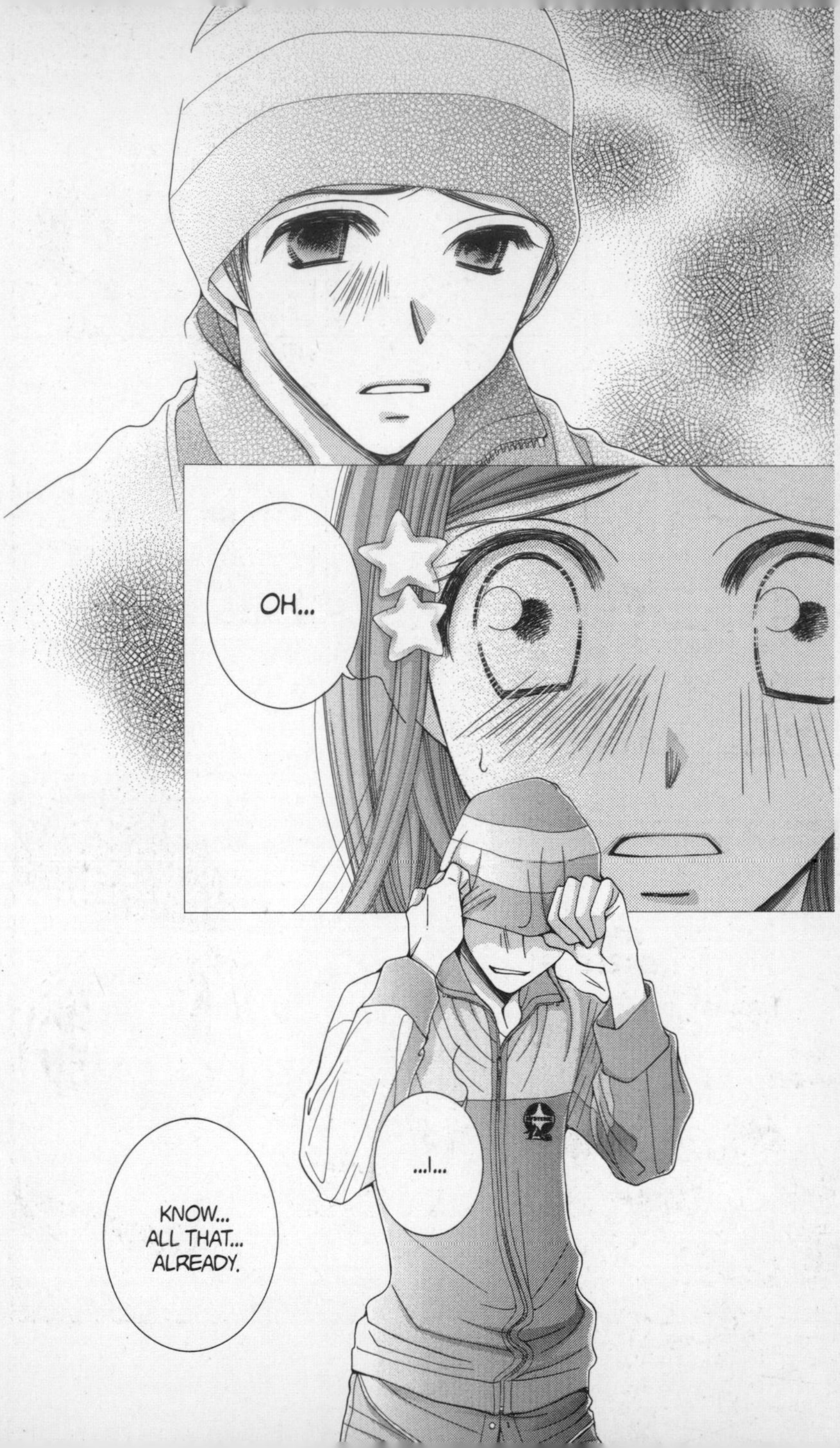
OH...
...I...
KNOW... ALL THAT... ALREADY.

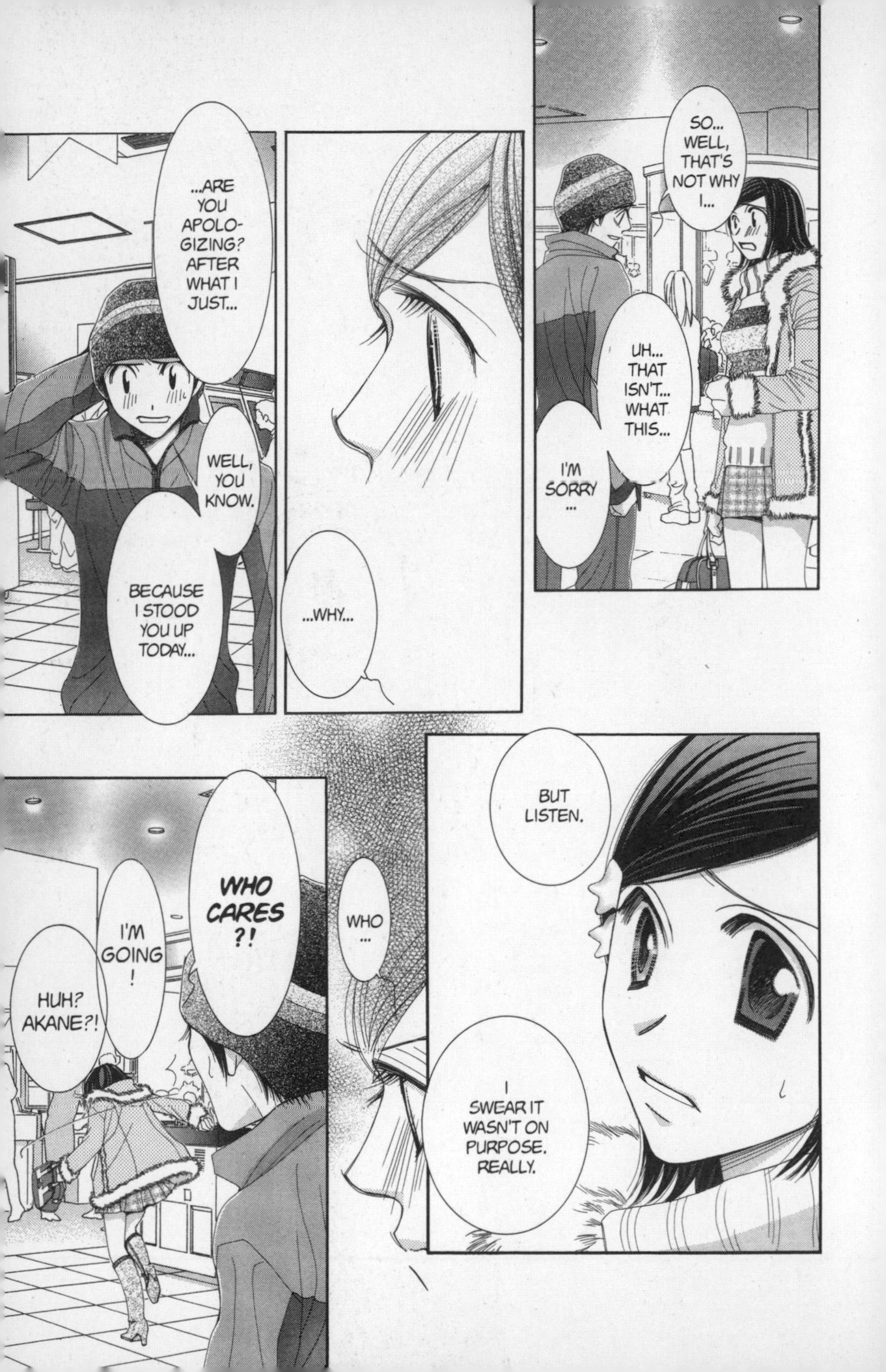
SO... WELL, THAT'S NOT WHY I...
UH... THAT ISN'T... WHAT THIS...
I'M SORRY ...
...WHY...
...ARE YOU APOLOGIZING? AFTER WHAT I JUST...
WELL, YOU KNOW.
BECAUSE I STOOD YOU UP TODAY...
BUT LISTEN.
I SWEAR IT WASN'T ON PURPOSE. REALLY.
WHO ...
WHO CARES?!
I'M GOING!
HUH? AKANE?!

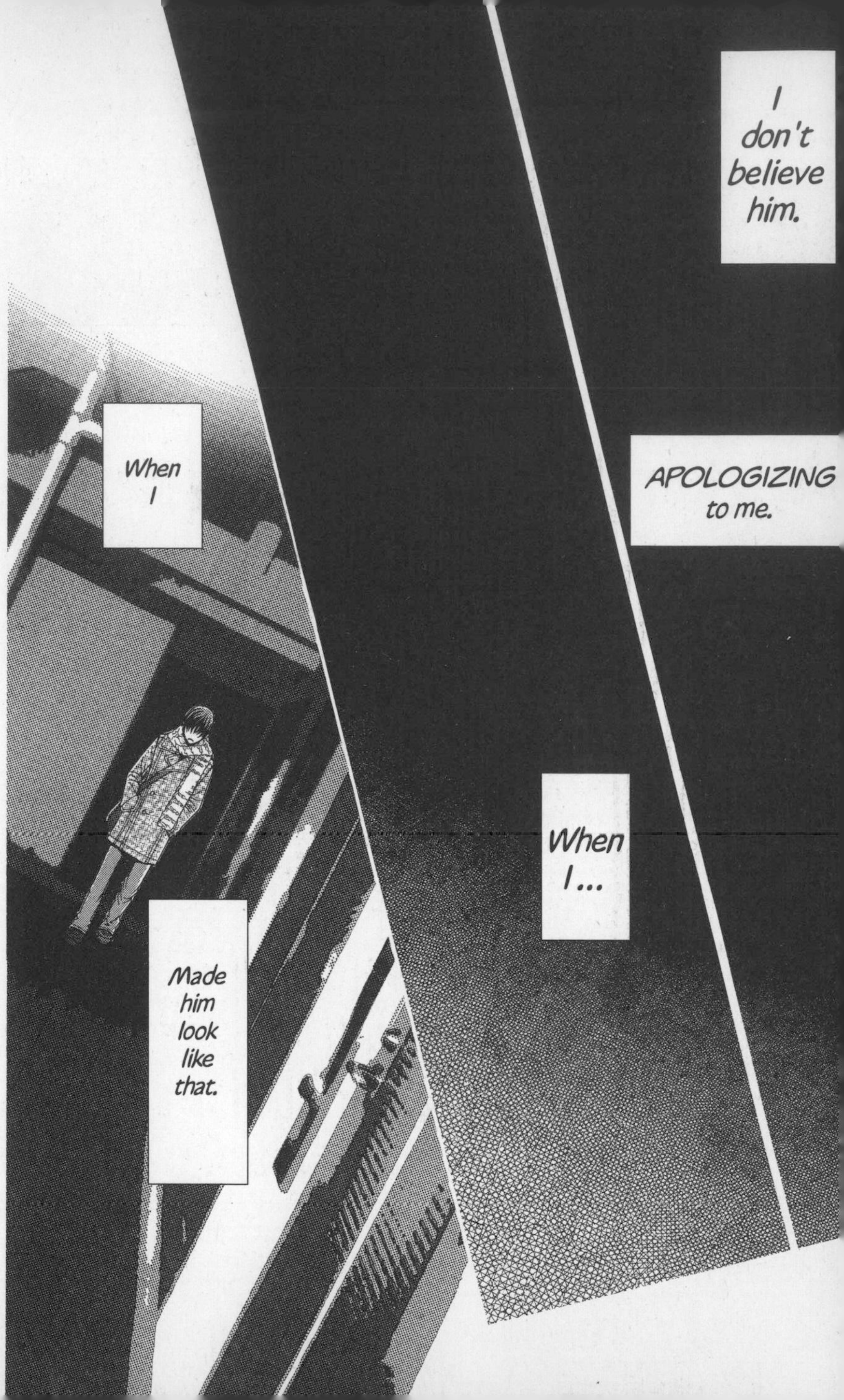
I don't believe him.
APOLOGIZING to me.
When I...
When I
Made him look like that.

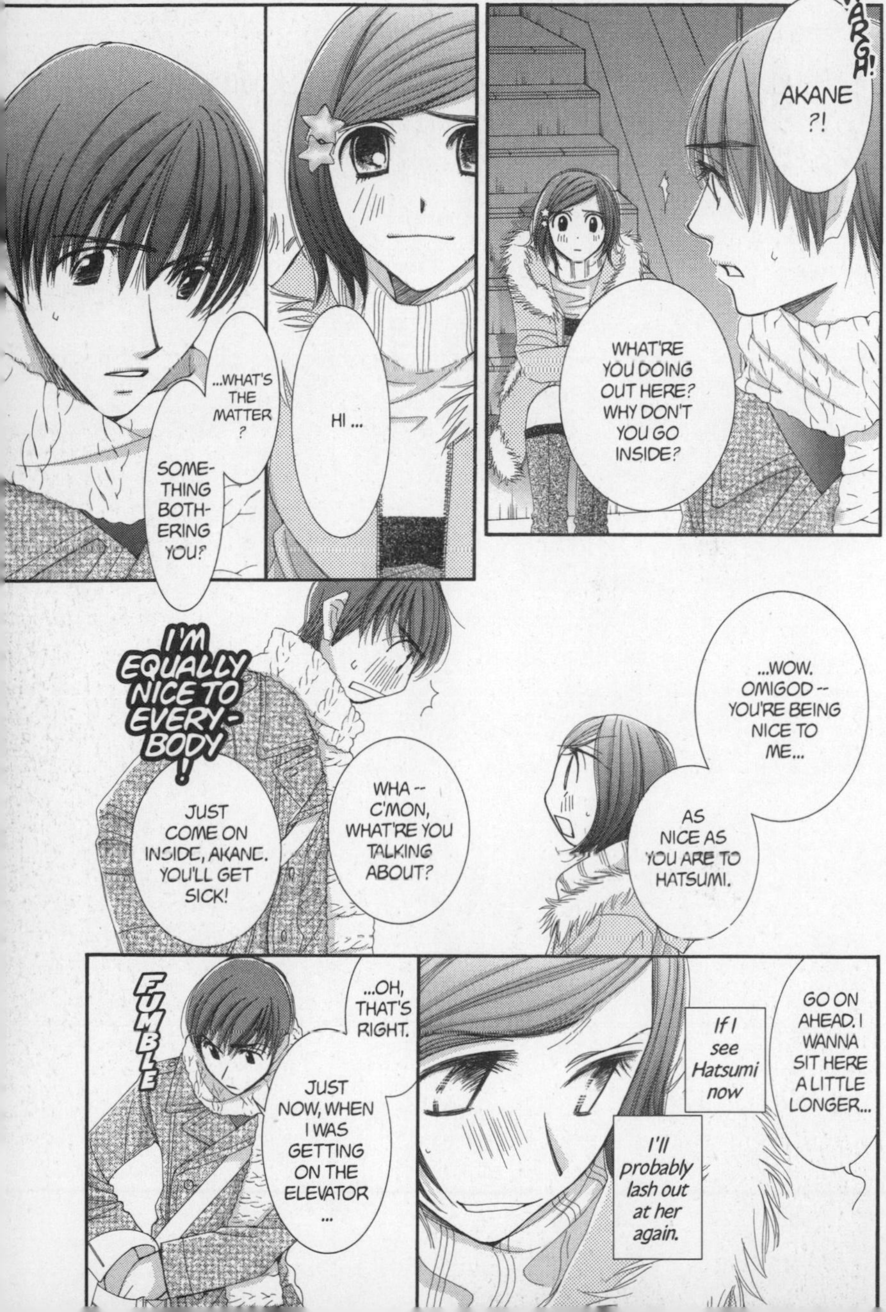
WARGH!
AKANE ?!
WHAT'RE YOU DOING OUT HERE? WHY DON'T YOU GO INSIDE?
HI ...
...WHAT'S THE MATTER ?
SOME-THING BOTH-ERING YOU?
...WOW. OMIGOD -- YOU'RE BEING NICE TO ME...
AS NICE AS YOU ARE TO HATSUMI.
WHA -- C'MON, WHAT'RE YOU TALKING ABOUT?
I'M EQUALLY NICE TO EVERY-BODY!
JUST COME ON INSIDE, AKANE. YOU'LL GET SICK!
GO ON AHEAD. I WANNA SIT HERE A LITTLE LONGER...
If I see Hatsumi now
I'll probably lash out at her again.
...OH, THAT'S RIGHT.
JUST NOW, WHEN I WAS GETTING ON THE ELEVATOR ...
FUMBLE

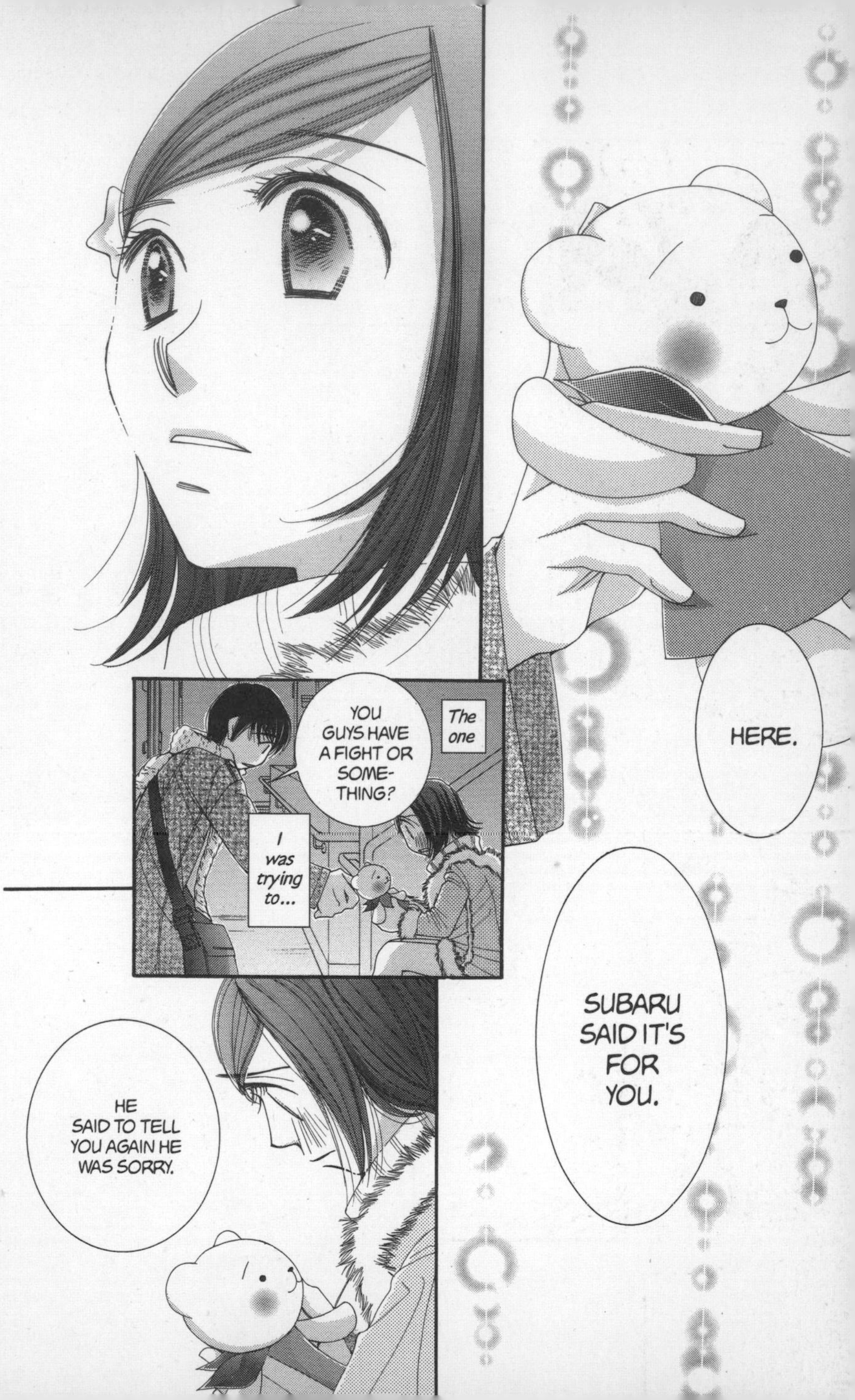
HERE.
SUBARU SAID IT'S FOR YOU.
The one
YOU GUYS HAVE A FIGHT OR SOME-THING?
I was trying to...
HE SAID TO TELL YOU AGAIN HE WAS SORRY.

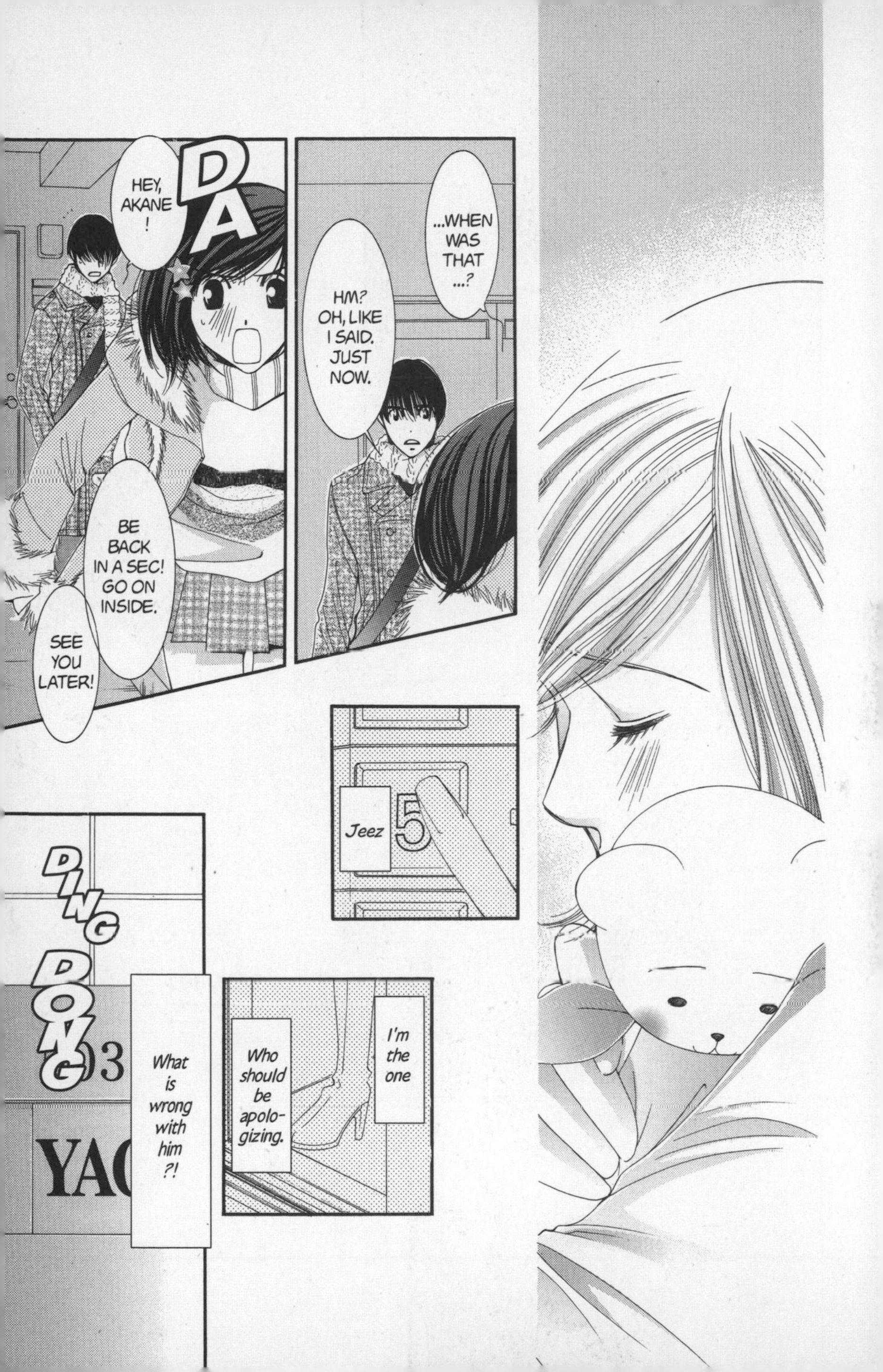
...WHEN WAS THAT ...?
HM? OH, LIKE I SAID. JUST NOW.
DA
HEY, AKANE !
BE BACK IN A SEC! GO ON INSIDE.
SEE YOU LATER!
Jeez
I'm the one
Who should be apolo-gizing.
DING DONG
What is wrong with him ?!

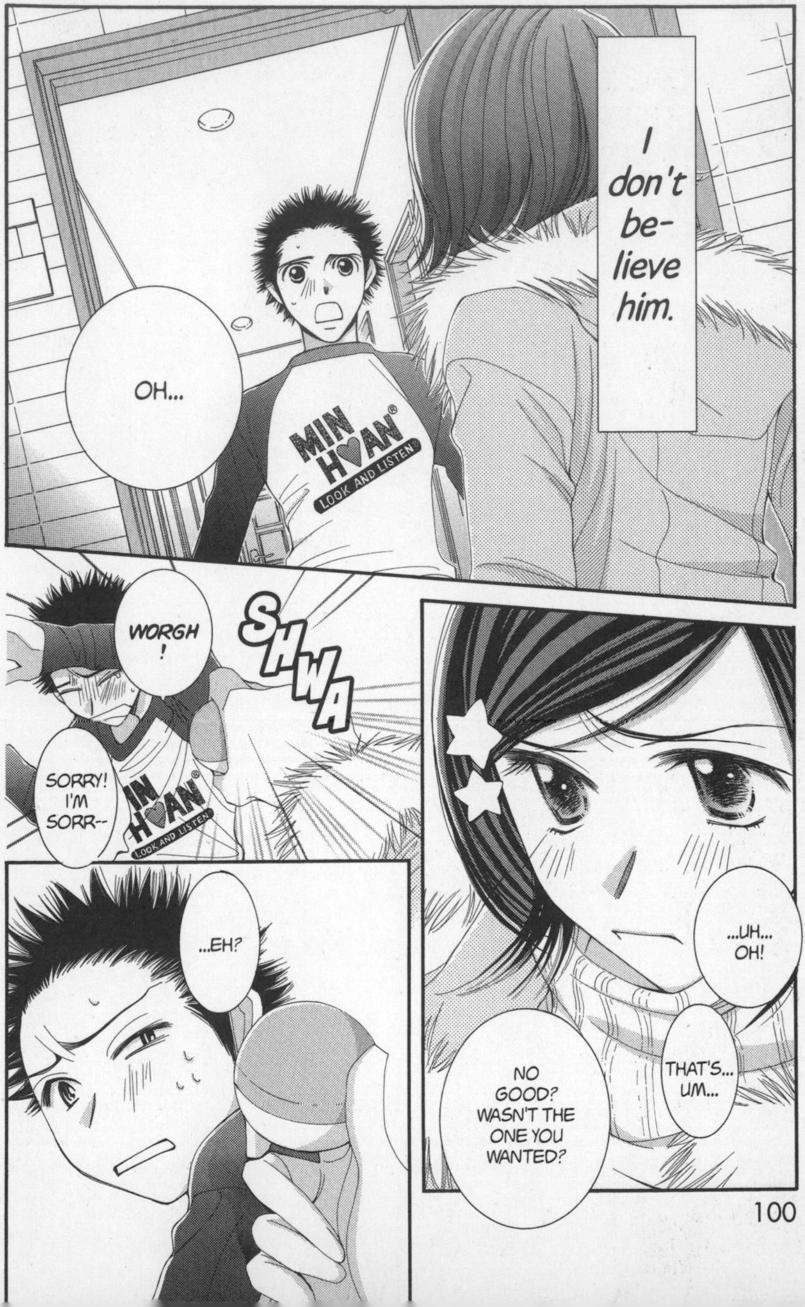
I don't be-lieve him.
OH...
...UH... OH!
THAT'S... UM...
NO GOOD? WASN'T THE ONE YOU WANTED?
SHWA
WORGH!
SORRY! I'M SORR--
MIN H♥AN LOOK AND LISTEN
...EH?

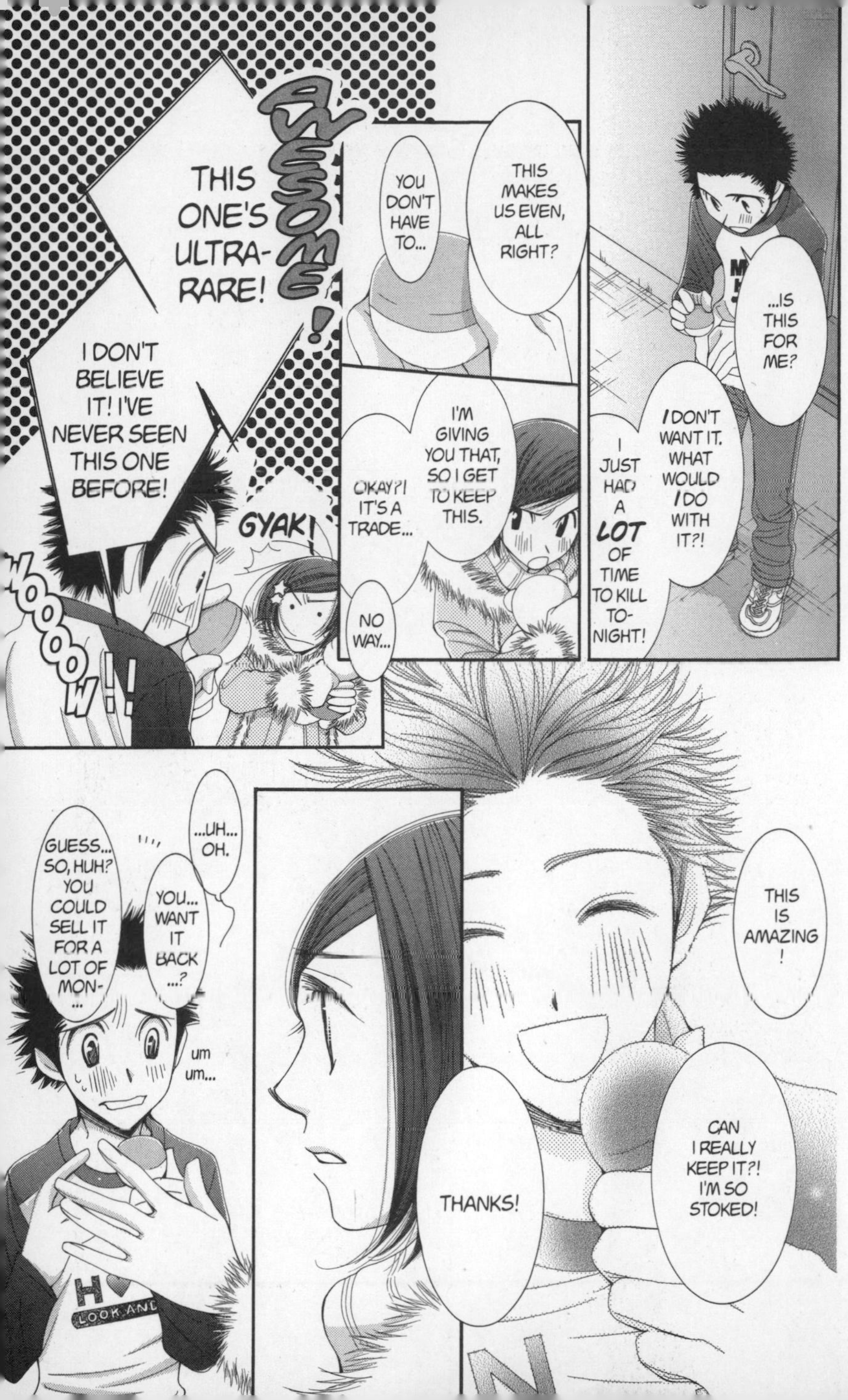
...IS THIS FOR ME?
I DON'T WANT IT. WHAT WOULD I DO WITH IT?!
I JUST HAD A LOT OF TIME TO KILL TO-NIGHT!
THIS MAKES US EVEN, ALL RIGHT?
YOU DON'T HAVE TO...
I'M GIVING YOU THAT, SO I GET TO KEEP THIS.
OKAY?! IT'S A TRADE...
NO WAY...
THIS ONE'S ULTRA-RARE!
AWESOME!
I DON'T BELIEVE IT! I'VE NEVER SEEN THIS ONE BEFORE!
GYAK!
WOOOOOW!!
THIS IS AMAZING!
CAN I REALLY KEEP IT?! I'M SO STOKED!
THANKS!
...UH... OH.
YOU... WANT IT BACK...?
GUESS... SO, HUH? YOU COULD SELL IT FOR A LOT OF MON-...
um um...

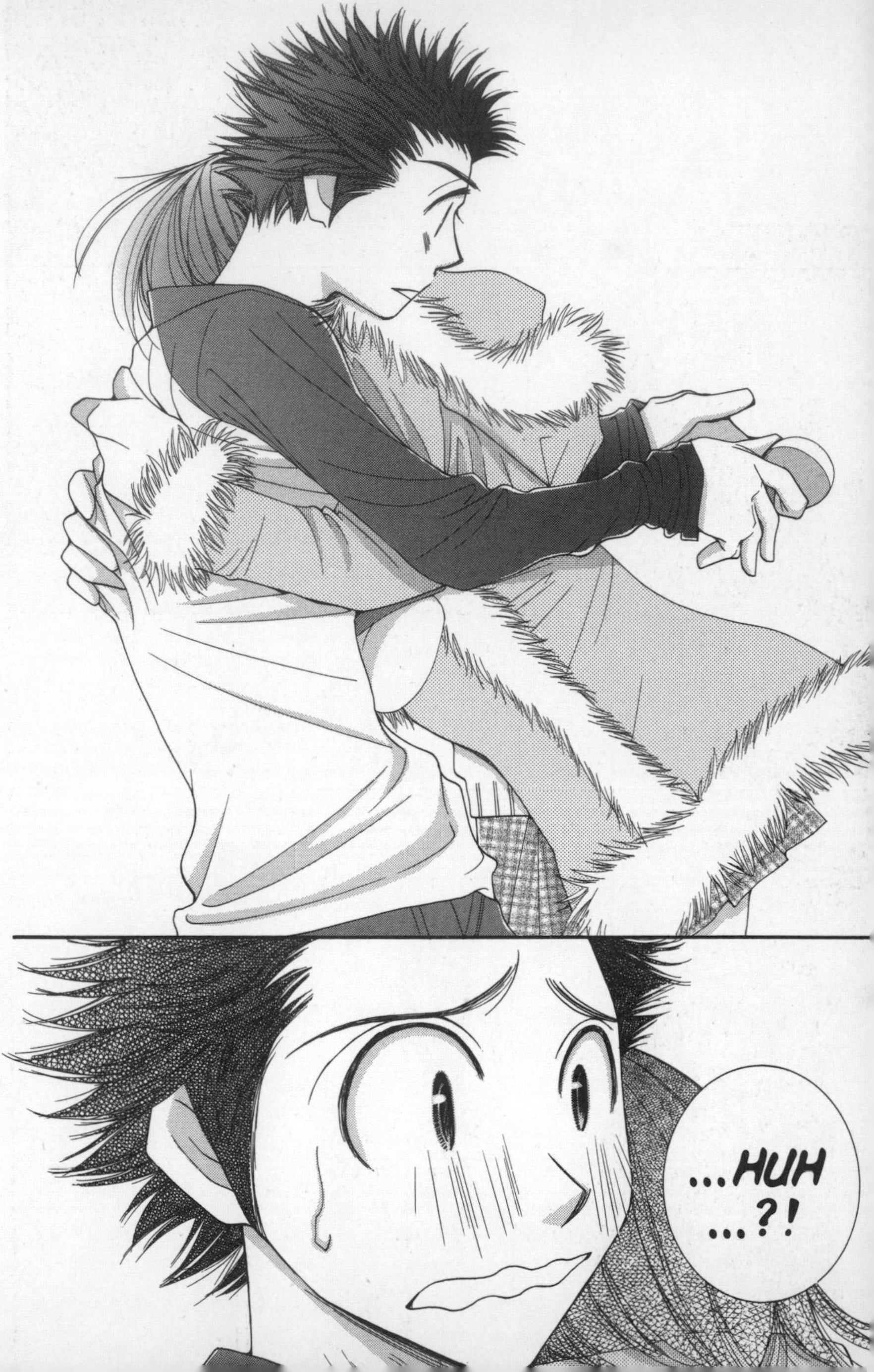
...HUH ...?!

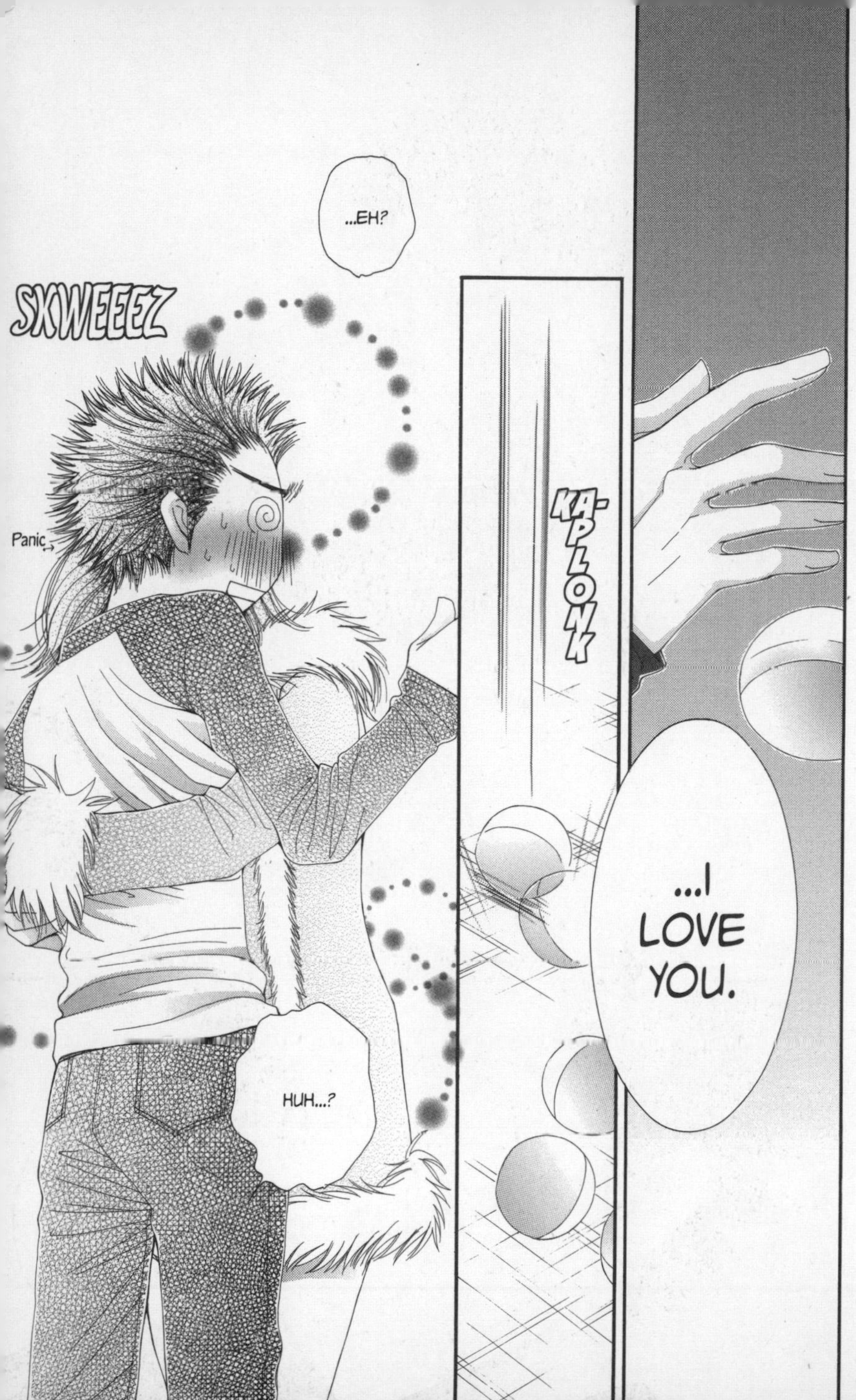
...I LOVE YOU.
KA-PLONK
...EH?
SKWEEEZ
Panic
HUH...?

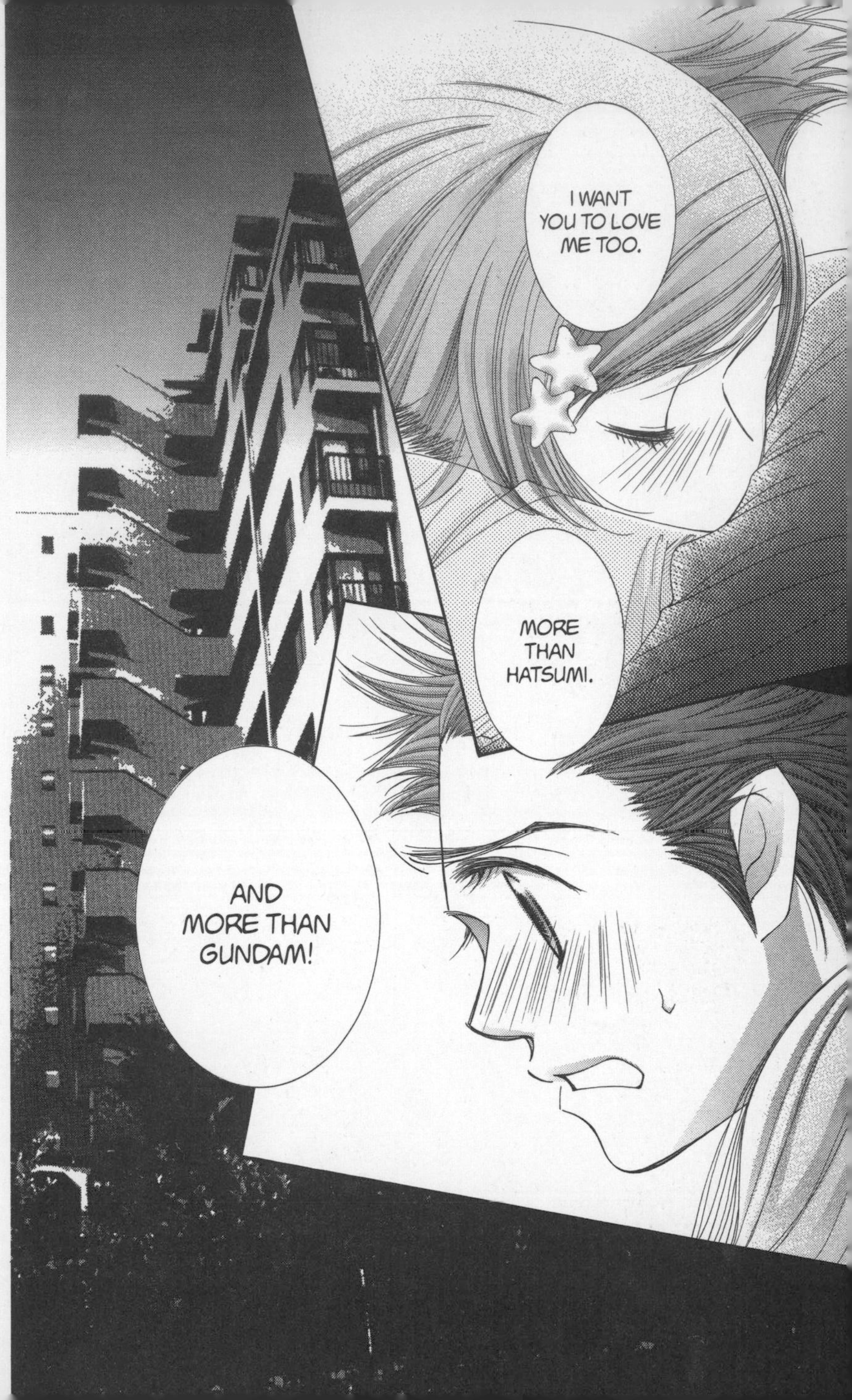
I WANT YOU TO LOVE ME TOO.
MORE THAN HATSUMI.
AND MORE THAN GUNDAM!

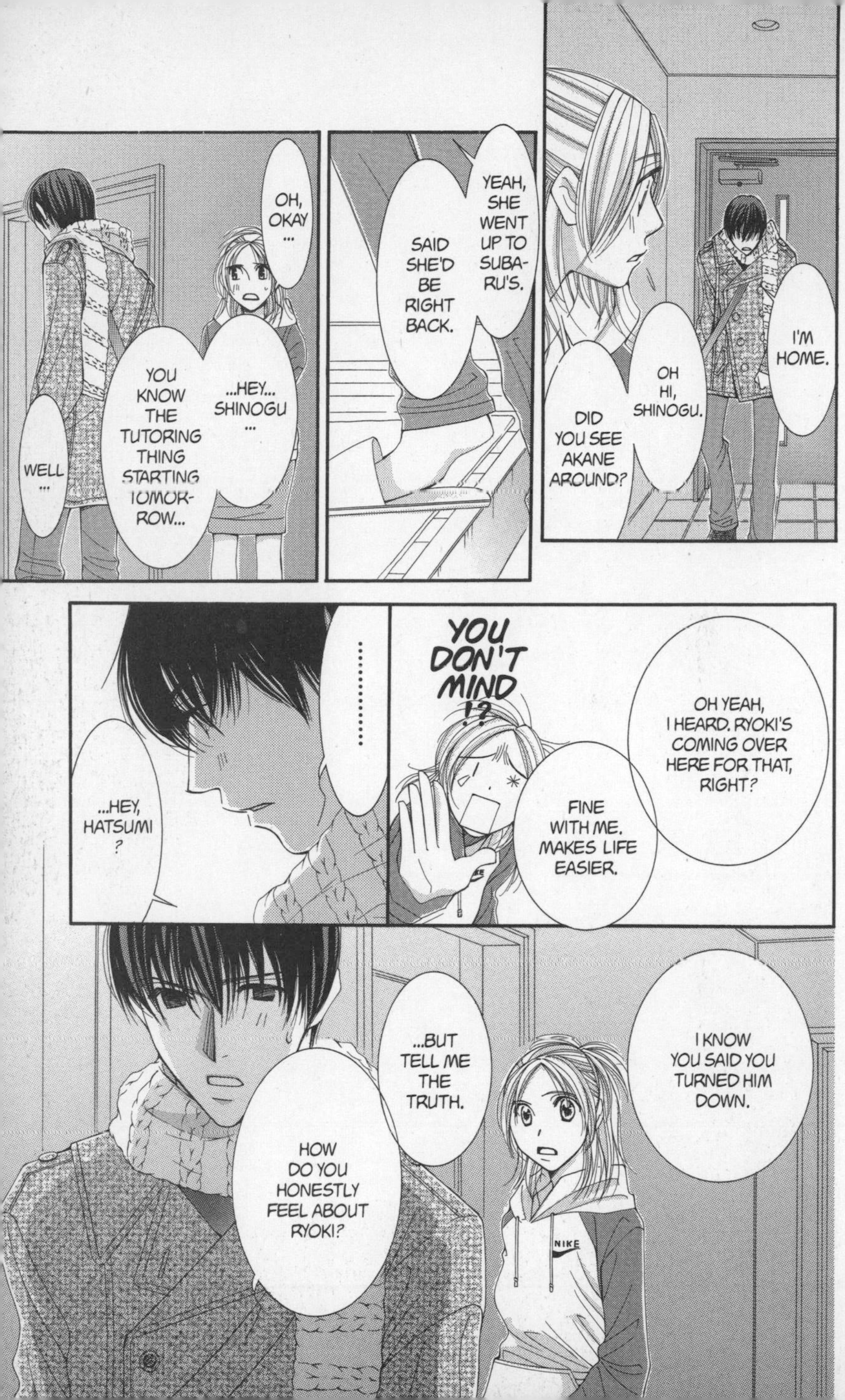
I'M HOME.
OH HI, SHINOGU.
DID YOU SEE AKANE AROUND?
YEAH, SHE WENT UP TO SUBARU'S.
SAID SHE'D BE RIGHT BACK.
OH, OKAY ...
...HEY... SHINOGU ...
YOU KNOW THE TUTORING THING STARTING TOMORROW...
WELL ...
OH YEAH, I HEARD. RYOKI'S COMING OVER HERE FOR THAT, RIGHT?
FINE WITH ME. MAKES LIFE EASIER.
YOU DON'T MIND !?
....
...HEY, HATSUMI ?
I KNOW YOU SAID YOU TURNED HIM DOWN.
...BUT TELL ME THE TRUTH.
HOW DO YOU HONESTLY FEEL ABOUT RYOKI?

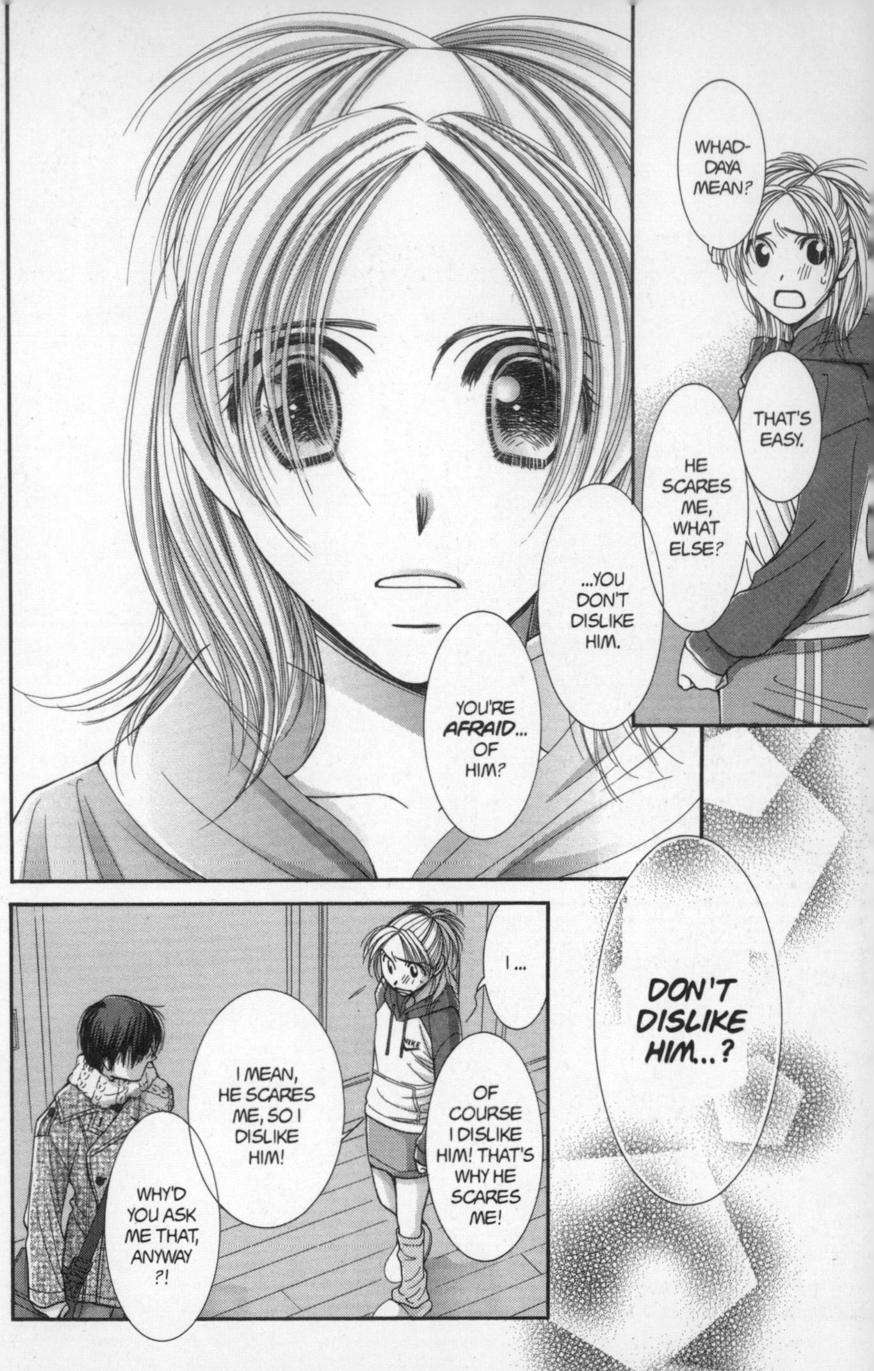
WHAD-DAYA MEAN?
THAT'S EASY.
HE SCARES ME, WHAT ELSE?
...YOU DON'T DISLIKE HIM.
YOU'RE AFRAID... OF HIM?
DON'T DISLIKE HIM...?
I...
OF COURSE I DISLIKE HIM! THAT'S WHY HE SCARES ME!
I MEAN, HE SCARES ME, SO I DISLIKE HIM!
WHY'D YOU ASK ME THAT, ANYWAY?!

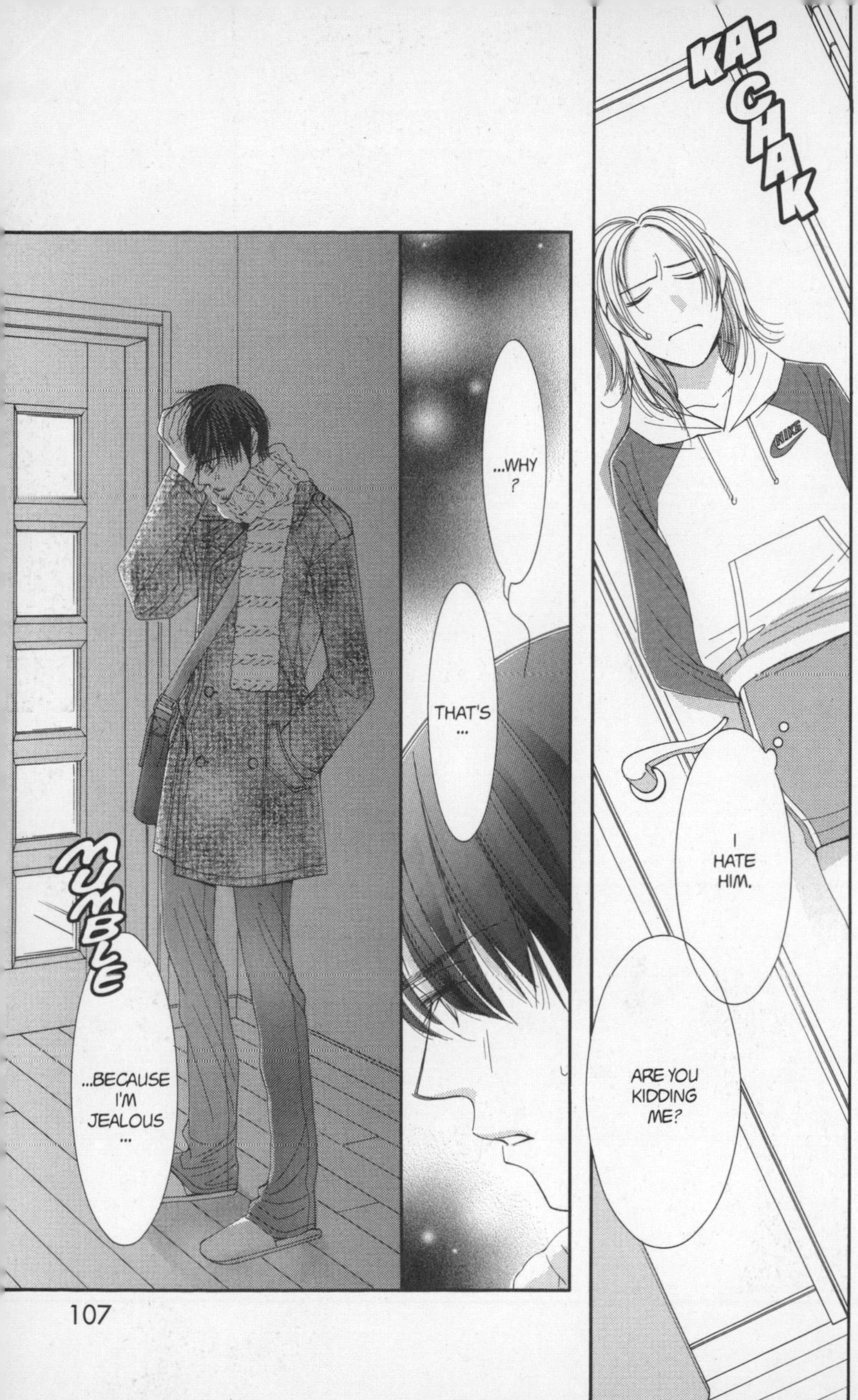
KA-CHAK
I HATE HIM.
ARE YOU KIDDING ME?
...WHY?
THAT'S...
MUMBLE
...BECAUSE I'M JEALOUS...

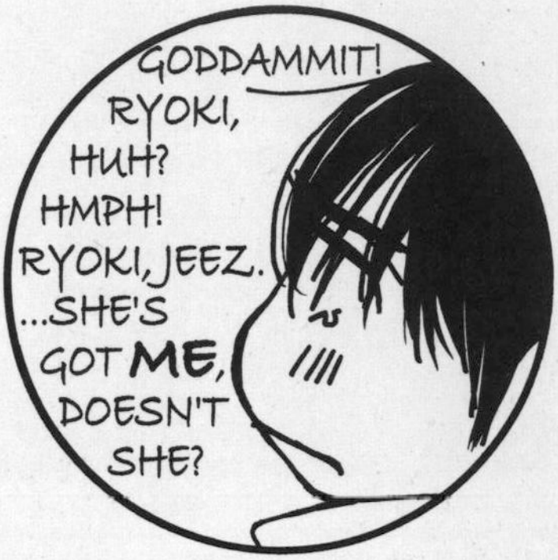
GODDAMMIT!
RYOKI,
HUH?
HMPH!
RYOKI, JEEZ.
...SHE'S
GOT **ME**,
DOESN'T
SHE?

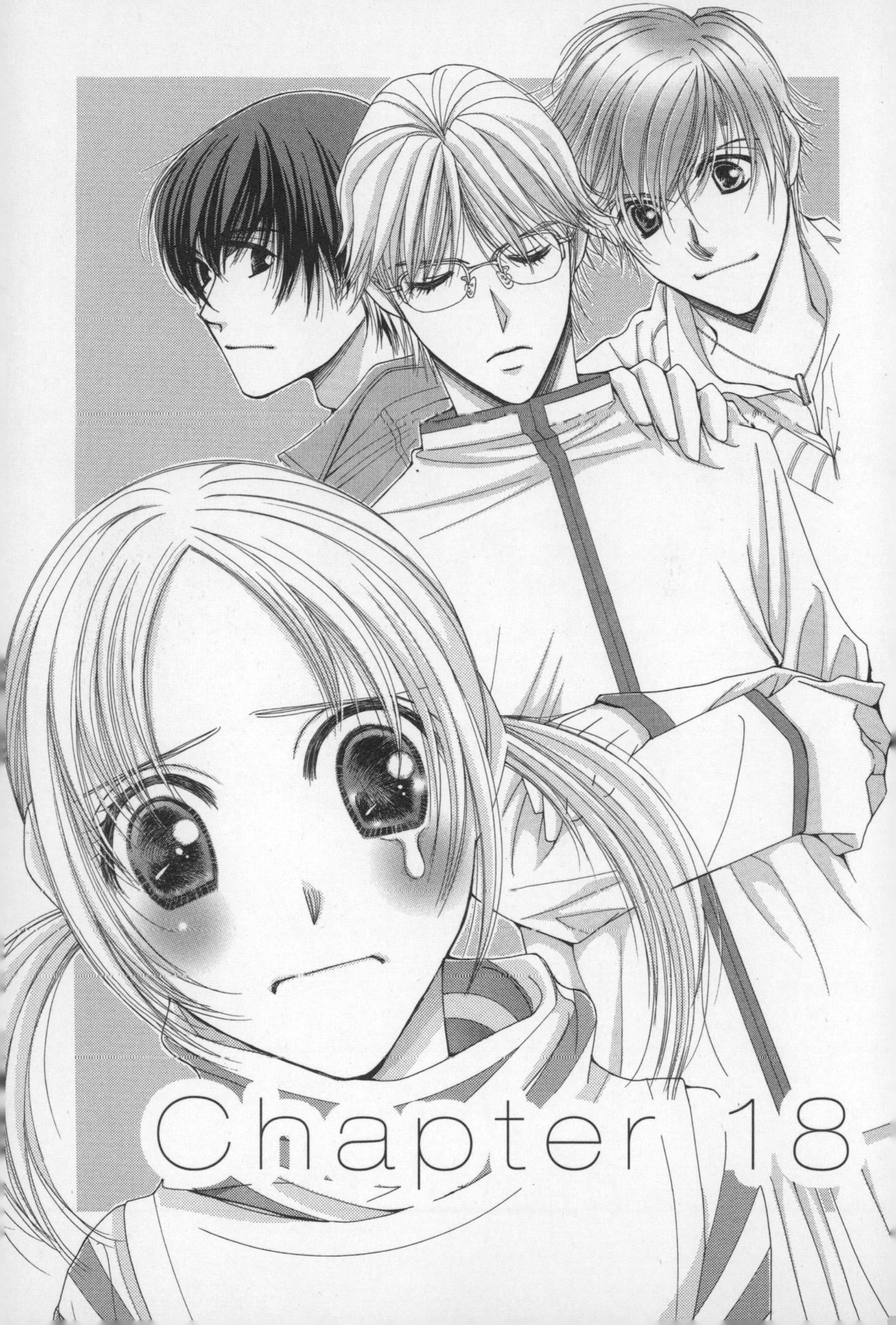
Chapter 18

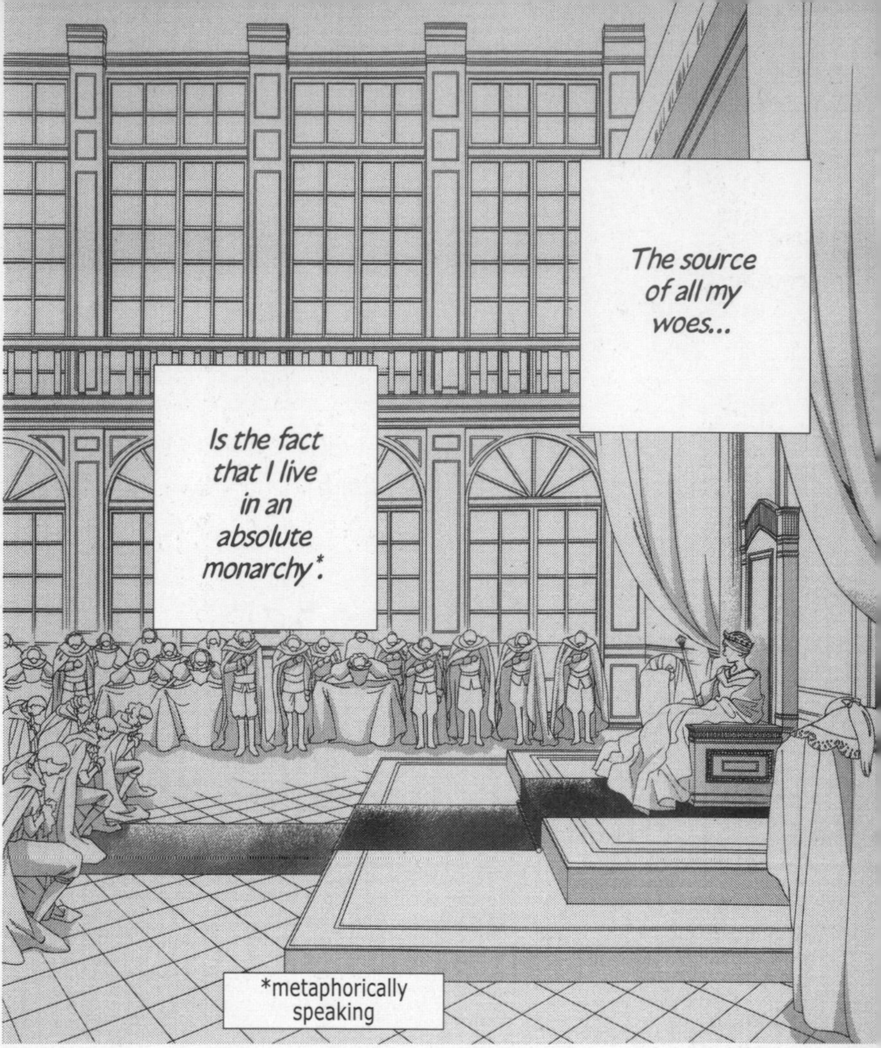
The source of all my woes...
Is the fact that I live in an absolute monarchy*.
*metaphorically speaking

hot gimmick

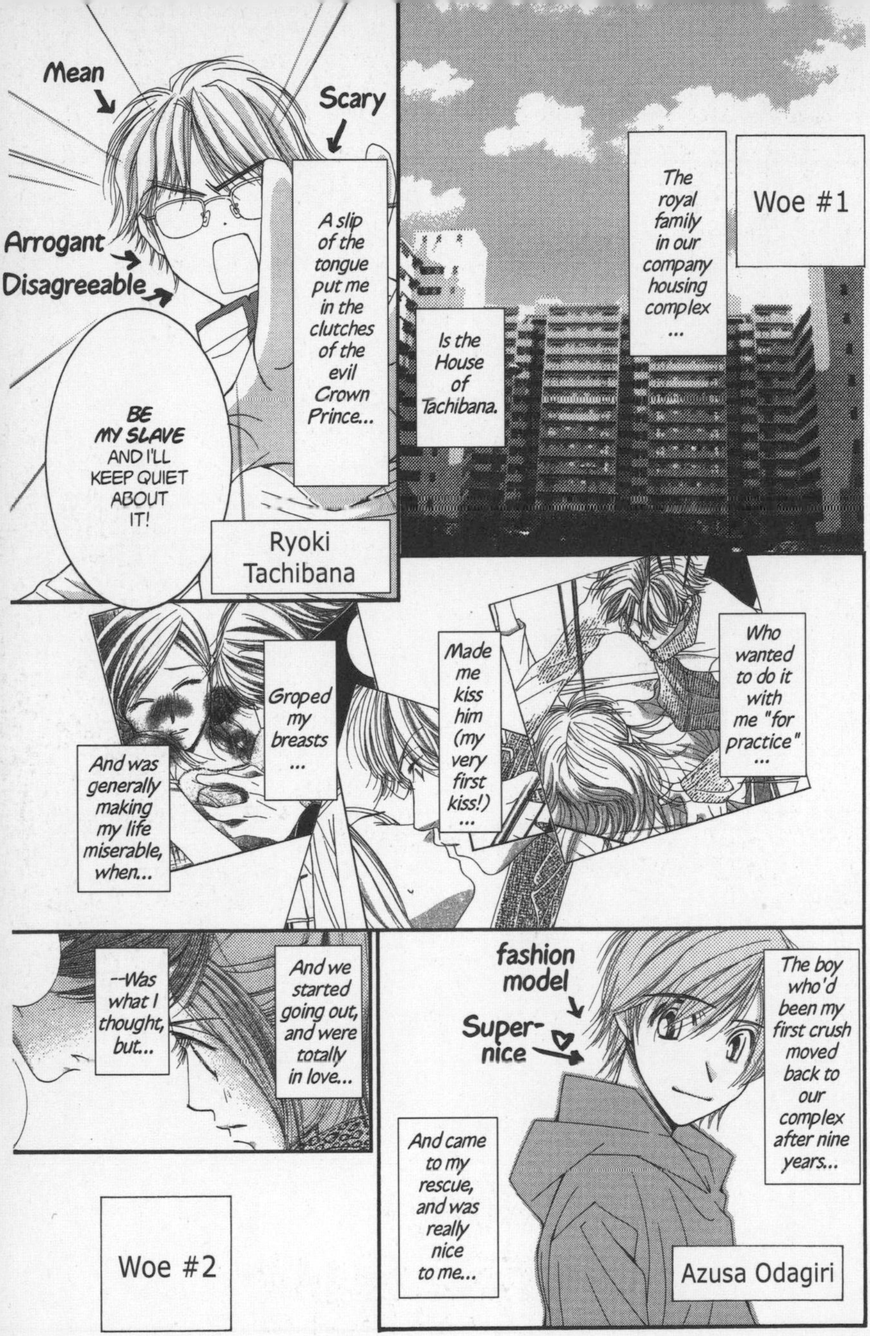
Woe #1
The royal family in our company housing complex ...
Is the House of Tachibana.
Scary
Mean
A slip of the tongue put me in the clutches of the evil Crown Prince...
Arrogant
Disagreeable
BE MY SLAVE AND I'LL KEEP QUIET ABOUT IT!
Ryoki Tachibana
Who wanted to do it with me "for practice" ...
Made me kiss him (my very first kiss!) ...
Groped my breasts ...
And was generally making my life miserable, when...
The boy who'd been my first crush moved back to our complex after nine years...
fashion model
Super-nice
And came to my rescue, and was really nice to me...
Azusa Odagiri
And we started going out, and were totally in love...
--Was what I thought, but...
Woe #2

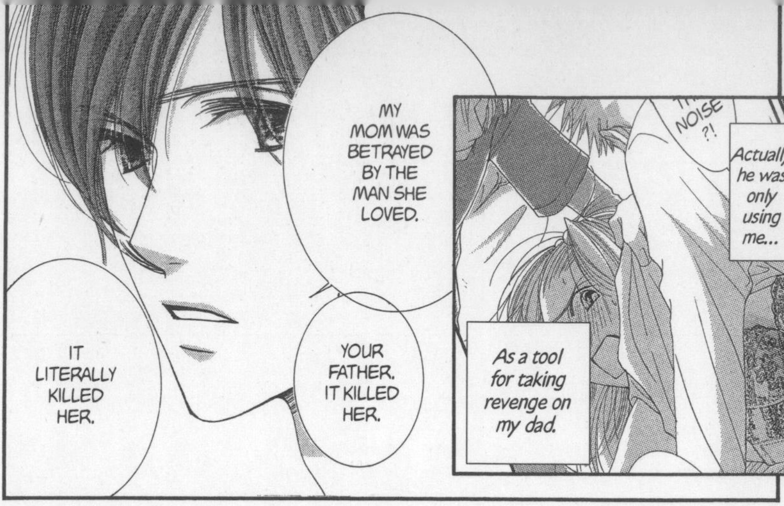
NOISE ?!
Actually he was only using me...
As a tool for taking revenge on my dad.
MY MOM WAS BETRAYED BY THE MAN SHE LOVED.
YOUR FATHER. IT KILLED HER.
IT LITERALLY KILLED HER.

While the truth about my dad is still a big mystery...

WOE #3

Just when I was really depressed about being duped by Azusa...

Ryoki Tachibana suddenly tells me...

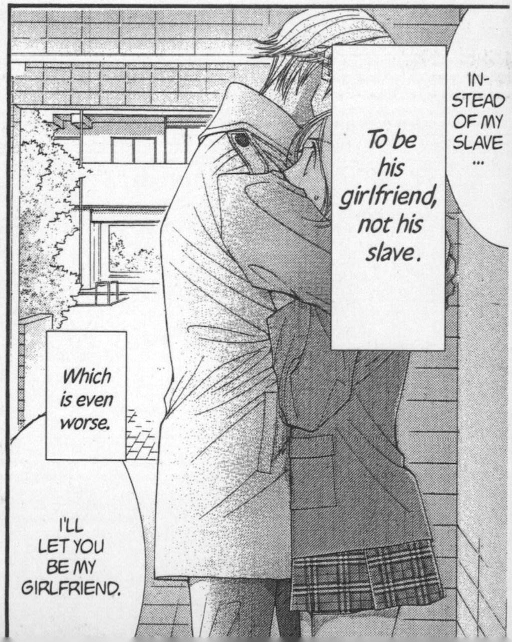
INSTEAD OF MY SLAVE...
To be his girlfriend, not his slave.
Which is even worse.
I'LL LET YOU BE MY GIRLFRIEND.

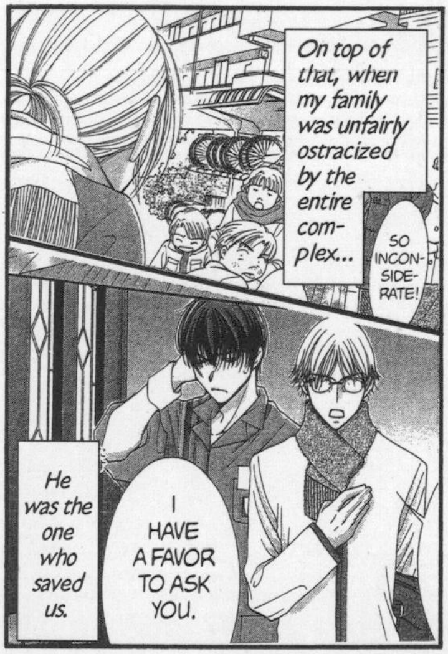
On top of that, when my family was unfairly ostracized by the entire complex...
SO INCONSIDERATE!
He was the one who saved us.
I HAVE A FAVOR TO ASK YOU.

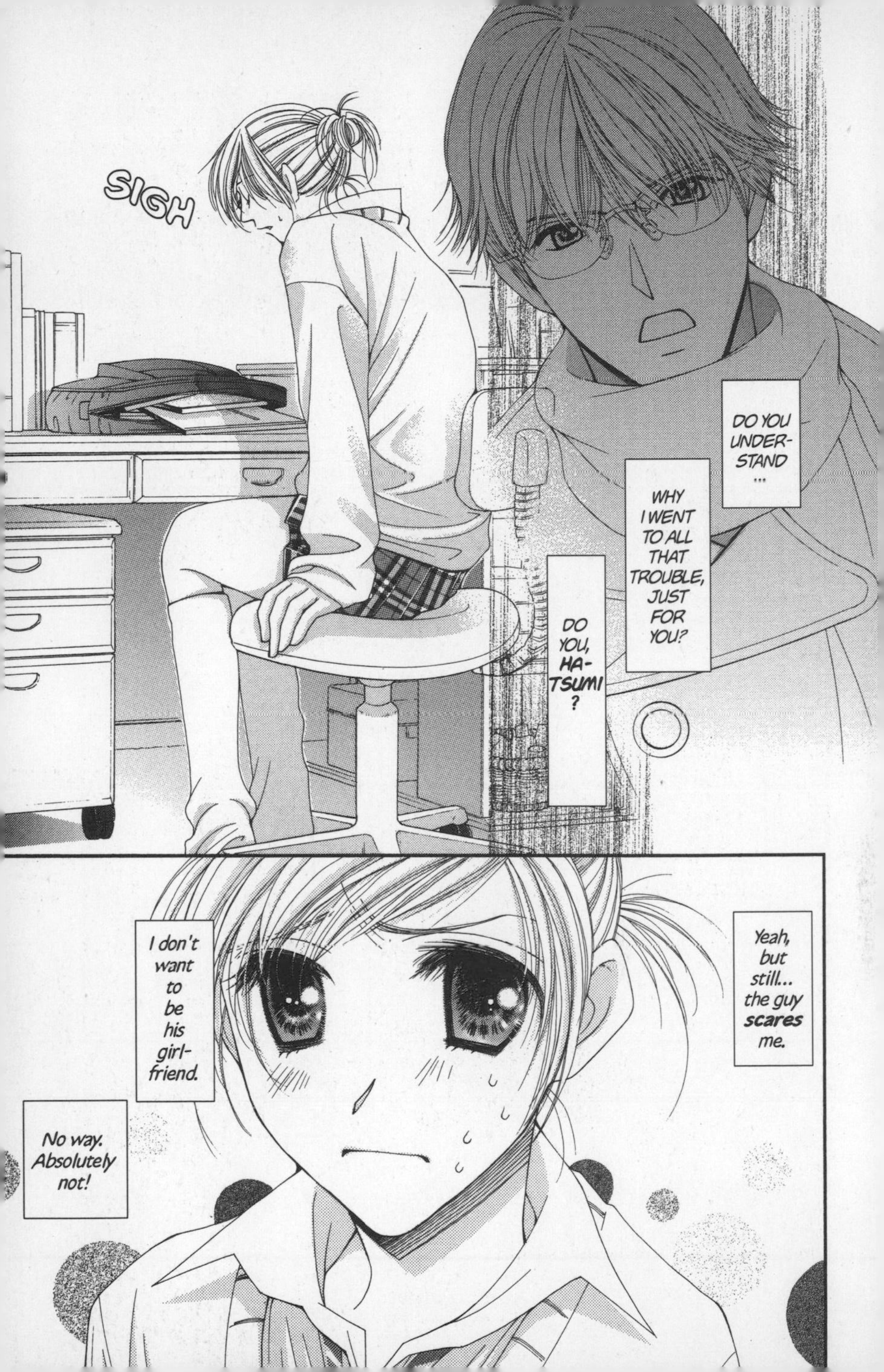
DO YOU UNDER-STAND ...
WHY I WENT TO ALL THAT TROUBLE, JUST FOR YOU?
DO YOU, HA-TSUMI?
SIGH
Yeah, but still... the guy scares me.
I don't want to be his girl-friend.
No way. Absolutely not!

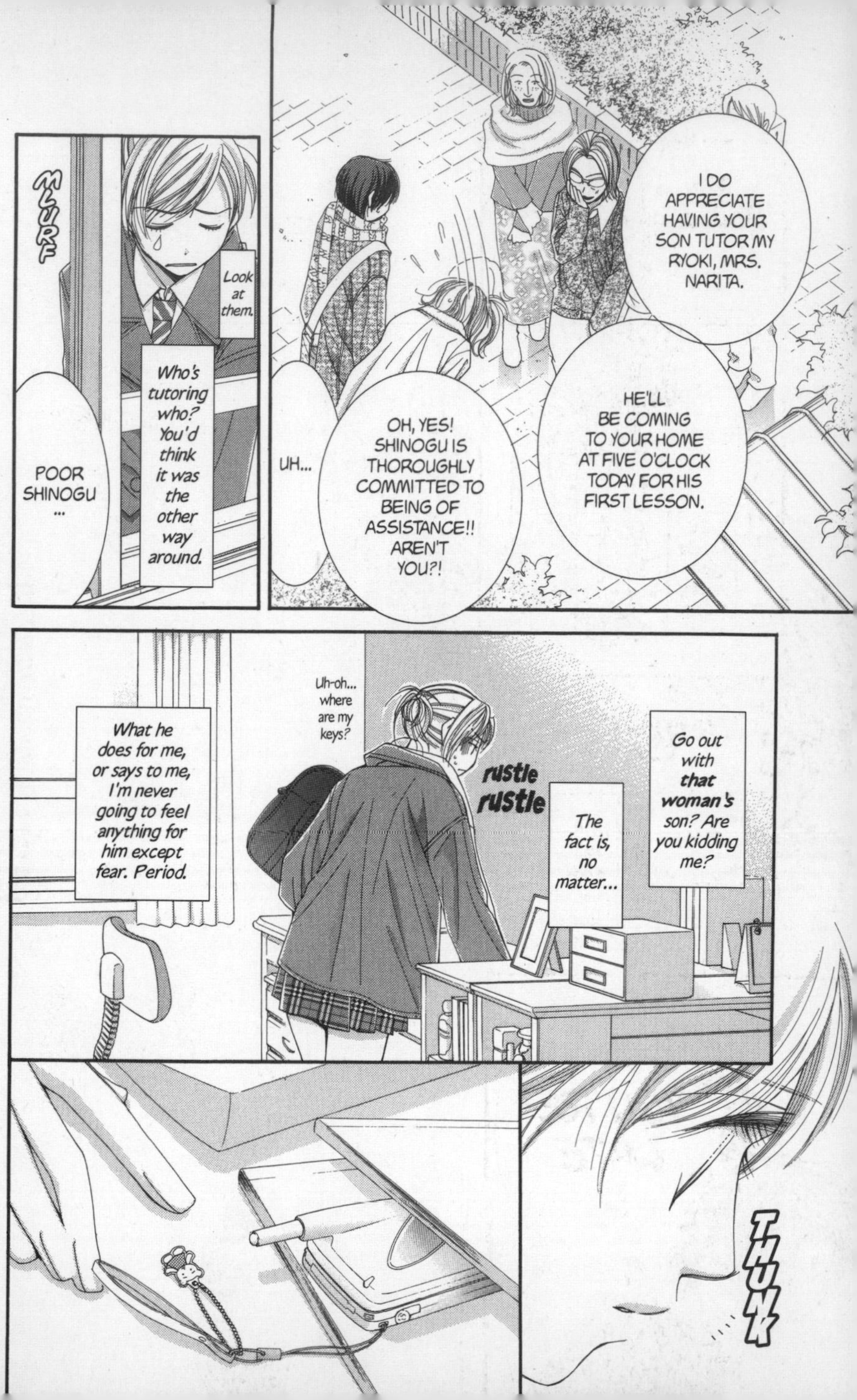
I DO APPRECIATE HAVING YOUR SON TUTOR MY RYOKI, MRS. NARITA.
HE'LL BE COMING TO YOUR HOME AT FIVE O'CLOCK TODAY FOR HIS FIRST LESSON.
OH, YES! SHINOGU IS THOROUGHLY COMMITTED TO BEING OF ASSISTANCE!! AREN'T YOU?!
UH...
MLURF
Look at them.
Who's tutoring who? You'd think it was the other way around.
POOR SHINOGU ...
Go out with **that woman's** son? Are you kidding me?
The fact is, no matter...
rustle rustle
Uh-oh... where are my keys?
What he does for me, or says to me, I'm never going to feel anything for him except fear. Period.
THUNK

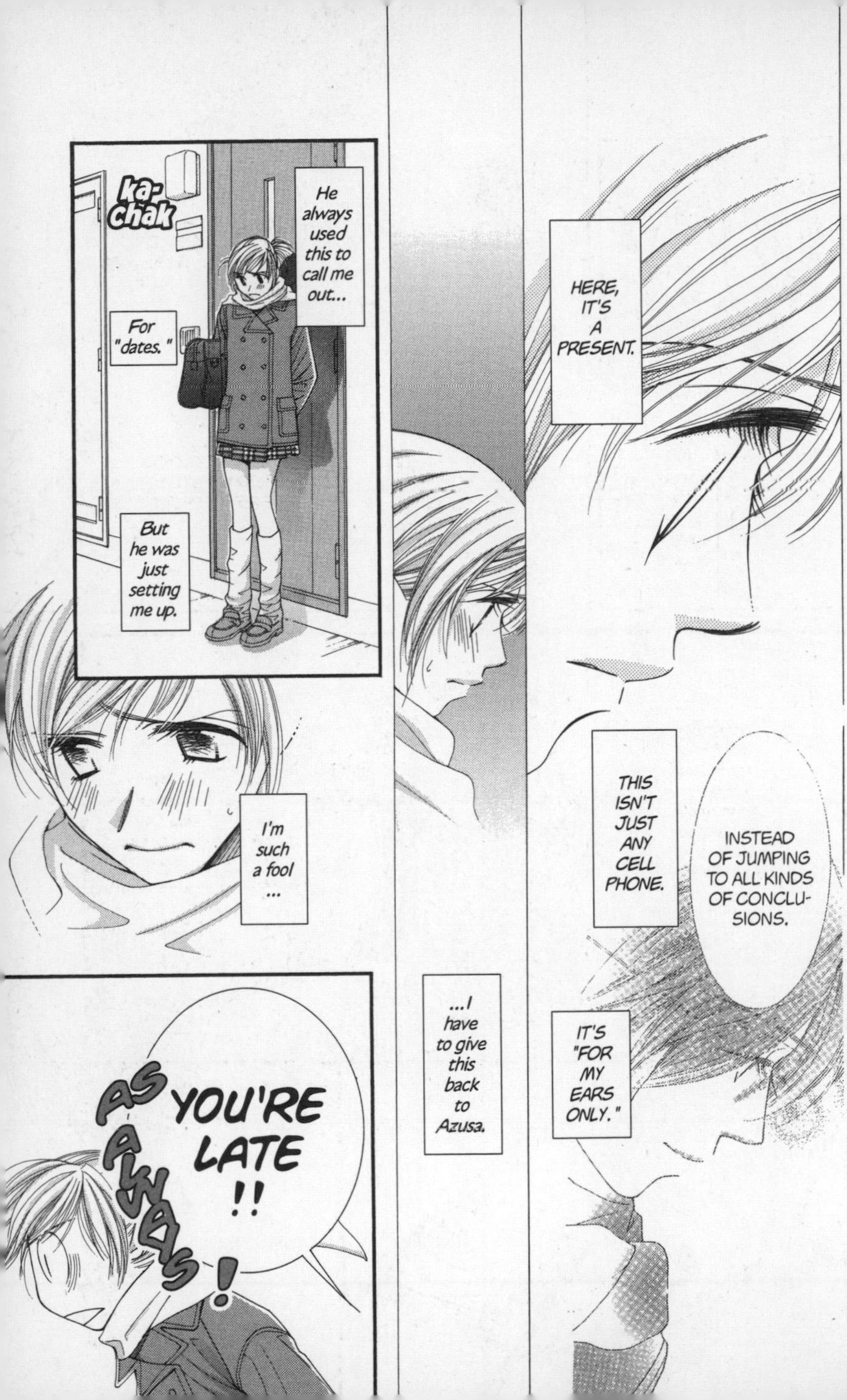
HERE, IT'S A PRESENT.
INSTEAD OF JUMPING TO ALL KINDS OF CONCLU-SIONS.
THIS ISN'T JUST ANY CELL PHONE.
IT'S "FOR MY EARS ONLY."
...I have to give this back to Azusa.
He always used this to call me out...
ka-chak
For "dates."
But he was just setting me up.
I'm such a fool ...
YOU'RE LATE !!
AS ALWAYS!

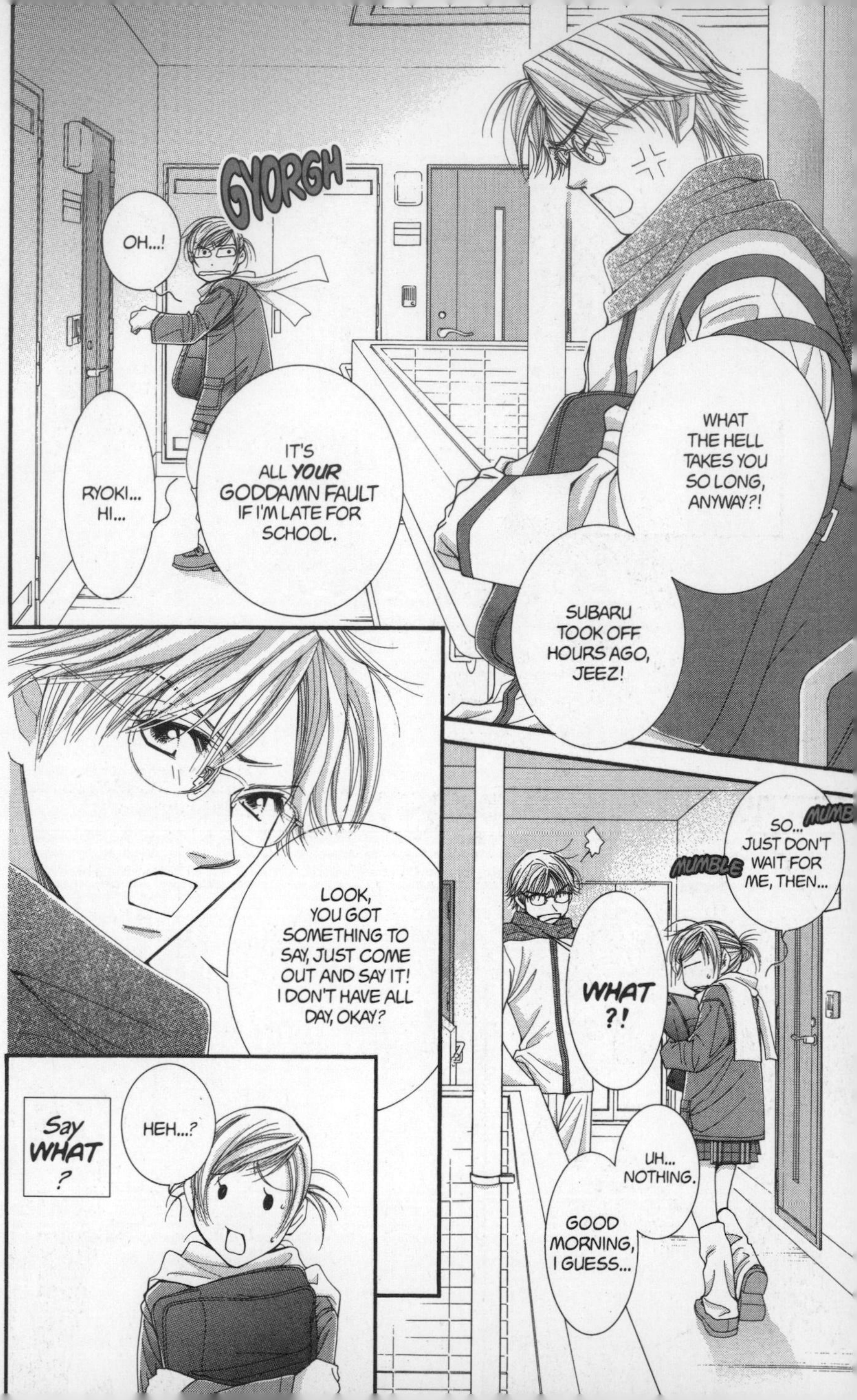
WHAT THE HELL TAKES YOU SO LONG, ANYWAY?!
SUBARU TOOK OFF HOURS AGO, JEEZ!
GYORGH
OH...!
IT'S ALL YOUR GODDAMN FAULT IF I'M LATE FOR SCHOOL.
RYOKI... HI...
MUMB
SO... JUST DON'T WAIT FOR ME, THEN...
MUMBLE
WHAT?!
UH... NOTHING.
GOOD MORNING, I GUESS...
LOOK, YOU GOT SOMETHING TO SAY, JUST COME OUT AND SAY IT! I DON'T HAVE ALL DAY, OKAY?
HEH...?
Say WHAT?

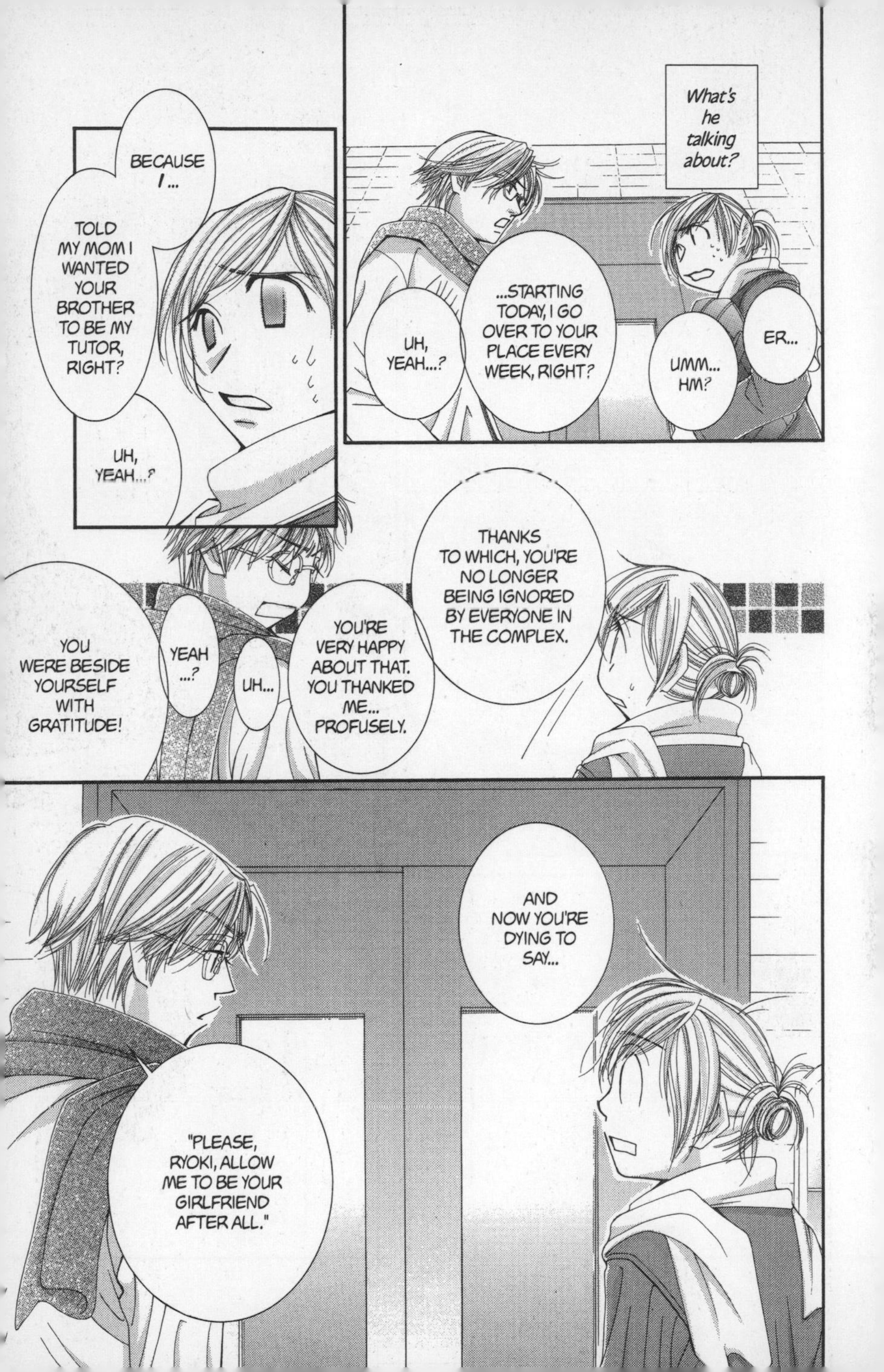
What's he talking about?
ER...
UMM... HM?
...STARTING TODAY, I GO OVER TO YOUR PLACE EVERY WEEK, RIGHT?
UH, YEAH...?
BECAUSE I...
TOLD MY MOM I WANTED YOUR BROTHER TO BE MY TUTOR, RIGHT?
UH, YEAH...?
THANKS TO WHICH, YOU'RE NO LONGER BEING IGNORED BY EVERYONE IN THE COMPLEX.
YOU'RE VERY HAPPY ABOUT THAT. YOU THANKED ME... PROFUSELY.
UH...
YEAH ...?
YOU WERE BESIDE YOURSELF WITH GRATITUDE!
AND NOW YOU'RE DYING TO SAY...
"PLEASE, RYOKI, ALLOW ME TO BE YOUR GIRLFRIEND AFTER ALL."

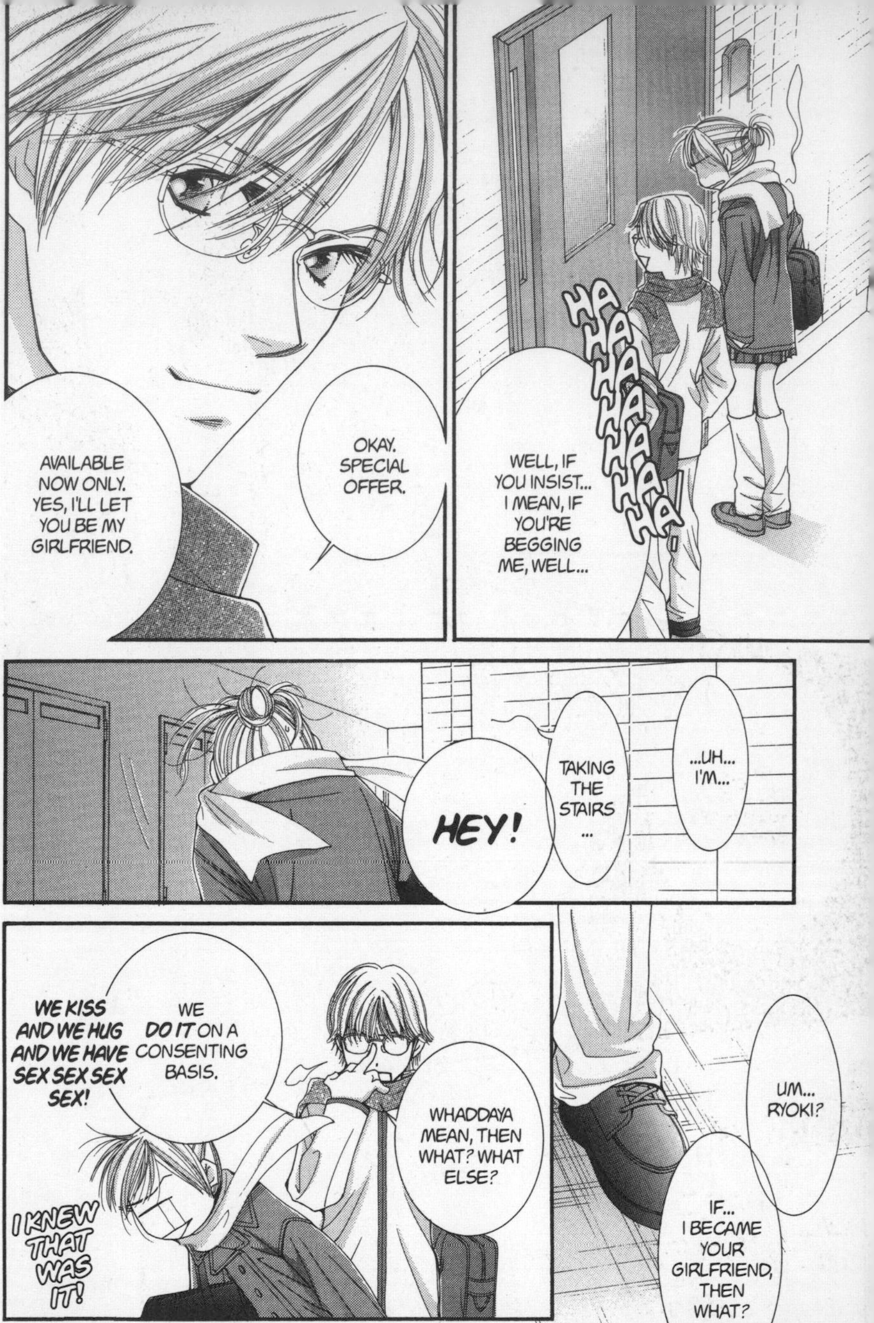
WELL, IF YOU INSIST... I MEAN, IF YOU'RE BEGGING ME, WELL...
HA HA HA HA HA HA HA HA!
OKAY. SPECIAL OFFER.
AVAILABLE NOW ONLY. YES, I'LL LET YOU BE MY GIRLFRIEND.
...UH... I'M...
TAKING THE STAIRS ...
HEY!
UM... RYOKI?
IF... I BECAME YOUR GIRLFRIEND, THEN WHAT?
WHADDAYA MEAN, THEN WHAT? WHAT ELSE?
WE DO IT ON A CONSENTING BASIS.
WE KISS AND WE HUG AND WE HAVE SEX SEX SEX SEX!
I KNEW THAT WAS IT!

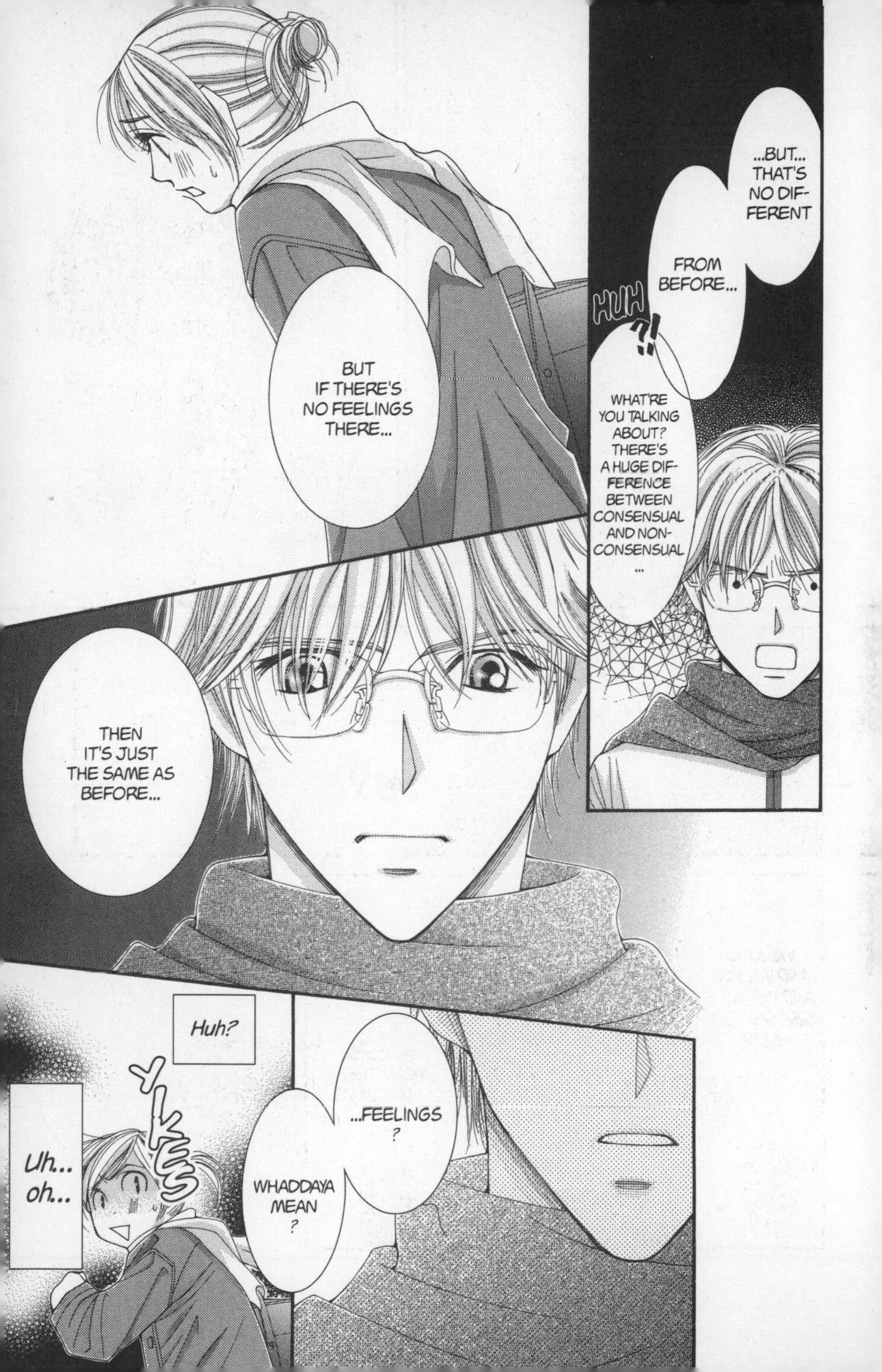
...BUT... THAT'S NO DIF-FERENT
FROM BEFORE...
HUH ?!
WHAT'RE YOU TALKING ABOUT? THERE'S A HUGE DIF-FERENCE BETWEEN CONSENSUAL AND NON-CONSENSUAL ...
BUT IF THERE'S NO FEELINGS THERE...
THEN IT'S JUST THE SAME AS BEFORE...
...FEELINGS ?
WHADDAYA MEAN ?
Huh?
YIKES
Uh... oh...

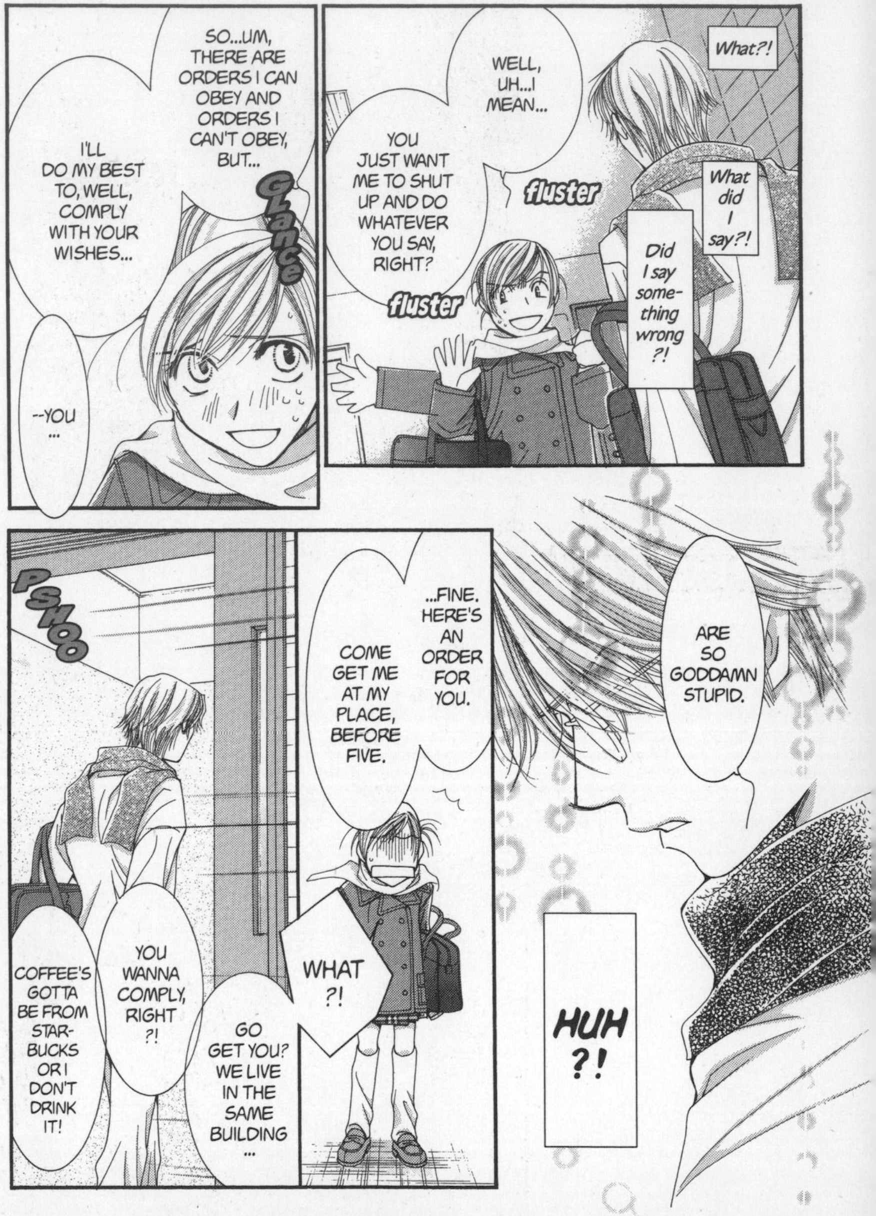
What?!
What did I say?!
Did I say some-thing wrong?!
WELL, UH...I MEAN...
YOU JUST WANT ME TO SHUT UP AND DO WHATEVER YOU SAY, RIGHT?
fluster
fluster
SO...UM, THERE ARE ORDERS I CAN OBEY AND ORDERS I CAN'T OBEY, BUT...
Glance
I'LL DO MY BEST TO, WELL, COMPLY WITH YOUR WISHES...
--YOU ...
ARE SO GODDAMN STUPID.
HUH ?!
...FINE. HERE'S AN ORDER FOR YOU.
COME GET ME AT MY PLACE, BEFORE FIVE.
WHAT ?!
GO GET YOU? WE LIVE IN THE SAME BUILDING ...
PSHOO
YOU WANNA COMPLY, RIGHT ?!
COFFEE'S GOTTA BE FROM STAR-BUCKS OR I DON'T DRINK IT!

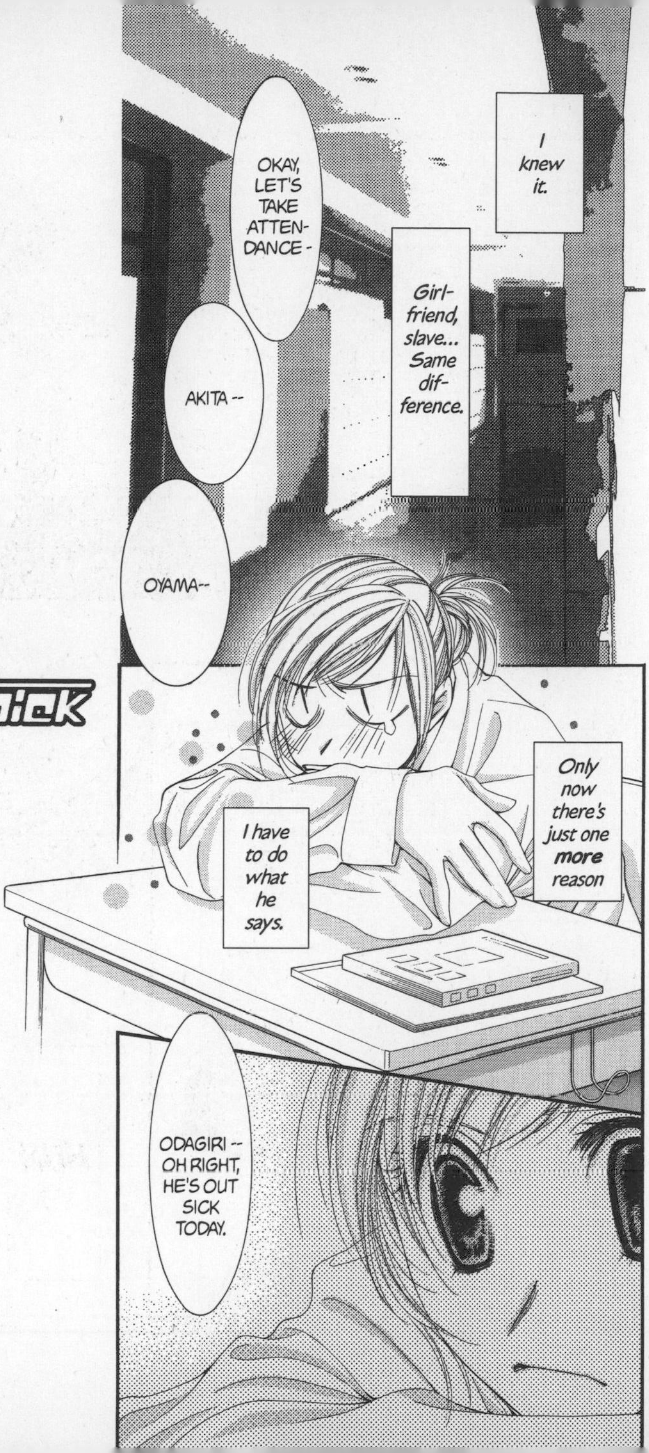
I knew it.
Girlfriend, slave... Same difference.
OKAY, LET'S TAKE ATTENDANCE -
AKITA --
OYAMA--
Only now there's just one **more** reason
I have to do what he says.
ODAGIRI -- OH RIGHT, HE'S OUT SICK TODAY.

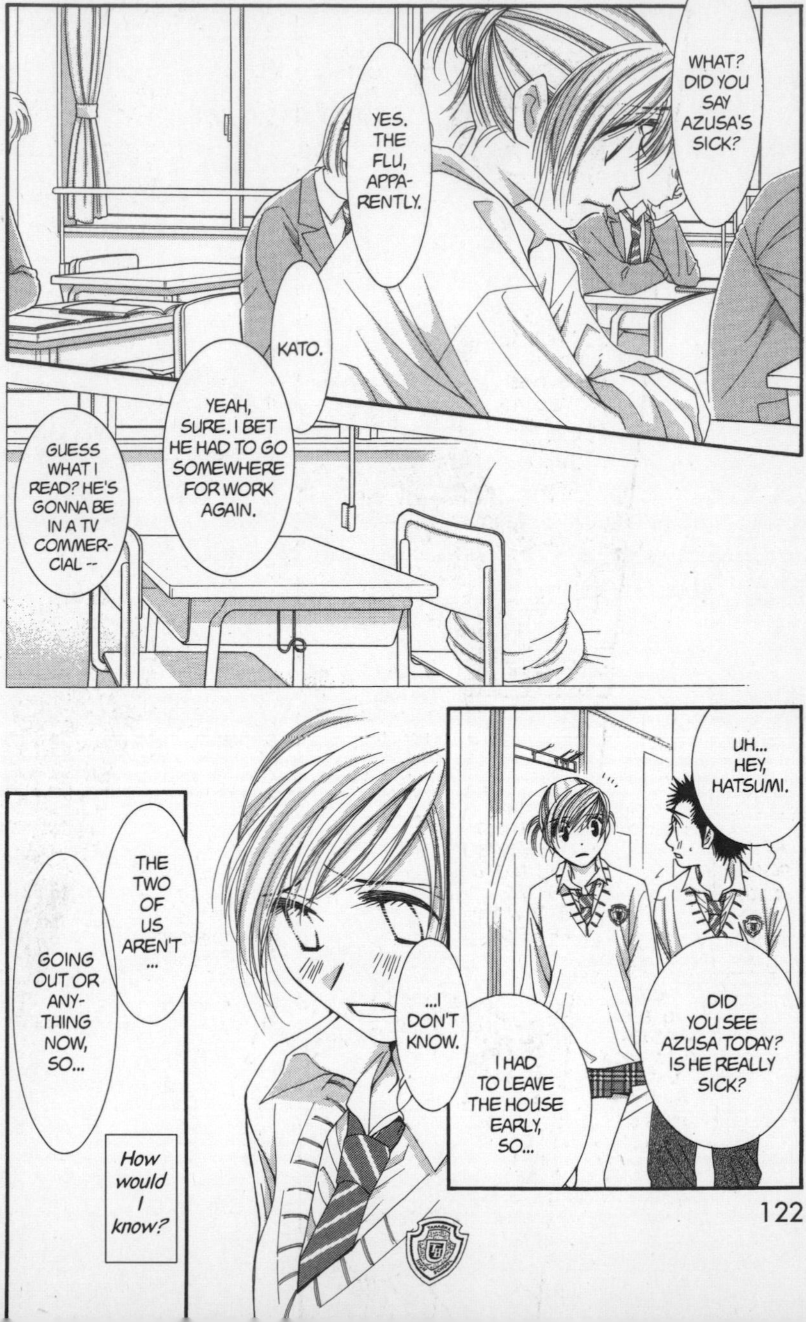
WHAT? DID YOU SAY AZUSA'S SICK?
YES. THE FLU, APPA-RENTLY.
KATO.
YEAH, SURE. I BET HE HAD TO GO SOMEWHERE FOR WORK AGAIN.
GUESS WHAT I READ? HE'S GONNA BE IN A TV COMMER-CIAL --
UH... HEY, HATSUMI.
DID YOU SEE AZUSA TODAY? IS HE REALLY SICK?
I HAD TO LEAVE THE HOUSE EARLY, SO...
...I DON'T KNOW.
THE TWO OF US AREN'T ...
GOING OUT OR ANY-THING NOW, SO...
How would I know?

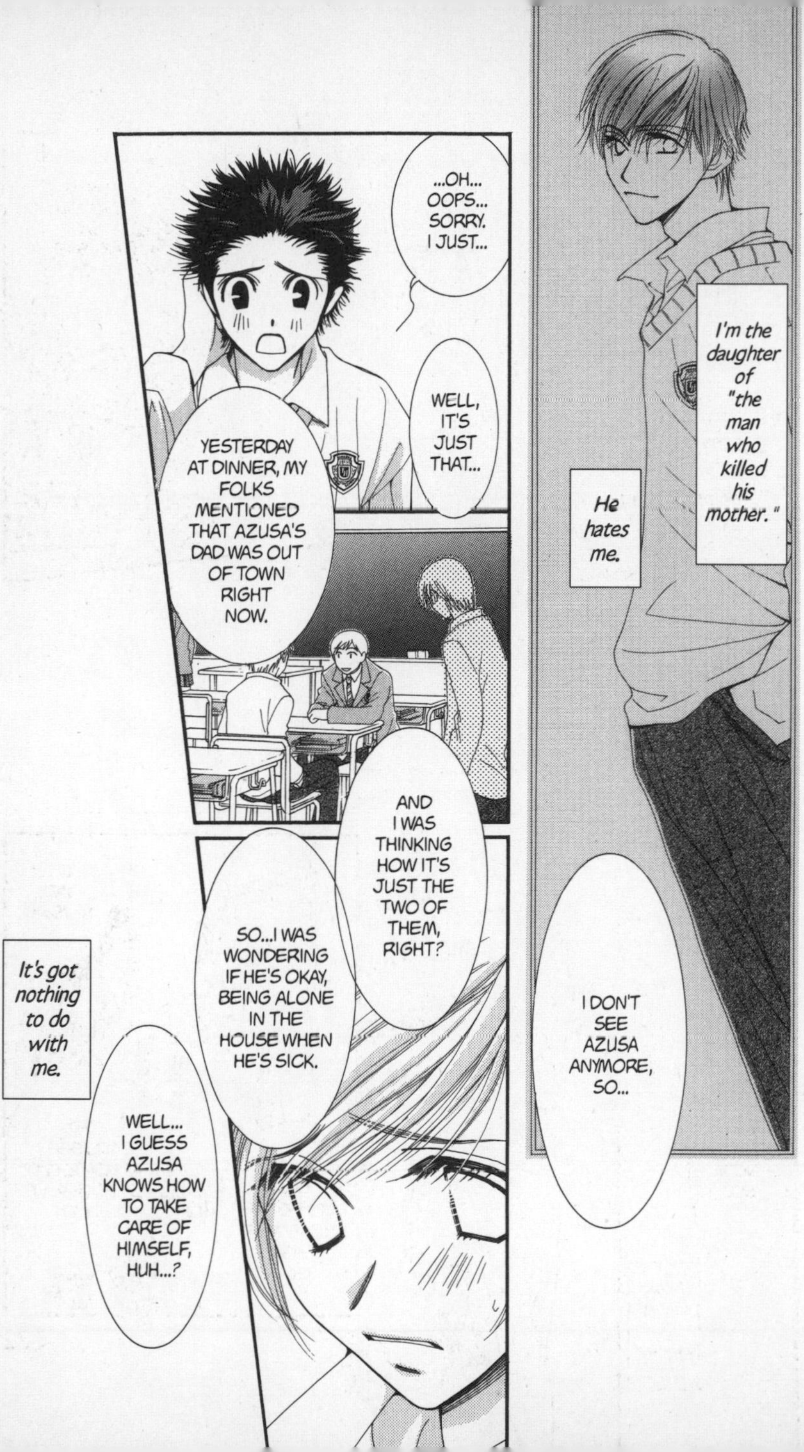
I'm the daughter of "the man who killed his mother."
He hates me.
...OH... OOPS... SORRY. I JUST...
WELL, IT'S JUST THAT...
YESTERDAY AT DINNER, MY FOLKS MENTIONED THAT AZUSA'S DAD WAS OUT OF TOWN RIGHT NOW.
AND I WAS THINKING HOW IT'S JUST THE TWO OF THEM, RIGHT?
SO...I WAS WONDERING IF HE'S OKAY, BEING ALONE IN THE HOUSE WHEN HE'S SICK.
I DON'T SEE AZUSA ANYMORE, SO...
WELL... I GUESS AZUSA KNOWS HOW TO TAKE CARE OF HIMSELF, HUH...?
It's got nothing to do with me.

I'M HOME --
OH...
Guess Shinogu isn't here yet...
PATISSIER TAKAGI
ROAST
STARBUCKS COFFEE
Hatsumi -
I don't get off work till 7:00 today, so please take good care of Ryoki until I get home.
I bought the coffee beans he likes, and some cake to go with.
← These
Mom
COME GET ME AT FIVE!
UGH!
I guess
There's still some time--

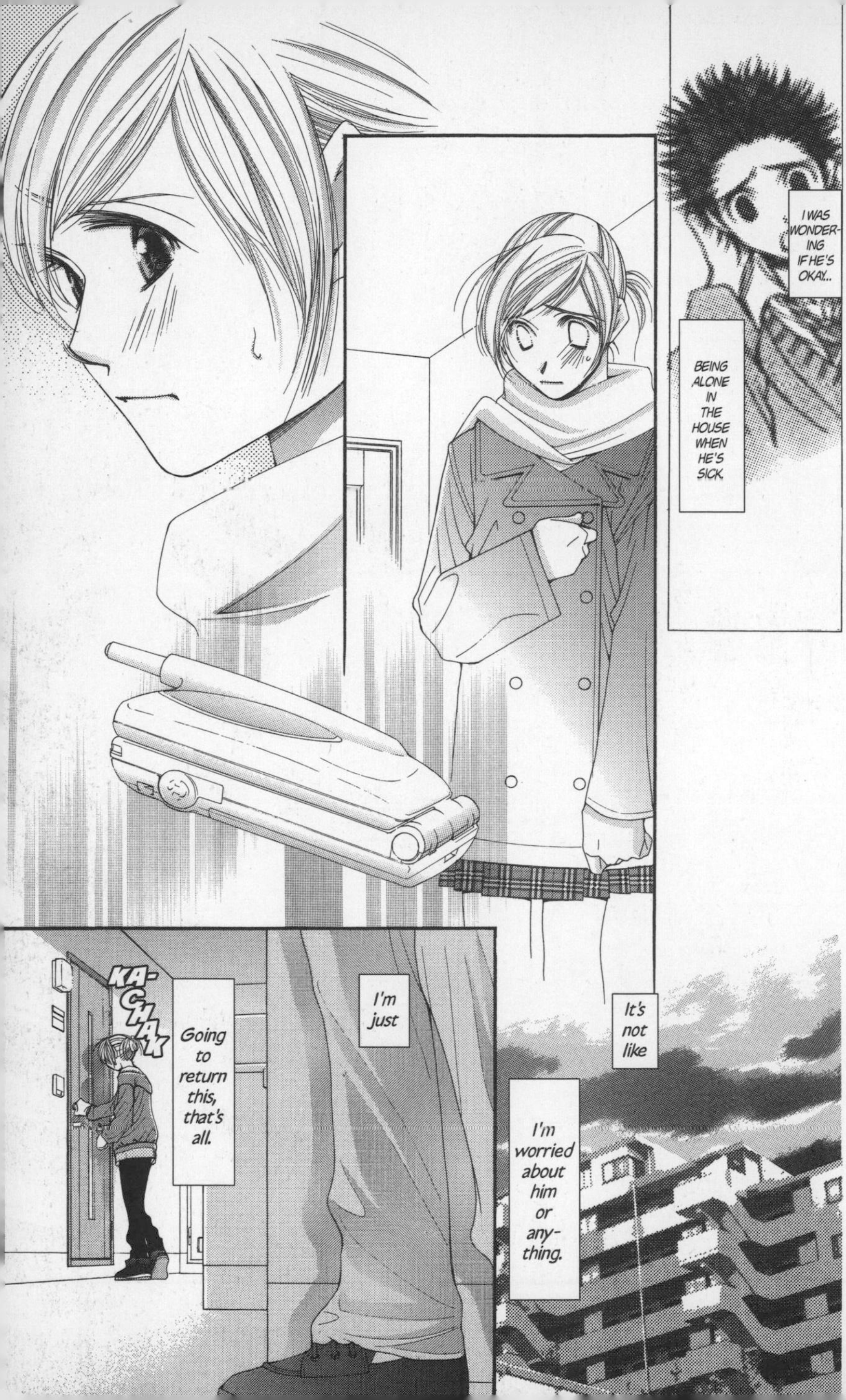
I WAS WONDERING IF HE'S OKAY...
BEING ALONE IN THE HOUSE WHEN HE'S SICK.
It's not like
I'm worried about him or anything.
I'm just
Going to return this, that's all.
KA-CHAK

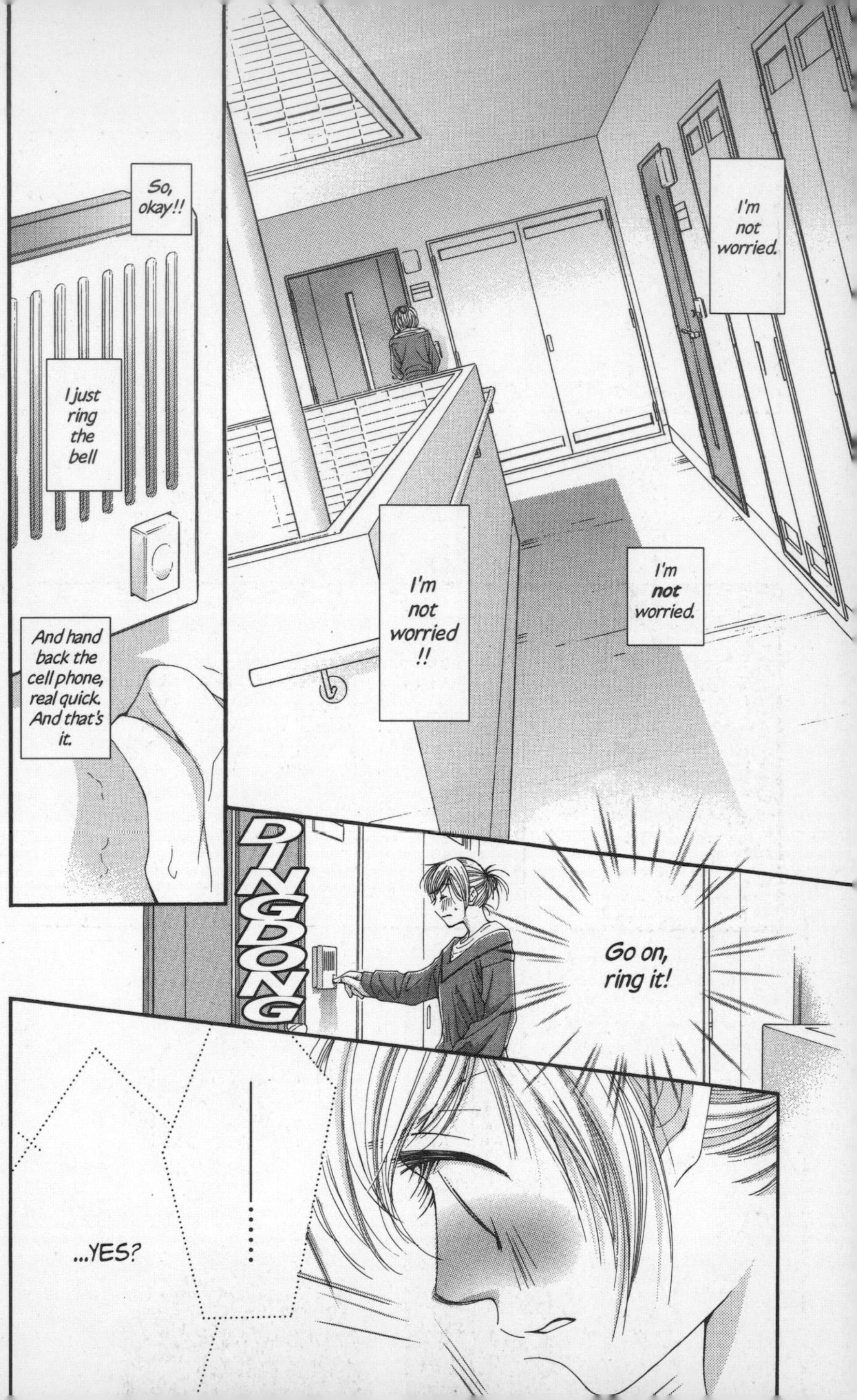
I'm not worried.
I'm **not** worried.
I'm not worried !!
So, okay!!
I just ring the bell
And hand back the cell phone, real quick. And that's it.
Go on, ring it!
DINGDONG
......
...YES?

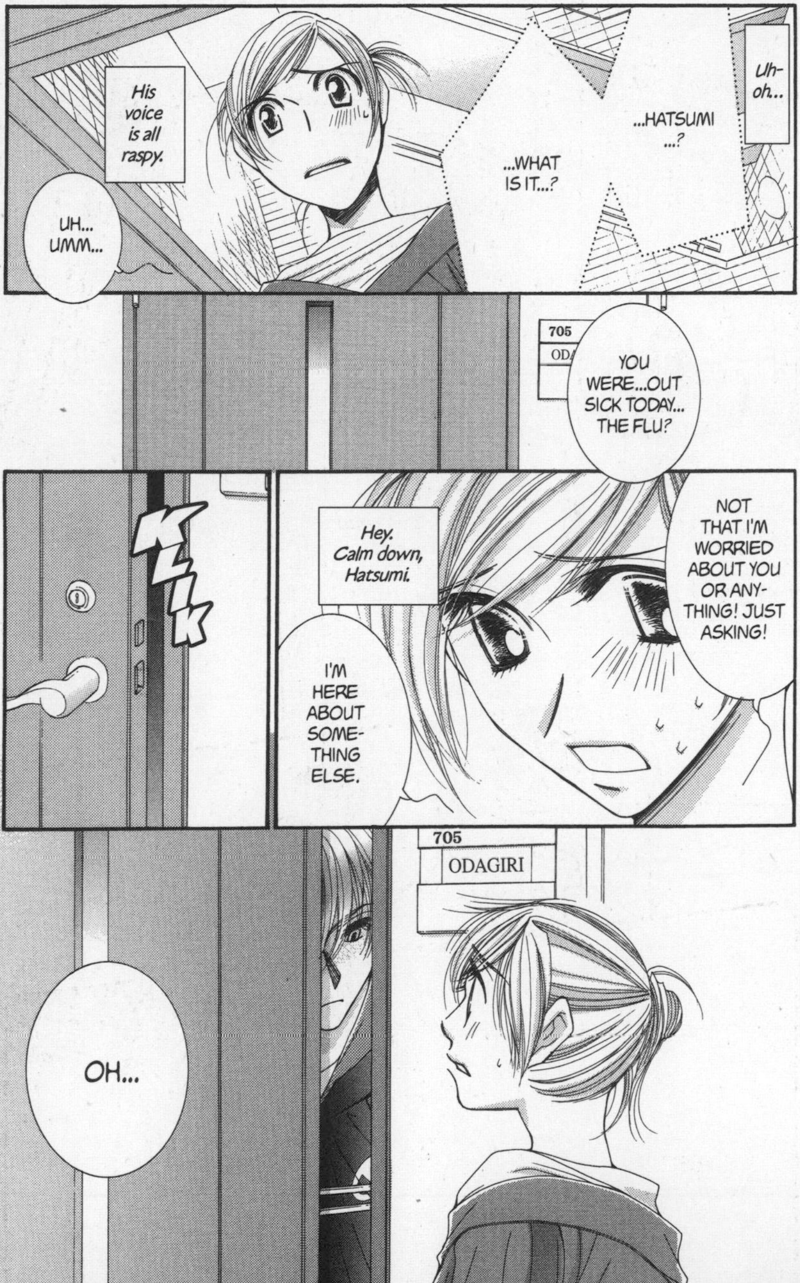
Uh-oh...
...HATSUMI ...?
...WHAT IS IT...?
His voice is all raspy.
UH... UMM...
705
YOU WERE...OUT SICK TODAY... THE FLU?
NOT THAT I'M WORRIED ABOUT YOU OR ANY-THING! JUST ASKING!
Hey. Calm down, Hatsumi.
I'M HERE ABOUT SOME-THING ELSE.
KLIK
705
ODAGIRI
OH...

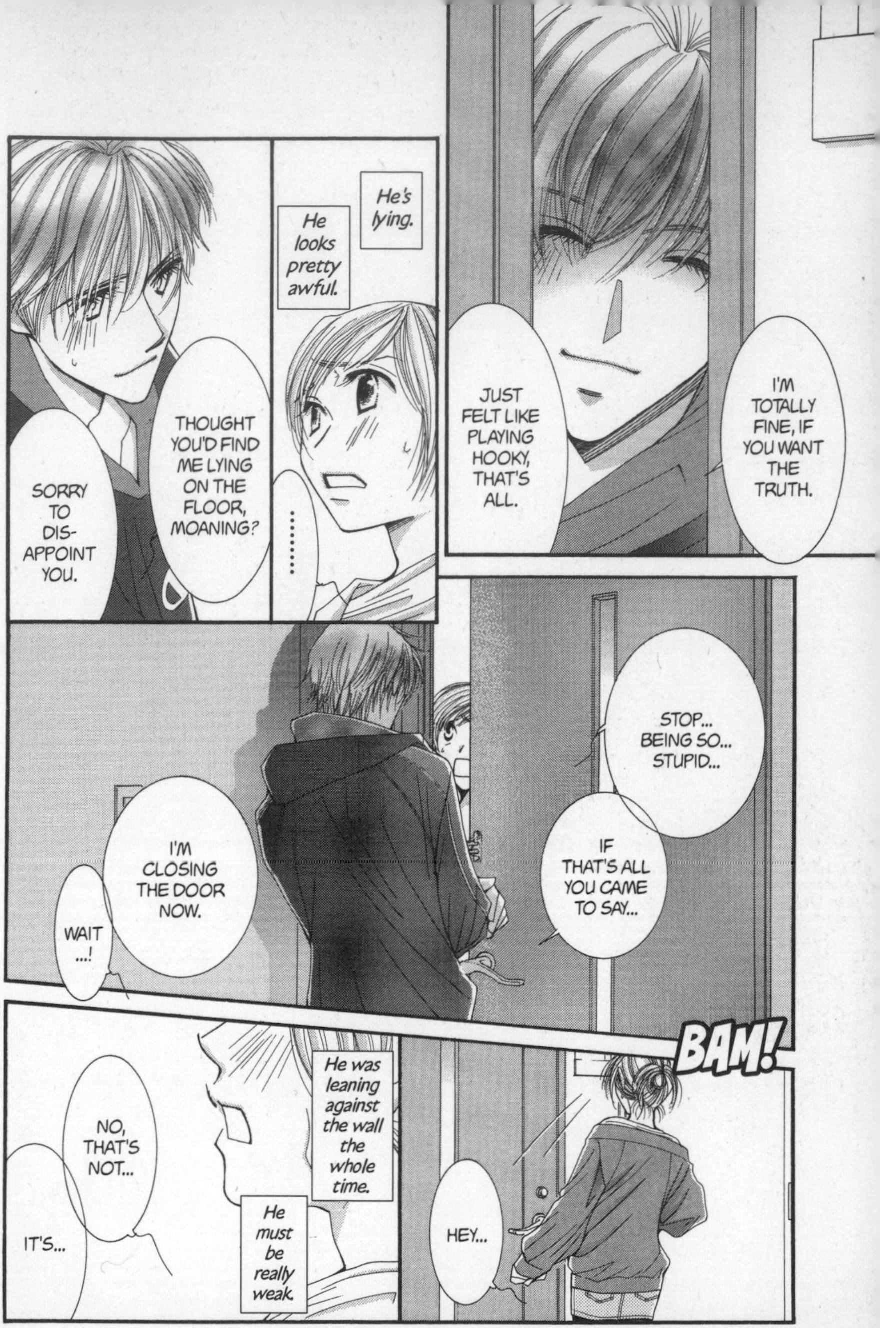
I'M TOTALLY FINE, IF YOU WANT THE TRUTH.
JUST FELT LIKE PLAYING HOOKY, THAT'S ALL.
He's lying.
He looks pretty awful.
......
THOUGHT YOU'D FIND ME LYING ON THE FLOOR, MOANING?
SORRY TO DIS-APPOINT YOU.
STOP... BEING SO... STUPID...
IF THAT'S ALL YOU CAME TO SAY...
I'M CLOSING THE DOOR NOW.
WAIT...!
BAM!
HEY...
He was leaning against the wall the whole time.
He must be really weak.
NO, THAT'S NOT...
IT'S...

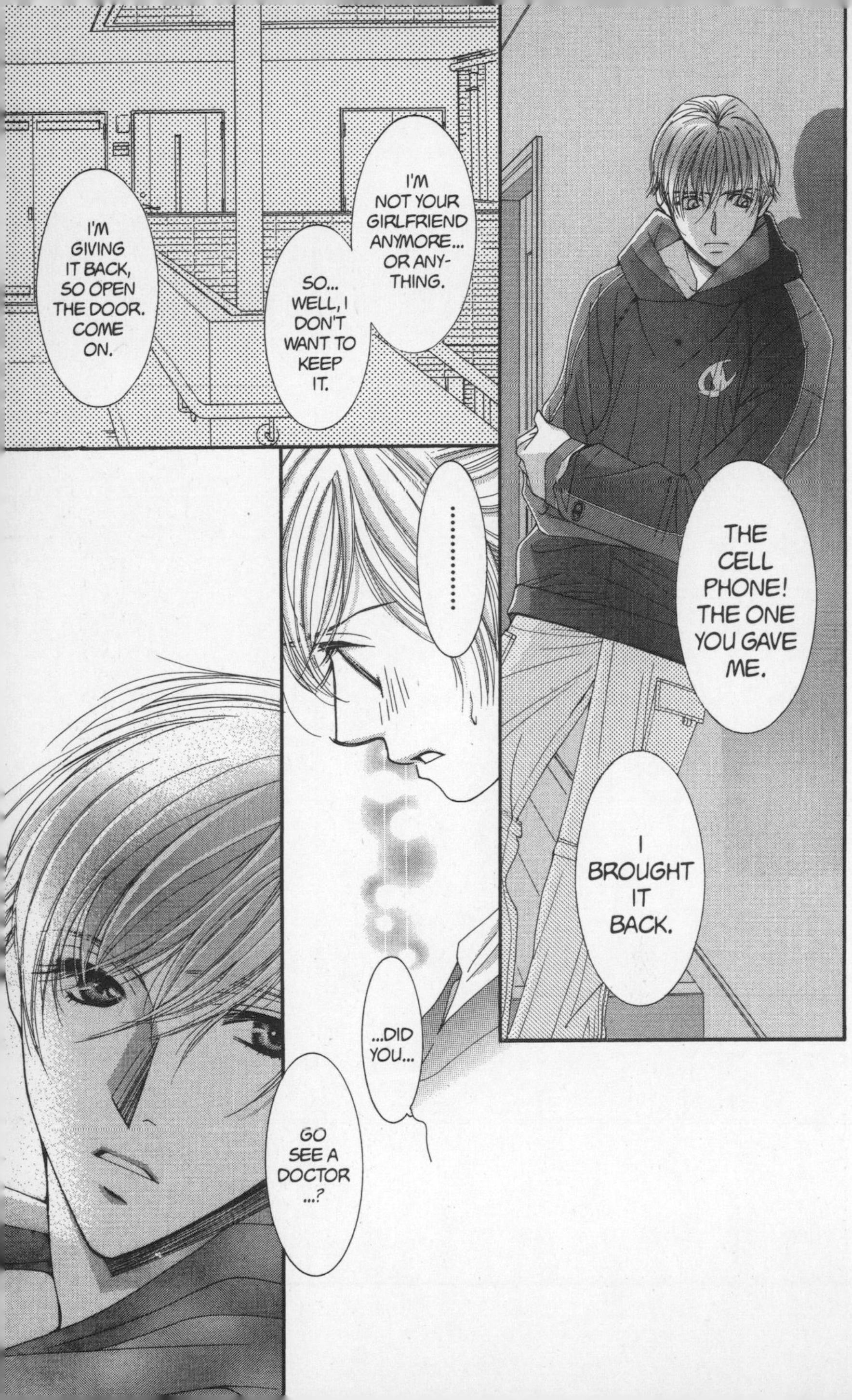
THE CELL PHONE! THE ONE YOU GAVE ME.
I BROUGHT IT BACK.
I'M NOT YOUR GIRLFRIEND ANYMORE... OR ANY-THING.
SO... WELL, I DON'T WANT TO KEEP IT.
I'M GIVING IT BACK, SO OPEN THE DOOR. COME ON.
......
...DID YOU...
GO SEE A DOCTOR ...?

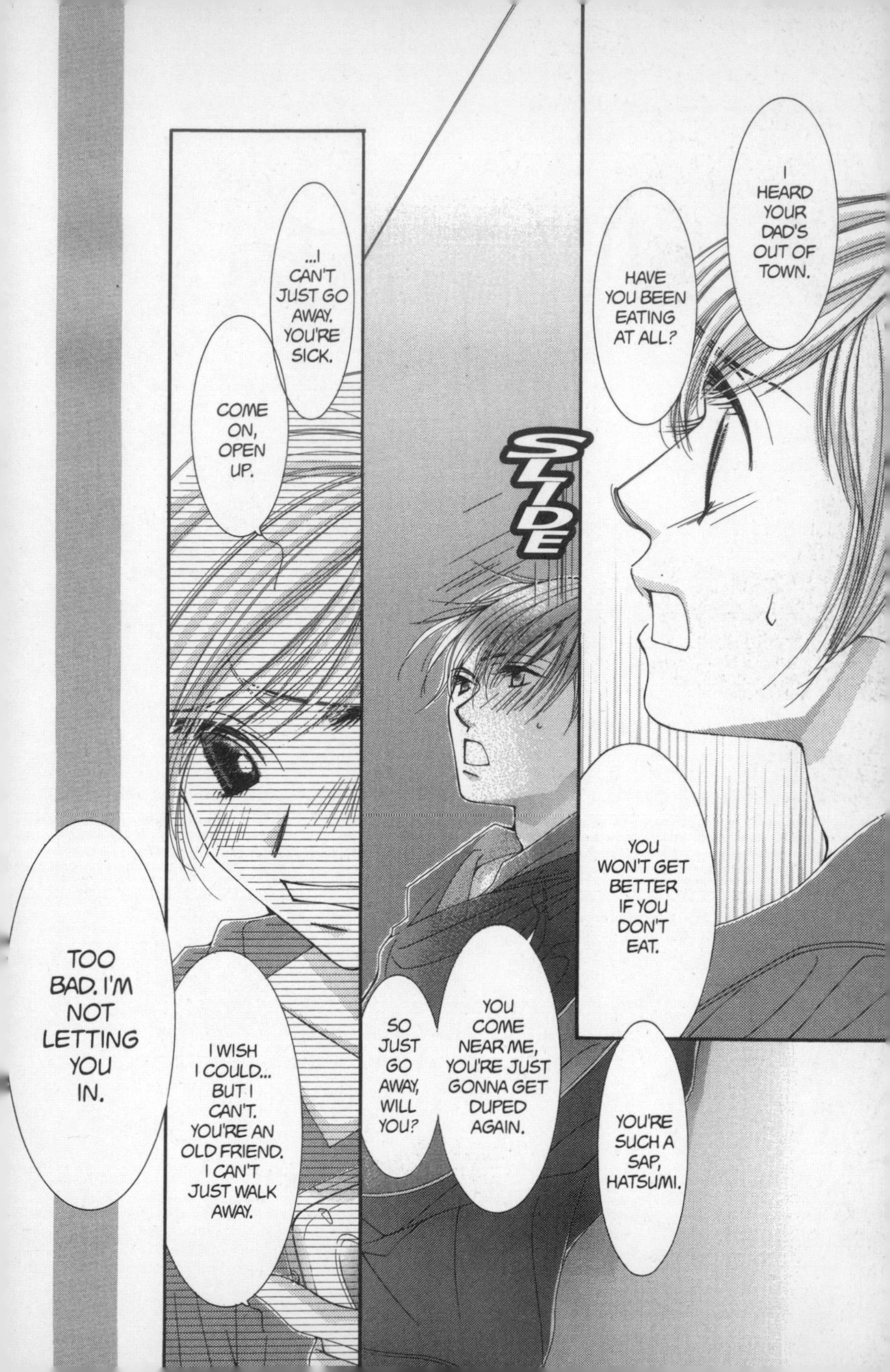
I HEARD YOUR DAD'S OUT OF TOWN.
HAVE YOU BEEN EATING AT ALL?
YOU WON'T GET BETTER IF YOU DON'T EAT.
SLIDE
YOU'RE SUCH A SAP, HATSUMI.
YOU COME NEAR ME, YOU'RE JUST GONNA GET DUPED AGAIN.
SO JUST GO AWAY, WILL YOU?
...I CAN'T JUST GO AWAY. YOU'RE SICK.
COME ON, OPEN UP.
I WISH I COULD... BUT I CAN'T. YOU'RE AN OLD FRIEND. I CAN'T JUST WALK AWAY.
TOO BAD. I'M NOT LETTING YOU IN.

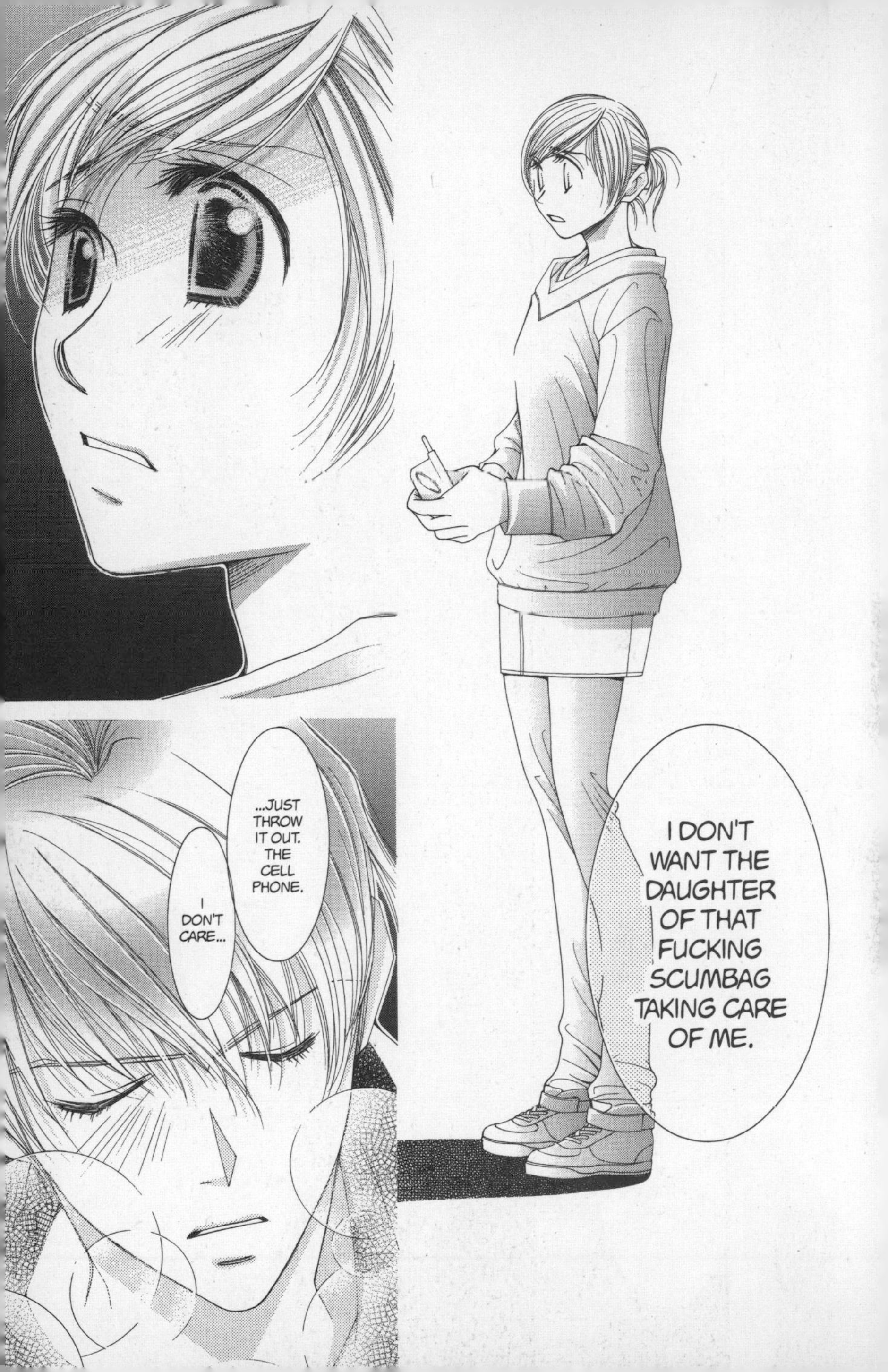
I DON'T WANT THE DAUGHTER OF THAT FUCKING SCUMBAG TAKING CARE OF ME.
...JUST THROW IT OUT. THE CELL PHONE.
I DON'T CARE...

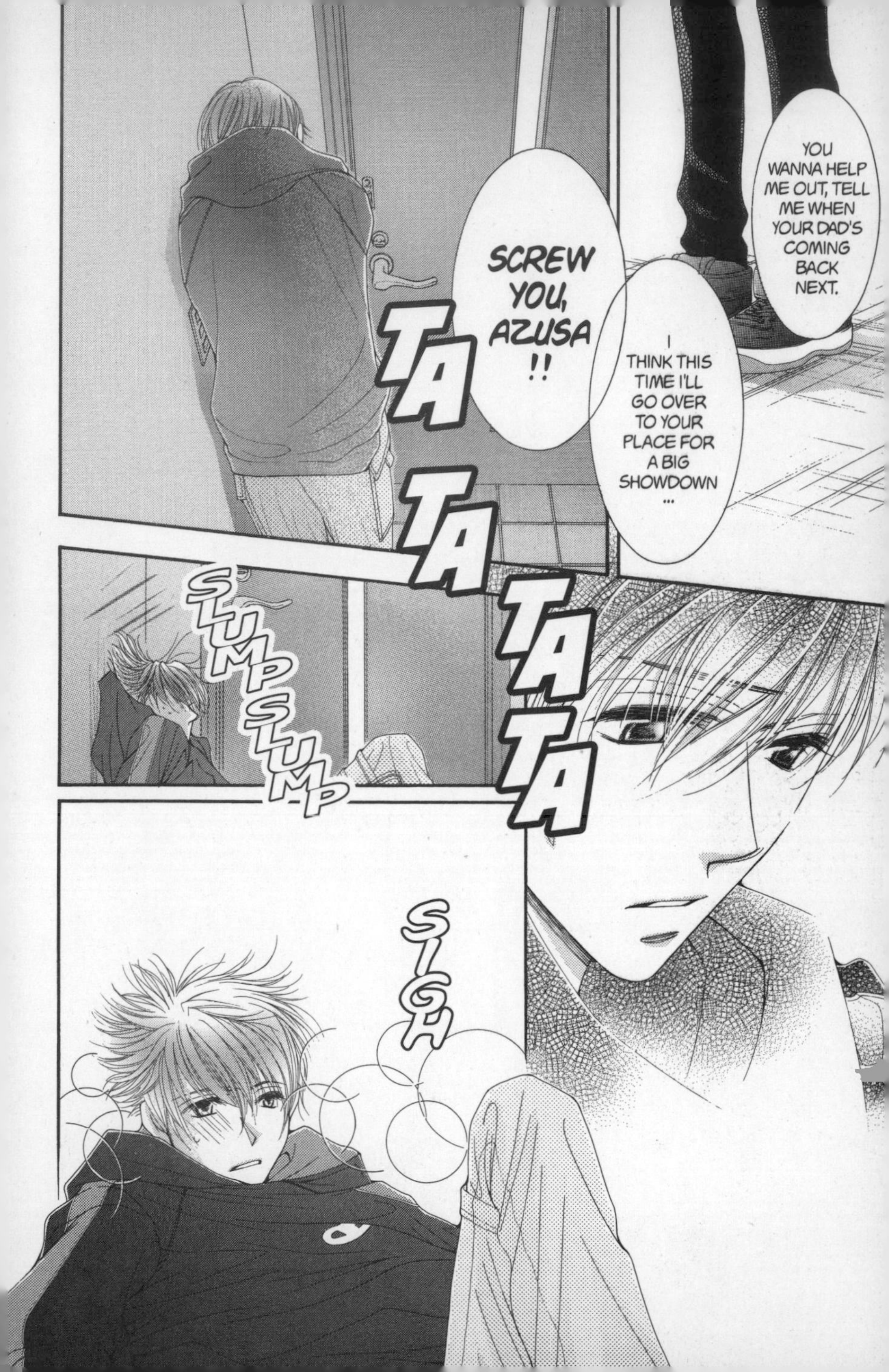
YOU WANNA HELP ME OUT, TELL ME WHEN YOUR DAD'S COMING BACK NEXT.
I THINK THIS TIME I'LL GO OVER TO YOUR PLACE FOR A BIG SHOWDOWN ...
SCREW YOU, AZUSA !!
TA TA TA TA TA
SLUMP SLUMP
SIGH

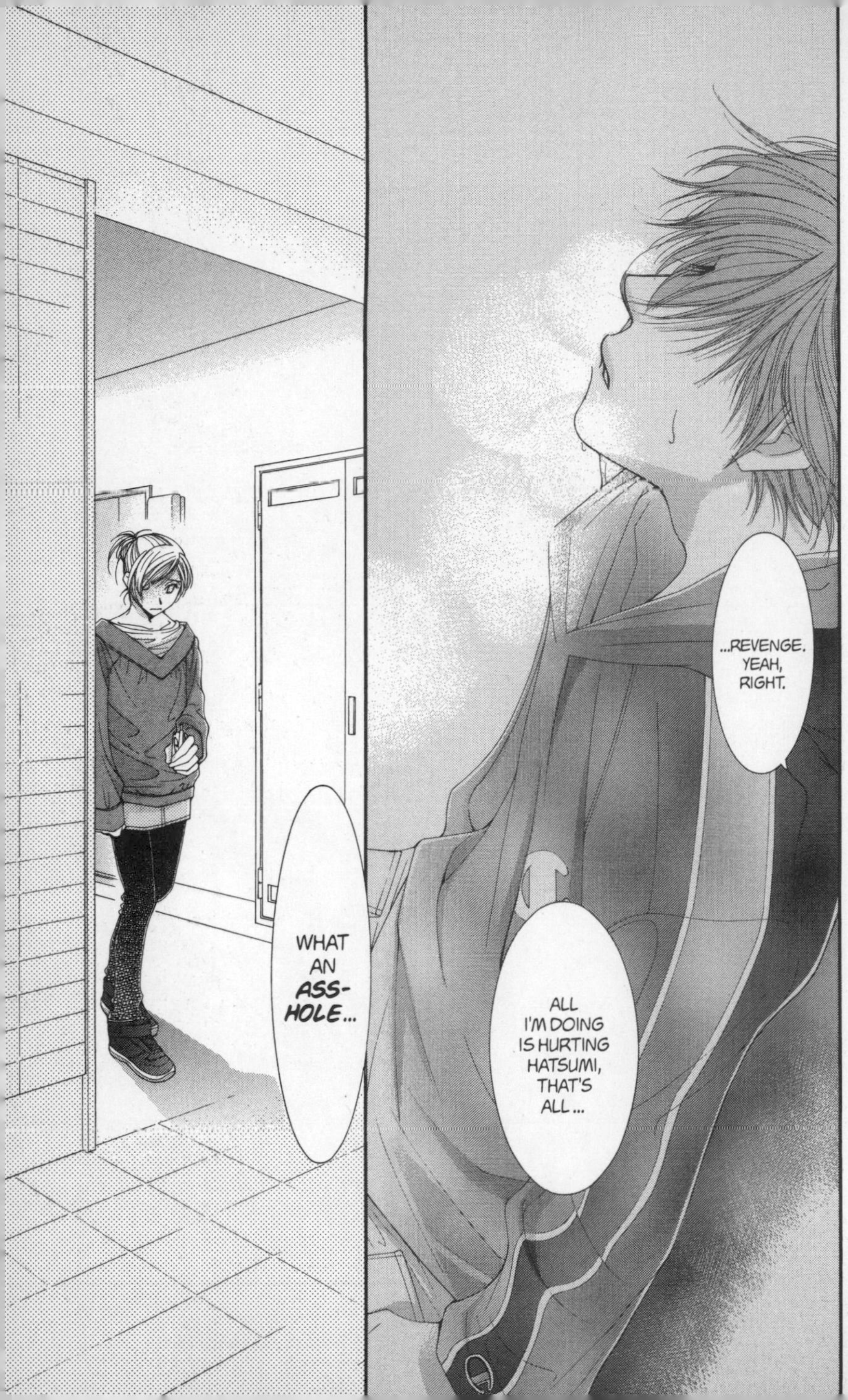
...REVENGE. YEAH, RIGHT.
ALL I'M DOING IS HURTING HATSUMI, THAT'S ALL...
WHAT AN ASS-HOLE...

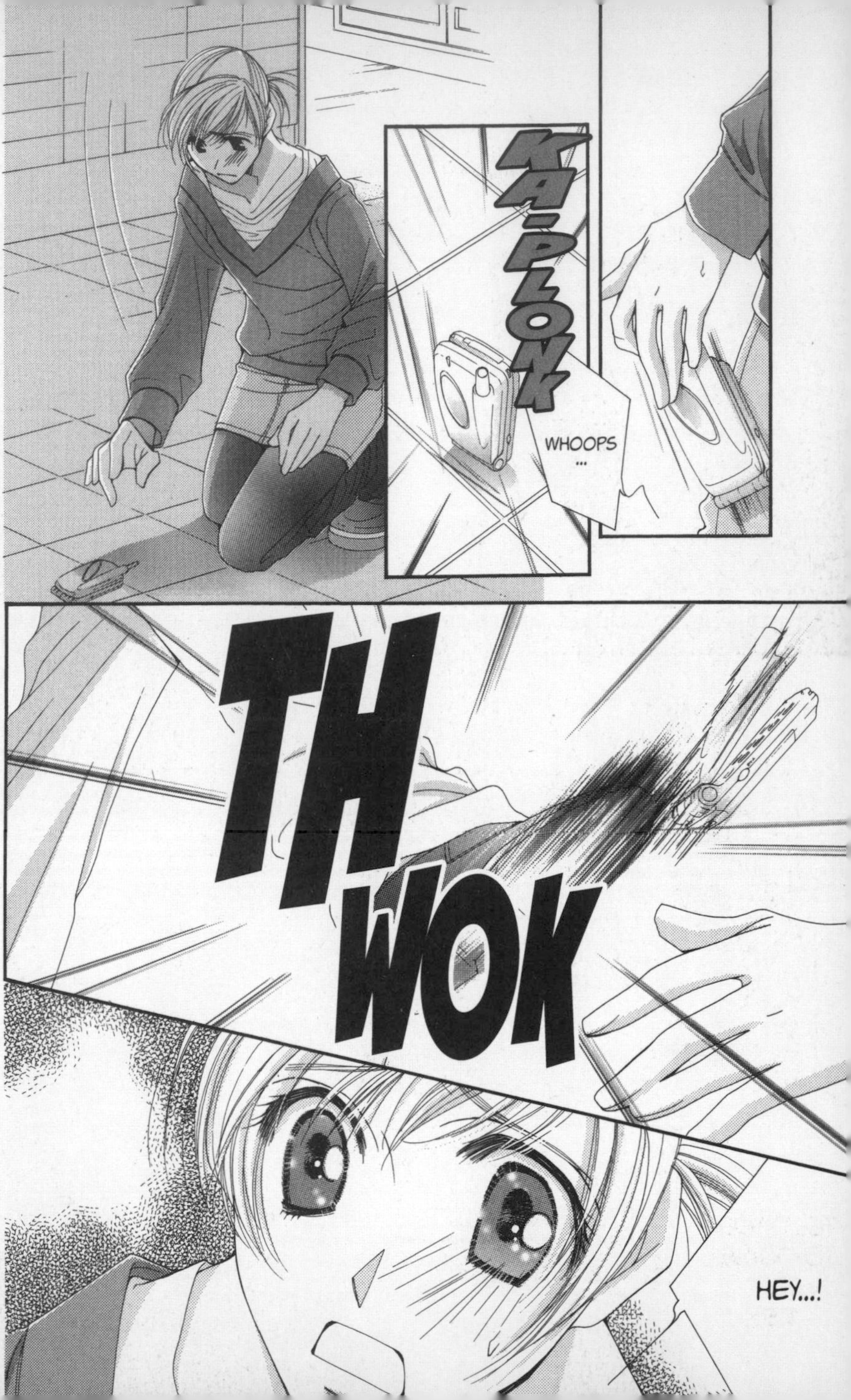
KA-PLONK
WHOOPS ...
TH WOK
HEY...!

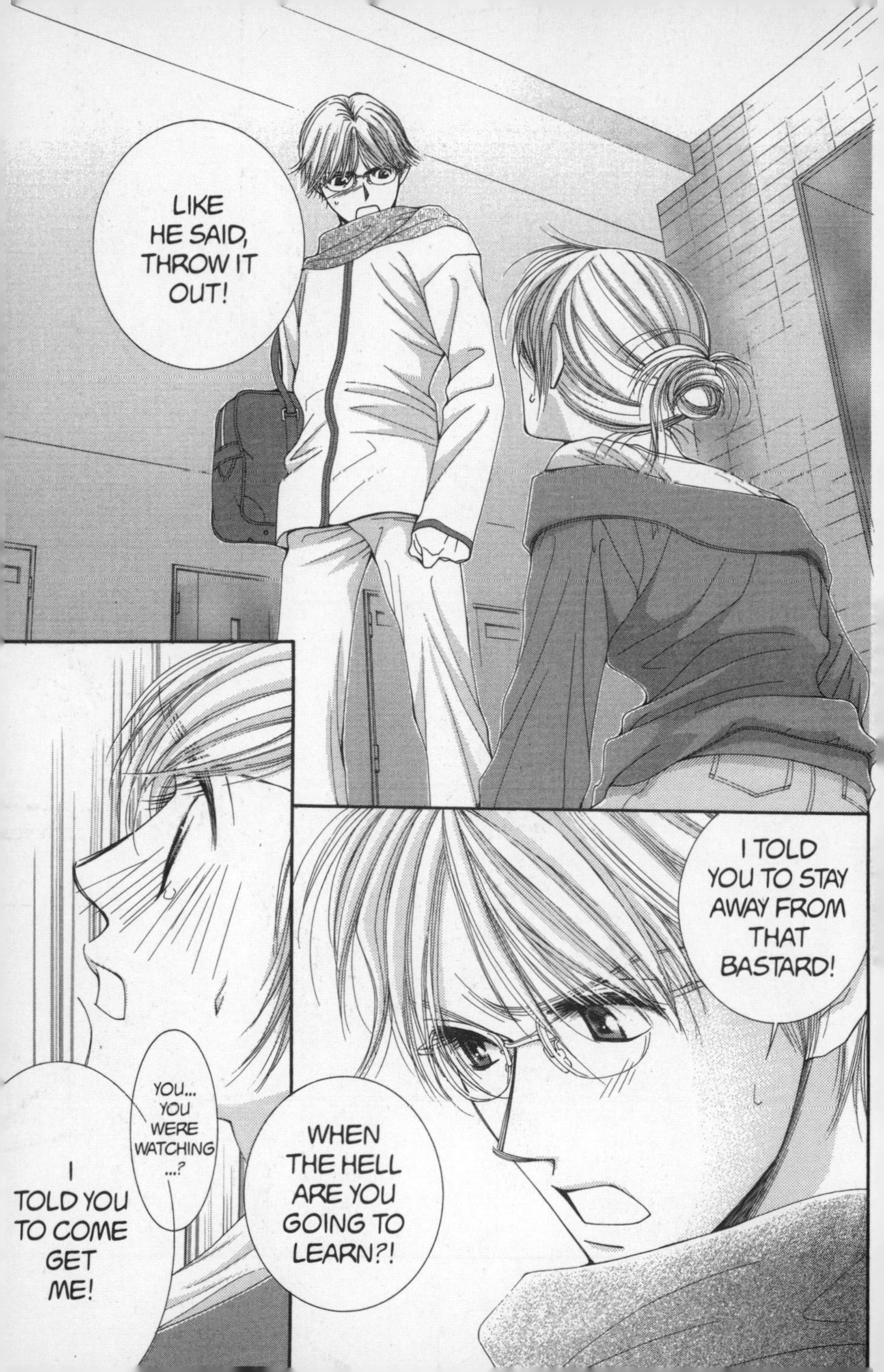
LIKE HE SAID, THROW IT OUT!
I TOLD YOU TO STAY AWAY FROM THAT BASTARD!
WHEN THE HELL ARE YOU GOING TO LEARN?!
YOU... YOU WERE WATCHING ...?
I TOLD YOU TO COME GET ME!

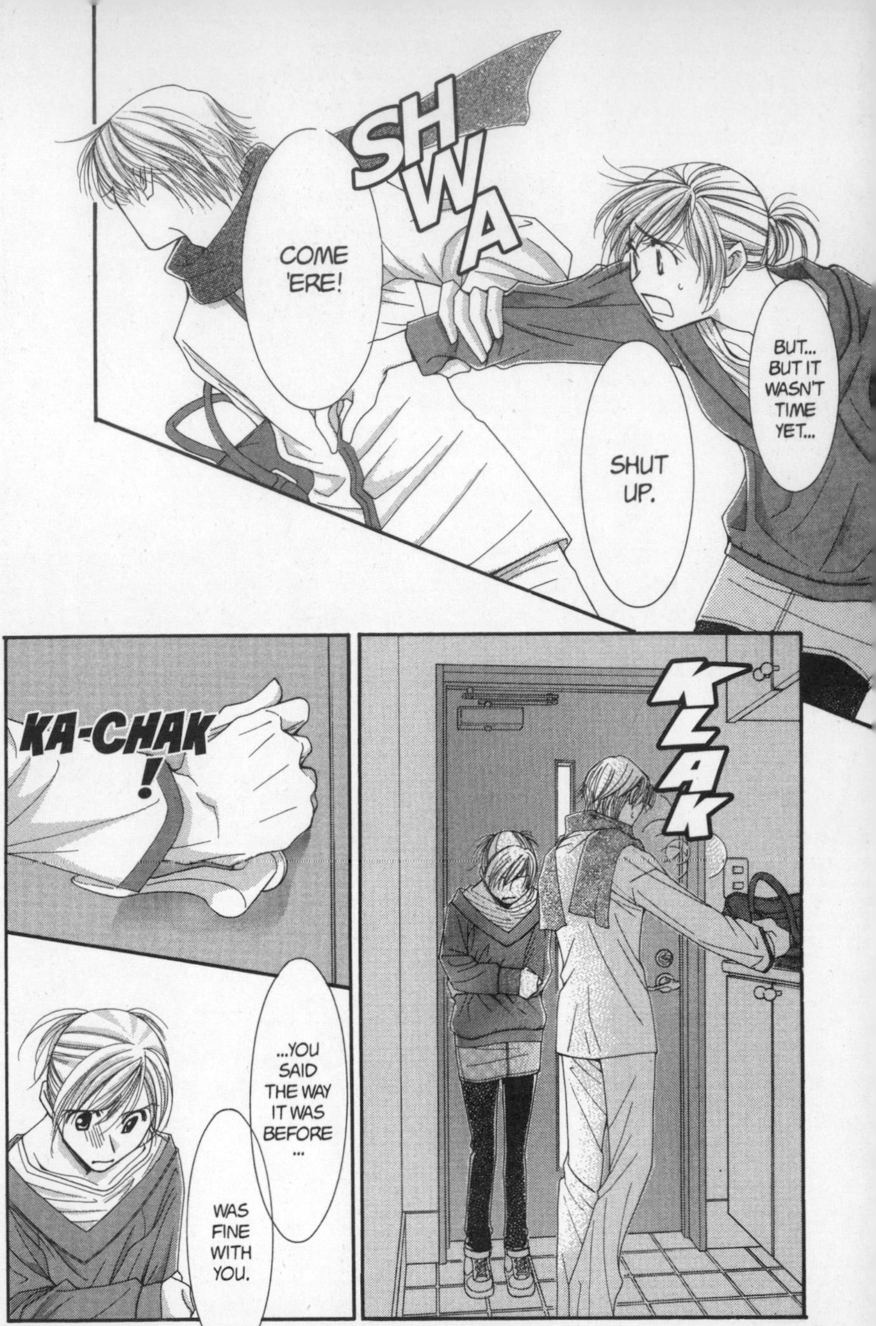
BUT... BUT IT WASN'T TIME YET...
SHWA
COME 'ERE!
SHUT UP.
KLAK
KA-CHAK!
...YOU SAID THE WAY IT WAS BEFORE...
WAS FINE WITH YOU.

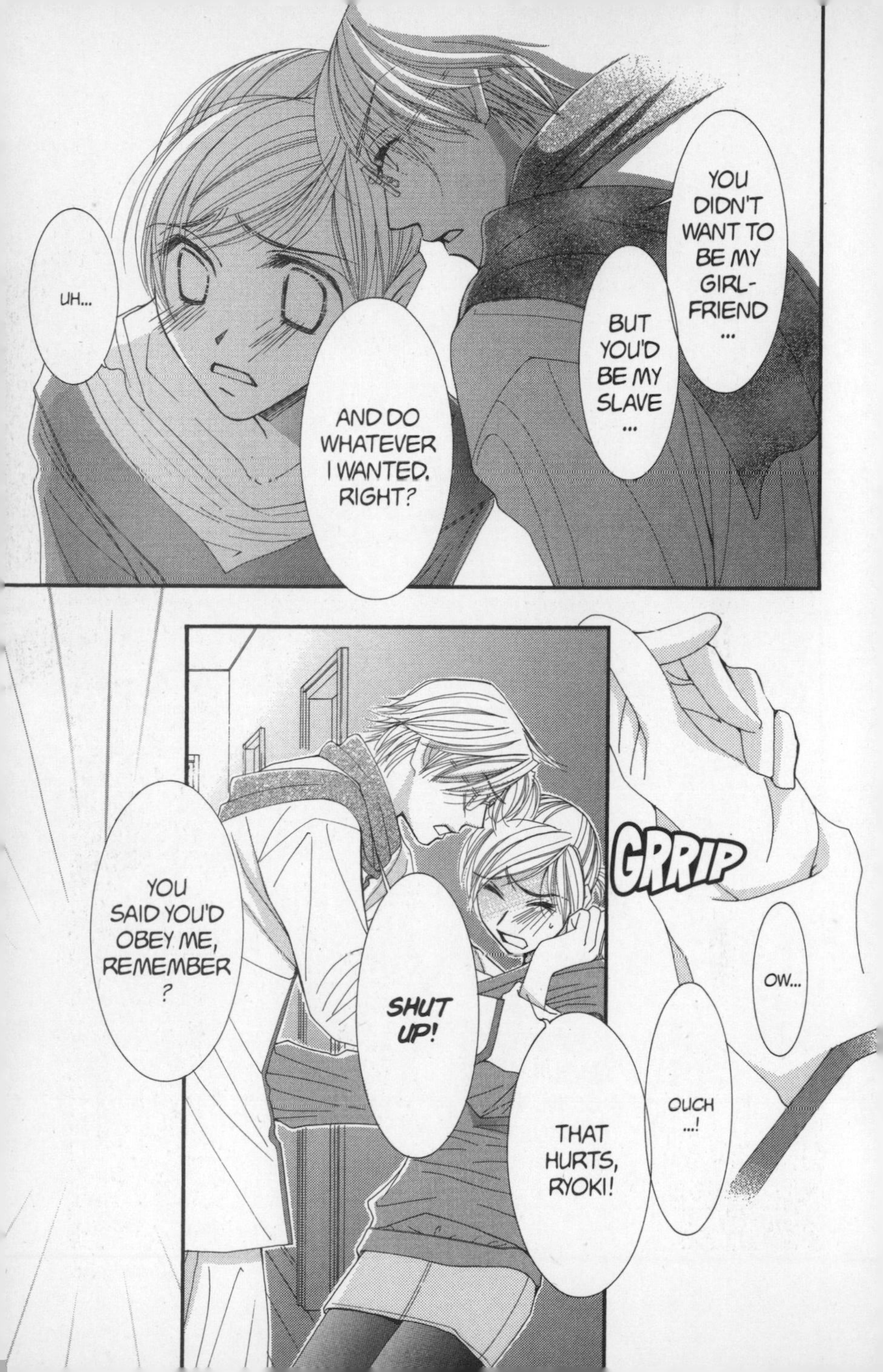
YOU DIDN'T WANT TO BE MY GIRL-FRIEND ...
BUT YOU'D BE MY SLAVE ...
AND DO WHATEVER I WANTED. RIGHT?
UH...
GRRIP
OW...
OUCH ...!
THAT HURTS, RYOKI!
SHUT UP!
YOU SAID YOU'D OBEY ME, REMEMBER ?

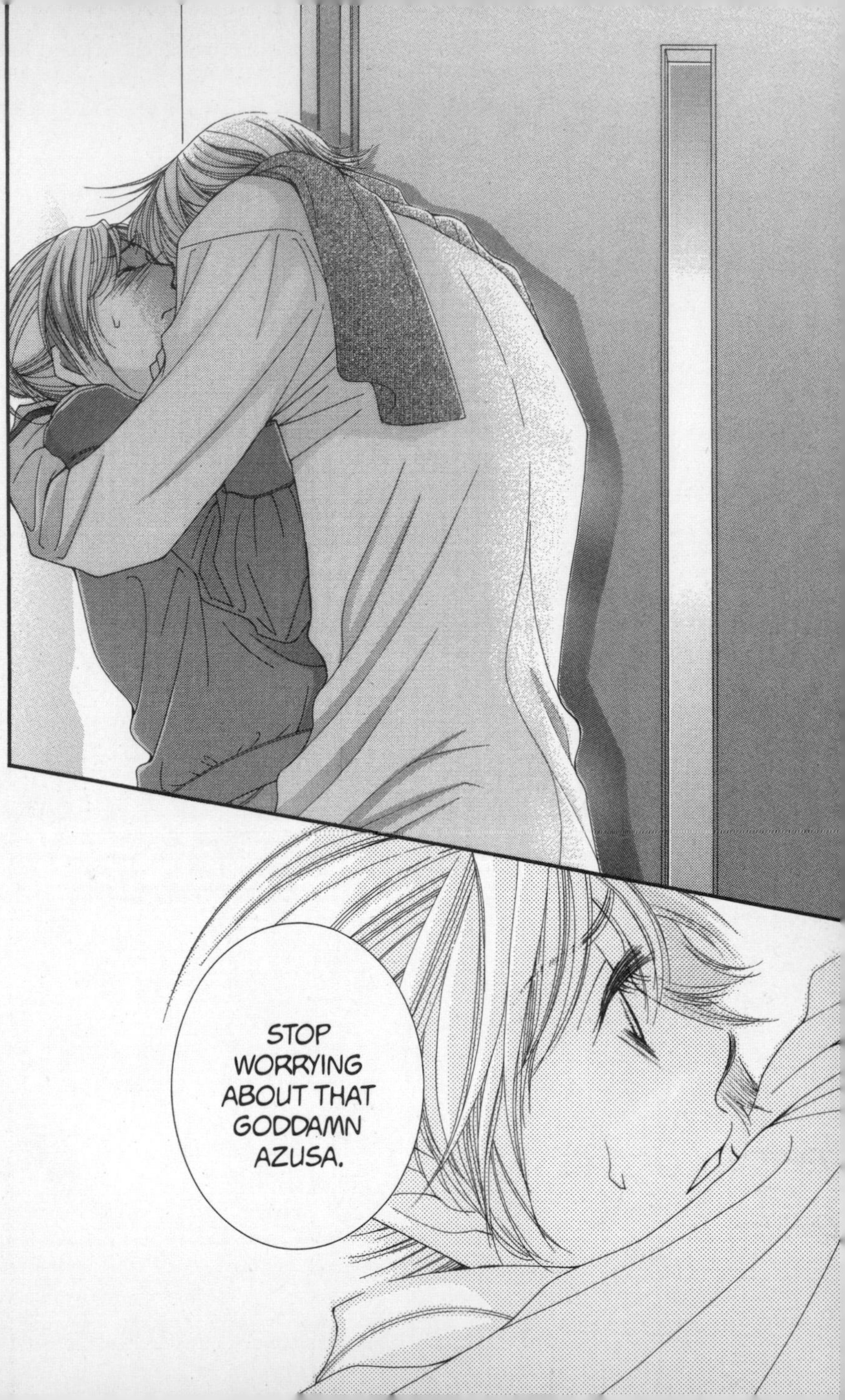
STOP WORRYING ABOUT THAT GODDAMN AZUSA.

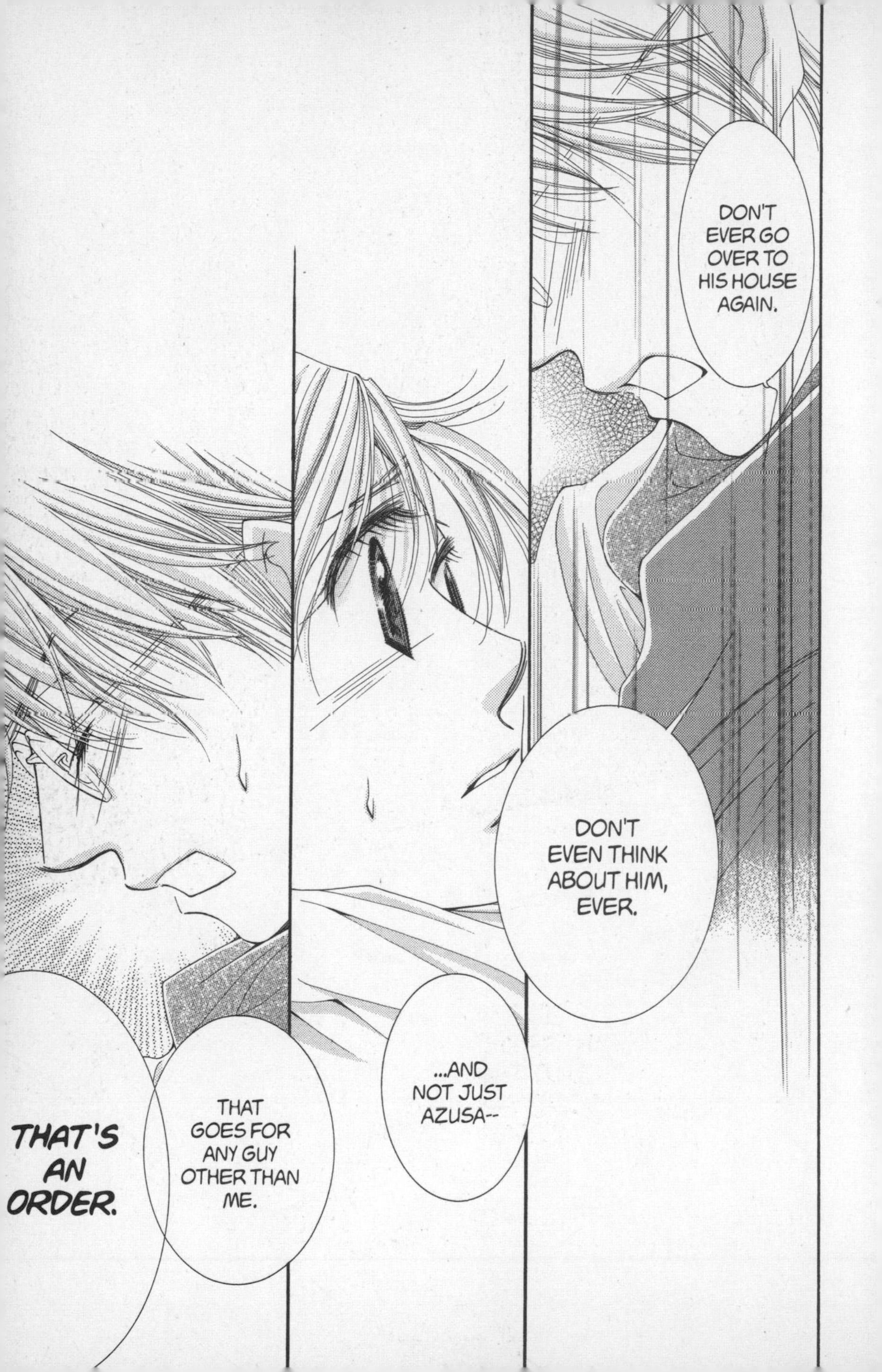
DON'T EVER GO OVER TO HIS HOUSE AGAIN.
DON'T EVEN THINK ABOUT HIM, EVER.
...AND NOT JUST AZUSA--
THAT GOES FOR ANY GUY OTHER THAN ME.
THAT'S AN ORDER.

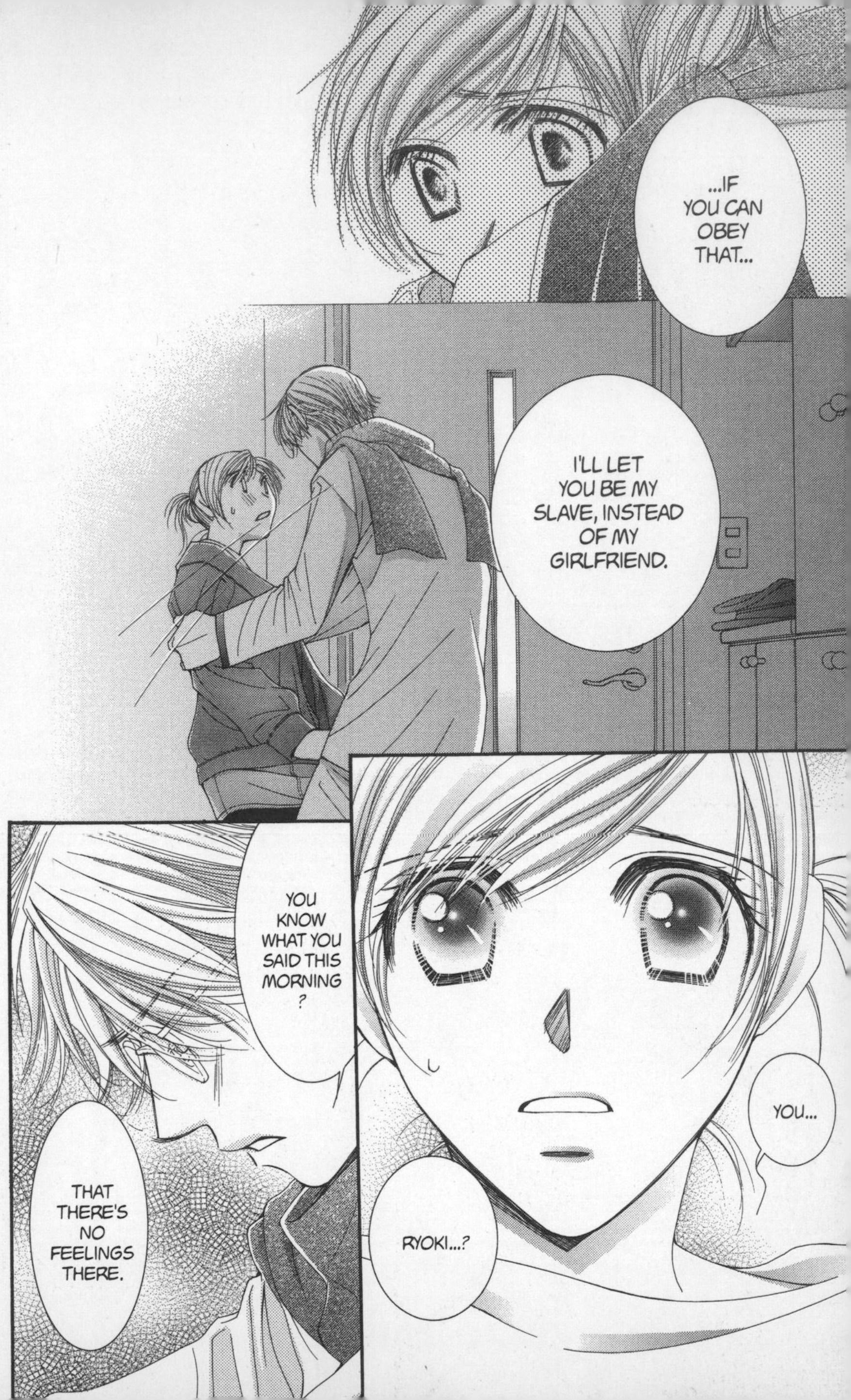
...IF YOU CAN OBEY THAT...
I'LL LET YOU BE MY SLAVE, INSTEAD OF MY GIRLFRIEND.
YOU...
RYOKI...?
YOU KNOW WHAT YOU SAID THIS MORNING?
THAT THERE'S NO FEELINGS THERE.

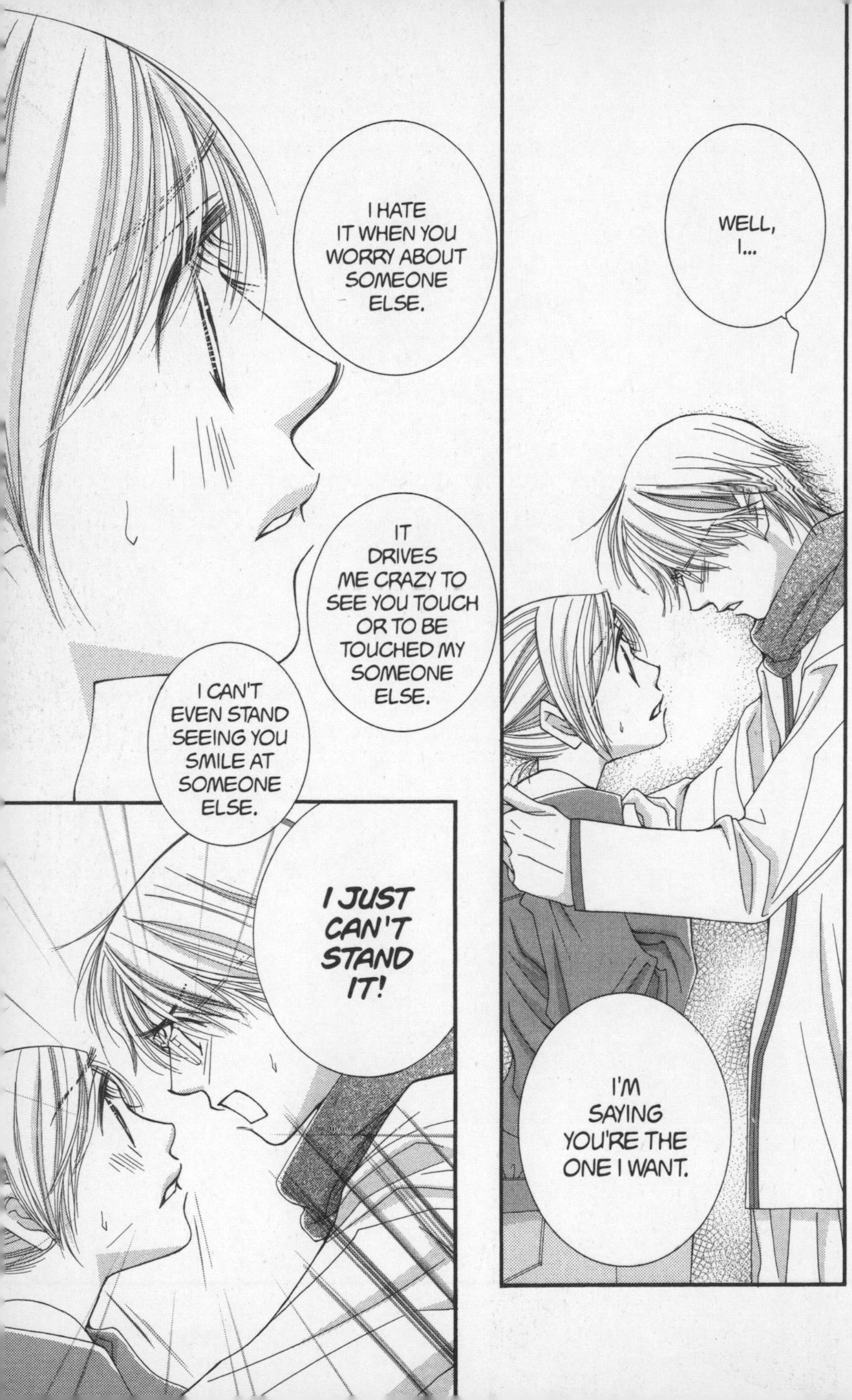
WELL, I...
I'M SAYING YOU'RE THE ONE I WANT.
I HATE IT WHEN YOU WORRY ABOUT SOMEONE ELSE.
IT DRIVES ME CRAZY TO SEE YOU TOUCH OR TO BE TOUCHED MY SOMEONE ELSE.
I CAN'T EVEN STAND SEEING YOU SMILE AT SOMEONE ELSE.
I JUST CAN'T STAND IT!

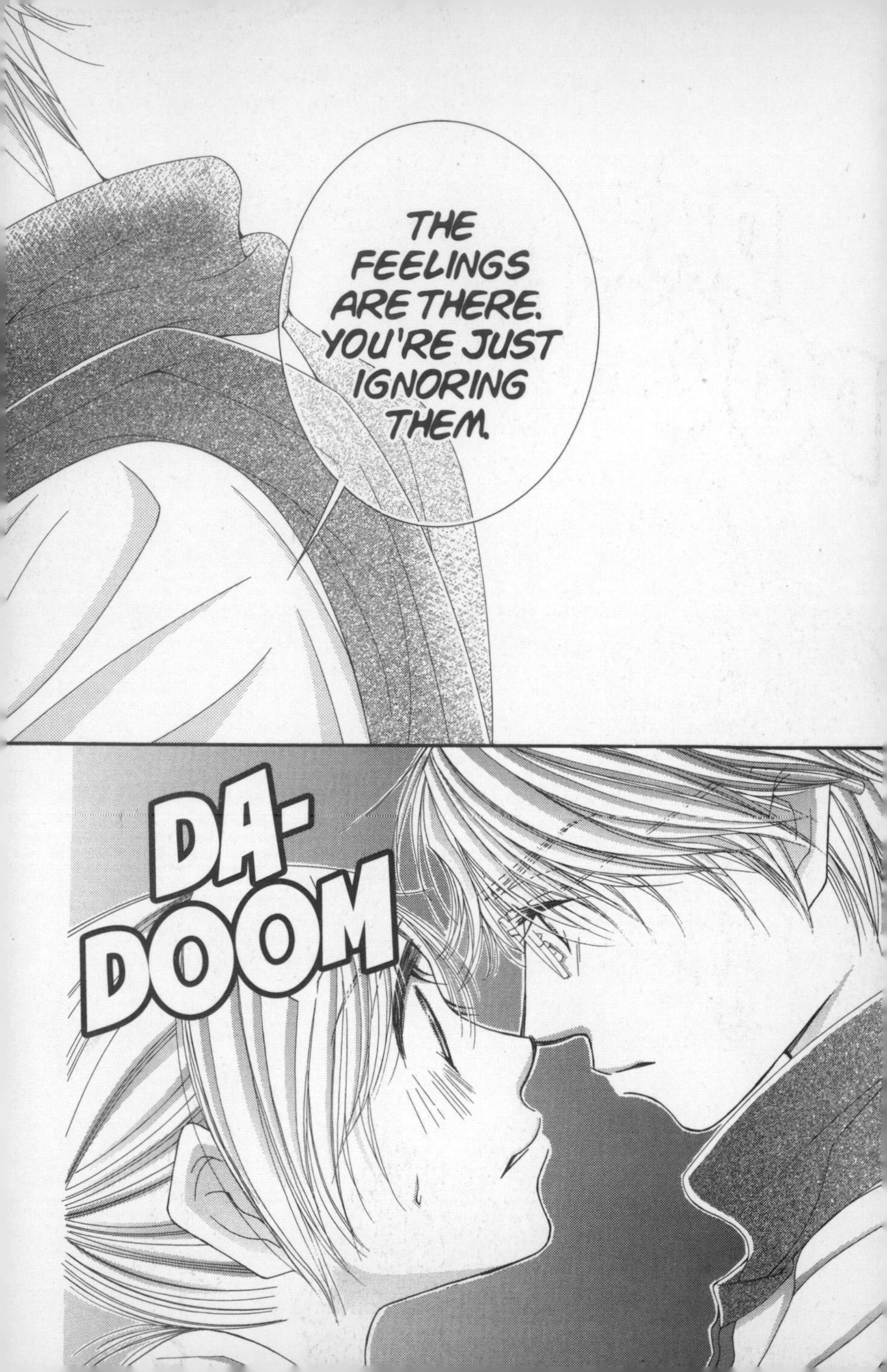
THE FEELINGS ARE THERE. YOU'RE JUST IGNORING THEM.
DA-DOOM

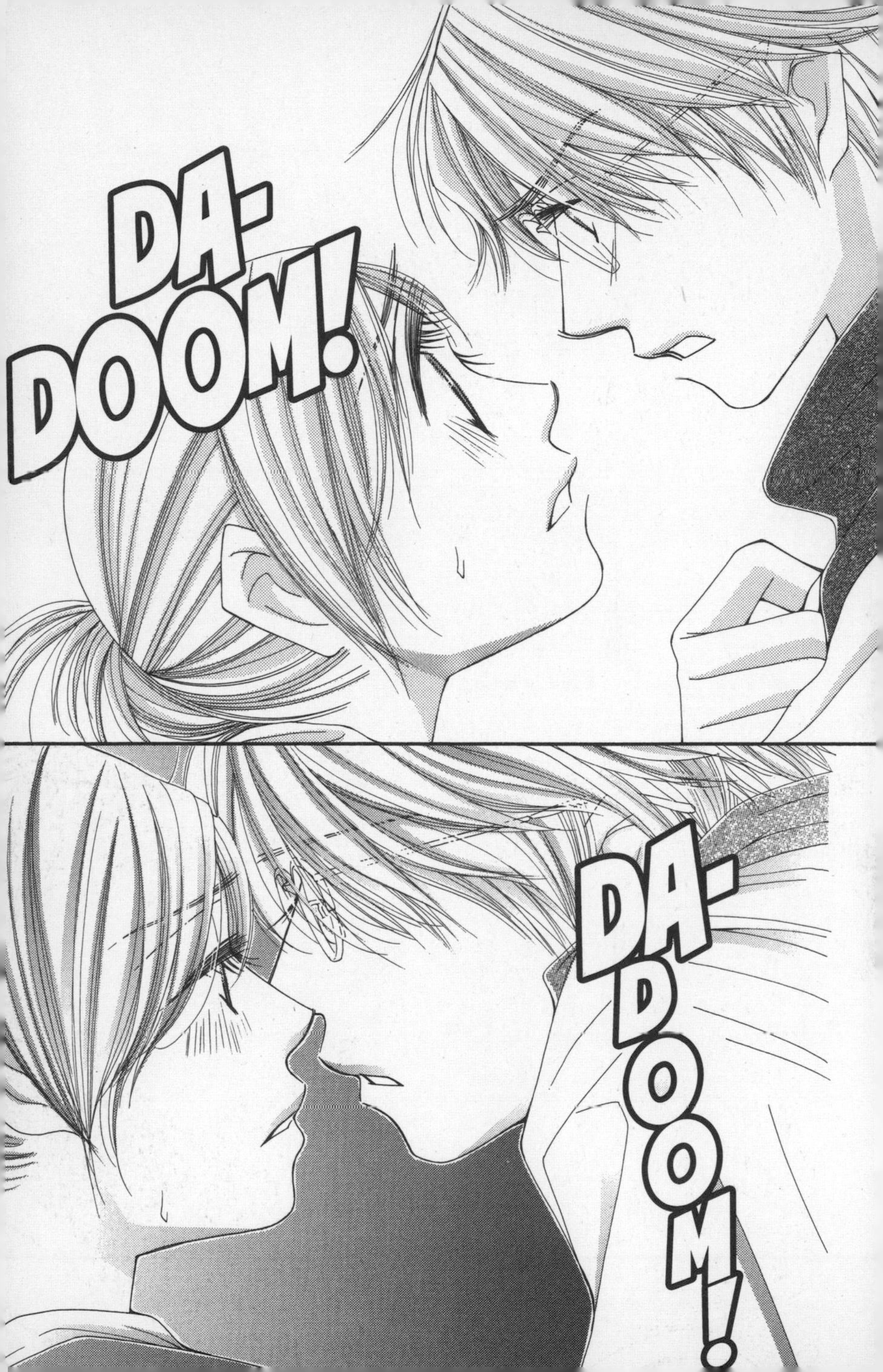
DA-DOOM!
DA-DOOM!

DA-DOOM

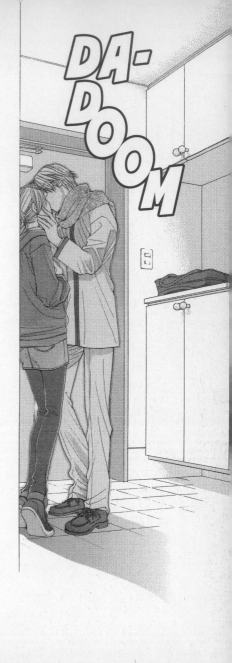

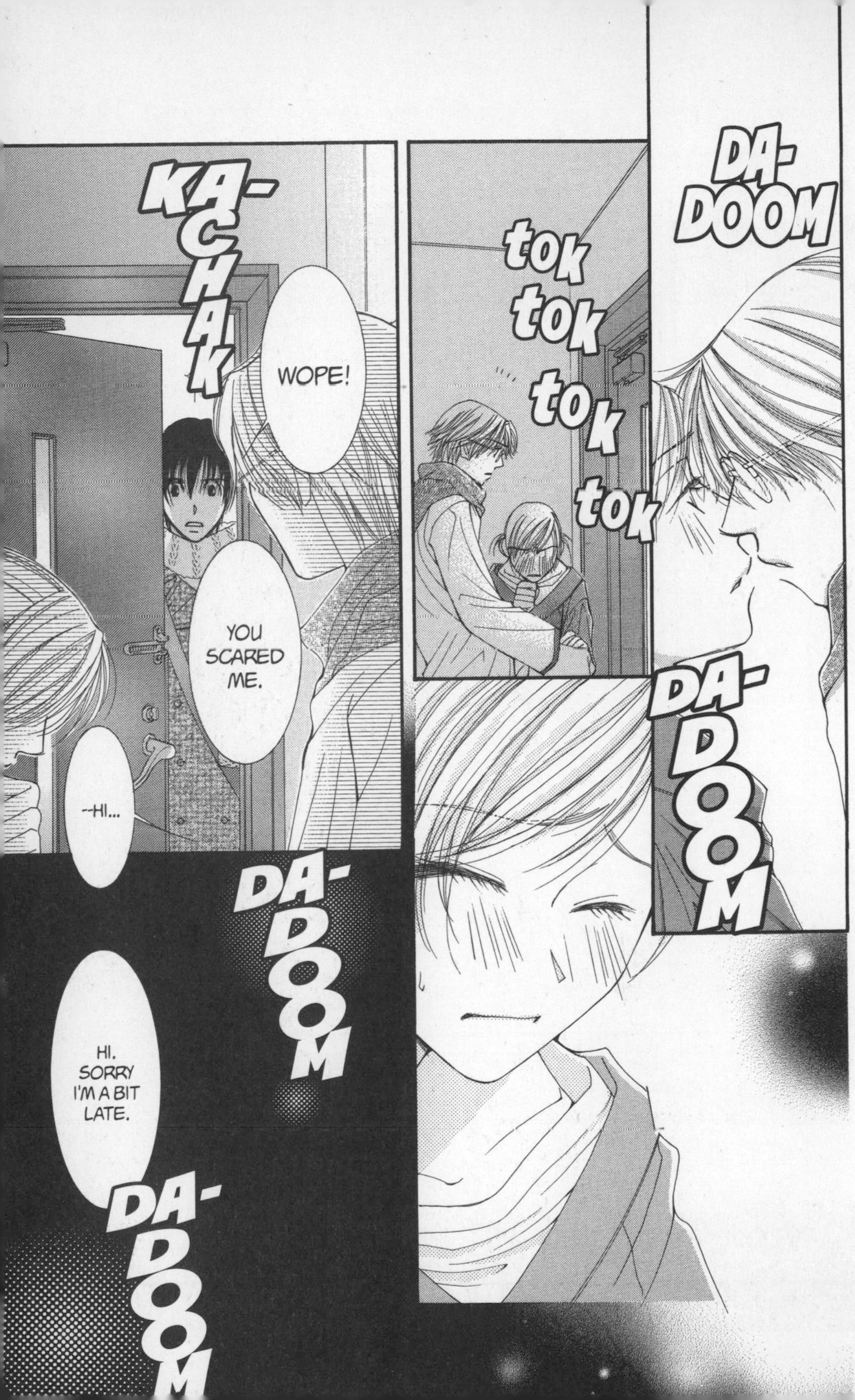
DA-DOOM
DA-DOOM
tok tok tok tok
KA-CHAK
WOPE!
YOU SCARED ME.
--HI...
DA-DOOM
HI. SORRY I'M A BIT LATE.
DA-DOOM

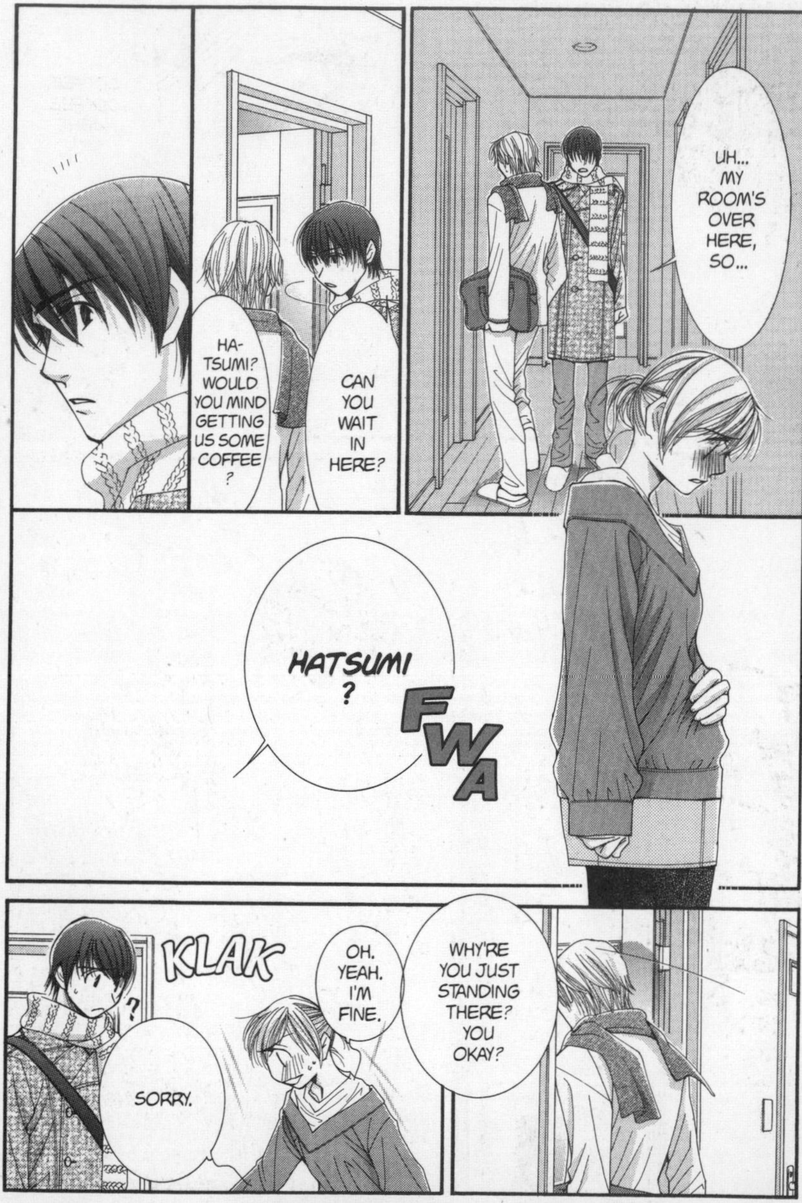
UH... MY ROOM'S OVER HERE, SO...
CAN YOU WAIT IN HERE?
HA-TSUMI? WOULD YOU MIND GETTING US SOME COFFEE?
HATSUMI?
FWA
WHY'RE YOU JUST STANDING THERE? YOU OKAY?
OH. YEAH. I'M FINE.
KLAK
SORRY.

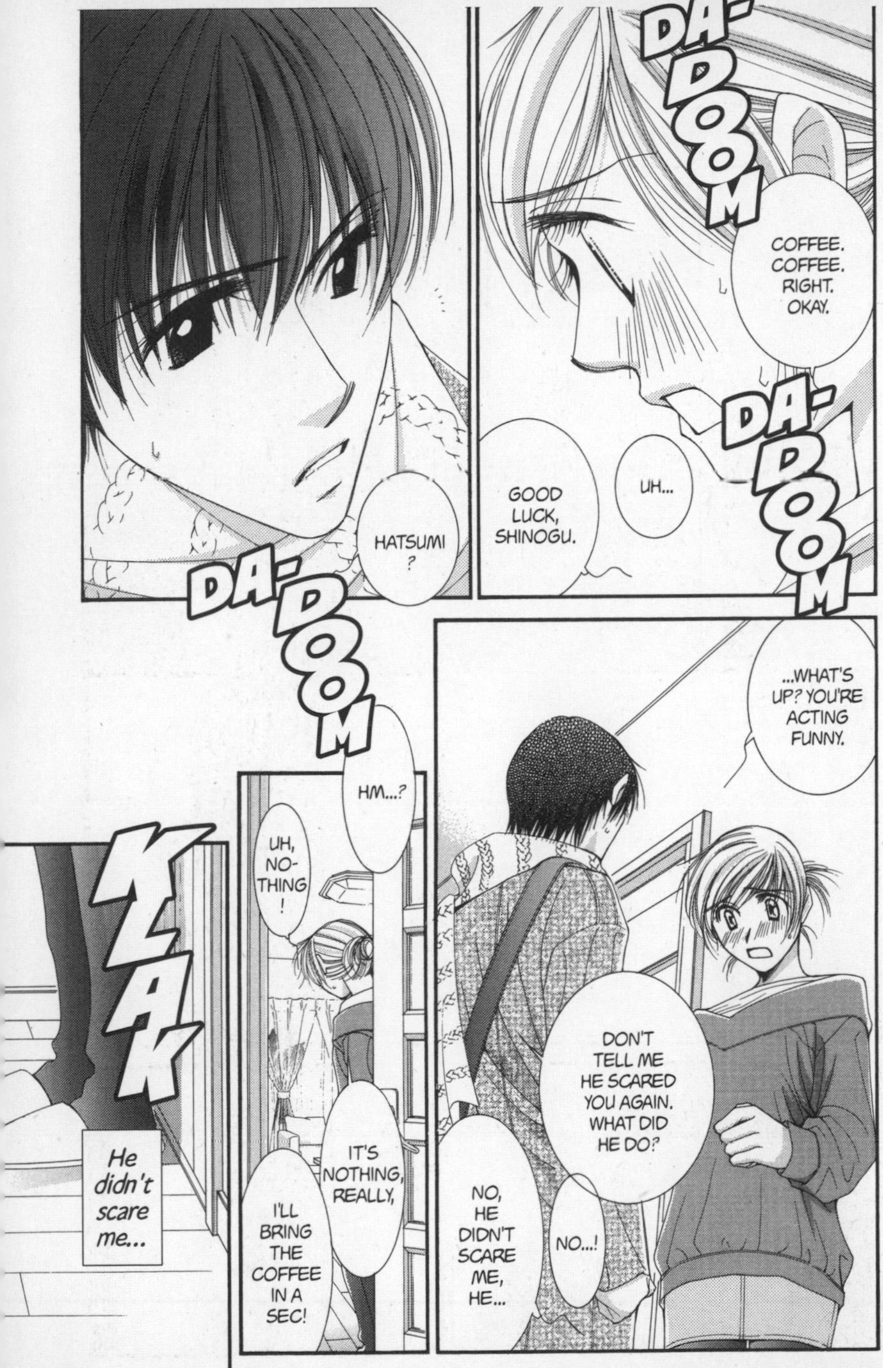
DA-DOOM
COFFEE. COFFEE. RIGHT. OKAY.
DA-DOOM
UH...
GOOD LUCK, SHINOGU.
HATSUMI?
DA-DOOM
...WHAT'S UP? YOU'RE ACTING FUNNY.
DON'T TELL ME HE SCARED YOU AGAIN. WHAT DID HE DO?
NO...!
NO, HE DIDN'T SCARE ME, HE...
HM...?
UH, NOTHING!
IT'S NOTHING, REALLY,
I'LL BRING THE COFFEE IN A SEC!
KLAK
He didn't scare me...

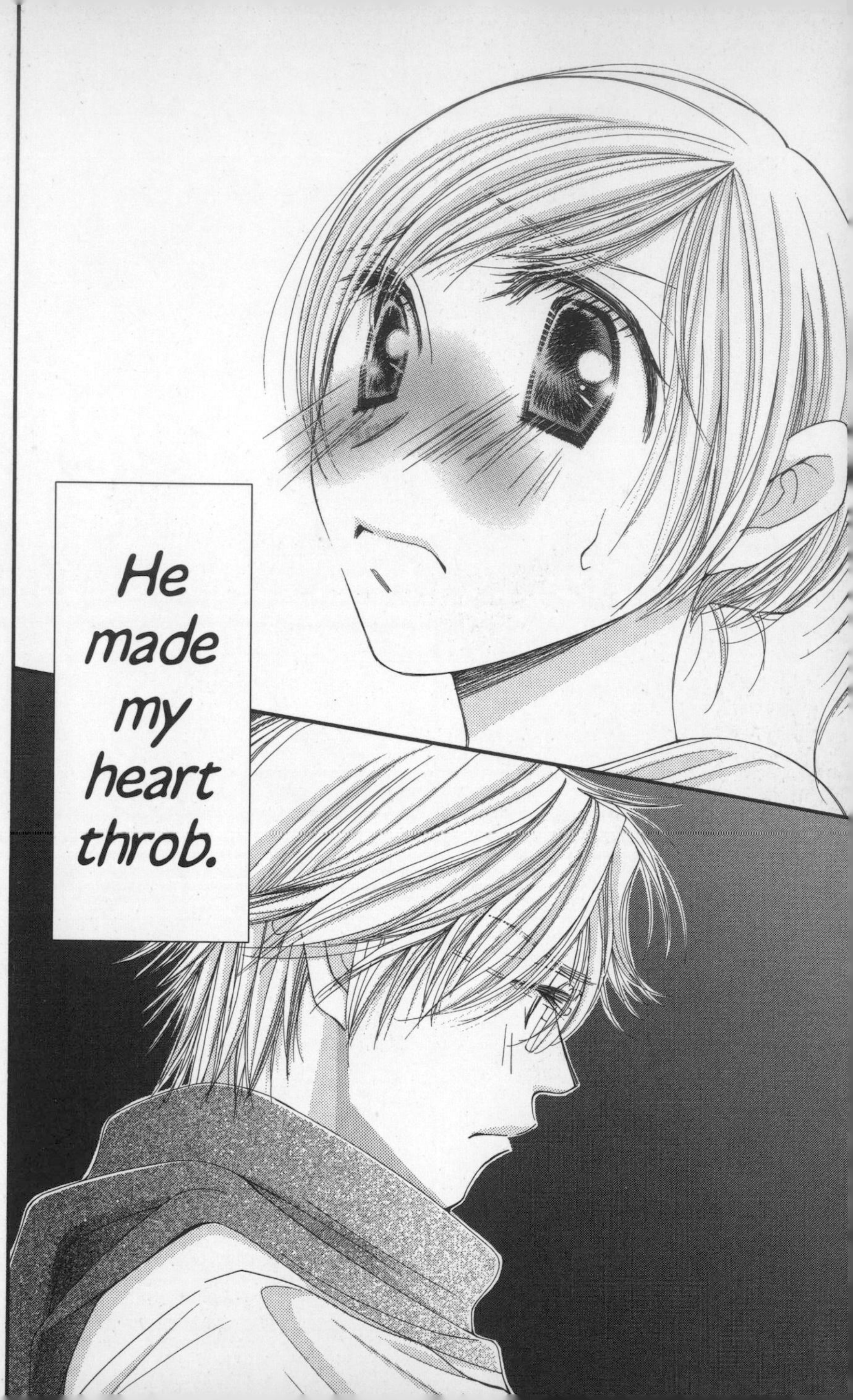
He made my heart throb.

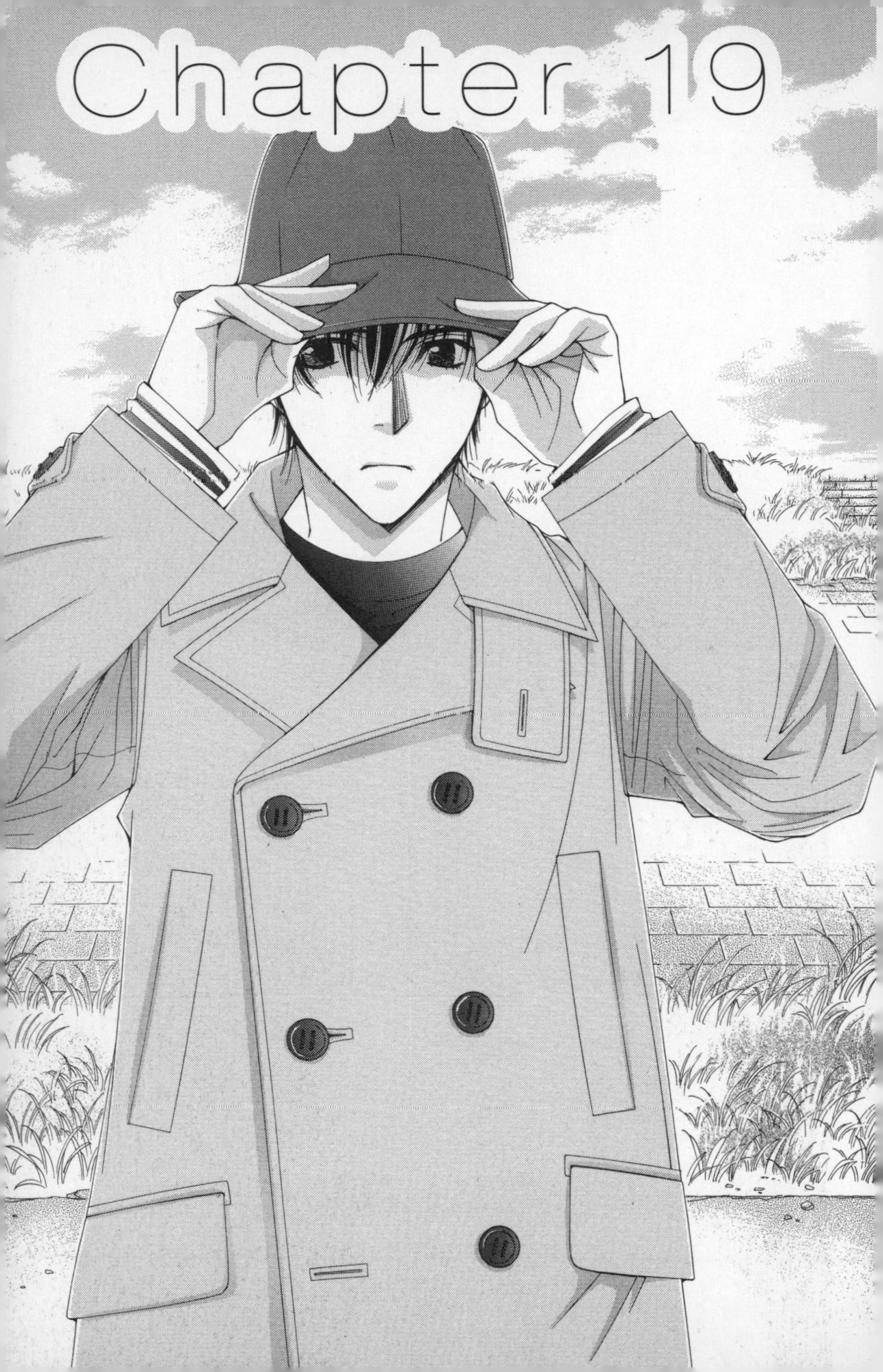
Chapter 19

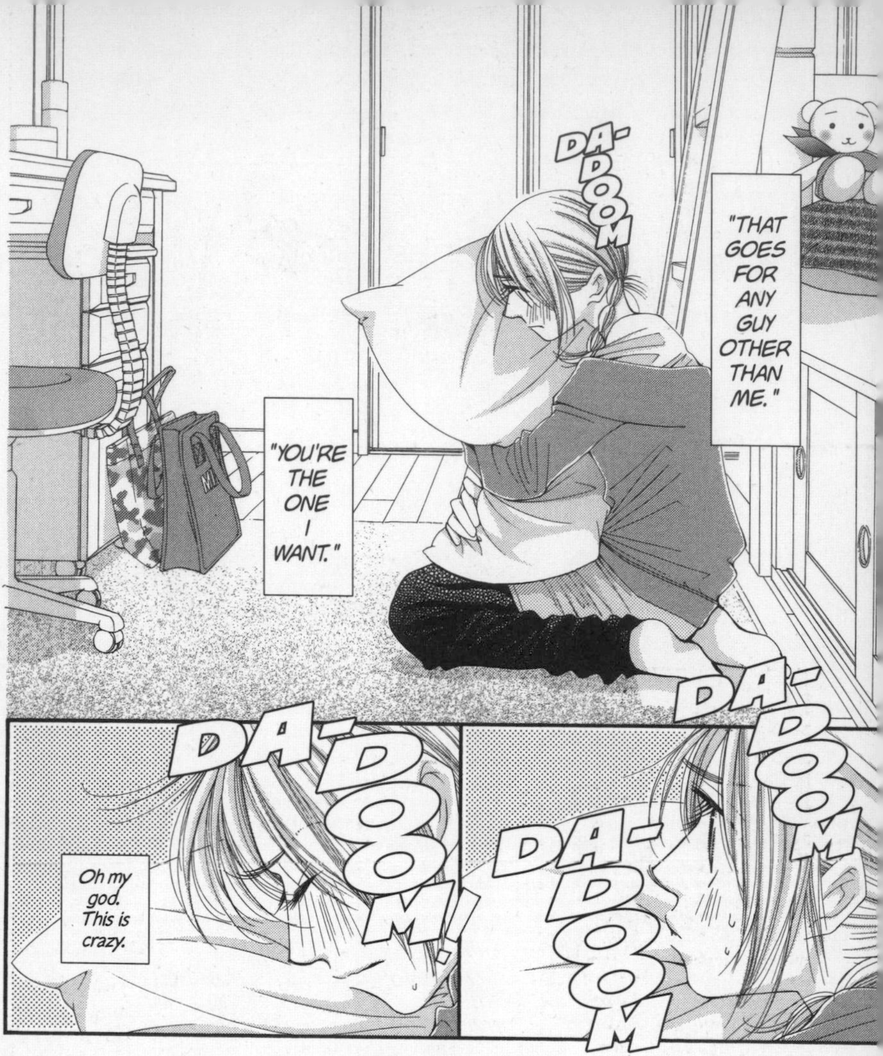
"THAT GOES FOR ANY GUY OTHER THAN ME."
DA-DOOM
"YOU'RE THE ONE I WANT."
DA-DOOM
DA-DOOM
DA-DOOM!
Oh my god. This is crazy.

hot gimmick

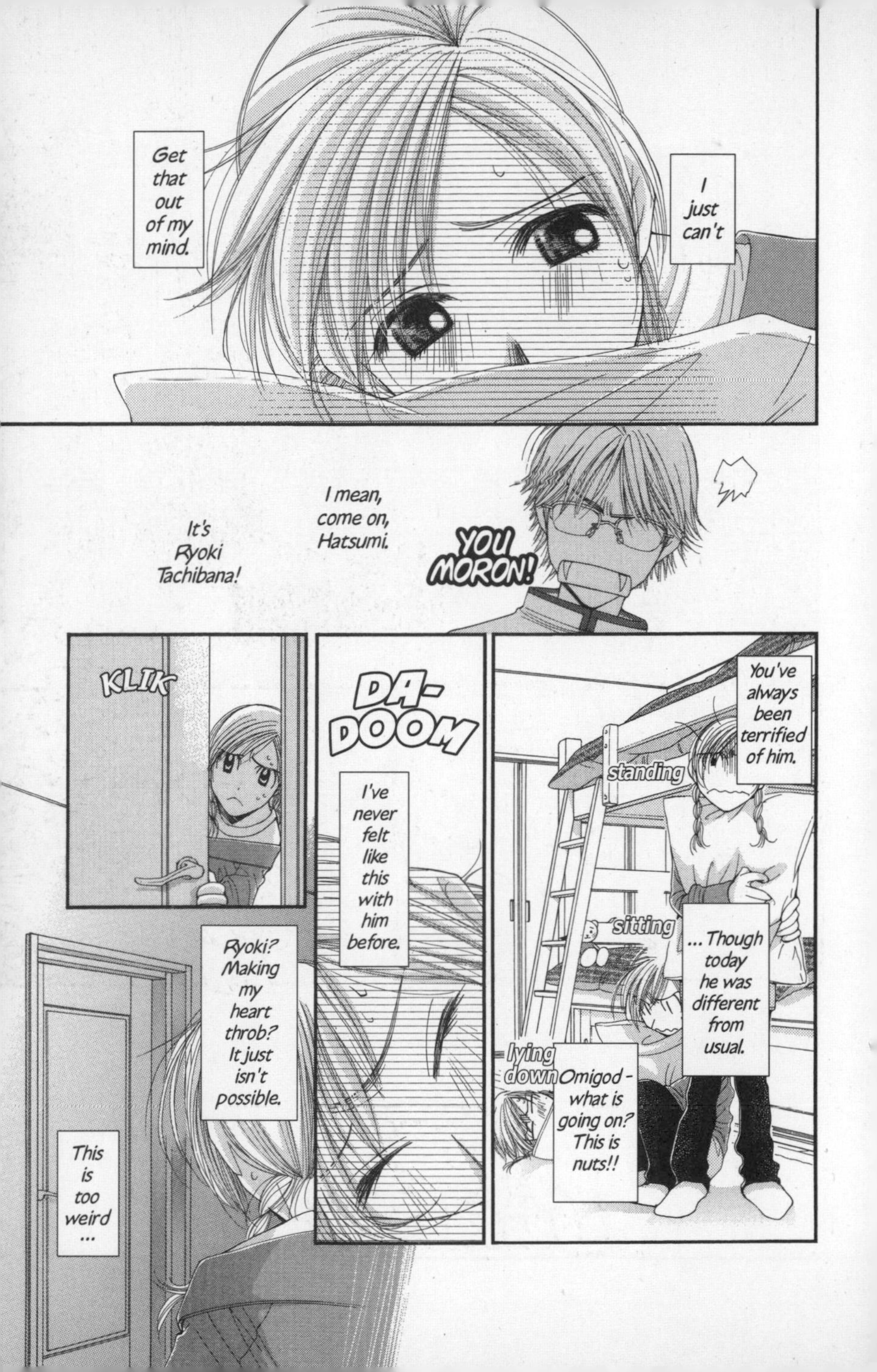

I just can't
Get that out of my mind.
YOU MORON!
I mean, come on, Hatsumi.
It's Ryoki Tachibana!
You've always been terrified of him.
standing
'sitting'
...Though today he was different from usual.
lying down
Omigod - what is going on? This is nuts!!
DA-DOOM
I've never felt like this with him before.
KLIK
Ryoki? Making my heart throb? It just isn't possible.
This is too weird ...

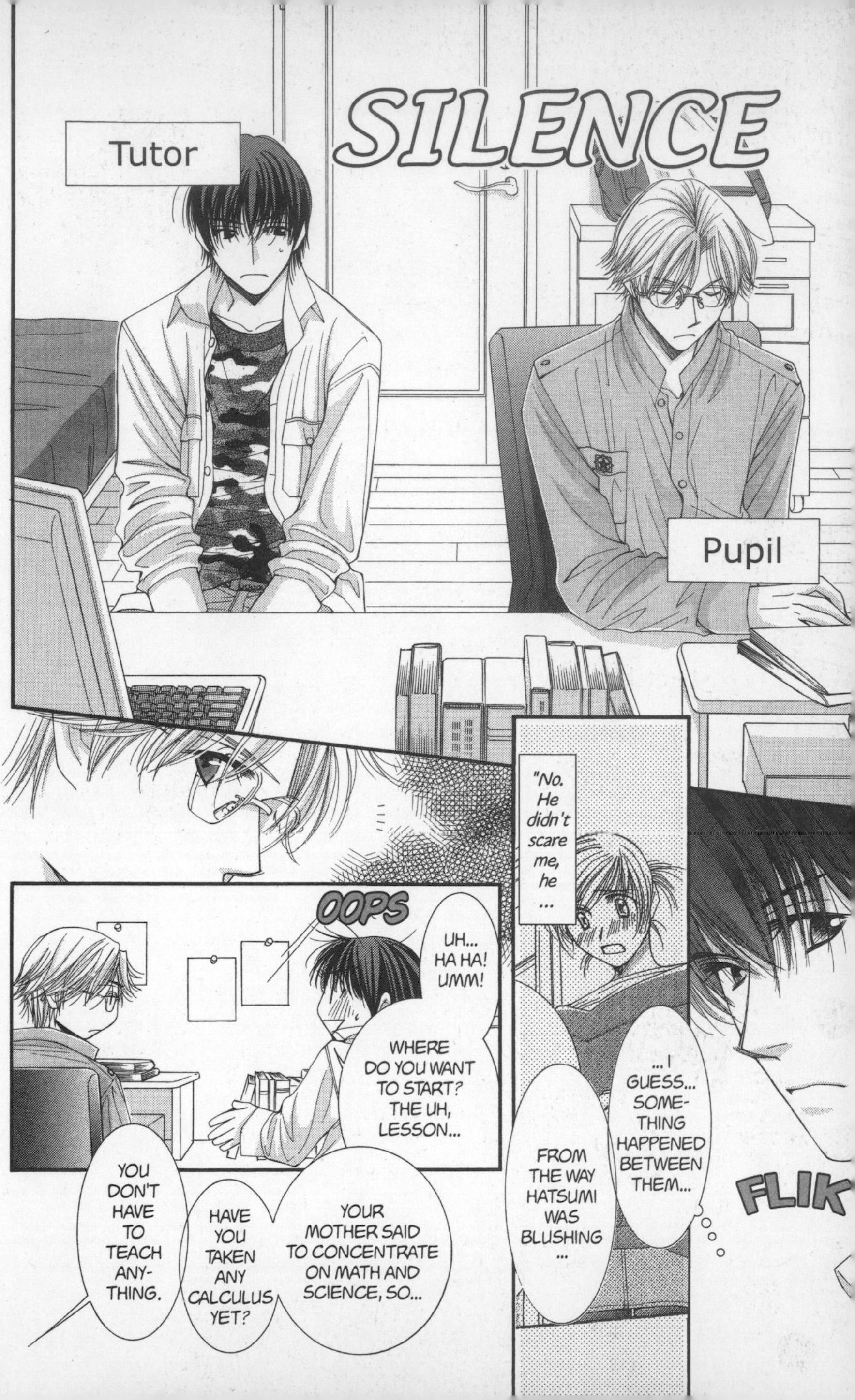
SILENCE
Pupil
Tutor
"No. He didn't scare me, he ...
FLIK
...I GUESS... SOME-THING HAPPENED BETWEEN THEM...
FROM THE WAY HATSUMI WAS BLUSHING ...
OOPS
UH... HA HA! UMM!
WHERE DO YOU WANT TO START? THE UH, LESSON...
YOUR MOTHER SAID TO CONCENTRATE ON MATH AND SCIENCE, SO...
HAVE YOU TAKEN ANY CALCULUS YET?
YOU DON'T HAVE TO TEACH ANY-THING.

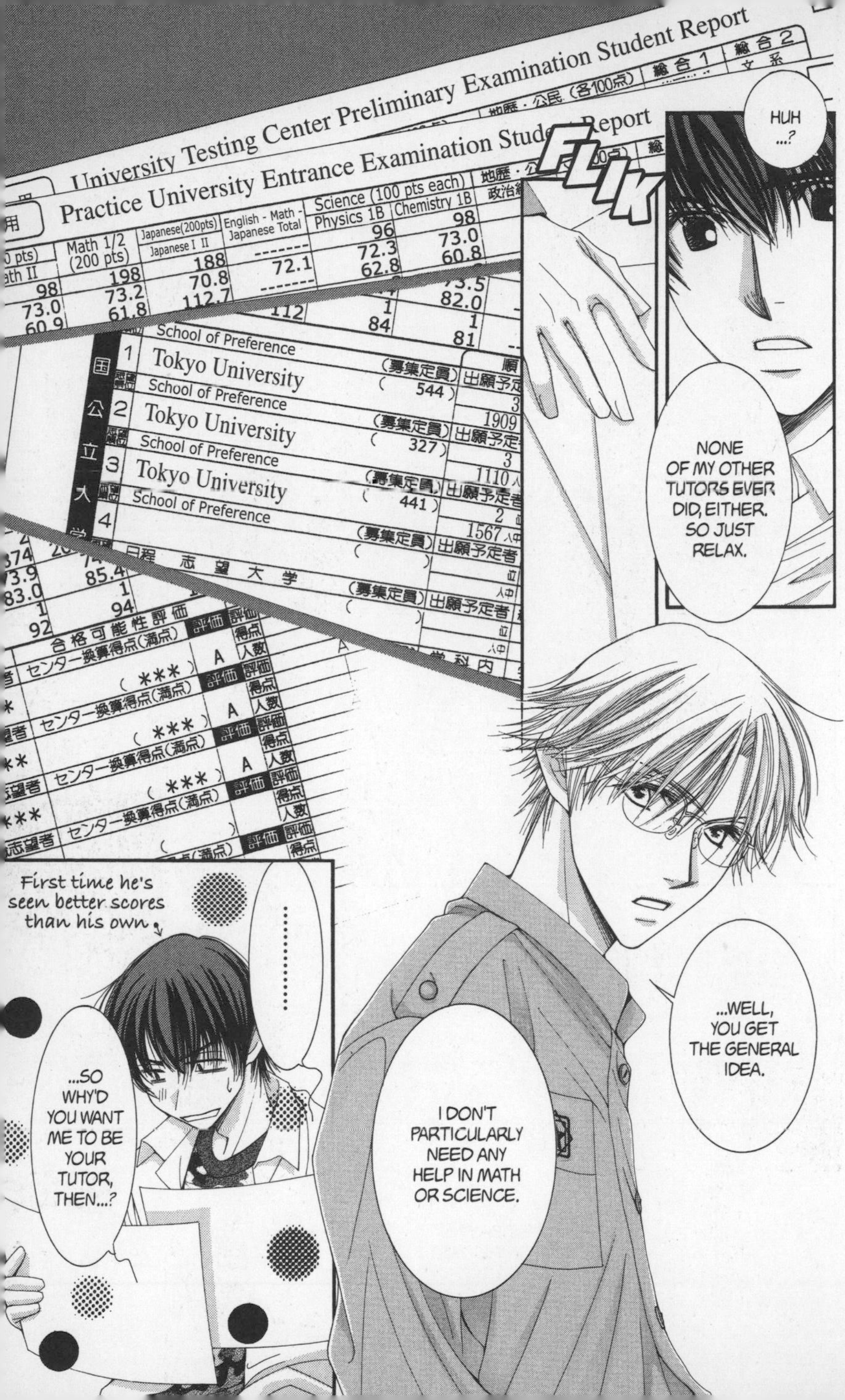
University Testing Center Preliminary Examination Student Report
Practice University Entrance Examination Student Report
Math 1/2 (200 pts)
Japanese(200pts) Japanese I II
English - Math - Japanese Total
Science (100 pts each)
Physics 1B
Chemistry 1B
School of Preference
Tokyo University
School of Preference
Tokyo University
School of Preference
Tokyo University
School of Preference
HUH ...?
FLIK
NONE OF MY OTHER TUTORS EVER DID, EITHER. SO JUST RELAX.
...WELL, YOU GET THE GENERAL IDEA.
I DON'T PARTICULARLY NEED ANY HELP IN MATH OR SCIENCE.
First time he's seen better scores than his own
......
...SO WHY'D YOU WANT ME TO BE YOUR TUTOR, THEN...?

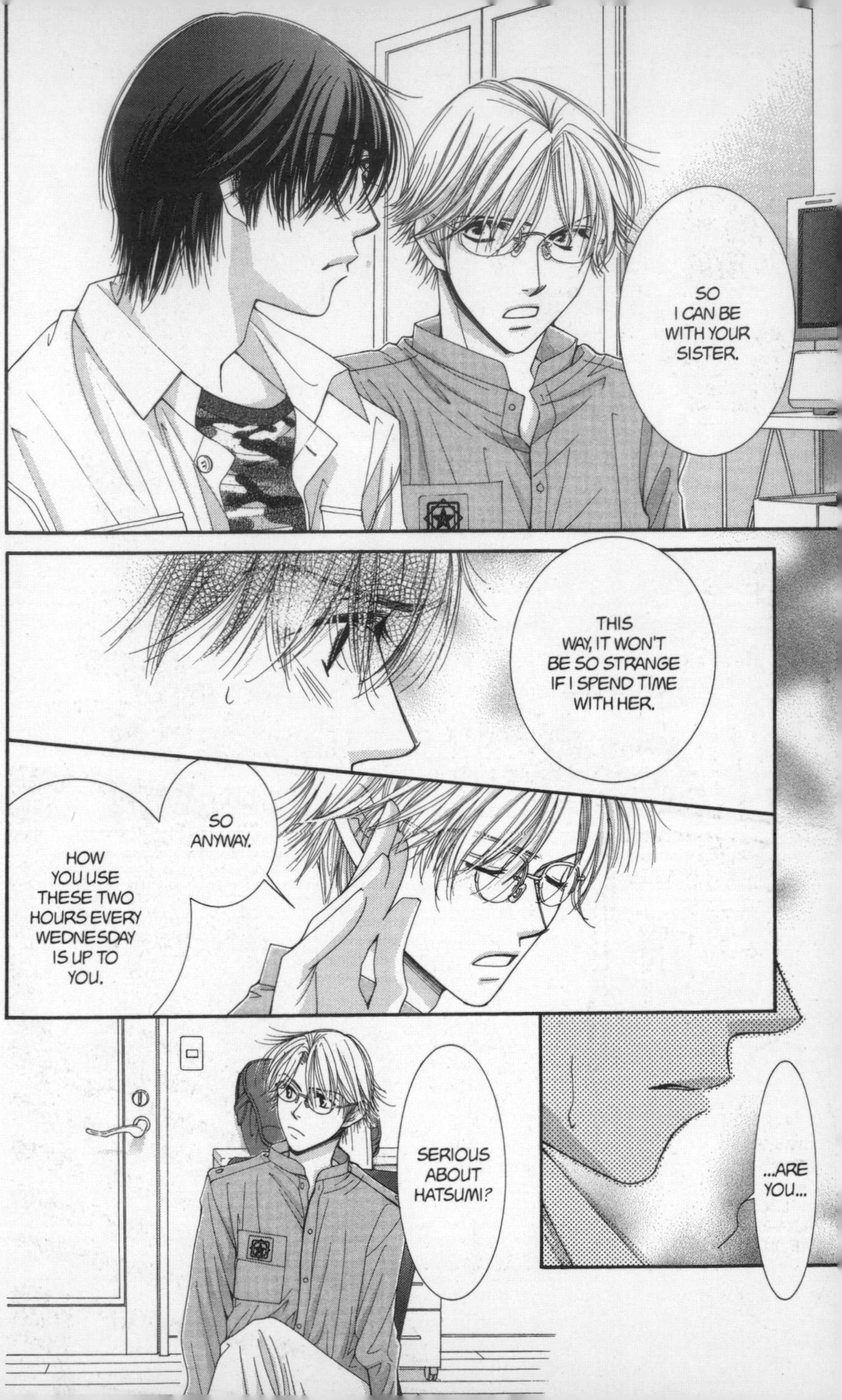
SO I CAN BE WITH YOUR SISTER.
THIS WAY, IT WON'T BE SO STRANGE IF I SPEND TIME WITH HER.
SO ANYWAY.
HOW YOU USE THESE TWO HOURS EVERY WEDNESDAY IS UP TO YOU.
...ARE YOU...
SERIOUS ABOUT HATSUMI?

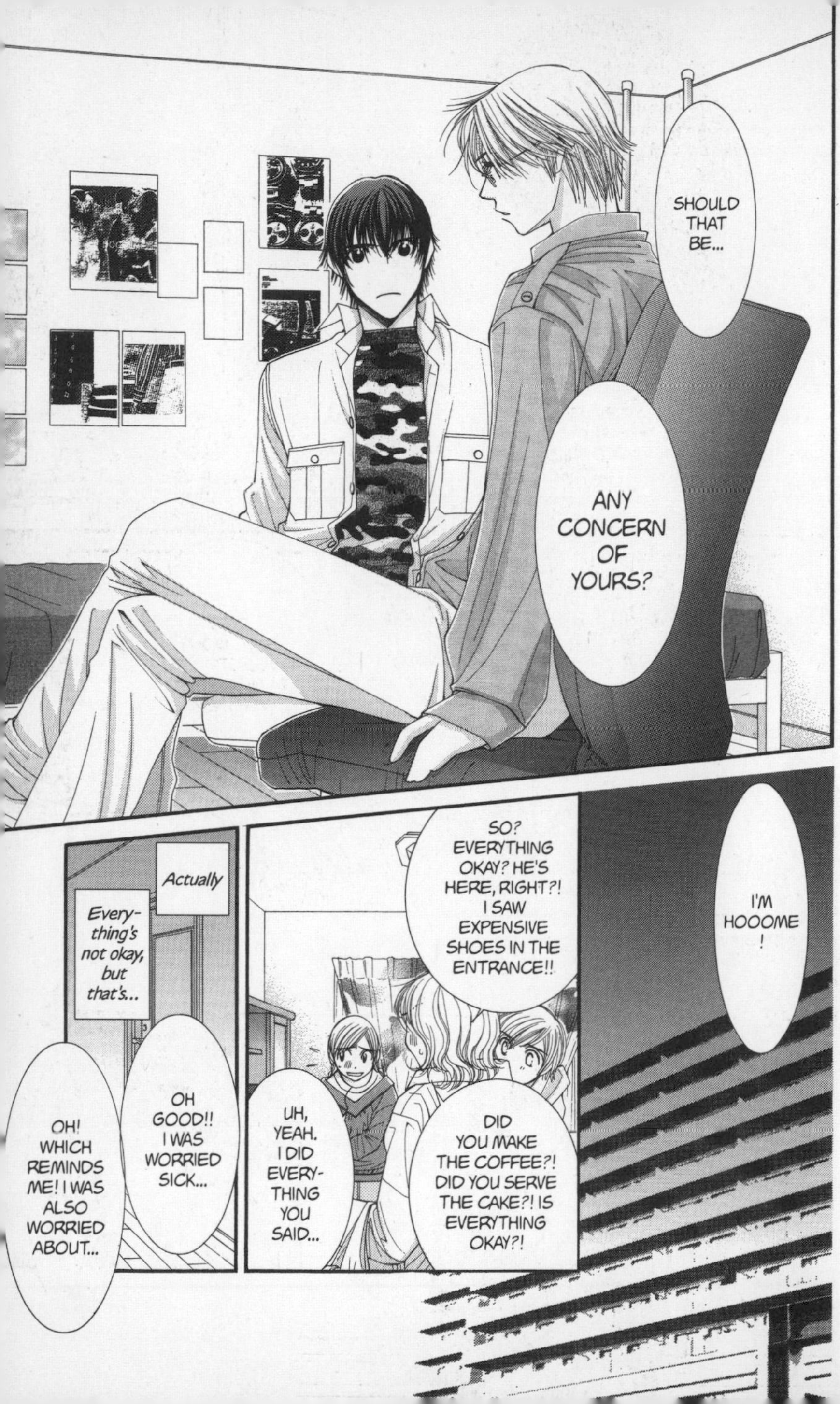
SHOULD THAT BE...
ANY CONCERN OF YOURS?
I'M HOOOME!
SO? EVERYTHING OKAY? HE'S HERE, RIGHT?! I SAW EXPENSIVE SHOES IN THE ENTRANCE!!
DID YOU MAKE THE COFFEE?! DID YOU SERVE THE CAKE?! IS EVERYTHING OKAY?!
UH, YEAH. I DID EVERY-THING YOU SAID...
Actually
Every-thing's not okay, but that's...
OH GOOD!! I WAS WORRIED SICK...
OH! WHICH REMINDS ME! I WAS ALSO WORRIED ABOUT...

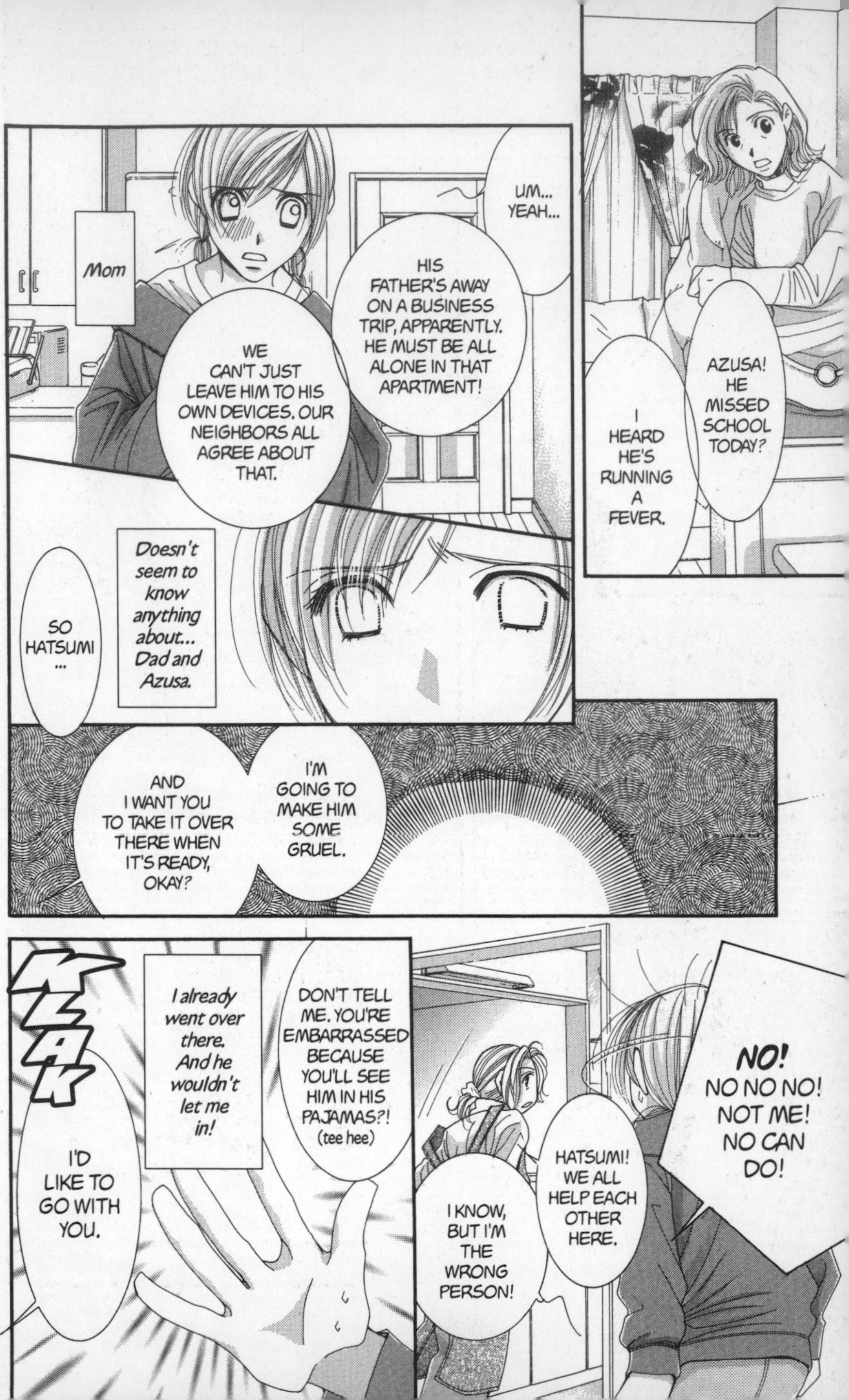

AZUSA! HE MISSED SCHOOL TODAY?
I HEARD HE'S RUNNING A FEVER.
UM... YEAH...
HIS FATHER'S AWAY ON A BUSINESS TRIP, APPARENTLY. HE MUST BE ALL ALONE IN THAT APARTMENT!
WE CAN'T JUST LEAVE HIM TO HIS OWN DEVICES. OUR NEIGHBORS ALL AGREE ABOUT THAT.
Mom
Doesn't seem to know anything about... Dad and Azusa.
SO HATSUMI ...
I'M GOING TO MAKE HIM SOME GRUEL.
AND I WANT YOU TO TAKE IT OVER THERE WHEN IT'S READY, OKAY?
NO! NO NO NO! NOT ME! NO CAN DO!
HATSUMI! WE ALL HELP EACH OTHER HERE.
I KNOW, BUT I'M THE WRONG PERSON!
DON'T TELL ME. YOU'RE EMBARRASSED BECAUSE YOU'LL SEE HIM IN HIS PAJAMAS?! (tee hee)
I already went over there. And he wouldn't let me in!
KLAK
I'D LIKE TO GO WITH YOU.

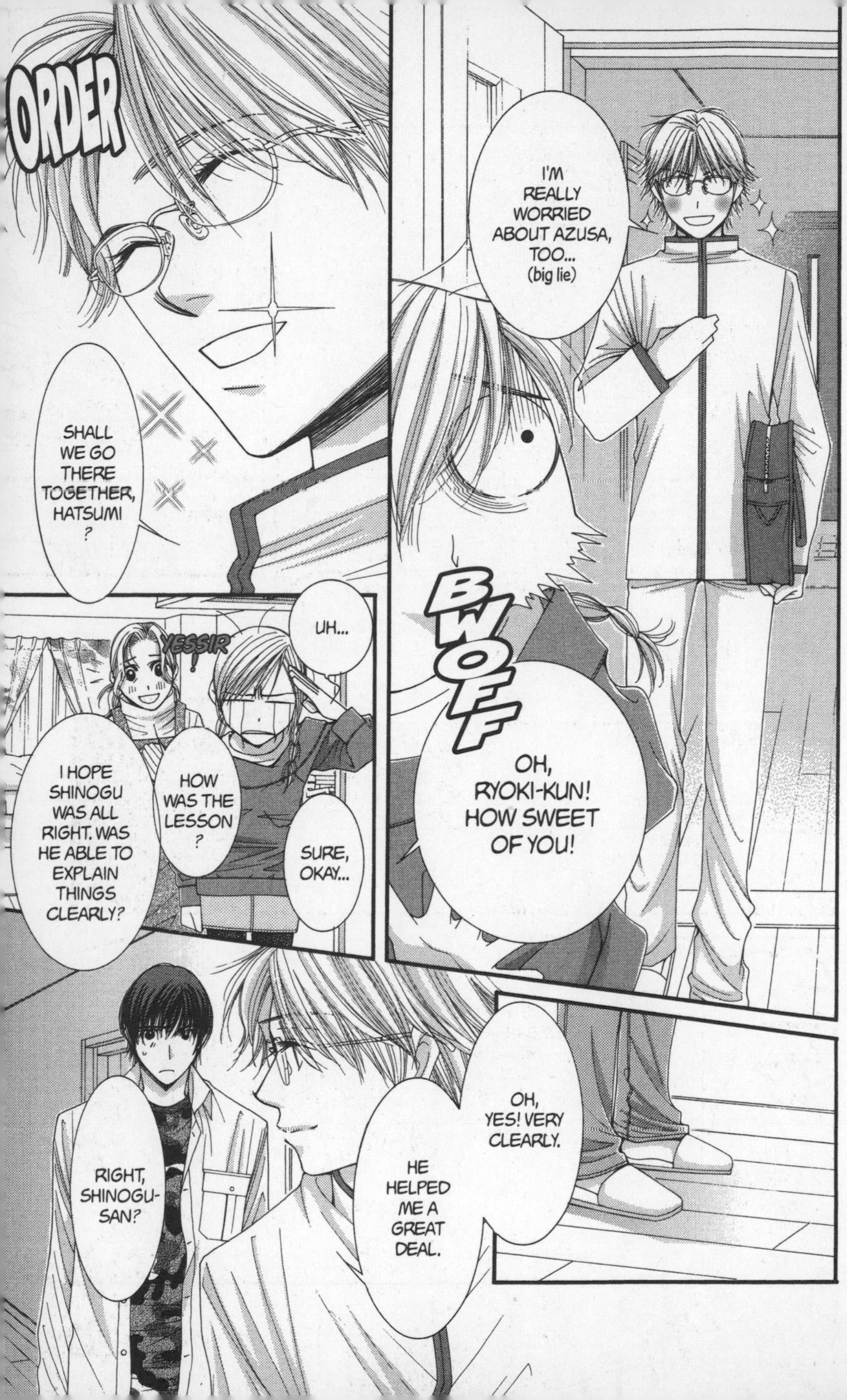
I'M REALLY WORRIED ABOUT AZUSA, TOO...
(big lie)
BWOFF
OH, RYOKI-KUN! HOW SWEET OF YOU!
ORDER
SHALL WE GO THERE TOGETHER, HATSUMI?
UH...
YESSIR
!
SURE, OKAY...
HOW WAS THE LESSON?
I HOPE SHINOGU WAS ALL RIGHT. WAS HE ABLE TO EXPLAIN THINGS CLEARLY?
OH, YES! VERY CLEARLY.
HE HELPED ME A GREAT DEAL.
RIGHT, SHINOGU-SAN?

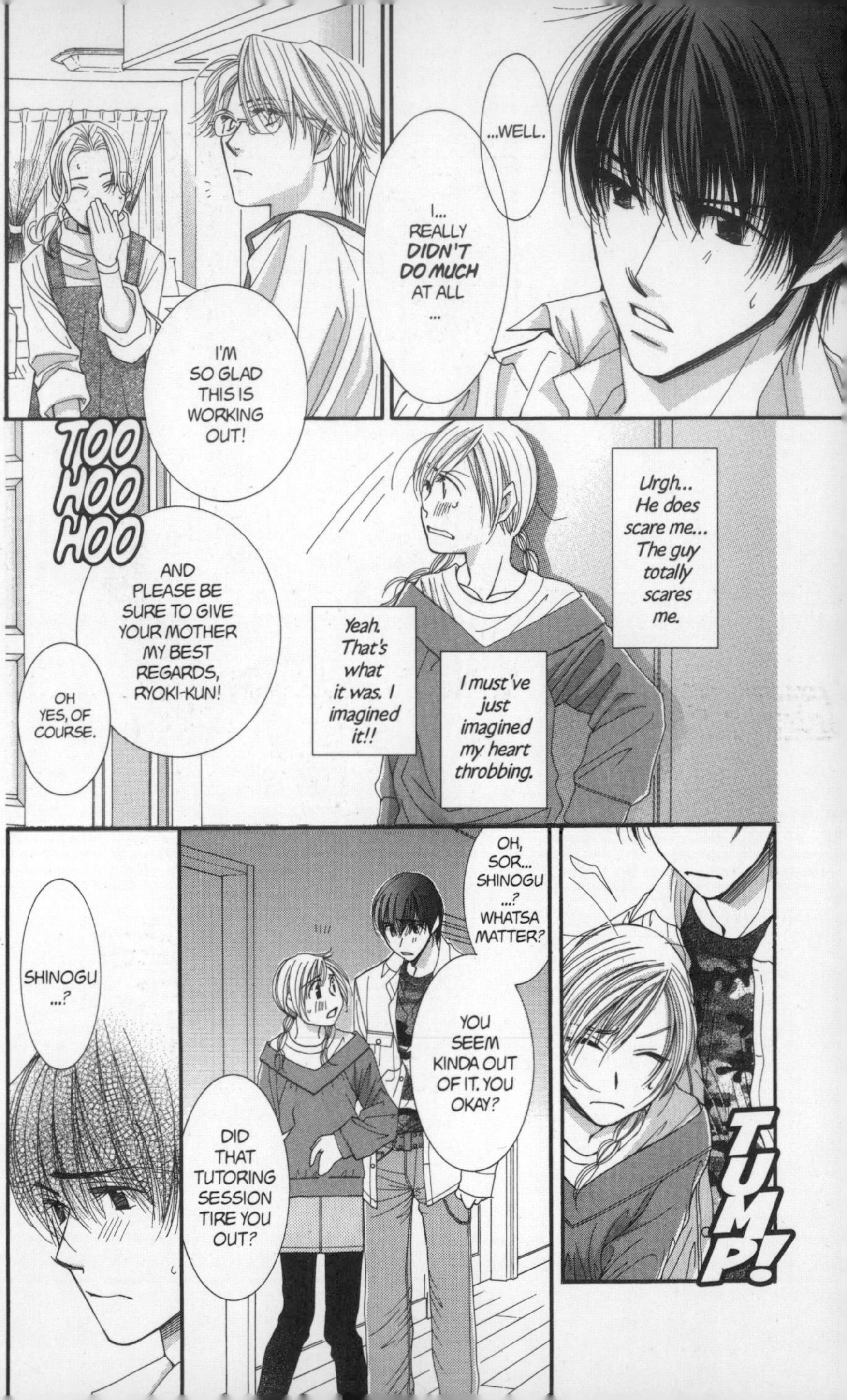
...WELL.
I... REALLY **DIDN'T DO MUCH** AT ALL ...
I'M SO GLAD THIS IS WORKING OUT!
Urgh... He does scare me... The guy totally scares me.
I must've just imagined my heart throbbing.
Yeah. That's what it was. I imagined it!!
TOO HOO HOO
AND PLEASE BE SURE TO GIVE YOUR MOTHER MY BEST REGARDS, RYOKI-KUN!
OH YES, OF COURSE.
TUMP!
OH, SOR... SHINOGU ...? WHATSA MATTER?
YOU SEEM KINDA OUT OF IT. YOU OKAY?
DID THAT TUTORING SESSION TIRE YOU OUT?
SHINOGU ...?

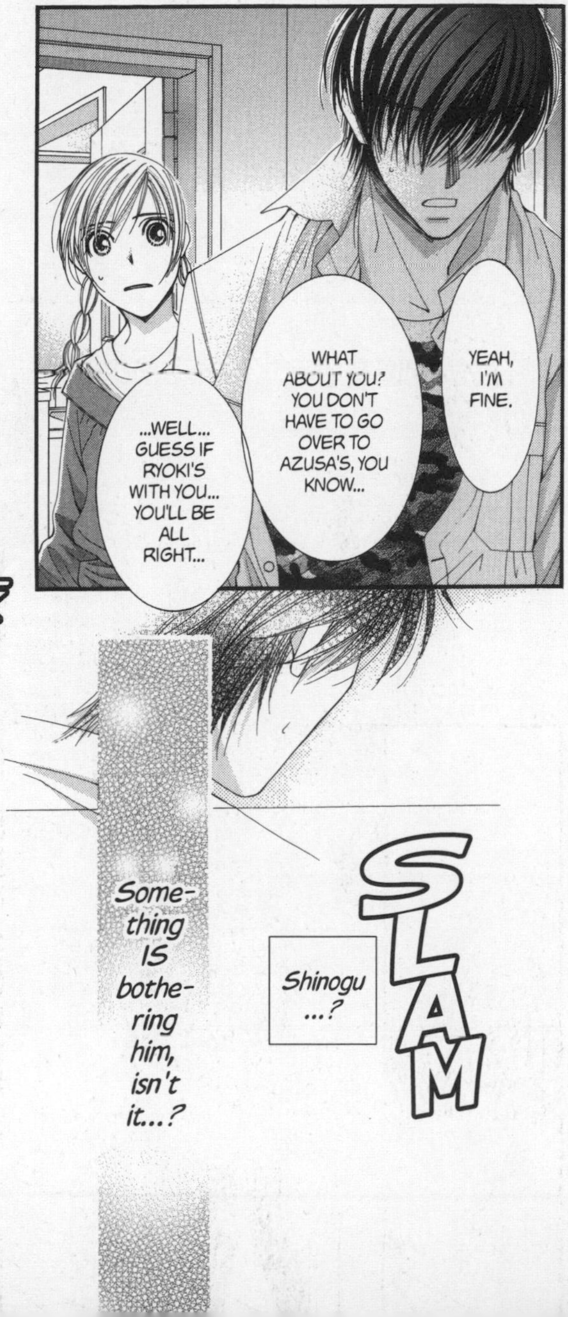
YEAH, I'M FINE.
WHAT ABOUT YOU? YOU DON'T HAVE TO GO OVER TO AZUSA'S, YOU KNOW...
...WELL... GUESS IF RYOKI'S WITH YOU... YOU'LL BE ALL RIGHT...
SLAM
Shinogu ...?
Some-thing IS bothe-ring him, isn't it...?

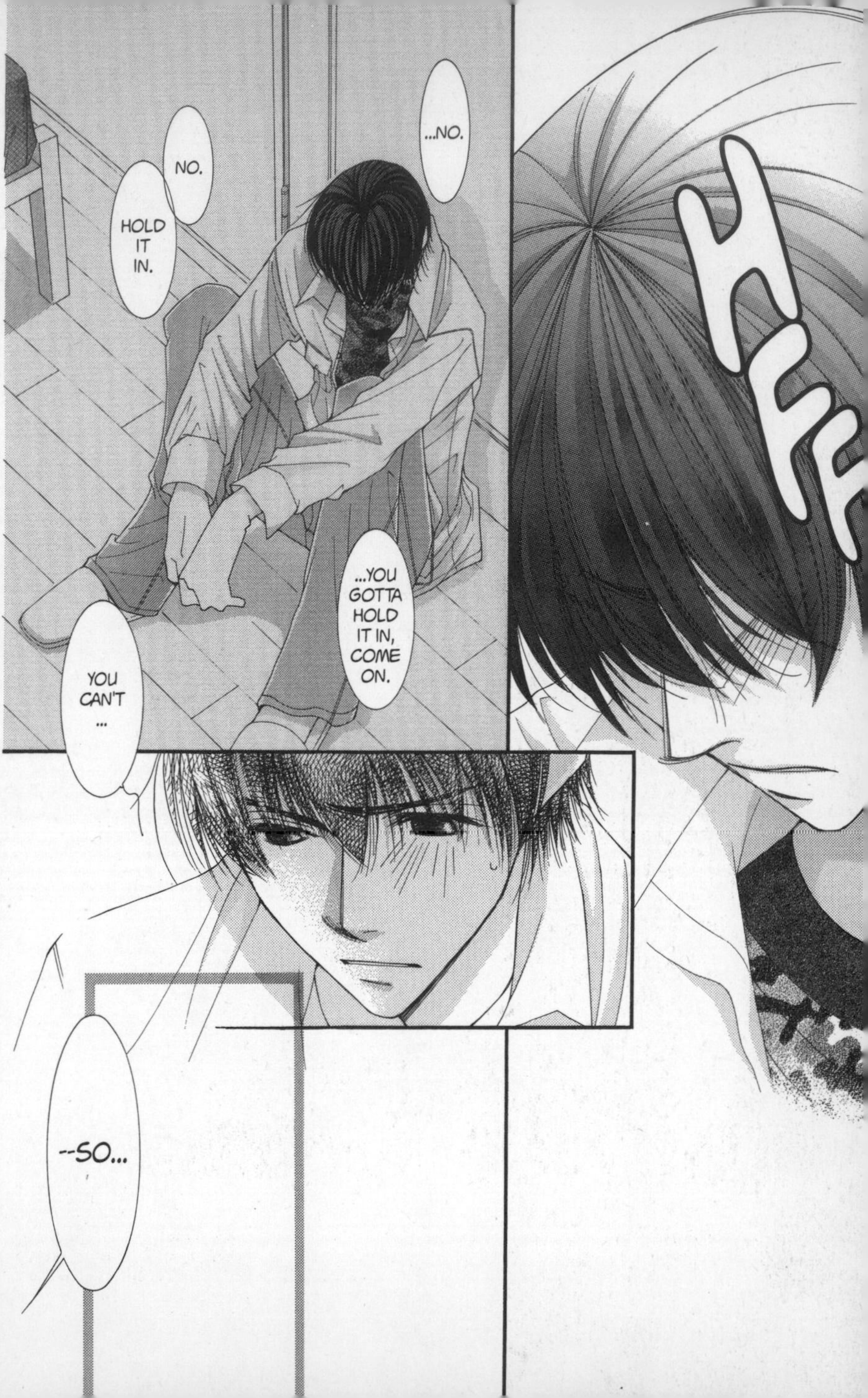
...NO.
NO.
HOLD IT IN.
...YOU GOTTA HOLD IT IN, COME ON.
YOU CAN'T ...
--SO...

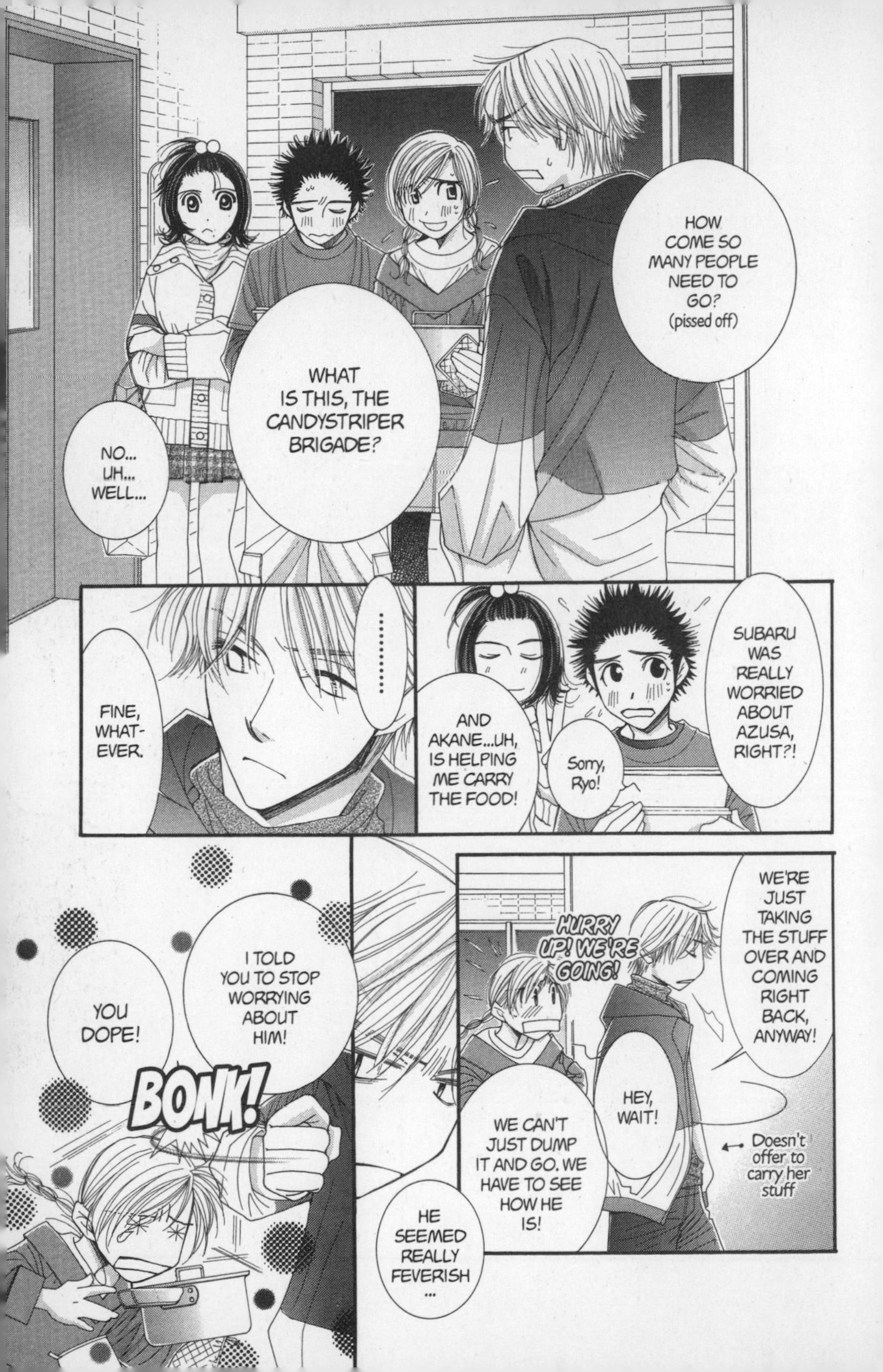
HOW COME SO MANY PEOPLE NEED TO GO? (pissed off)
WHAT IS THIS, THE CANDYSTRIPER BRIGADE?
NO... UH... WELL...
SUBARU WAS REALLY WORRIED ABOUT AZUSA, RIGHT?!
Sorry, Ryo!
AND AKANE...UH, IS HELPING ME CARRY THE FOOD!
......
FINE, WHAT-EVER.
WE'RE JUST TAKING THE STUFF OVER AND COMING RIGHT BACK, ANYWAY!
HURRY UP! WE'RE GOING!
HEY, WAIT!
WE CAN'T JUST DUMP IT AND GO. WE HAVE TO SEE HOW HE IS!
Doesn't offer to carry her stuff
HE SEEMED REALLY FEVERISH ...
I TOLD YOU TO STOP WORRYING ABOUT HIM!
YOU DOPE!
BONK!

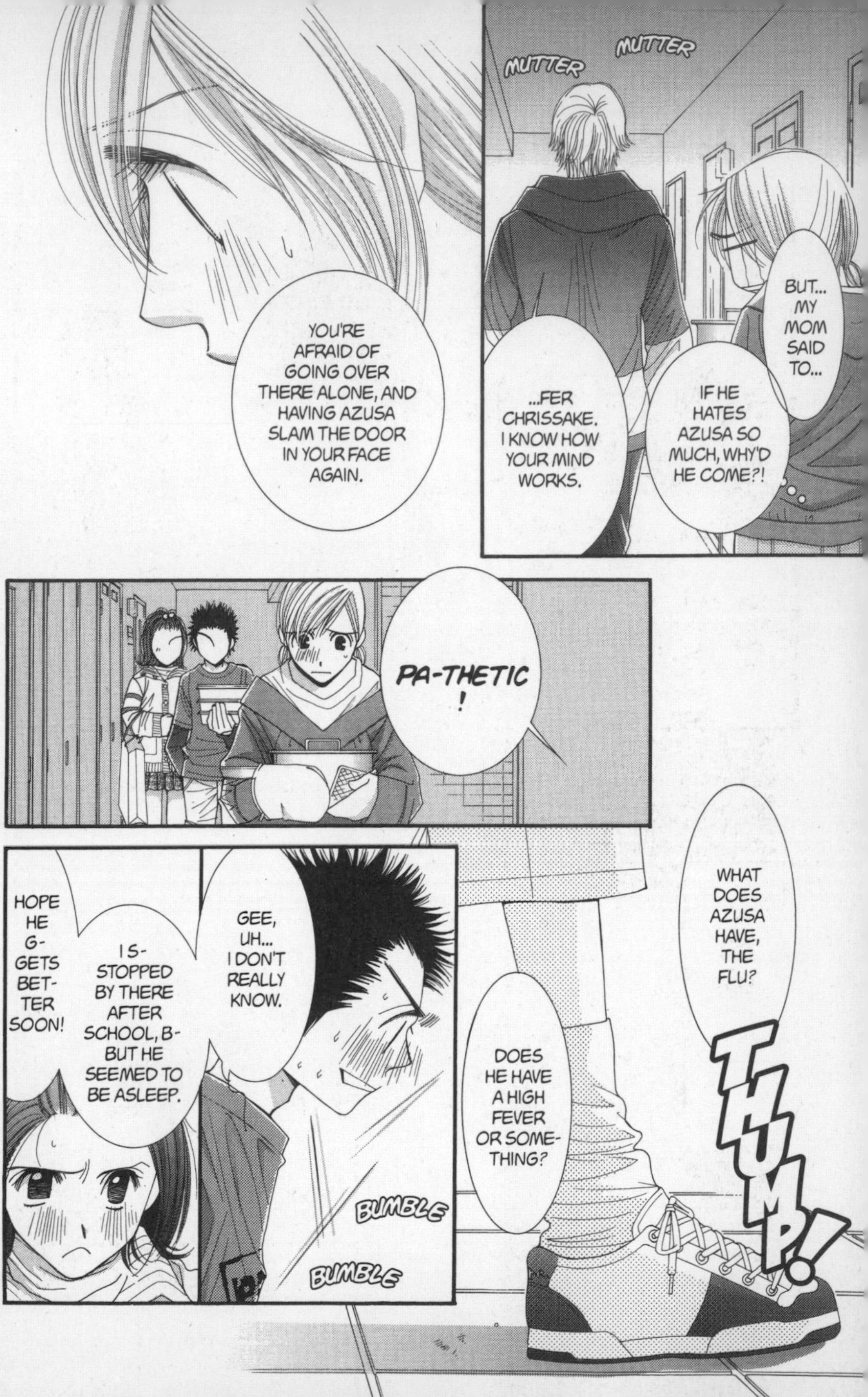
MUTTER
MUTTER
BUT... MY MOM SAID TO...
IF HE HATES AZUSA SO MUCH, WHY'D HE COME?!
...FER CHRISSAKE. I KNOW HOW YOUR MIND WORKS.
YOU'RE AFRAID OF GOING OVER THERE ALONE, AND HAVING AZUSA SLAM THE DOOR IN YOUR FACE AGAIN.
PA-THETIC!
WHAT DOES AZUSA HAVE, THE FLU?
DOES HE HAVE A HIGH FEVER OR SOMETHING?
THUMP!
GEE, UH... I DON'T REALLY KNOW.
BUMBLE
BUMBLE
I S-STOPPED BY THERE AFTER SCHOOL, B-BUT HE SEEMED TO BE ASLEEP.
HOPE HE G-GETS BET-TER SOON!

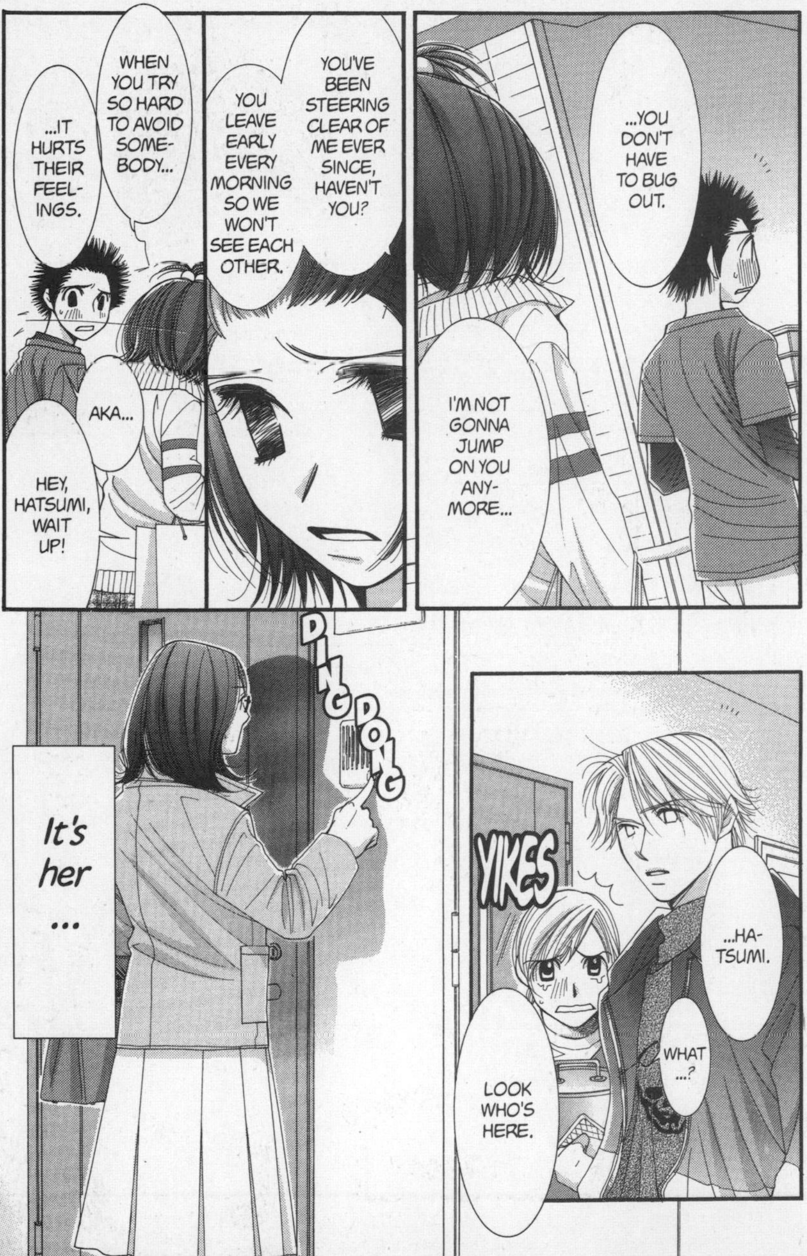
...YOU DON'T HAVE TO BUG OUT.
I'M NOT GONNA JUMP ON YOU ANYMORE...
YOU'VE BEEN STEERING CLEAR OF ME EVER SINCE, HAVEN'T YOU?
YOU LEAVE EARLY EVERY MORNING SO WE WON'T SEE EACH OTHER.
WHEN YOU TRY SO HARD TO AVOID SOME-BODY...
...IT HURTS THEIR FEEL-INGS.
AKA...
HEY, HATSUMI, WAIT UP!
...HA-TSUMI.
YIKES
WHAT ...?
LOOK WHO'S HERE.
DING DONG
It's her ...

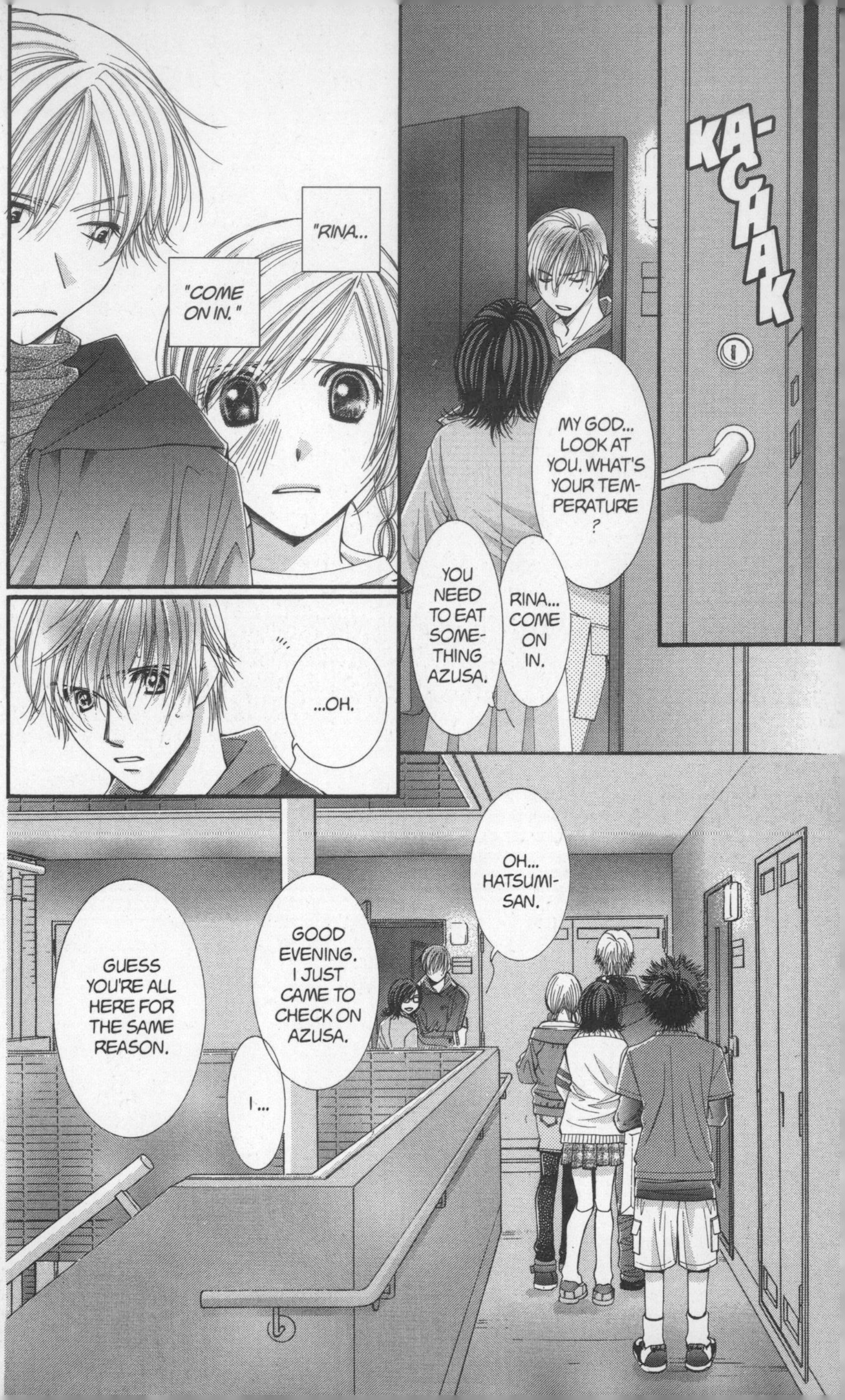
KA-CHAK
MY GOD... LOOK AT YOU. WHAT'S YOUR TEMPERATURE?
RINA... COME ON IN.
YOU NEED TO EAT SOMETHING AZUSA.
"RINA...
"COME ON IN."
...OH.
OH... HATSUMI-SAN.
GOOD EVENING. I JUST CAME TO CHECK ON AZUSA.
I...
GUESS YOU'RE ALL HERE FOR THE SAME REASON.

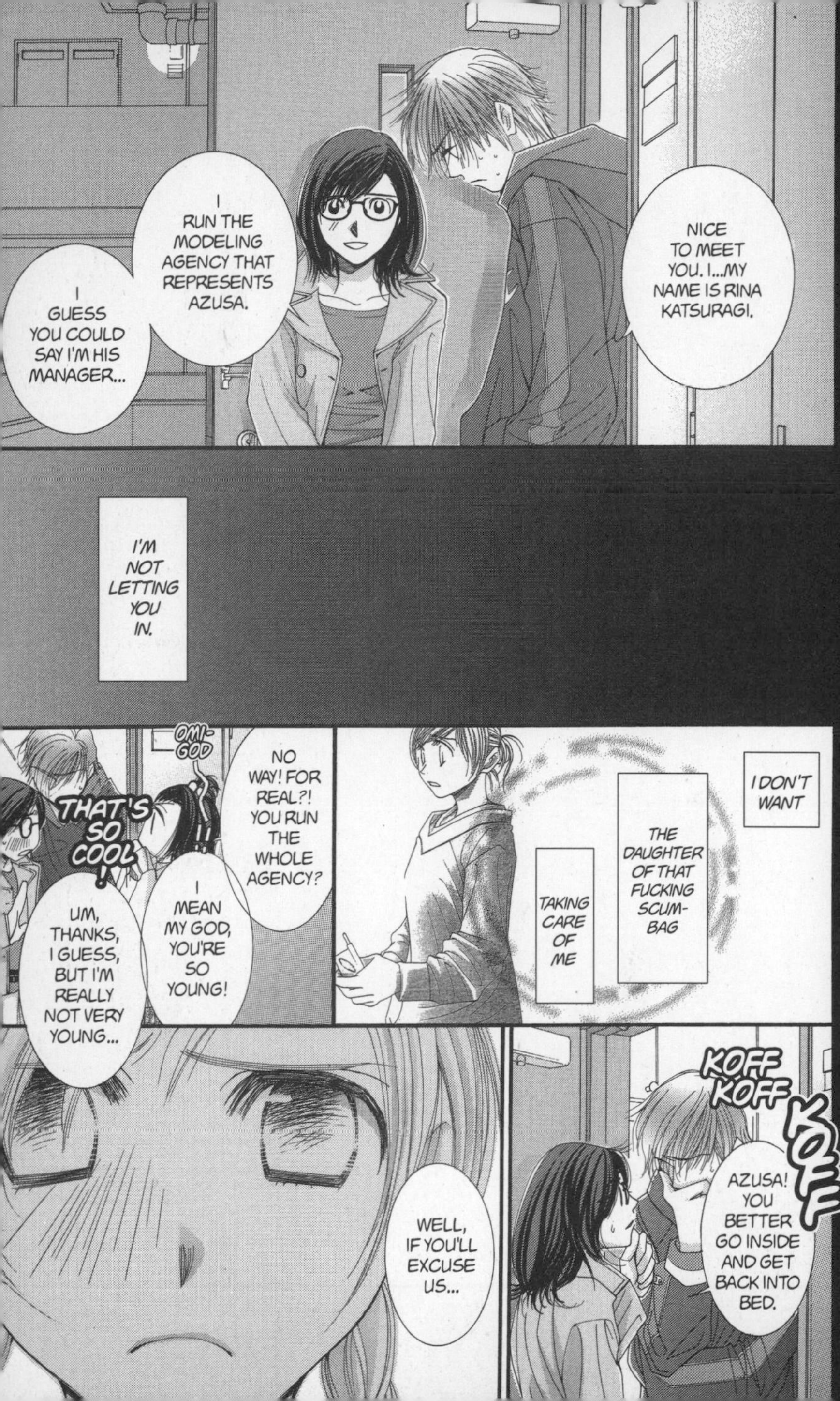
NICE TO MEET YOU. I...MY NAME IS RINA KATSURAGI.
I RUN THE MODELING AGENCY THAT REPRESENTS AZUSA.
I GUESS YOU COULD SAY I'M HIS MANAGER...
I'M NOT LETTING YOU IN.
I DON'T WANT
THE DAUGHTER OF THAT FUCKING SCUM-BAG
TAKING CARE OF ME
NO WAY! FOR REAL?! YOU RUN THE WHOLE AGENCY?
OMI-GOD
THAT'S SO COOL!
I MEAN MY GOD, YOU'RE SO YOUNG!
UM, THANKS, I GUESS, BUT I'M REALLY NOT VERY YOUNG...
KOFF KOFF
KOFF
AZUSA! YOU BETTER GO INSIDE AND GET BACK INTO BED.
WELL, IF YOU'LL EXCUSE US...

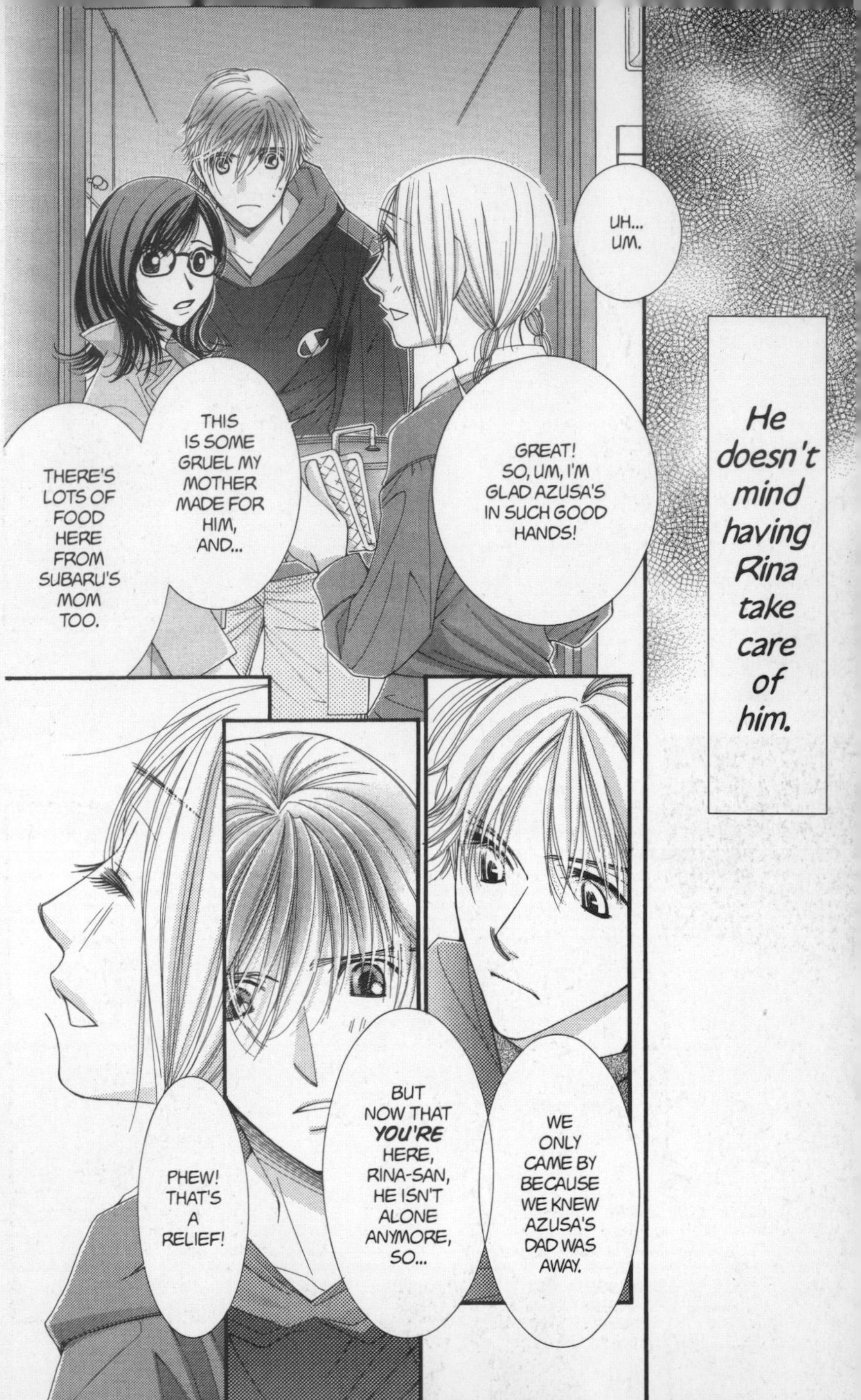
He doesn't mind having Rina take care of him.
UH... UM.
GREAT! SO, UM, I'M GLAD AZUSA'S IN SUCH GOOD HANDS!
THIS IS SOME GRUEL MY MOTHER MADE FOR HIM, AND...
THERE'S LOTS OF FOOD HERE FROM SUBARU'S MOM TOO.
WE ONLY CAME BY BECAUSE WE KNEW AZUSA'S DAD WAS AWAY.
BUT NOW THAT YOU'RE HERE, RINA-SAN, HE ISN'T ALONE ANYMORE, SO...
PHEW! THAT'S A RELIEF!

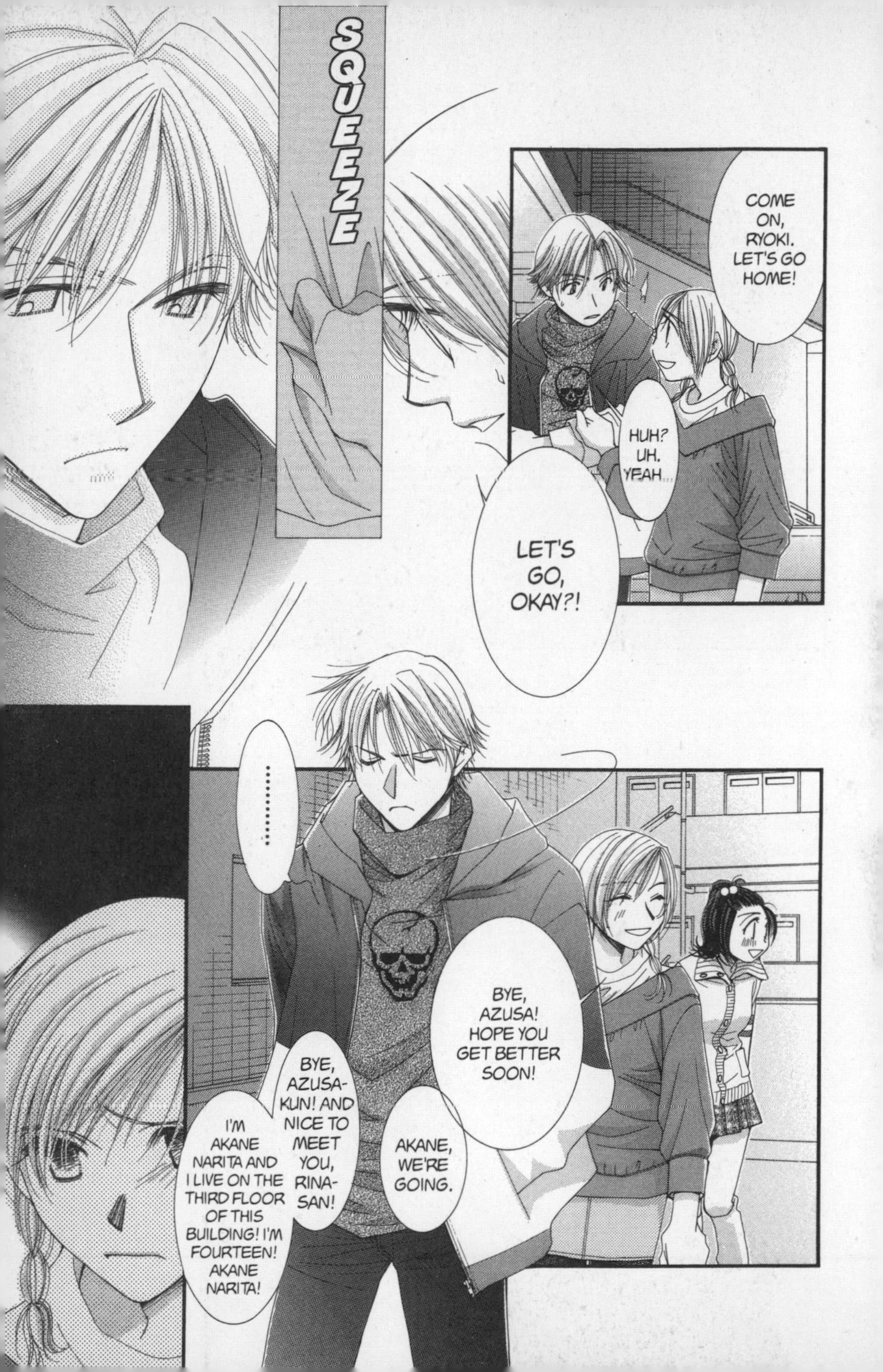
COME ON, RYOKI. LET'S GO HOME!
HUH? UH. YEAH...
LET'S GO, OKAY?!
SQUEEZE
......
BYE, AZUSA! HOPE YOU GET BETTER SOON!
AKANE, WE'RE GOING.
BYE, AZUSA-KUN! AND NICE TO MEET YOU, RINA-SAN!
I'M AKANE NARITA AND I LIVE ON THE THIRD FLOOR OF THIS BUILDING! I'M FOURTEEN! AKANE NARITA!

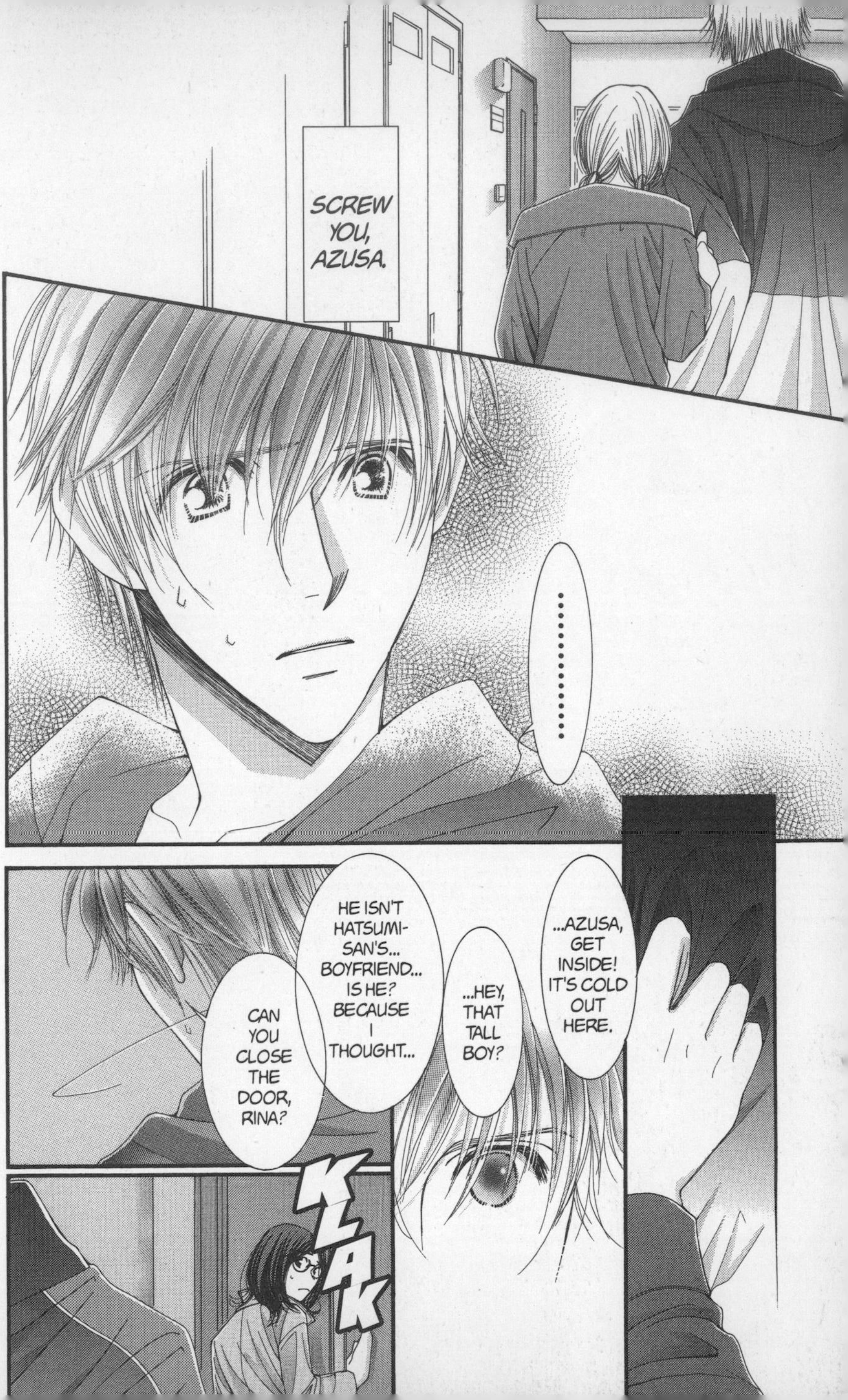
SCREW YOU, AZUSA.
......
...AZUSA, GET INSIDE! IT'S COLD OUT HERE.
...HEY, THAT TALL BOY?
HE ISN'T HATSUMI-SAN'S... BOYFRIEND... IS HE? BECAUSE I THOUGHT...
CAN YOU CLOSE THE DOOR, RINA?
KLAK

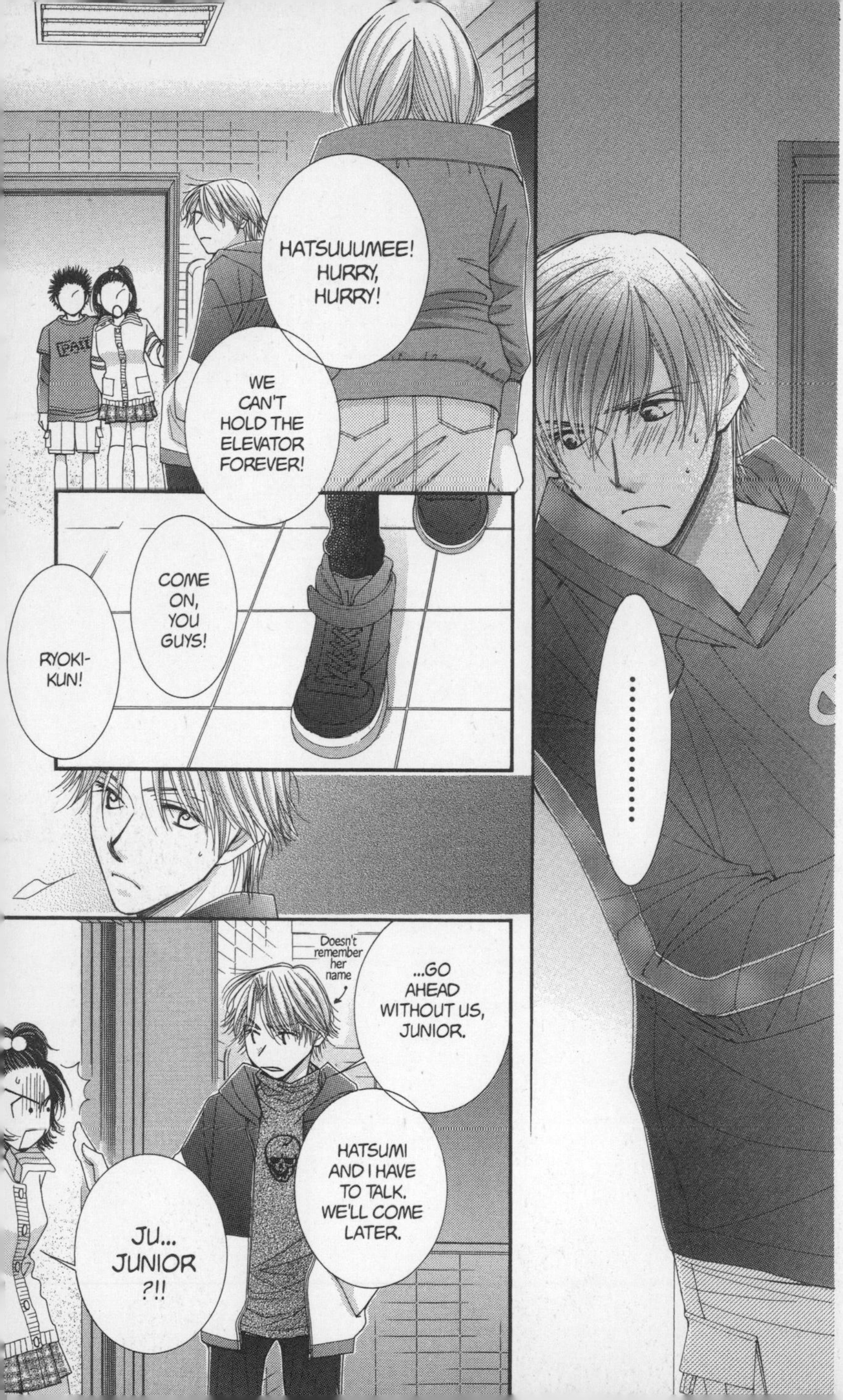
....
HATSUUUMEE! HURRY, HURRY!
WE CAN'T HOLD THE ELEVATOR FOREVER!
COME ON, YOU GUYS!
RYOKI-KUN!
Doesn't remember her name
...GO AHEAD WITHOUT US, JUNIOR.
HATSUMI AND I HAVE TO TALK. WE'LL COME LATER.
JU... JUNIOR ?!!

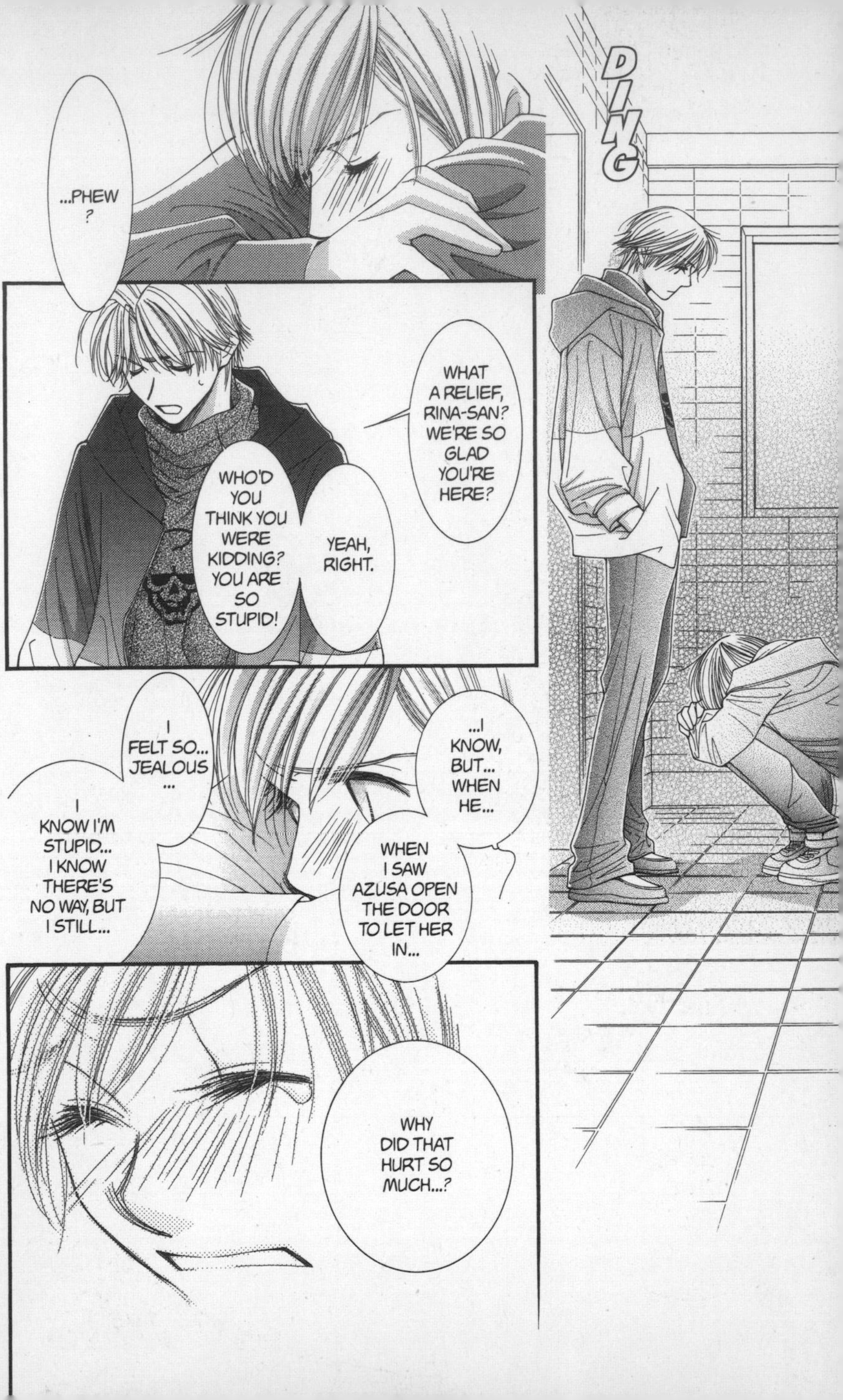
DING
...PHEW?
WHAT A RELIEF, RINA-SAN? WE'RE SO GLAD YOU'RE HERE?
YEAH, RIGHT.
WHO'D YOU THINK YOU WERE KIDDING? YOU ARE SO STUPID!
...I KNOW, BUT... WHEN HE...
WHEN I SAW AZUSA OPEN THE DOOR TO LET HER IN...
I FELT SO... JEALOUS...
I KNOW I'M STUPID... I KNOW THERE'S NO WAY, BUT I STILL...
WHY DID THAT HURT SO MUCH...?

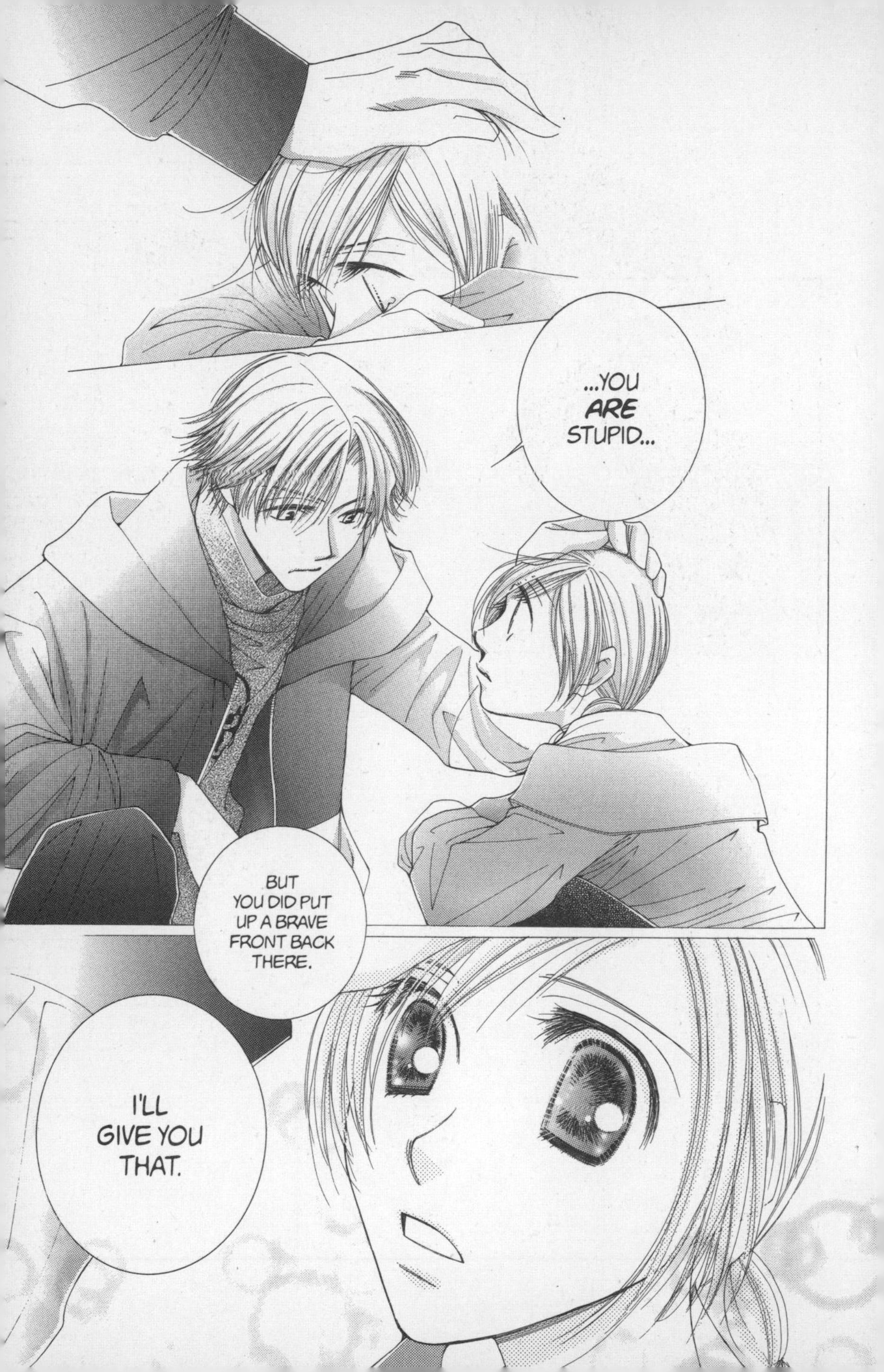
...YOU **ARE** STUPID...
BUT YOU DID PUT UP A BRAVE FRONT BACK THERE.
I'LL GIVE YOU THAT.

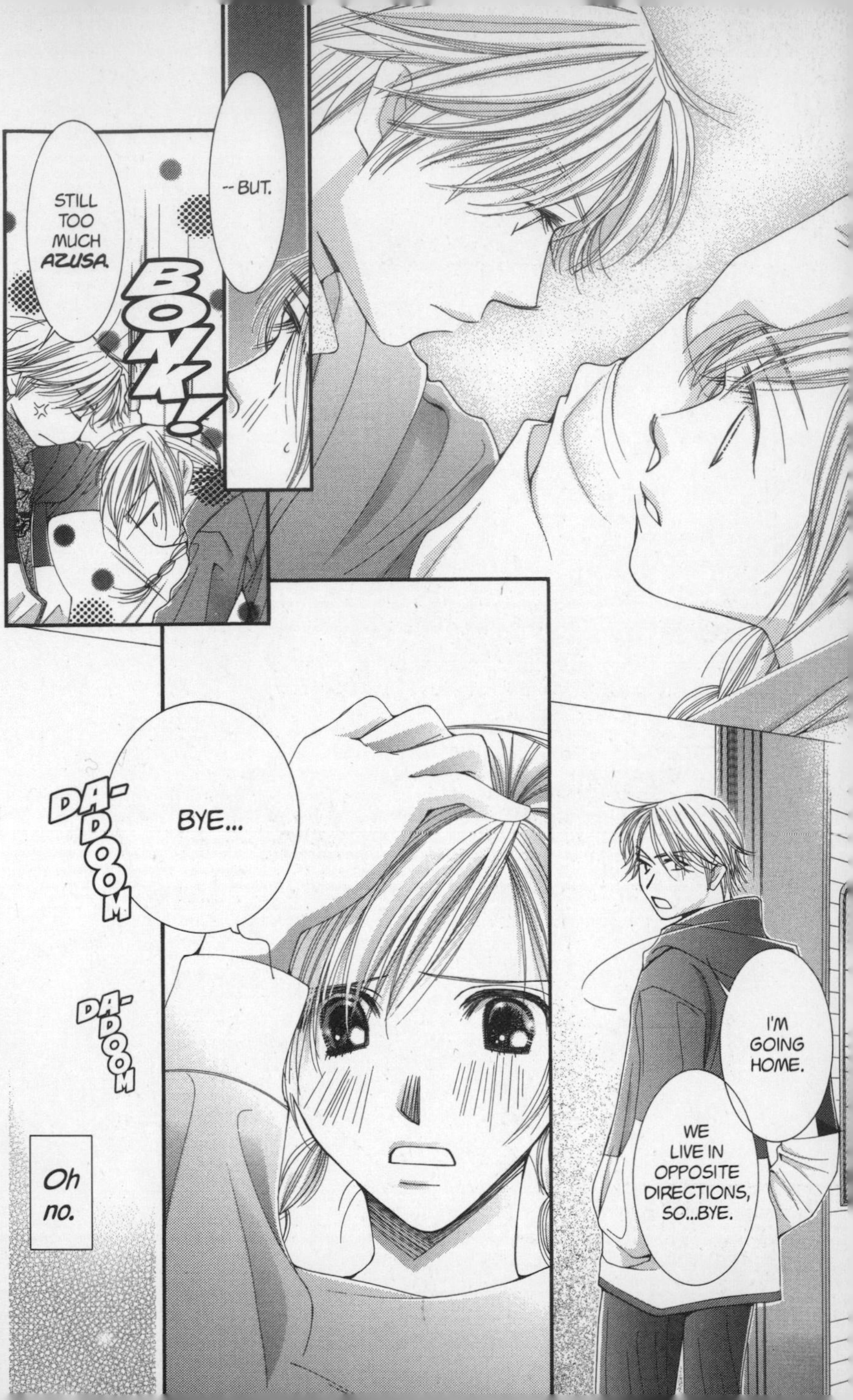
--BUT.
STILL TOO MUCH AZUSA.
BONK!
I'M GOING HOME.
WE LIVE IN OPPOSITE DIRECTIONS, SO...BYE.
BYE...
DA-DOOM
DA-DOOM
Oh no.

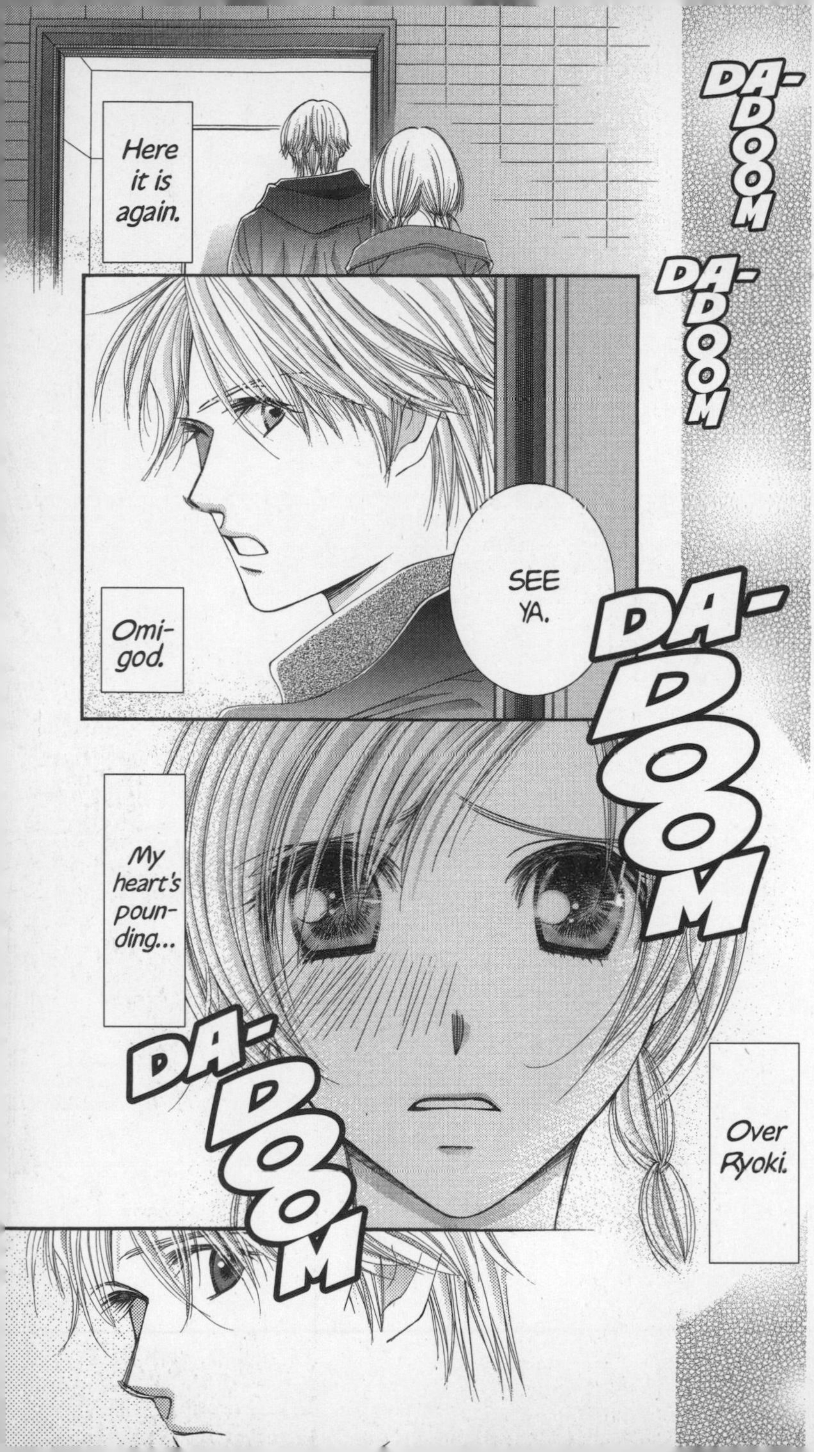
DA-DOOOM
DA-DOOOM
Here it is again.
SEE YA.
Omi-god.
DA-DOOOM
Over Ryoki.
My heart's pounding...
DA-DOOOM

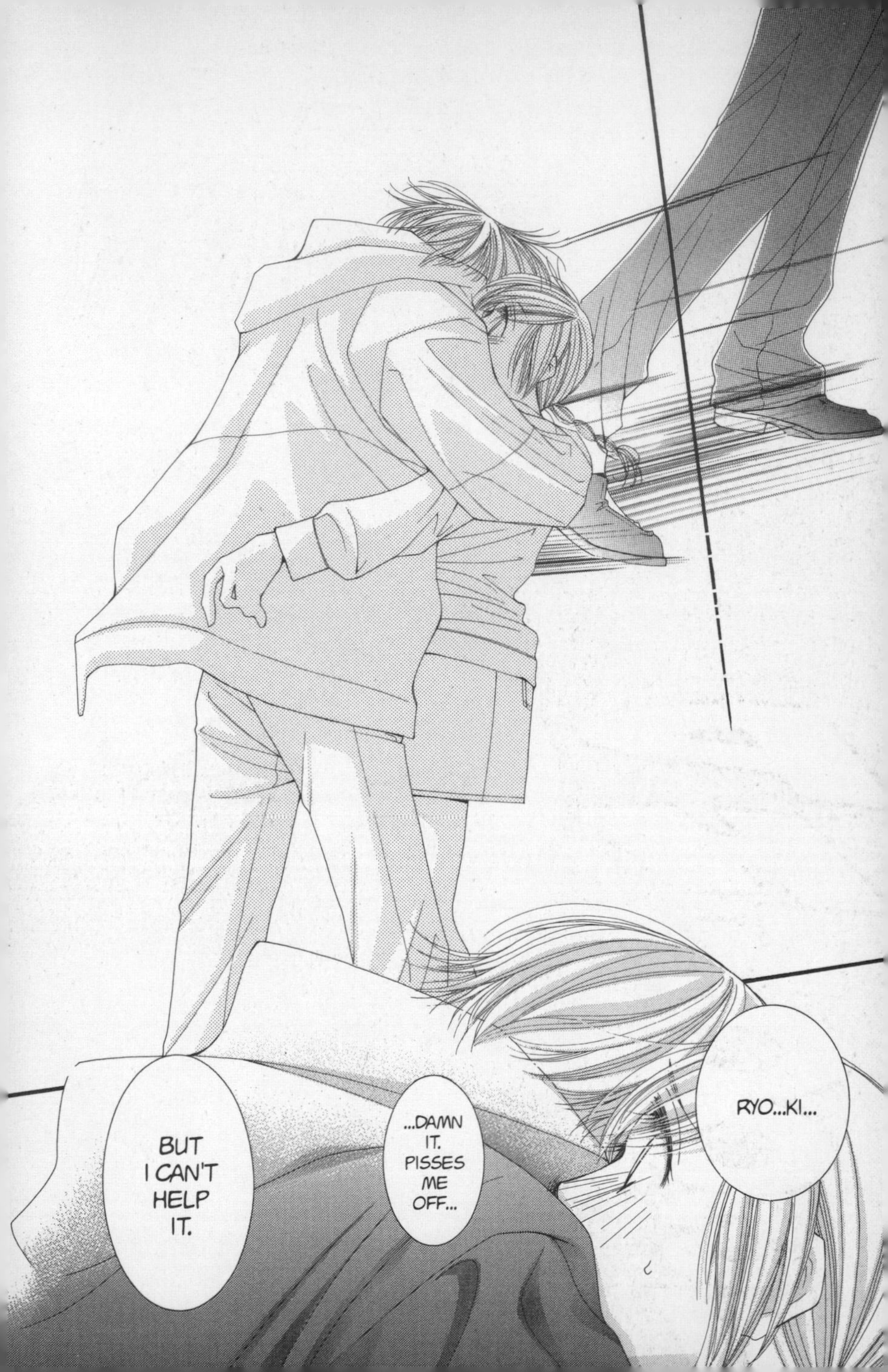
RYO...KI...
...DAMN IT. PISSES ME OFF...
BUT I CAN'T HELP IT.

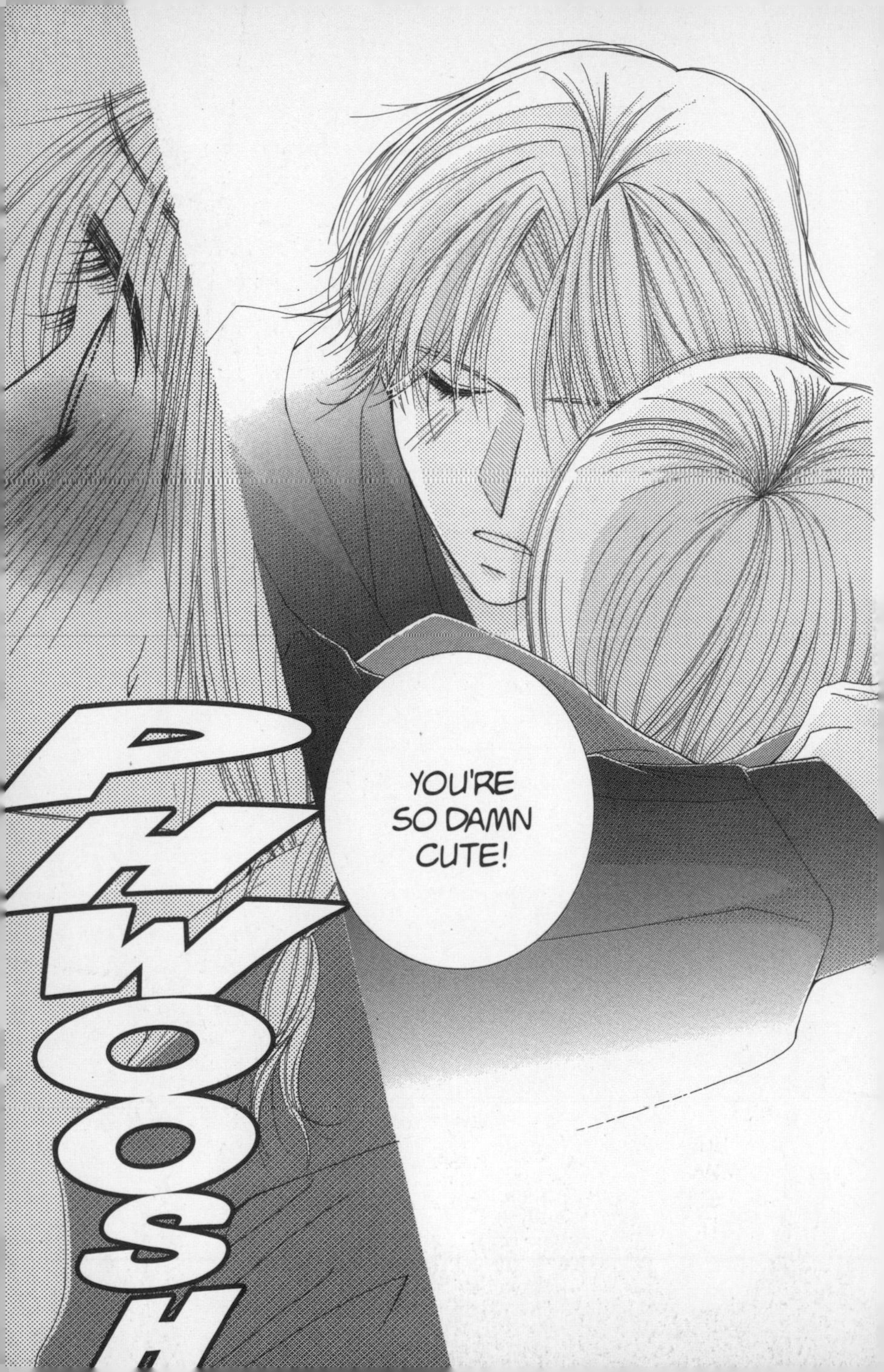
YOU'RE SO DAMN CUTE!
PHWOOSH

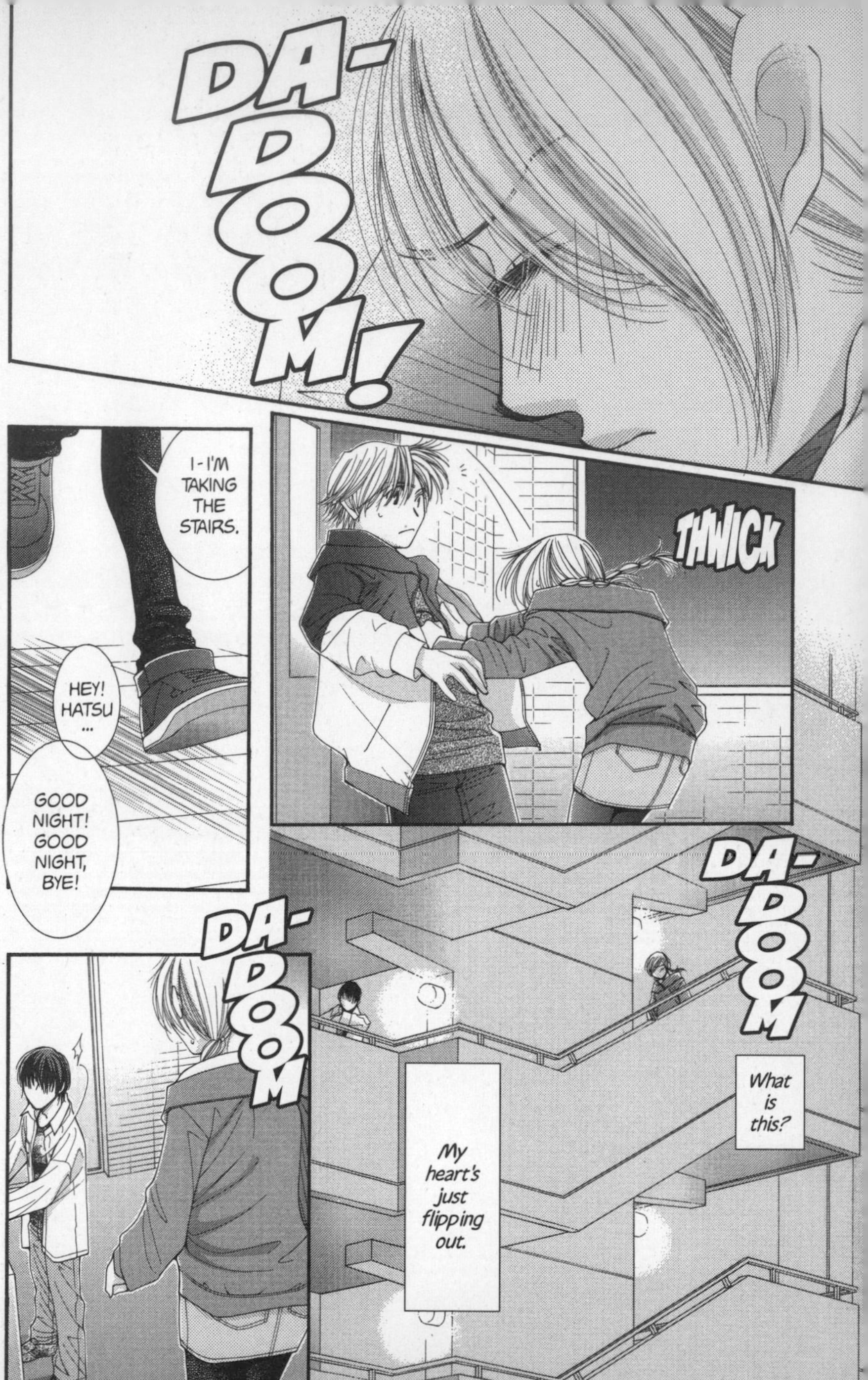
DA-DOOM!
THWICK
I-I'M TAKING THE STAIRS.
HEY! HATSU...
GOOD NIGHT! GOOD NIGHT, BYE!
DA-DOOM
What is this?
My heart's just flipping out.
DA-DOOM

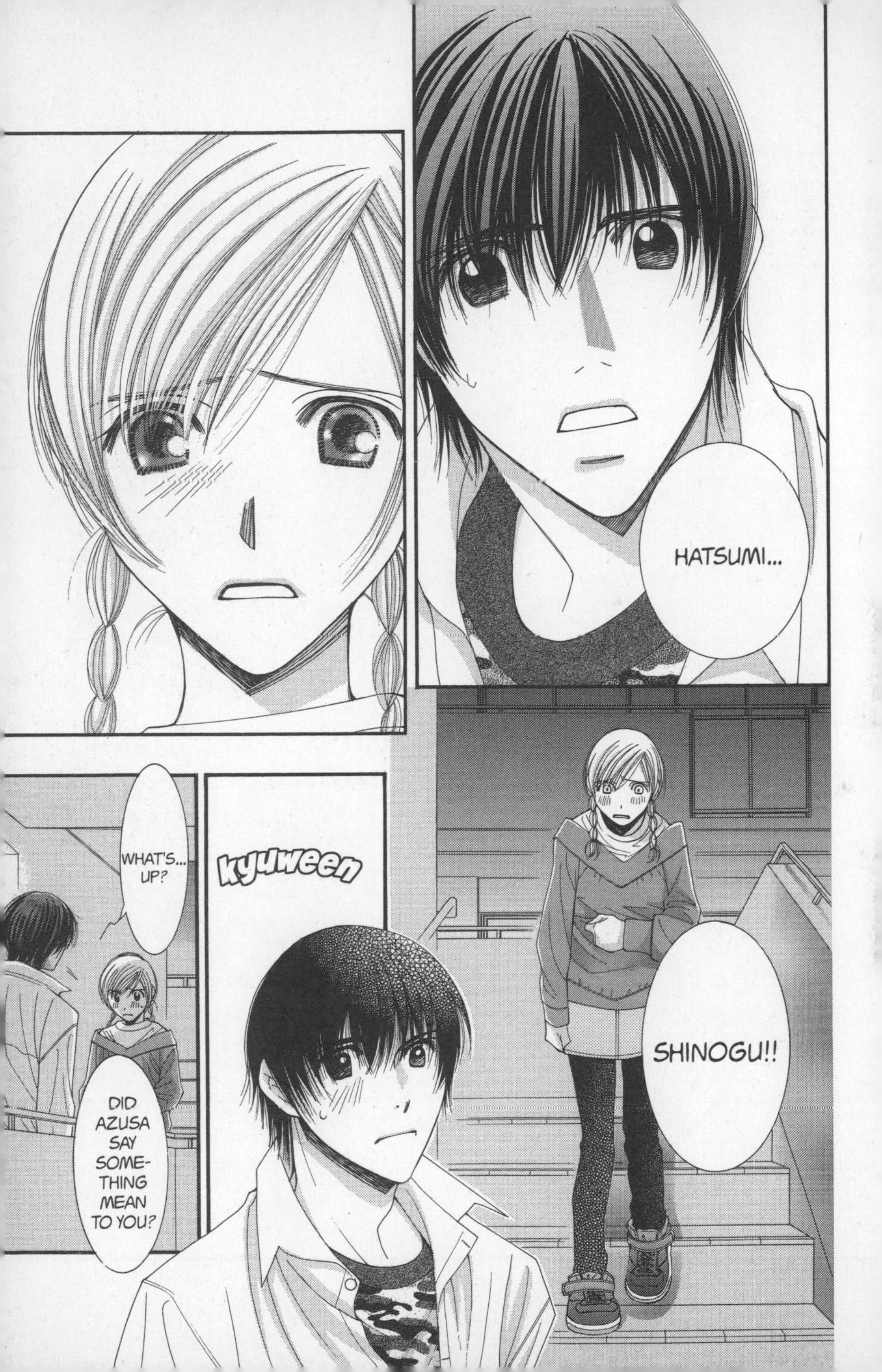
HATSUMI...
SHINOGU!!
kyuween
WHAT'S... UP?
DID AZUSA SAY SOME-THING MEAN TO YOU?

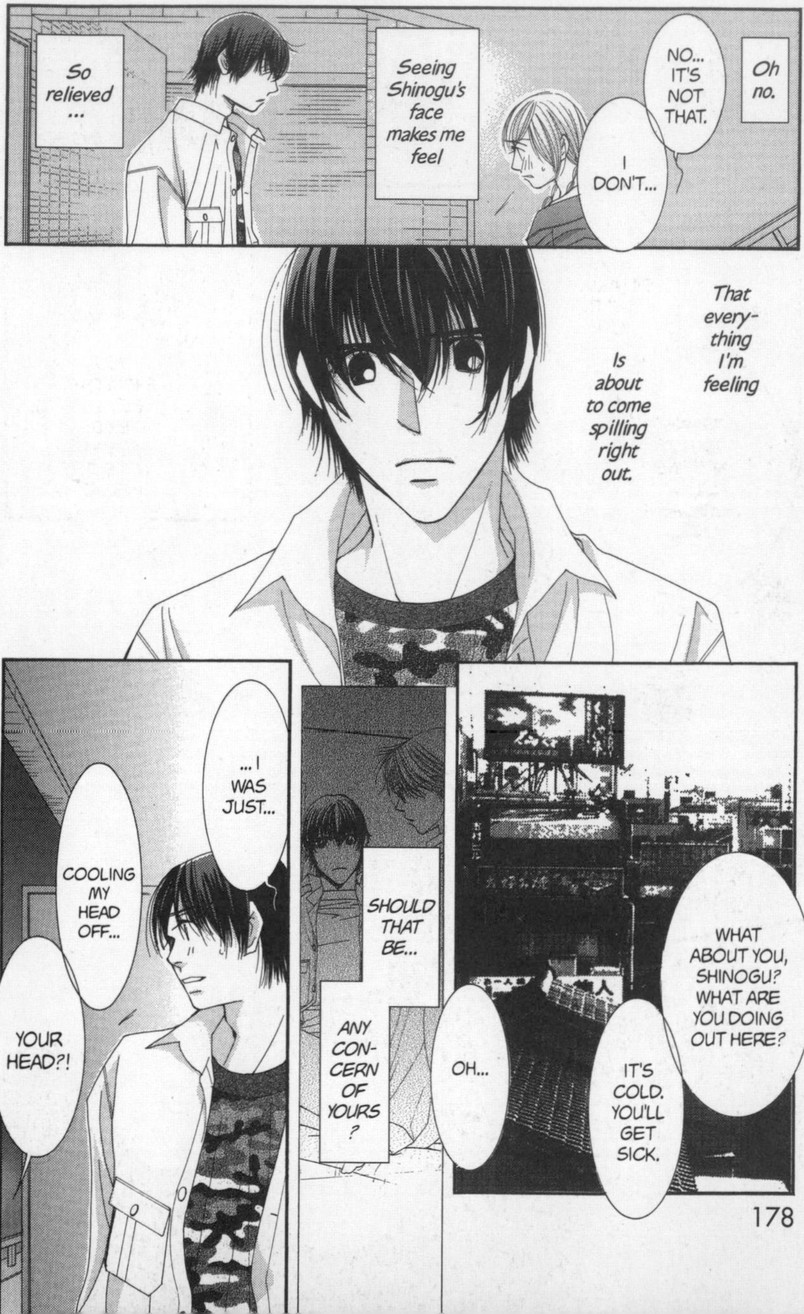

Oh no.
NO... IT'S NOT THAT.
I DON'T...
Seeing Shinogu's face makes me feel
So relieved ...
That every-thing I'm feeling
Is about to come spilling right out.
WHAT ABOUT YOU, SHINOGU? WHAT ARE YOU DOING OUT HERE?
IT'S COLD. YOU'LL GET SICK.
OH...
SHOULD THAT BE...
ANY CON-CERN OF YOURS?
...I WAS JUST...
COOLING MY HEAD OFF...
YOUR HEAD?!

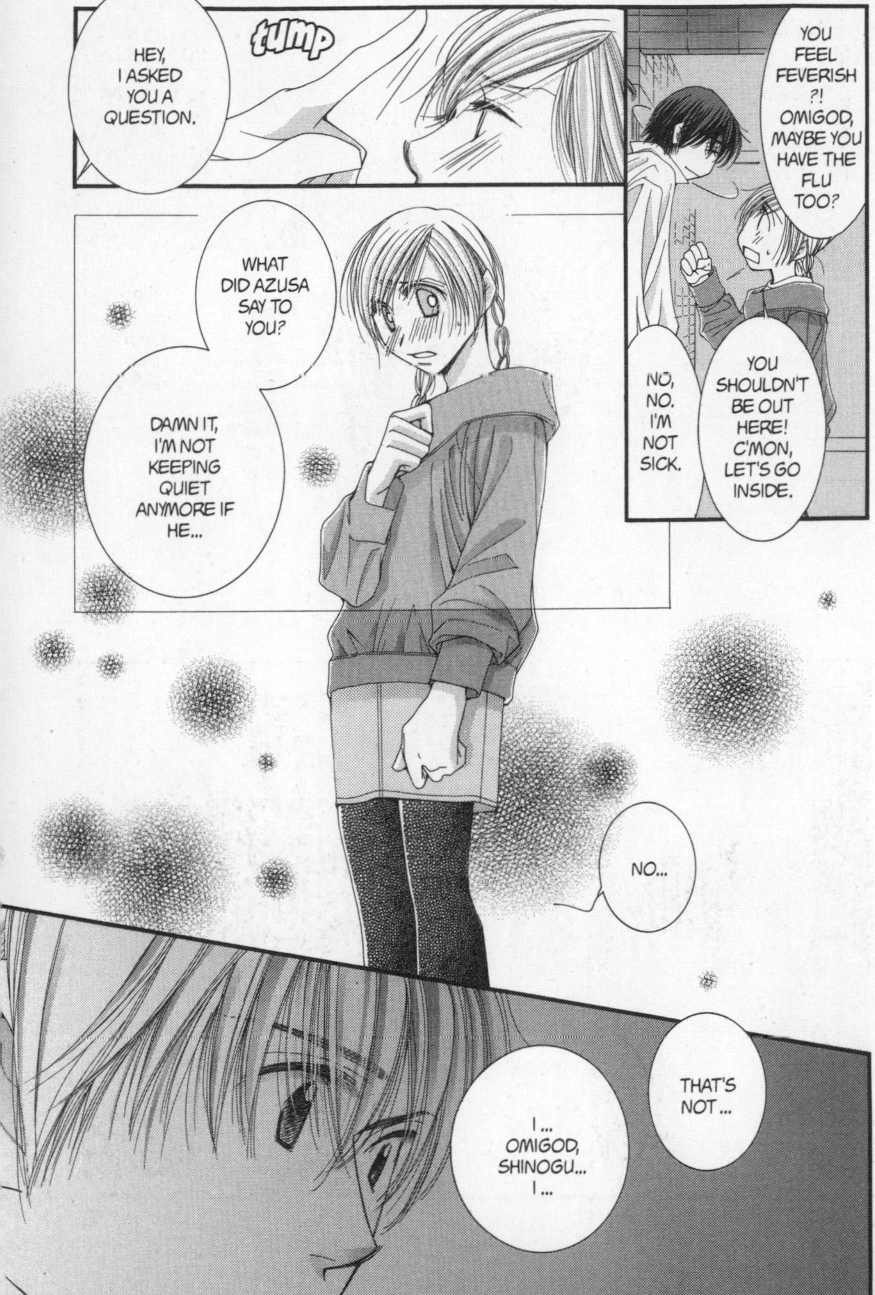
YOU FEEL FEVERISH?! OMIGOD, MAYBE YOU HAVE THE FLU TOO?
YOU SHOULDN'T BE OUT HERE! C'MON, LET'S GO INSIDE.
NO, NO. I'M NOT SICK.
tump
HEY, I ASKED YOU A QUESTION.
WHAT DID AZUSA SAY TO YOU?
DAMN IT, I'M NOT KEEPING QUIET ANYMORE IF HE...
NO...
THAT'S NOT...
I... OMIGOD, SHINOGU... I...

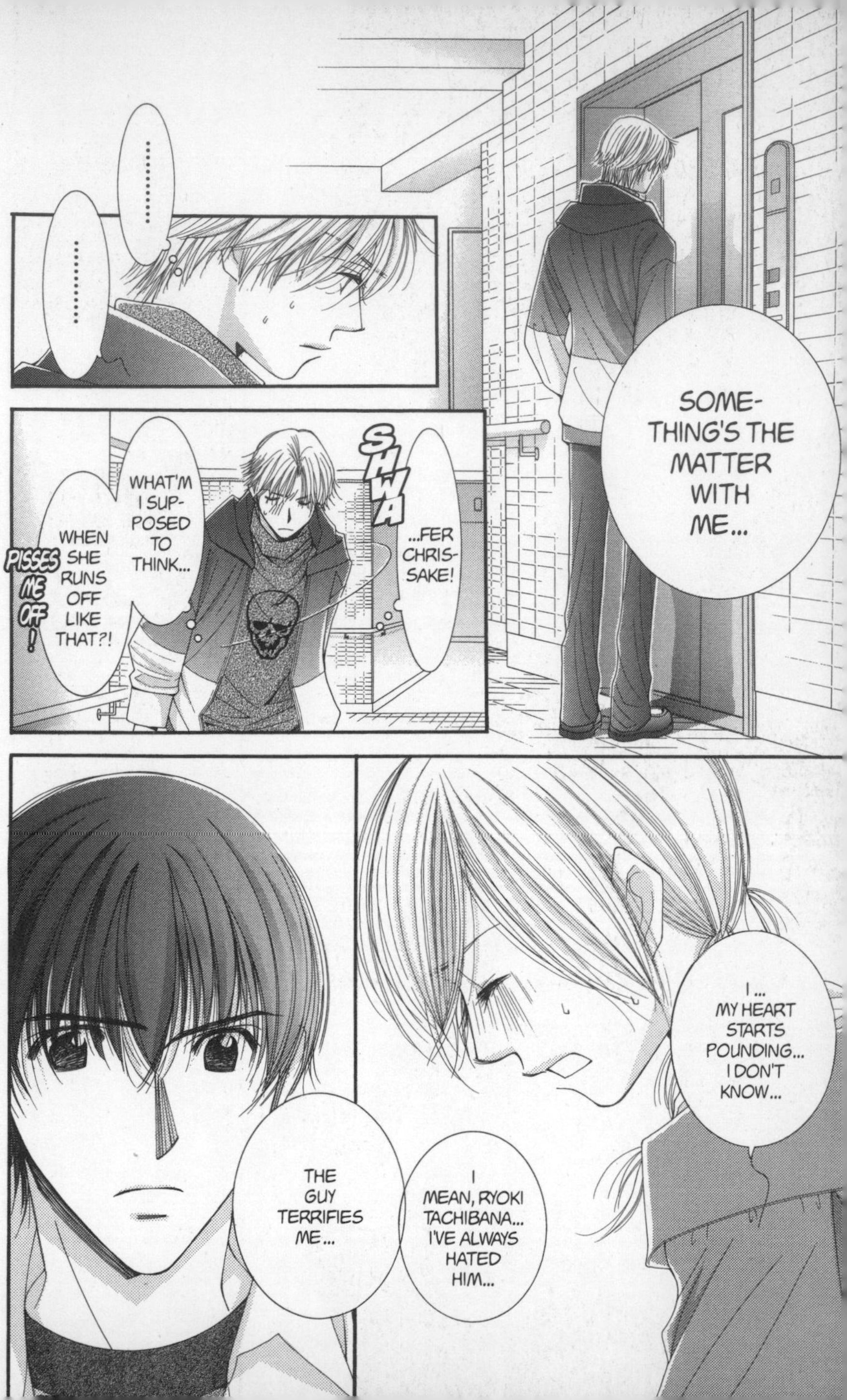
SOME-THING'S THE MATTER WITH ME...
......
......
SHWA
...FER CHRIS-SAKE!
WHAT'M I SUP-POSED TO THINK...
WHEN SHE RUNS OFF LIKE THAT?!
PISSES ME OFF!
I... MY HEART STARTS POUNDING... I DON'T KNOW...
I MEAN, RYOKI TACHIBANA... I'VE ALWAYS HATED HIM...
THE GUY TERRIFIES ME...

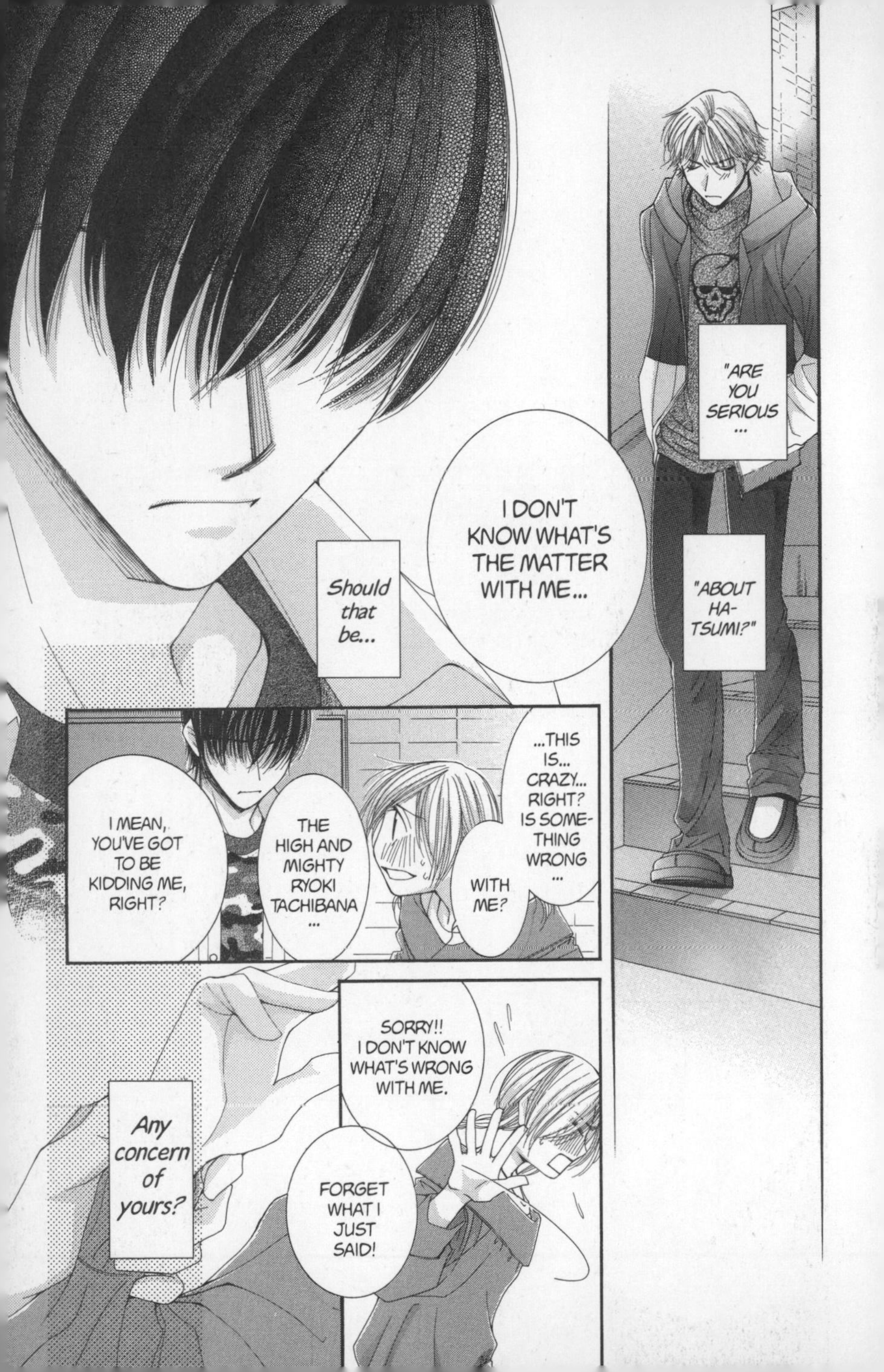
"ARE YOU SERIOUS ...
"ABOUT HA-TSUMI?"
I DON'T KNOW WHAT'S THE MATTER WITH ME...
Should that be...
...THIS IS... CRAZY... RIGHT? IS SOME-THING WRONG ...
WITH ME?
THE HIGH AND MIGHTY RYOKI TACHIBANA ...
I MEAN, YOU'VE GOT TO BE KIDDING ME, RIGHT?
SORRY!! I DON'T KNOW WHAT'S WRONG WITH ME.
FORGET WHAT I JUST SAID!
Any concern of yours?

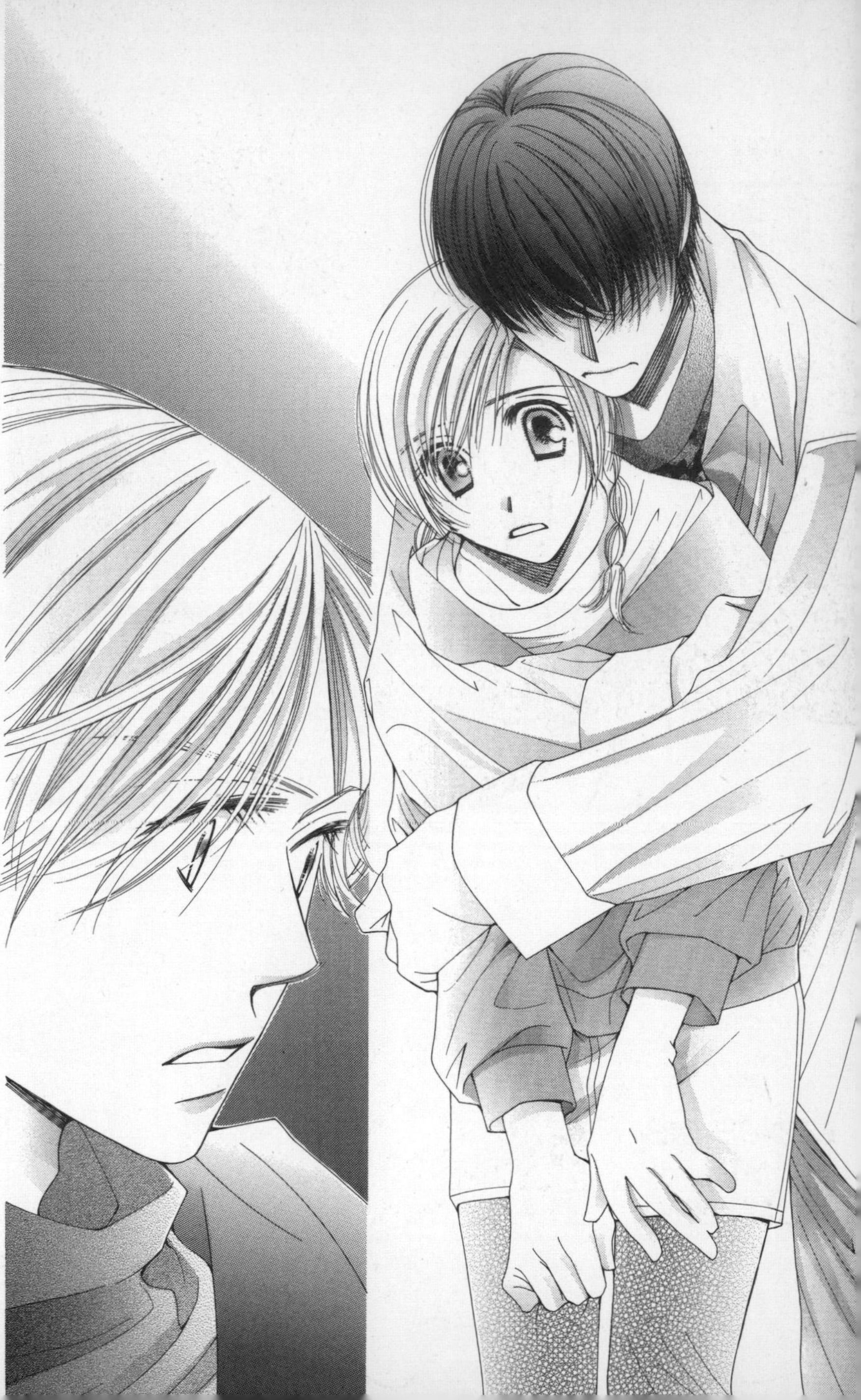

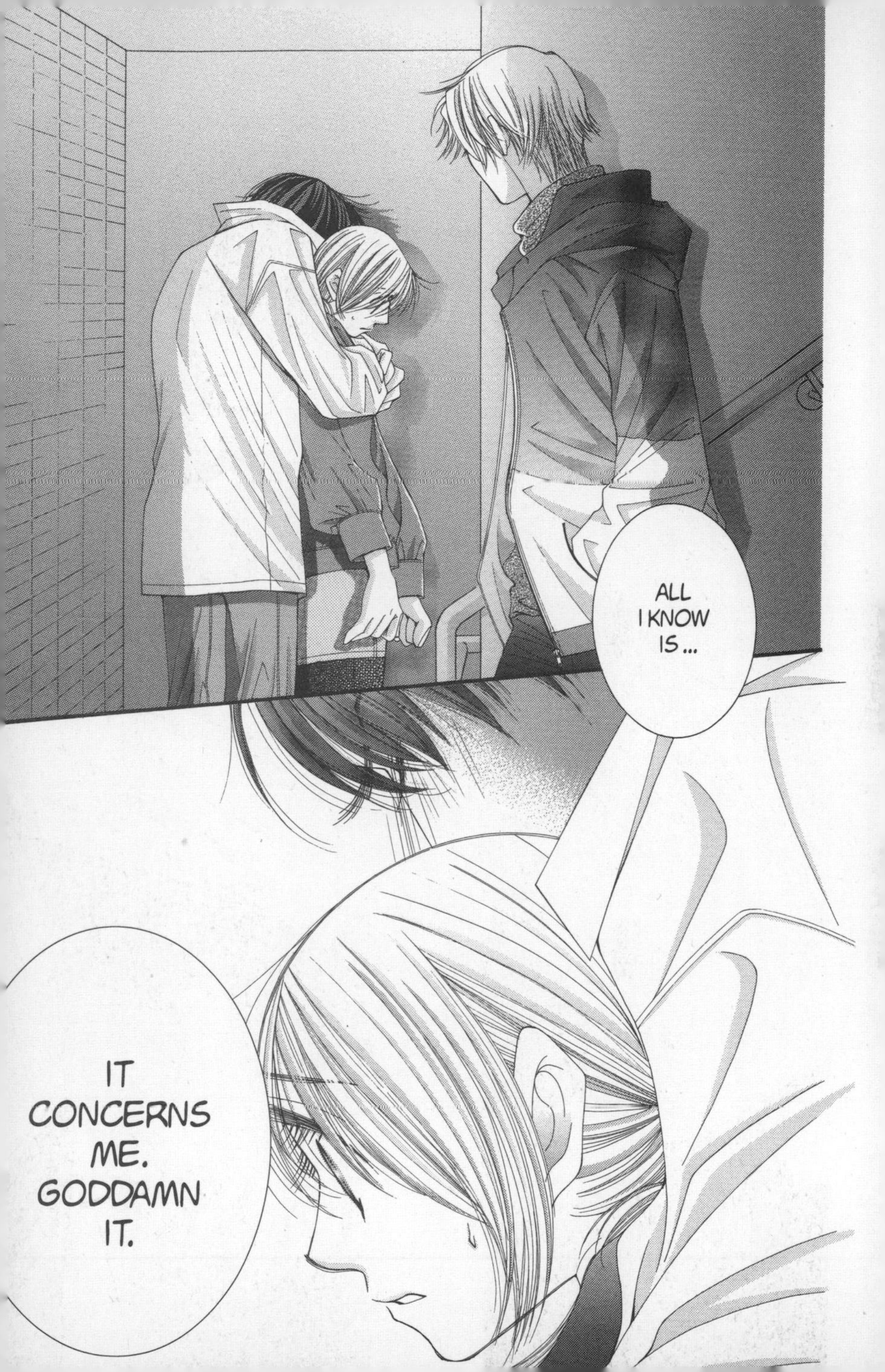
ALL I KNOW IS...
IT CONCERNS ME. GODDAMN IT.

To be continued

HOT GIMMICK
Vol. 4

Shôjo Edition

STORY & ART BY MIKI AIHARA

ENGLISH ADAPTATION BY POOKIE ROLF

Touch-Up Art & Lettering/Rina Mapa
Design/Judi Roubideaux
Editor/Kit Fox

Managing Editor/Annette Roman
Editorial Director/Alvin Lu
Director of Production/Noboru Watanabe
Sr. Director of Licensing and Acquisitions/Rika Inouye
V.P. of Sales & Marketing/Liza Coppola
Executive V.P./Hyoe Narita
Publisher/Seiji Horibuchi

Printed in Canada

Published by VIZ, LLC, P.O. Box 77010, San Francisco, CA 94107

Shôjo Edition
10 9 8 7 6 5 4 3
First printing, April 2004
Second printing, July 2004
Third printing, October 2004

Hot Gimmick

EDITOR'S RECOMMENDATIONS

More manga!
More manga!

Did you like *Hot Gimmick*? Here's what VIZ recommends you try next:

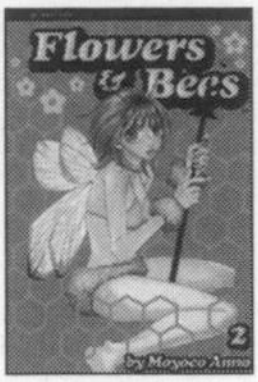
Flowers & Bees
2
by Moyoco Anno

© 2000 Moyoco Anno/ Kodansha Ltd.

FLOWERS AND BEES Moyoco Anno's painfully hilarious chronicle of a normal guy attempting to unleash his inner metrosexual is as funny as it is incisive. Hoping to spruce up his image (and at the same time, increase his chances of "gettin' some"), Komatsu becomes a regular at the World of Beautiful Men salon. The salon's proprietresses, a pair of sexy fashionistas, adopt Komatsu as their own private slave and shadow his myriad failed attempts at scoring some points with the opposite sex. Will this hapless hero ever get some lovin'? More importantly, will he ever get his shit together?

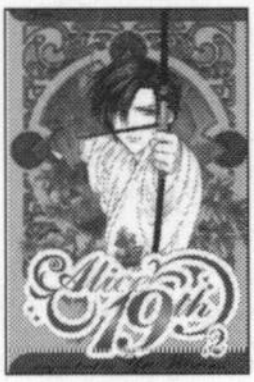
Alice 19th
2

© 2001 Yuu Watase/ Shogakukan, Inc.

ALICE 19TH is the latest completed series by the manga fan-favorite Yû Watase. Alice is the forgotten younger sister of one of the most popular girls in school and at home. And when Alice falls in love with the handsome Kyô Wakayama, it's only natural that Alice's sister, Mayura, would be his most likely girlfriend. Then a magical white rabbit enters Alice's life to tell her that she can be a master of the world-changing Lotis Words–a power that can change the world into a dream, or a nightmare!

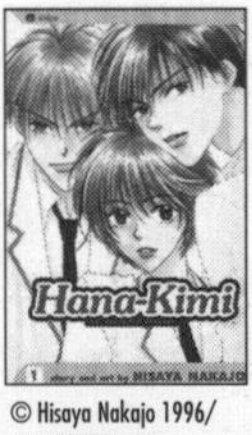
Hana-Kimi
1
HISAYA NAKAJO

© Hisaya Nakajo 1996/ HAKUSENSHA, Inc.

HANA-KIMI: FOR YOU IN FULL BLOSSOM is the story of Mizuki, a young athlete who's so besotted with her track-and-field idol that she dresses as a boy and transfers to an all boys' school just to be close to him. But life is never easy (especially in manga), so imagine Mizuki's surprise when her roommate turns out to be none other than Izumi Sano, the very person she's gone topsy-turvy over. What's a cross-dressing, gender-bending girl to do?

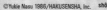

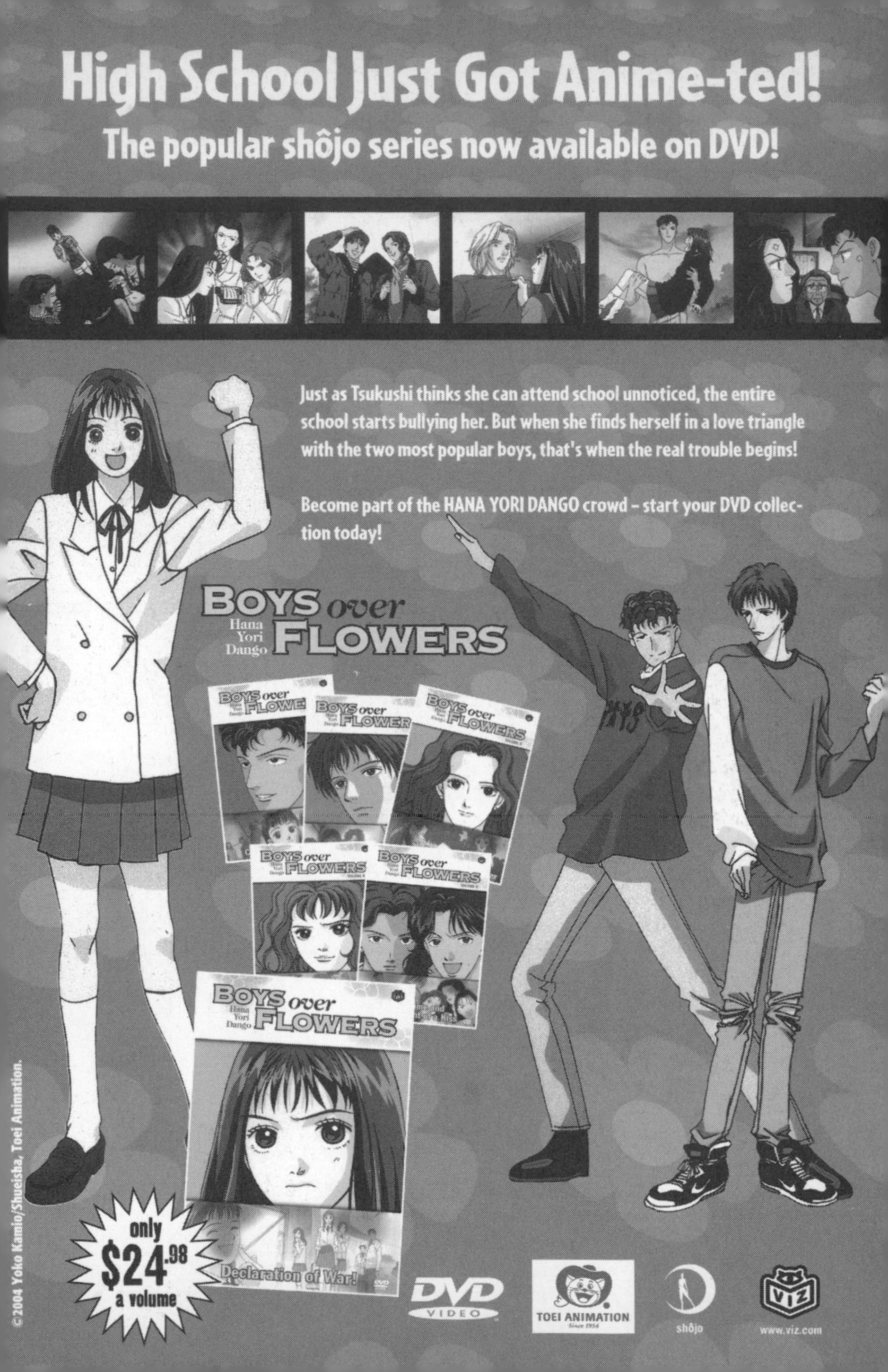
High School Just Got Anime-ted!
The popular shôjo series now available on DVD!
Just as Tsukushi thinks she can attend school unnoticed, the entire school starts bullying her. But when she finds herself in a love triangle with the two most popular boys, that's when the real trouble begins!
Become part of the HANA YORI DANGO crowd – start your DVD collection today!
BOYS over FLOWERS
Hana Yori Dango
Declaration of War!
only $24.98 a volume
DVD VIDEO
TOEI ANIMATION
Since 1956
shôjo
VIZ
www.viz.com
©2004 Yoko Kamio/Shueisha, Toei Animation.

The Power of a Kiss

Soon after her first kiss, Yuri is pulled into a puddle and transported to an ancient Middle Eastern village. Surrounded by strange people speaking a language she can't understand, Yuri has no idea how to get back home and is soon embroiled in the politics and romance of the ancient Middle East. If a kiss helped get Yuri into this mess, can a kiss get her out?

RED RIVER

Start your graphic novel collection today!

ONLY $9.95!

www.viz.com
store.viz.com

COMPLETE OUR SURVEY AND LET US KNOW WHAT YOU THINK!

☐ Please do NOT send me information about VIZ products, news and events, special offers, or other information.

☐ Please do NOT send me information from VIZ's trusted business partners.

Name: _____

Address: _____

City: _____ **State:** _____ **Zip:** _____

E-mail: _____

☐ **Male** ☐ **Female**   **Date of Birth** (mm/dd/yyyy): ___/___/_____ (Under 13? Parental consent required)

What race/ethnicity do you consider yourself? (please check one)

☐ Asian/Pacific Islander   ☐ Black/African American   ☐ Hispanic/Latino

☐ Native American/Alaskan Native   ☐ White/Caucasian   ☐ Other: _____

What VIZ product did you purchase? (check all that apply and indicate title purchased)

☐ DVD/VHS _____

☐ Graphic Novel _____

☐ Magazines _____

☐ Merchandise _____

Reason for purchase: (check all that apply)

☐ Special offer   ☐ Favorite title   ☐ Gift

☐ Recommendation   ☐ Other _____

Where did you make your purchase? (please check one)

☐ Comic store   ☐ Bookstore   ☐ Mass/Grocery Store

☐ Newsstand   ☐ Video/Video Game Store ☐ Other: _____

☐ Online (site: _____)

What other VIZ properties have you purchased/own? _____

_____

How many anime and/or manga titles have you purchased in the last year? How many were VIZ titles? **(please check one from each column)**

ANIME	MANGA	VIZ
☐ None	☐ None	☐ None
☐ 1-4	☐ 1-4	☐ 1-4
☐ 5-10	☐ 5-10	☐ 5-10
☐ 11+	☐ 11+	☐ 11+

I find the pricing of VIZ products to be: **(please check one)**

☐ Cheap ☐ Reasonable ☐ Expensive

What genre of manga and anime would you like to see from VIZ? **(please check two)**

☐ Adventure ☐ Comic Strip ☐ Science Fiction ☐ Fighting

☐ Horror ☐ Romance ☐ Fantasy ☐ Sports

What do you think of VIZ's new look?

☐ Love It ☐ It's OK ☐ Hate It ☐ Didn't Notice ☐ No Opinion

Which do you prefer? **(please check one)**

☐ Reading right-to-left

☐ Reading left-to-right

Which do you prefer? **(please check one)**

☐ Sound effects in English

☐ Sound effects in Japanese with English captions

☐ Sound effects in Japanese only with a glossary at the back

THANK YOU! Please send the completed form to:

NJW Research
42 Catharine St.
Poughkeepsie, NY 12601

All information provided will be used for internal purposes only. We promise not to sell or otherwise divulge your information.